CAUGHT OFF GUARD

CAUGHT OFF GUARD

Teachers Rethinking Censorship and Controversy

Ellen Henson Brinkley
Western Michigan University

Allyn and Bacon

Boston ∎ London ∎ Toronto ∎ Sydney ∎ Tokyo ∎ Singapore

Senior Editor: Virginia Lanigan
Series Editorial Assistant: Bridget Keane
Marketing Managers: Ellen Dolberg/Brad Parkins
Manufacturing Buyer: Suzanne Lareau

Library of Congress Cataloging-in-Publication Data

Brinkley, Ellen Henson.
   Caught off guard : teachers rethinking censorship and controversy
 / Ellen Henson Brinkley.
     p.   cm.
   Includes bibliographical references and index.
   ISBN 0-205-18529-0
   1. Teaching, freedom of--United States.   2. Public schools--United
States--Curricula--Censorship.   3. Textbook--Censorship--United
States.   4. Academic freedom--United States.   I. Title.
LC72.2.B75   1999
379.1'56'0973--dc21   98-46508
                              CIP

Printed in the United States of America

10 9 8 7 6 5 4 3 2 1   02 01 00 99

Figure 2.3 on page 41 and McDonald paraphrases on pages 42–43 are adapted from *Teaching Literature in the Secondary School* by Richard W. Beach and James D. Marshall, copyright © 1991 by Harcourt Brace & Company, reprinted by permission of the publisher.

To Max, Matthew, and Sarah, with love and thanks

CONTENTS

Preface   xv

1 Teaching in a Changing Classroom World   1

What Is a Classroom Teacher to Do?   5

Facts about Curricular Challenges and Controversies   8

Circumstances That Invite Challenge and Controversy   11
New Curricula or Policies   12
Attention-Getting Classroom Projects   12
Curricula Linked to Personal Experience   12
Explicit Ideological and Political Stances   13
Politicized Pedagogical and School Reform Issues   13

Vulnerable Teachers   14
Risk-Taking Teachers   14
Playing-It-Safe Teachers   15
New Teachers   15
Experienced Teachers   16

Vulnerable Schools   17

Parent Protesters   18

First Signs and Impulses   21
Ignoring or Minimizing Signals   21
Making Concessions   22
Launching an Aggressive Counterattack   23
Searching for Appropriate Action   24

Living in a "Heads-Up" School World   24

Are There Other Possibilities?   25

Helpful Resources   26

References   27

2 Rethinking Classroom Censorship and Decision Making   29

Worst-Case Censorship Scenario   29
Lessons for Today   31

What Is Censorship?   32
Censorship Perspectives   32
Testing Ourselves   33
Librarians and Censorship   35

Acts of Censorship   35

The Power of Reading   38

Daily Classroom Judgment Calls   39

Censorship and Selection   40
Professional and Personal Selection Purposes   40
Choosing and Excluding   41
Free Thought and Thought Control   42
Thinking for Ourselves   42

Self- and School-Sponsored Censorship   43

Censorship of Learning   46

Rethinking Censorship   47

What Can You Do about Classroom Censorship?   47

Helpful Resources   49

References   49

3 Facing Classroom and Community Controversy   51

The "Good Old Days"   52

Perceptions about Public Schools   53
USA Today Poll   53
Citizens for Excellence in Education Survey   54
Public Agenda Report   54

Good News about Public Schools   56
National Science Foundation Report   56
Sandia National Laboratories Report   56
The Manufactured Crisis   57

Belief Systems That Put Pressure on Classroom Teachers   **57**

Pressure from and within the "Governing State"   **59**
Teachers Feeling Pressure from the Public   59

Pressure from the "Religious State"   **59**
Teachers Feeling Pressure from Religious Conservatives   60
The Christian Coalition   61
Citizens for Excellence in Education   61
Focus on the Family   62
The Eagle Forum   63
Other Groups   63

Pressure from the "Capitalist State"   **63**
Responding to Corporate Pressures   65

Pressure from the "Transformation State"   **66**
Putting Pressure to Work   67

The Influence of New Age Spiritualists   **68**

Pressure from Extremists   **69**

Is There Any Common Ground?   **70**

What Can You Do about Pressures?   **71**

Helpful Resources   **72**

References   **73**

4   Reading, Writing, Research, and Expression   75

Fighting about Phonics and Meaning Making   **75**
Money, Religion, and Politics   77
Helping Others Make Sense of the Phonics Controversy   78

Misunderstandings about Purposes for Reading   **79**

What Can You Do about Reading Controversies?   **83**

Controversy about Student Writing, Research, and Expression   **86**
Personal Writing in Journals and Writing for Social Action   88
Writing, Inquiry, and Research   89
Challenging Students' Freedom of Speech and Expression   90
Students' Oral Expression in the Classroom   92

What Can You Do about Controversies about Writing, Research, and Expression?   **93**

Freedom of Press, the High School Newspaper, and Enlightened Administrators
by Dan Holt　94

Helpful Resources　96

References　98

5 **Censorship in Science and Science Education
by Ronald G. Good, James A. Shymansky, and
Larry D. Yore**　**101**

What Is Science?　102

Three Views of Knowledge　104

The Changing Complexion of Censorship　105

A Brief History of Censorship in Science　106

Unnecessary Conflicts　108

Two Sides of Science　109

New Forms of Censorship　110
Equal Time Arguments　110
Multicultural Arguments　112

Nature as the Ultimate Censor　115

Censoring Critical Thinking　115

What Can You Do about Censorship in Science?　117

Teaching Science in a Context of Change　119

References　120

6 **Literature and the Imagination**　**123**

Questioning the Value of Literature　124
How Literature Is Censored　125

Issues That Spark Literature Challenges　126
Offensive Language　127
Sexuality　127
Violence　128
Racial Stereotypes　129
Gender Stereotypes　129

Witchcraft and Satanism   130
New Age and the Imagination   131

Defending Literature Study   132
Defending Multicultural Literature   133
Defending Critical Literacy for All Students   134

What Can You Do about Literature Controversies?   135

Helpful Resources   141

References   144

**7 Censorship in Sexuality Education
by Jodi Brookins-Fisher   147**

Comprehensive Sexuality Education   148

Areas of Controversy   149

Why the Controversy?   151

New Movements: Abstinence-Based versus Abstinence-Only Curricula   154

What Can You Do about Censorship in Sexuality Education?   156

Other Considerations   159

What Else Can You Do?   160

References   161

8 Making a Place for Religion   163

Religion and the Role of Schooling   164

A Place for Religion   166

Teaching about Religions   168

Separation of Church and State   170
Prayer and Bible Reading   172
Continued Debate   173
Sorting Out the Historical Facts   174

Treating Religious and Nonreligious Beliefs in a Neutral Way   175
Rethinking Secular Humanism   176

Parents and Community Members   180

What Can You Do to Teach about Religions?   181

How Can You and Your School District Acknowledge Religion and Nonreligion?   183

How Can Students Express and Exercise Religious or Nonreligious Belief?   184

Appendix
Religion in the Public Schools: A Joint Statement of Current Law   186

Helpful Resources   191

References   192

9   Character, Values, and Intellectual Freedom   195

Views about Moral Character and Social Values   195

Controversy and Consensus   197

Teaching Character and Values   200
Redefining Values Clarification   200
In the Classroom and Beyond   201

What Can You Do to Teach Moral Character and Social Values?   203

Views about Intellectual Freedom   204

Exercising Academic Freedom   207

Children's Intellectual Rights   209

Students' Speech and Expression   211

Teaching Intellectual Freedom   213

What Can You Do to Preserve Intellectual Freedom?   215

Helpful Resources   216

References   217

10   Taking Action: Policies and Strategies   221

Making a Plan   222

Learning about Censorship   224
Teachers and Administrators   224
Students   225
Parents   227

Establishing Policies and Procedures   **228**

Philosophy Statements   **228**

Selection Policies and Procedures   **230**

Rationales   **233**
Rationale Guidelines   233

Reconsideration Policies and Procedures   **238**

Nonprint Media and the Internet   **241**

What Can You Do When Challenged?   **243**

Appendix
Selection and Reconsideration Policy of Riverside (California)
Unified School District—Plus Commentary   **245**

Helpful Resources   **250**

References   **251**

11   **Taking Action as Teacher, Citizen, and Advocate**   **253**

Perceived Problems and Real Needs   **253**

Crisis Rhetoric   **255**

Control of Education   **257**
Legislative Agendas   258
Religious Freedom   258
Parental Rights   259

Public, Private, and For-Profit Schools   **260**

A Dangerous Trend   **262**
Parents Training Children to Resist Classroom Ideas   262
Taking Control of Local and State School Boards   263
"Family-Friendly" Libraries   263
Technology as a Form of Parental Control   265

Taking Action as a Teacher and a Citizen   **266**
Public Charter Schools   266
Regaining Public Confidence   267

Inviting the Public Back into Public Education
by Jan Loveless   **267**
Positive School Reform   270

Taking Action as a Citizen and an Advocate   271
Grass-Roots Organizations   271
Moral Will   272

What Can You Do as a Teacher and a Citizen?   273

Helpful Resources   274

References   275

Index   277

PREFACE

Almost daily, the national media report on what are generally regarded as the failures of public education. Professional journals and local newspapers regularly describe parent protests and conflicts among a variety of education stakeholders over basic disagreements about classroom materials, methods, and philosophies. Some teachers boldly ignore all the hubbub, confident that they can defend themselves if necessary. Others seem to close their eyes and hold their breath, hoping that what they do in the classroom will not attract the challengers' notice. I understand both perspectives because I have felt both impulses. And truth be told, I have taken both stances during my teaching career.

This book speaks both to the bold ignorers and to the blind worriers as well as to teachers who take a variety of other stances toward teaching and learning. It is a book to help teachers think through the issues that surround classroom decision making and to offer suggestions for meeting the challenges posed by sincere parents concerned about their children and by broader threats to intellectual freedom and to public education. It is a book that proposes specific strategies and remedies to address challenges, reduce conflict, teach intellectual freedom, and strengthen public education.

Do we, as teachers, need to spend our time focusing on what *might* happen someday? Clearly, the answer is yes. Serious protesters and would-be censors strike with greater impact when they are likely to catch classroom teachers off guard. And serious challengers often count on unprepared teachers to react with self-doubts. Any sign of uncertainty on the teachers' part can be used to advantage by those who align themselves with nationally organized protest groups whose underlying agendas go well beyond minor adjustments to a particular curriculum. Nothing pleases them more than teachers who fear censorship and controversy enough to make quick changes in classroom practices to avoid trouble.

In a hostile climate created by a crisis in education that is at least partially "manufactured" (Berliner & Biddle, 1995), potential censorship and controversy touch every classroom experience, every book and resource, and every word spoken in the classroom. Many books and articles about school censorship recount school war stories and court cases. I respect the work of educators, librarians, attorneys, and constitutional scholars who have devoted their careers to studying censorship and its effects. Some of what I have learned from them is reflected in this book. I have gathered information and ideas from a wealth of sources that reflect widely divergent viewpoints, but primarily this is a book about teaching and learning, about what happens in classrooms and school districts. It is about how we can defend what we do, work with parents, and promote students' intellectual growth and freedom.

I have written this book primarily from the perspective of a teacher and a teacher educator with a keen interest in censorship, school controversy, and intellectual freedom. As a teacher, I am influenced not only by professional experiences but also by other roles outside the classroom that serendipitously affect my teaching and philosophy of education. For example, part of my interest in censorship issues stems from growing up and then first teaching in Kanawha County, West Virginia, the site of a 1974 landmark censorship case (see Chapter 2). The teacher who had supervised my student teaching was a member of the

Kanawha County Textbook Review Committee and had delivered speeches to stunned audiences across the country about what James Moffett has called the "storm in the mountains" of Kanawha County.

Another part of my interest in these issues stems from growing up in a Christian fundamentalist church and home environment. At home and church, religious faith mattered a lot. But as a student, I lived in a public school world that seemed unconnected to my church experience. By the time I was married in the late 1960s to a man deeply interested in political and social issues, I had begun to reexamine the political and theological views with which I had been raised. These experiences have deepened my understanding of the Appalachian culture from which the Kanawha County censors acted and their theological perspective, as well. I no longer hold the ultraconservative theological and political views I once held, but I have a deep sense of the theological motivations of the influential national protest groups that so often generate headlines. More important, I maintain a strong faith and continue to identify with some of the faith-related concerns expressed by parents.

As a parent, I have watched my children's school experiences—often with delight as I have applauded their acquisition of new knowledge and achievements. On rare occasions, however, I have experienced the frustration that comes from feeling that my concerns as a parent (and as an educator, since it is impossible in such circumstances to separate the two) have been more or less disregarded by a teacher or administrator. Therefore, since I have written this book from a teacher's perspective, I have also tried not to forget how it feels to be a parent who disagrees with a teacher about the needs of a particular child.

Finally, this book was written while I was teaching my university courses for preservice teachers of English language arts, directing the Third Coast Writing Project, and participating in several other major professional projects. Since 1995, I have also worked with a handful of passionate and committed colleagues and acquaintances to create a statewide grass-roots organization to support and strengthen public education. In that role, I have testified before legislative committees, produced newsletters, and networked with a wide range of individuals and groups to achieve common goals. These advocacy experiences have enriched and refined my understanding of issues, political processes, and people's concerns and agendas; they have also influenced the focus and content of this book.

My intention is to get beyond the superficial, highly charged, and divisive rhetoric that is too often associated with challenges to classroom materials and teaching methods. I hope instead to explore and to explain why teachers today are so often confronted by disapproving parents and community members and how to avoid being caught by surprise. You will learn from the testimonials of those who have lived through major curricular controversies and who understand retrospectively when it is wise to confront boldly and when it is wiser to accommodate, when distinctions between "us" and "them" are essential and when they poison hope for constructive change. I invite you to read actively—pausing to examine your own beliefs about the issues and to think through the implications and effects of possible decisions and actions. I invite you to rethink what you already know about school censorship and controversy, and to consider new possibilities for yourself as a teacher and as a citizen.

Each chapter provides practical information and insights to help you be ready to respond to the concerns, fears, and demands of parents and organized groups. Each chapter offers specific suggestions and resources to help you make wise classroom decisions without self-censoring. Chapters 4 through 7 focus on issues and topics within particular content areas that have drawn the protesters' fire.

I offer special thanks to the knowledgeable and wise contributing authors: Jodi Brookins-Fisher (Central Michigan University), who wrote Chapter 5 about sexuality education; and coauthors Ronald G. Good (Louisiana State University), James A. Shymansky (University of Missouri), and Larry D. Yore (University of Victoria), who wrote Chapter 7 about science and science education. Thanks also to Dan Holt (St. Joseph High School, Michigan) for explaining the perspective that has guided his experience as advisor for award-winning student publications, and to Jan Loveless (Midland, Michigan) for describing a practical and effective plan that reconnects communities and their public schools.

Many others, whose work is cited, have made important contributions to enrich the resources this book provides. A sabbatical leave and a grant from the Western Michigan University Faculty Research and Creative Activities Support Fund provided the time that made publication possible. Also, the response and suggestions offered by friends and colleagues kept me coming back to the manuscript in the midst of a range of other demanding tasks. My appreciation goes to Lynda Griffiths for her careful copyediting and to the following reviewers for their helpful comments on the manuscript: Alice Naylor (Appalachian State University) and Patt Graff (La Cueva High School). I especially thank Jean Tittle, Lyla Fox, Charles Israel, Aedìn Clements, and Connie Weaver, who read portions of the manuscript and/or offered helpful insights, ideas, and encouragement.

REFERENCES

Berliner, D. C., & B. J. Biddle. (1995). *The manufactured crisis: Myths, fraud, and the attack on America's public schools*. Reading, MA: Addison-Wesley.

Moffett, J. (1988). *Storm in the mountains: A case study of censorship, conflict, and consciousness*. Carbondale, IL: Southern Illinois University Press.

CAUGHT OFF GUARD

1 Teaching in a Changing Classroom World

What we will never be able to measure is how many books were not taught, how many topics were not discussed, how many newspaper articles were not brought into the classroom that would have been very valuable for kids to have read and learned about because of the fear that teacher had that they might become the object of another challenge.

—Kevin Teeley (cited in Feldman, 1994)

Classroom teachers have traditionally depended heavily on textbooks and accompanying materials produced by publishers for direction in long-term and day-by-day curriculum planning. Detailed scope and sequence charts prescribe when and how we should "cover" each part of the curriculum. Many of us, however, use scope and sequence materials more as suggestions to be considered, reshaped, or abandoned as we work with our colleagues to design school or school district curricula. Although school boards have the final say, we make many classroom decisions based on our own professional preparation and knowledge about students, about content, and about teaching and learning. Ultimately, we depend on our skills and artistry as teachers.

In best-practice classrooms, we learn theory and research well enough to work on our own or with teaching colleagues to make many, but not all, day-by-day curricular decisions. We learn from our students how to gauge what they know and need to learn. We provide at least limited choice based on students' interests. And we build into our curricula opportunities for both individual and group inquiries involving research and experiences that often go well beyond materials found inside classroom or library walls.

Teachers of our grandparents' and even parents' generations were often limited to using a single hard-covered textbook, but teachers today seldom face such limitations. Teachers' choices of materials have been changed forever by inexpensive paperback books, photocopying machines, and computers. An article appearing in yesterday's newspaper or on an online news service can spark today's discussion of the possibility of life on other planets or the impact of a Supreme Court ruling.

The fact that textbooks are no longer the primary resource represents a dramatic shift in education with far-reaching implications. Teachers and students have access to almost unlimited potential curricular materials that can free teachers and students alike from the limited materials and outdated information that constrained people in the past. Classroom teachers are constrained, nevertheless, by school districts' budgets and districts' willingness to purchase and use particular classroom materials and resources. More significantly, teachers are sometimes constrained rather than supported by district-established policies and curricula and by community pressures to censor materials and technology. Three true-story vignettes illustrate the range of challenges that classroom teachers face:

Vignette 1

Computers are bringing dramatic change to classrooms, but with computers comes less teacher and parental control over the materials and learning experiences students have available to them. Consider, for example, the potential dilemma faced by a group of Canadian teachers and students who found a poem titled "inborn consent" waiting for them online. This particular poem showed up within a national online program called Writers in Electronic Residence (Owen, 1995, p. 50). (I caution you about the violent nature and language found in the poem, but a milder substitution would not illustrate my point.)

> *inborn consent**
>
> Hey Bitch—
>   wanna fuck?
> Hey Bitch—
>   yeah you!
> wanna fuck?
> I know you do
>   you yelled it to me
>   with your slutwalk
> you screamed
>   your obscene desire to me
>   with your whoreclothes
> Hey Bitch—
>   wanna fuck?
> I don't give a shit
>   that your girlvoice
>   whispers no
> Your womanbody already
>   said yes
>   —Delacey Tedesco

*Reprinted with permission by Delacey Tedesco.

What happens when students are the first to encounter such messages online? Can or should teachers limit students' access to ideas like this that offend so many? Although we hear discussion about online etiquette as well as guidelines and rules, the interactive nature of the Internet—which gives "voice" to anyone who has access to the equipment and the service—means that teachers and parents have little control over what students read and have no control over what they write or "publish" for others to read.

When Trevor Owen (1995) discussed his students' discovery of the poem "inborn consent," he warned that teachers should "be prepared to deal with the work that comes" (p. 50). The high school and college students in this case responded to the "inborn consent" poet online: "I suppose we need questionable stuff like this to define what 'acceptable' is"; "Your verse feels ironic, as though the words are turning back against the speaker"; and even, "I don't think your poem is offensive or gross at all—except perhaps to those who actually think this way. Poems were made to change the world. Maybe this one will make a difference" (p. 51). Owen did not say whether any parents heard about or protested students' reactions to this poem. If they had, he could have pointed to the students' thoughtful and insightful responses and insisted that poems *are* meant to change the world and that "inborn consent" did make a difference by generating thoughtful responses about the nature of poetry as well as resistance to the ideas being expressed.

Many high school teachers would not be surprised if parents raised questions about the offensive language of "inborn consent," since language is a favorite target for many protesters. What is more offensive and chilling to those who look beyond the offensive language, of course, is the apparent theme of condoned violent assault against women.

Vignette 2
Most middle and high school teachers know to expect complaints about violence in literature selections. Today, even elementary teachers—who once were protected from censorship by lifeless and bloodless basal reader stories—are encountering objections to violence in the children's literature in their classrooms.

Such complaints are described in a California classroom story. Third-graders read or listened to several versions of the Cinderella story from a variety of cultures, including Indian, French, Egyptian, and Chinese. By comparing these stories and the Disney cartoon version that many students had seen, the children became more thoughtful readers as they tested one version of the story against another (Meade, 1990, p. 42). With their teacher's guidance, they were able to learn a bit more about different cultures and, perhaps by contrast, to learn more about their own.

There is more to this story, however. One of the Cinderella stories the teacher read aloud was Grimm's "Aschenputtel," a version that the teacher later admitted is "a little bloody." (The Queen told the sisters to cut off a part of their feet to try to fit into the lost slipper but the prince noticed in both cases "how the blood was running out of her shoe, and how it had stained her white stocking quite red.") During their final discussion of all the stories, the teacher called attention to the stories' similar plots and themes and commented that "at different times, [similar] thoughts are expressed by different cultures, by people from different ethnic backgrounds" (Meade, 1990, p. 42).

Classroom conversations like this one are clearly aligned with current best practice. But on this particular day, in this classroom, a parent observer sat in on the reading and discussion. The next day, the teacher discovered that the parent had called a school board member to complain.

The principal who subsequently looked over the teacher's curricular materials was so impressed that she arranged for the teacher to share her ideas with her colleagues. I hope the teacher also had the chance to discuss the matter with the protesting parent. If so, I hope she was able to explain what her students were learning. I hope she had student-produced art and writing that would show that the students had not been disturbed by the "bloody" story. More important, I hope the teacher invited the parent to explain what he or she objected to about the literature and/or the lesson. Was it the bloody foot or the cross-cultural fairy tale? And why was the parent concerned? I also hope the teacher really listened before she responded.

Vignette 3

A group of parents objected to a proposed schoolwide emphasis on technology in their local schools. The parents, all members of a local church, used their objection to technology to argue for a separate school-within-a-school for their children. Their concern was based in their belief that "regular classrooms with their emphasis on technology, such as computers and television, would lead their children away from Bible teachings" (Associated Press, 1995). To accommodate the parents' requests, the public school proposed an amazing solution: The 22 children involved would be provided entirely segregated classes and a separate schedule that would take place within an existing elementary school but that would provide separate doors, separate classrooms, separate lunch accommodations, a separate teacher, and a separate curriculum that would emphasize "reading, writing, math, English, cooking, sewing and crafts" (p. A6).

As it turns out, these children had not previously attended the local schools but had been home schooled. The parents used their protest of technology as a vehicle to obtain a separate public school classroom and curriculum, and they did so with the blessing of school officials. Why? The local school district administrators saw the proposal "as a way to add new students and about $160,000 in state money to a school with declining enrollment." Conservative State Board of Education members who favored providing public funds for semipublic charter schools applauded the program as "just another example of trying to make government more 'customer friendly'" (Associated Press, 1995).

On first glance, you may wonder why anyone would object to such a plan that promises benefits to students, parents, and the school district. However, this story raises important questions: How far should teachers, administrators, and school board members be willing to go to accommodate the concerns, requests, and demands of a small cluster of parents? Which requests should be honored? To what extent are we, as members of a democratic society, ready to alter school schedules and curricula?

What Is a Classroom Teacher to Do?

No matter the kind of pressure or its source, no teacher welcomes personal or professional criticism. Many good teachers, whose everyday lives are filled both with the joys of learning and the hassles of bureaucracy, do not feel they can spend much time or energy worrying about potential complaints or challenges to their teaching practices. No one wants to be caught off guard, though.

At some point during the day when the Cinderella teacher heard that her classroom practice had been challenged, she probably paused to question the wisdom of her classroom choices. In the course of a day, we teachers make hundreds of decisions, perform countless tasks, and interact hour by hour with students individually and in groups. In spite of good intentions, we all occasionally make mistakes. And even when we do not make mistakes, we are extremely vulnerable to criticism.

Given the three true-story vignettes, we might be tempted to become discouraged, thinking that such conflicts present circumstances over which classroom teachers have little, if any, control. Given the poem "inborn consent," some teachers may even agree that schools might be better off not to open Pandora's box—that is, not to give students access to materials that so many consider objectionable. These stories, however, point to the need for teachers to anticipate when curricular pressures and protests might arise and to think through questions that do not have easy answers, such as the following:

- Is it possible for teachers to use only those classroom materials and experiences of which no parent would disapprove?
- How might teachers decide to handle controversial and/or offensive items that are transmitted online?
- What inkling might teachers have that parents, who normally welcome technology and its use, might object so strenuously as to insist on separate classrooms and instruction?
- What part does intellectual freedom play for students and for teachers?

These and many other questions will be discussed in the chapters ahead. In the meantime, the following "Teacher's Self-Test #1: Defending Classroom Decisions" (Figure 1.1) is offered to help you begin to sort out and think through the issues sur-

FIGURE 1.1   Teacher's Self-Test #1: Defending Classroom Decisions

What do you know about issues of censorship and school controversy within the context of your own school setting? Test yourself with the questions below. Then read the "Responses to Teacher's Self-Test #1" in the chapter text. Encourage your teaching colleagues to respond to the self-test, as well. Then compare notes with each other as you begin to consider how to address the issues more effectively.

1. How well can you defend what and how you teach? How do you do it?

   _____

2. On what occasions during the last 12 months have you explained your philosophy of teaching and learning? To whom?

   _____

3. How well do you understand the views of those who might oppose you? Try articulating what you believe their views to be.

   _____

4. How would you describe your own political views and theological perspective or philosophical worldview? To what extent are your views and perspective shared by other teachers in your district? By those in your community?

   _____

5. How familiar are you with your school or district's materials selection policy and procedures? With reconsideration policy and procedures?

   _____

6. If you were challenged tomorrow morning by someone objecting to a particular text or class experience, what would you do first? Second? Third?

   _____

7. Who can you identify as trusted colleagues you could count on to support you in the midst of a personal challenge?

   _____

8. How would you describe your own views about intellectual freedom? Where do you personally draw the line in terms of appropriate and inappropriate materials and class experiences?

   _____

9. What seems at this moment to be your own or your district's greatest need in terms of rethinking issues of classroom decision making and potential censorship and school controversy?

   _____

Note: May be photocopied for use; source must be cited: Ellen Brinkley, *Caught off Guard: Teachers Rethinking Censorship and Controversy* (Boston: Allyn and Bacon, 1999).

rounding classroom censorship and controversy. It can serve as a nudge to help you become more aware, better informed, and more articulate about issues that too many of us never think much about until a challenger's questions and complaints catch us off guard. Given the significance of the questions posed, each may require considerably more thought and writing than the space provided. The point is to tap quickly into your first responses. I encourage you to return to these questions again as you and your teaching colleagues continue to rethink the issues.

Responses to Teacher's Self-Test #1

1. Clearly you need to be able to explain and defend what you teach as well as how you teach it. You need specific strategies for explaining your curricular choices and classroom experiences.

2. If you know what you do in the classroom and why, but seldom spend much time talking about it, you need to take the time to make explicit the assumptions that guide your teaching. In fact, you need to be able to explain in a convincing manner and in detail to parents and others what you do and why.

3. Censorship issues change over time. It is crucial to read local and national news reports about censorship and controversy issues so that you are better equipped to understand and respond to those with different views. Aristotle said one needs to know one's opponent's position as well as or better than one's own. It was good advice then and it is good advice now.

4. You need to think through and be able to articulate, at least for yourself, your own philosophical or theological worldviews. It is not that you need to go public with your personal perspective, but it is essential for you, at least privately, to consider how your own views may intersect and conflict with the views of your teaching colleagues and the views of the community where you teach.

5. It sounds self-evident, but some teachers actually do not know if their districts have a formal academic freedom policy or policies and procedures for materials selection and reconsideration (see Chapter 10). If such policies and procedures are in place, you need to be well informed about them. If not, you can volunteer to work with your colleagues and administrators to create them—not to constrain what and how you and your colleagues teach but to clarify for yourselves and others the process by which parents and others in the community can question what happens in the local schools.

6. This question asks you to face the uncomfortable likelihood that, in spite of everything, your materials and practices will be challenged. It is the assumption with which you have to start. Do your school's official policies and procedures really work? You need to decide ahead of time what your personal options might be and what sources of support you could count on.

7. Too often, teachers report feeling alienated when challenged. You need to cultivate professional friendships that will serve as much-needed resources when there is a need for someone to listen, advise, and provide support. The time to identify and develop that support is, of course, before the need arises.

8. Many teachers fall woefully short in terms of understanding what intellectual freedom they have as teachers (see Chapter 9). You may remember too little of your undergraduate education classes in which such issues were discussed. If you have considerable teaching experience, you may tend to make curricular decisions intuitively, or so it seems. If so, you need to think through carefully the classroom values that influence how you determine what to include and what to omit.

9. This question invites you to reflect on issues raised in earlier questions and on your own local school circumstances and community climate so that gaps in knowledge and planning can be addressed.

Facts about Curricular Challenges and Controversies

Although we teachers have always been more or less accountable for what happens in our classrooms, we enter the twenty-first century with increasing awareness that each decision we make—big or little—is subject to scrutiny by persons whose perspectives or agendas we may not agree with or even understand. As we search for some way to live daily with the prospect of potential challenge or complaint, we understandably ask: When are complaints apt to surface? How likely are curricular protests in my school district?

We can begin to consider such questions by studying available data. The American Library Association (ALA) keeps records of challenges that might result in the removal or restriction of books and nonprint materials. Each year, ALA produces a list of books most often challenged as well as the number of challenges to public library, school library, and school materials reported to the ALA Office for Intellectual Freedom. For example, in 1991, ALA's Office for Intellectual Freedom reported 514 total challenges to school and school library materials. By 1994, that number had risen to 760 but then dropped to 482 in 1995 (see Figure 1.2).

People for the American Way (PFAW) uses a strict set of criteria in their reporting challenges, which exclude (1) parents' attempts to prevent only their own child from using materials or participating in a program; (2) citizens who first request removal but promptly accept offers to remove their children from the activities in question and who then withdraw their complaints; and (3) incidents that are clear issues of pedagogy or methodology. Given these guidelines, in order to be included in the PFAW "attempted censorship" category, a challenge "must attempt to control what *other parents' children* [emphasis added] may have access to" (PFAW, 1996, p. 10). PFAW reports that usually such challenges involve opposition to issues of religion or ideology.

Each year, PFAW tracks which texts and topics have drawn the greatest number of challenges and annually publishes a list of the year's most frequently challenged books. PFAW also provides a cumulative report beginning with 1982 (see Figure 1.3).

It is interesting to notice that over the years the list tends not to change a great deal. Time and time again, district after district fights slightly different battles over the

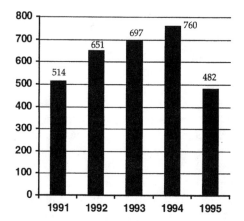

FIGURE 1.2   Number of Challenges to Schools and School Library Materials

Source: Reprinted by permission of the American Library Association.

Note: The Office for Intellectual Freedom does not claim comprehensiveness in recording challenges. Research suggests that for each challenge reported, there are as many as four or five that go unreported.

same books. The same is true for the cumulative report for the year's most frequently challenged materials, which includes commercially published curricular materials, popular magazines, state curriculum materials, and films (see Figure 1.3).

 People for the American Way recognizes that it has become increasingly important to monitor challenges or protest incidents beyond those that focus on restricting or removing particular school texts and materials. Therefore, PFAW's annual reports separate school-based incidents of attempted censorship from a broader range of chal-

FIGURE 1.3   Most Frequently Challenged Books and Materials, 1982–1996

Books	*Materials*
Of Mice and Men, John Steinbeck	*Impressions* [textbook series]
The Catcher in the Rye, J. D. Salinger	*Pumsy in Pursuit of Excellence* [self-esteem
The Chocolate War, Robert Cormier	program]
I Know Why the Caged Bird Sings, Maya	*Quest* [self-esteem program]
Angelou	*Developing Understanding of Self and Others*
Scary Stories To Tell in the Dark, Alvin	[self-esteem program]
Schwartz	*Rolling Stone* [magazine]
The Adventures of Huckleberry Finn, Mark	*Romeo and Juliet* [film]
Twain	*YM* [magazine]
More Scary Stories to Tell in the Dark, Alvin	*Schindler's List* [film]
Schwartz	*Michigan Model for Comprehensive School*
Go Ask Alice, anonymous	*Health Education*
Bridge to Terabithia, Katherine Paterson	*Junior Great Book Series* [reading texts]
The Witches, Roald Dahl	

Source: People for the American Way Foundation. Reprinted by permission.

lenges that include "attempts by individuals or organizations to inject their own ideological or sectarian agenda into the educational process" (1996, p. 10). These more politicized incidents include "efforts to distort textbook selection processes by bringing ideological or sectarian pressure, or advancing legislation or other initiatives that would inject such considerations" (1996, p. 10).

For the 1995–96 school year, PFAW (1996, p. 11) reported a 46 percent increase (175 of the 475 reported challenges) in "broad-based" complaints. When school-based incidents of attempted censorship are combined with broad-based challenges, People for the American Way recorded 264 incidents in 1990–91 with numbers rising in subsequent years to 475 in 1995–96 (PFAW, 1990, 1991, 1992, 1993, 1994, 1995, 1996).

The ALA and PFAW data overall reveal a clear rising trend in the number of incidents reported. Part of the increase may result from educators being more alert to censorship attempts and their significance. If so, that means we are doing a better job of knowing the truth. Neither ALA nor PFAW, however, claim to report comprehensive data. In fact, because they have to rely to a great extent on information provided by the general public, both groups make a point to emphasize that there is every indication that the data are significantly underreported. ALA's research suggests that for every one incident reported, there are as many as four or five unreported. I support this estimate, since I am surprised every year when the annual reports miss some of the challenges I am aware of in my state. Others place the unreported figure much higher. Edward B. Jenkinson, censorship monitor and scholar, speculated—on the basis of conversations with teachers, librarians, and administrators in 33 states—that "for every reported incident of censorship at least fifty go unreported" (1985, p. 28). Notice that this amazing figure is not a wild guess. Thus, when reading these annual reports, one needs to keep in mind the likelihood that the numbers represent merely the tip of the school censorship/controversy iceberg.

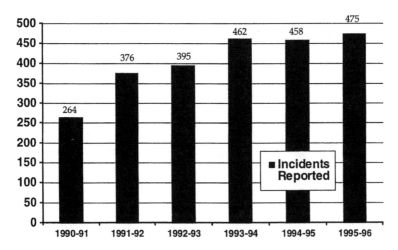

FIGURE 1.4   Number of Censorship and Related Challenges to Public Education

Source: People for the American Way Foundation. Reprinted by permission.

On the other hand, making a good-faith effort not to exaggerate problems and potential problems is also important. Few people listen to exaggerated claims, and most teachers learn quickly that it is not wise to overstate or to underestimate circumstances unnecessarily. I particularly appreciate PFAW's rigorous practice of separating censorship challenges involving removal or restriction from the wide-ranging possible actions that fall into the "broad-based" category. *Censorship* is such a pejorative term that almost no individual protester or organized group ever identifies its own actions as "censorship." Thus, it is helpful to be explicit in describing particular circumstances and to assign specific meanings to words such as *complaint, protest, challenge,* and *censorship.* I have tried to make these distinctions throughout the book, especially when identifying specific incidents and circumstances. When I address issues in a more general way, at times I use a range of terms, primarily because some broad-based complaints or protests eventually result in censorship of particular materials or experiences. Also, some single-text censorship challenges expand into broad controversies that encompass every school-related facet of the community.

Circumstances in such cases are often extremely fluid, and classroom teachers may not have access to up-to-the-minute reports on latest developments. Teachers cannot, therefore, be exactly clear at any moment when a parental complaint might become a protest, or when a protest might involve potential censorship, or even when censorship actually occurs. Chances are that the classroom teacher will not be present if parents register a complaint with the principal and may not immediately realize that other parents have joined in a protest or that the principal may have promised to get rid of the disapproved materials.

As a rule, librarians are better informed and organized by virtue of their training than classroom teachers to focus on issues of intellectual freedom. In fact, often the school librarian acts as the primary resource person in the midst of addressing particular issues and challenges. But efforts by the American Family Association, Focus on the Family, and the Family Research Council to discredit the ALA (Mizner, 1995, p. 6) have led to frightening rhetoric describing new threats to public libraries: "Right to read? It's a bunch of hogwash. . . . You don't have the right to read anything you want. We have to protect each other from dangerous material" (Burress, cited in Mizner, 1995). Most librarians and teachers believe that the "protection" promised is likely to be a lot more dangerous than access to the reading materials. Given the potential of these new challenges, classroom teachers will want to work together with school librarians to protect students' rights to intellectual freedom.

Circumstances That Invite Challenge and Controversy

We cannot predict with great accuracy when classroom materials and teaching practices will be challenged. Certain circumstances, however, can be identified in which school challenges and potential censorship are more likely to occur. These are discussed next.

New Curricula or Policies

Most school districts are alert to the possibility of challenges whenever they adopt new curricular materials, especially if those materials have been controversial in other school districts. National media attention to the censorship of the *Impressions* elementary language arts textbook series caught the attention of parents across North America who, once aware of the controversy, demanded that the series be removed from their own districts. This wildfire protest against an innovative curriculum that included culturally diverse reading selections was so extensive that *Impressions* still is listed first on PFAW's 1982–96 list of most frequently challenged materials. New policies can also generate controversy and protests, as occurred when the Lake County, Florida, school board enacted an "America-first" policy that would require teachers to teach that American culture is superior to all others (Rohter, 1994).

Attention-Getting Classroom Projects

Complaints tend to arise whenever teachers or students begin new classroom projects or become especially enthusiastic about what they are reading, discussing, and doing—that is, what they are learning—in the classroom. Enthusiasm often leads to talk in school and at home about what is happening. Talk creates attention and scrutiny, which can result in praise and/or criticism. For example, when a group of alternative high school students in my area, most of whom were reluctant or resistant readers, engaged in intense discussions about *Monster: The Autobiography of an LA Gang Member*, the word got out. When the word spread to the ears of those who questioned just what kind of book could be generating so much interest among previously disinterested students, new restrictions on classroom texts soon were put into place.

Curricula Linked to Personal Experience

Challenges occur whenever teachers simply share more of themselves—their knowledge, opinions, and life stories—with their students and whenever teachers encourage students to share from their own knowledge and experiences. Teachers of writing, for example, are encouraged to be writers themselves and to share their writing with their students. When they do, they communicate to students the importance of writing, they model writing strategies, and they celebrate the shared stories that emerge as students and teachers write about their experiences. Because the energy for writing often comes from topics close to student writers' own experiences, occasionally their writing includes personal or family stories about death or divorce. Students, especially young ones, have always volunteered both amusing and embarrassing details of family life in various formats of Show-and-Tell. What parents increasingly protest are teacher-initiated classroom activities or assignments that encourage students to draw on personal or family experience as an aid to learning.

Explicit Ideological and Political Stances

Challenges to classroom practices are likely to surface whenever teachers take an explicitly sociopolitical stance. A high school teacher of U.S. Government who is a Desert Storm veteran can provide real-life stories that will breathe life into otherwise dull textbook lessons. If this teacher also expresses strong personal views about why war in such cases is or is not justified, the teacher risks parental protest from those whose perspectives differ. Sadly, even if the teacher simply encourages an examination of pro and con sides of the issue, he or she might be challenged for that, as well, if he or she teaches in a district that has decided to emphasize uncritical praise for U.S. policy and actions.

Strong stands on sociopolitical issues can generate complaints regardless of whether the perspective taken is from the political right or left, as a group of conservative Colorado teachers found out (Shanahan, 1994). They were criticized by a more liberal parent who objected to an antiabortion video being shown in his son's seventh-grade class, an objection raised especially because the video had been produced by the Christian Coalition. Clearly, teachers who take overtly political stands in the classroom can expect to be challenged by those with opposing views.

Politicized Pedagogical and School Reform Issues

Pervasive crisis rhetoric about public schools (see Chapter 3) has created an atmosphere in which major reform initiatives are quickly challenged by anxious parents and organized groups. Pedagogical and school reform movements, such as Outcomes Based Education and whole language, have been especially targeted by radio talk-show hosts and leaders of conservative national organizations, such as Citizens for Excellence in Education (CEE). The Summer 1996 issue of CEE's *Newsline* featured articles titled "Goals 2000 Loses Ground," "Charter Schools Catch On," and "Is Self-Esteem Really Good for You?" On radio talk shows, school reform movements typically are defined in a few sentences or less. Frequently, talk-show hosts use only a single negative catchphrase, such as *the dumbing down of education* or *reading as a guessing game,* to politicize the issues and rally support for views on issues that I feel sure they know almost nothing about. Seldom is there any information offered that might help the listeners or readers sort out issues for themselves. But such strategies get people's attention, fan the flames of controversy, and generate income for the lambasters. Popular news magazines do a better job of covering such topics but often provide just enough information so that people from many walks of life feel qualified to take a position and to express opinions on the basis of one or two articles in *Time* or *Newsweek.*

More often than not, the net result, especially of the political rhetoric, is increased discontent and controversy directed at public schools. When some churches form local parent committees that take direction from national conservative Christian organizations, there is often a protest surrounding a single issue or a steady drumbeat of complaints and protests targeting any number of school district curricula and practices. Jenkinson (1990, p. 15) has identified at least 200 targets of individuals or groups during a 17-year study. Since the early 1980s, the ultimate goal of such ongoing complaints has frequently been an explicitly political one that goes well beyond changing the curriculum. Many of these protesters want to dismantle public education so that public money can be used to pay for private schooling (see Chapter 11).

The reality is that several of these factors usually exist at any given time in most school districts. Schools do adopt new curricula and policies, and classroom projects will attract attention. Most teachers today do draw on students' experiences whenever they can to strengthen learning. More and more teachers believe that all pedagogy is grounded at least to some extent in ideological and political philosophies. And today's media feed on crisis rhetoric and controversy. Given such circumstances, teachers sometimes question whether it is even remotely possible to feel safe against challenge and controversy. Indeed, most conclude that there is no guaranteed security.

This is not to say that there is nothing teachers can do to prevent some of the challenges and controversy or that there is no hope amidst the conflict. To begin, we can prepare for the likelihood of challenges and school controversy when any of these circumstances exist. We can learn to expect challenges at virtually any time. And no matter how elaborately we anticipate potential censorship or controversy, parents will always rightfully ask questions about school, and protesters will sometimes create controversy.

Vulnerable Teachers

Although all teachers are at risk, clearly some are more likely to be confronted by parent or community protestors. Unfortunately, as the following categories indicate, all teachers seem to fall into at least one vulnerable category.

Risk-Taking Teachers

Some teachers seem to thrive on testing the edges of curricular decision making. With admirable determination, they arrange the desks in their classrooms to encourage cooperative group work, respect students' diverse abilities and interests, and organize daily schedules that allow for some student choice of what and how to learn. They try to provide engaging tasks and seek new ways to encourage students to take charge of their own learning, to question and solve problems. One elementary science teacher encourages his students to close their eyes and pretend they are floating in a cloud so they can imagine the effects of changing temperatures. A high school World History teacher shows and discusses *Schlinder's List*. She encourages her students to gather stories told by grandparents or great-grandparents about their own memories of World War II. She might invite a Holocaust survivor to speak. An especially bold teacher might even invite a speaker who discounts the events of the Holocaust so that students could consider the evidence for themselves.

The elementary science teacher and the high school history teacher are both likely to be praised by some parents and administrators for making learning come alive for their students. They may both believe that their praiseworthy methods will protect them from being criticized or challenged. Yet, they both are *more* subject to administrative criticism and parental protest for the very same practices that might earn them praise. They are at risk because they step outside routine expectations.

Playing-It-Safe Teachers

Some teachers, of course, work harder at "playing it safe" than others. Knowing the disruption that can accompany criticism or challenge, such teachers remind themselves how important it is to keep their own attention and that of their students focused on learning. They have no time or stomach for dealing with protests or complaints. As they teach earth science, they decide to stick to the school-approved text when they sense that students might raise questions about creationism and origins of the universe. As they select novels for whole-class assignments in English or language arts classes, they steer clear of Kurt Vonnegut or Judy Blume, insisting that there is no need for students to read them when there are so many other fine authors to choose from. When a colleague chooses a riskier path, play-it-safe teachers quietly reassure themselves that, chances are, the potential protesters will go after their risk-taking colleagues and leave them—the play-it-safers—in peace. Sometimes such a strategy works; however, teachers who try hardest to avoid controversy are just as much at risk because even they can find themselves embroiled in a debate that no one could have predicted. When they depend on playing it safe, such teachers are the ones most likely to be caught off guard.

New Teachers

New teachers are vulnerable teachers. Although they have had considerable preparation for teaching, including an intern teaching semester, their first real job is dramatically different from their intern experiences. They now bear the entire responsibility for what happens in their classrooms, just like the veteran teachers in the classrooms down the hall. As new teachers move through their first year, each school day is at least partially experimental as they begin to sort out what works for them individually as a teacher and for their students. Their lack of experience usually leaves them the least self-confident of professional educators.

School districts that provide induction programs for new teachers know that experienced and trained mentors can help beat the national odds that as many as 50 percent of new teachers leave the profession during their first five years of teaching. Unfortunately, new teachers in districts without induction programs too often find themselves with the most difficult teaching assignments in the district.

New teachers are especially at risk of being challenged because of the many complex demands. With so much to learn on the job and so much to handle at the same time, new teachers inevitably make mistakes. They are also the most scrutinized teachers in any building, the most likely to be watched by administrators and parents. Additionally, they lack the one thing that often protects experienced teachers from criticism: a professional reputation.

Experienced Teachers

Many experienced teachers seem—at least on the surface—confident and self-assured. They know how to organize and manage their classrooms and create what they believe are engaging learning experiences. They live out their beliefs about teaching and learning day by day, having learned along the way how to get along within the culture of their schools and communities. New teachers often envy veteran teachers' confidence and experience. Ironically, even nationally acclaimed classroom teachers—those with many years of successful classroom experience, with teaching awards to their credit or with articles or books published—harbor occasional fears that maybe they are not "good enough" at what they do. That is, they occasionally second-guess themselves and worry that maybe they do not have an adequate background in the discipline they are currently teaching. Or maybe they have not read enough research in their field (and who can read it all?). Or maybe they have not assessed a student's portfolio fairly . . . or maybe they could have said something that might have kept a reluctant learner from quitting school . . . or maybe . . . .

Some experienced teachers, however, take self-doubts as healthy signs that they are reflective practitioners, able to critique their own classroom decisions. Their confidence and self-respect are tempered by acceptance of their weaknesses as well as their strengths. They know what they *do not* know as well as what they *do* know. They know that teaching affords the opportunity to continue learning.

Experienced teachers are the least likely to have their curriculum and teaching practices challenged. More significantly, they are the best prepared to avoid criticism when possible, to predict when risk taking might result in being challenged, and to respond positively when protests occur. Having learned what "goes" and what does not in their schools and communities, experienced teachers develop a sense of where the boundaries are and when and how to work toward positive change. They have read articles in professional journals and in the public press. They have also heard stories from across the country about school districts that have been turned upside down by organized protests that demand enormous amounts of teachers' attention and drain teachers of much of their resolve. In many cases, experienced teachers have realized they need to plan ahead for ways to defend and protect the curricular materials they select, or those the school district committees have selected for them. Sometimes they have worked with colleagues to establish selection and reconsideration policies.

In general, experienced teachers tend to develop a certain comfort level that rests on the assurance that they have done everything they can toward preserving intellectual freedom in their classrooms and school districts. But experienced educators also know that even careful plans and precautions cannot provide fail-safe protection against the possibility of future challenges and confrontations.

Although risk-taking teachers and new teachers are most vulnerable—and risk-taking new teachers most of all—ultimately, all of us are susceptible to potential censorship. *All* of the teachers identified are likely to be challenged—risk-taking teachers, play-it-safe teachers, new teachers, and experienced teachers alike—at some points in their careers. Facing this truth does not mean that we must become reconciled to constant confrontation. Rather, it means that we must work together to (1) include academic and intellectual freedom clauses in student handbooks, teachers' contracts, and school mission statements; (2) increase support for new teachers and protect their right to use fresh ideas and materials; and (3) build into the school year occasions when parents, community members, and educators can talk about the real substance of curricular issues—teachers seeking to understand the community's perspectives and concerns, and community members seeking to understand the importance of protecting teachers' and students' intellectual freedom.

Vulnerable Schools

Some schools and districts do take more curricular and extracurricular risks than others, but there is no evidence that I am aware of to suggest that conservative, play-it-safe districts have fewer complaints from parent protesters. Parents' socioeconomic levels, parents' education levels, and whether a school district is urban, suburban, or rural, however, may be factors. Inner-city teachers seem to face fewer parental protests even when the curriculum includes "risky" topics, such as tolerance for homosexual lifestyles. If teachers have more education and more income than most of the families in the school district, chances are that the teachers will not be challenged as often as their counterparts in the suburbs. Inner-city parents' job and survival issues may demand so much attention that parents have little inclination to complain about curricula. And with less education and income, many urban parents seem somewhat more likely to defer to their children's teachers. Sometimes they are grateful when teachers address real-world issues, even controversial ones.

Teachers seem more likely to face challenges to curriculum in school districts where the socioeconomic status of the parents is equal to or higher than that of school faculty and administration. Although suburban parents are usually strongly supportive of their local schools, they often hold strong opinions about what should be happening in classrooms. If teachers in such districts have less income than many families in the school district, they may be impressed or intimidated by parents' wealth and comfortable lifestyles. They are likely to be challenged by bolder, self-confident parents who have the time to focus on school issues. In such cases, teachers may be tempted or even pressured to defer to parents' wishes.

Although parent protests may occur in any school at any time, most of what gets reported in the media are challenges that occur in public rather than in private schools. Parents of private and parochial school students always have the option of moving their children back to traditional public school classrooms. The same is true for magnet schools and charter schools. Although magnet and charter schools are often at least semipublic schools, teachers at such schools frequently have more say about designing curricula.

Ultimately, it may be that challenges are more likely in areas where sizable groups of parents, for one reason or another, believe they know more than teachers. Such views may be expressed by highly educated parents or by parents who are convinced of the superiority of their own views about education and/or life.

Parent Protesters

As Figure 1.5 shows, parents by far outnumber any other category of potential censor. This makes sense, of course, since parents are responsible for deciding how to raise their children, and children are generally considered the group most in need of protection. Many parent protests consist of individual parents expressing concern about an issue that affects their own child. But since the early 1980s, more and more parent protests consist of groups of disgruntled parents who are influenced by the agendas of national organizations. People for the American Way (1996, p. 7), for example, reports that 16 percent of its 1995–96 reported incidents were prompted by groups of parent protesters from the religious right. Another 16 percent of incidents "appear to be inspired by" religious-right groups of protesters (p. 7). Leftist groups of parent protest-

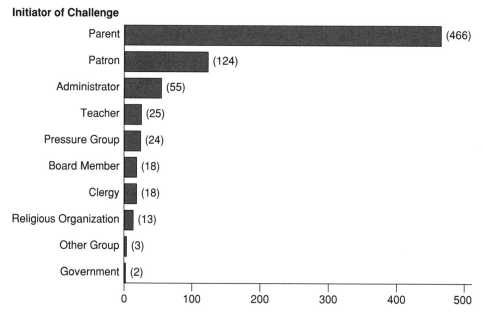

Initiator of Challenge

FIGURE 1.5   Office of Intellectual Freedom (OIF) Censorship Database, 1994

Source: Reprinted by permission of the American Library Association.

ers can be just as adamant in raising objections to curricula and teaching practices, but only 6 percent of PFAW's 1995–96 challenges reported came from the political left (p. 9). Group protests, however, often begin with one parent speaking out against classroom materials or experiences, so it is useful to consider the kinds of parents who protest, especially those who lead other parents into an expanded protest.

As individuals, parent protesters are not always known as chronic complainers but are likely instead to be parents sincerely concerned about sex education, offensive language, or any of a host of other issues. Sometimes, of course, the individual protester is not a parent but simply a local citizen or member of a local church. And sometimes the protester is a teaching colleague, such as a pacifist teacher who objects to using texts that might be interpreted as glorifying war (May & Slayton, 1994). The majority of school protests, however, are initiated by parents—particularly by parents who "misunderstand or disagree with most Americans' notion of public education" (PFAW, 1996, p. 9).

Parents' views are significantly shaped by their own school memories. Some individual parents, for example, remember their own school experience with pride, feeling their school years were their best—a time without adult worries when they could be themselves, enjoy friendships, and broaden their horizons. Parents with very positive memories often strongly support their children's teachers and schools and welcome classroom and curricular innovations. Ironically, some of the parents who are most vocal as protesters also frequently hold very positive school memories but want nothing more (or less, from their perspective) for their children than a duplication of what they experienced. (This "it-worked-for-me" attitude can sometimes be challenged by asking parents to consider whether they would be satisfied if their children's pediatricians prescribed only medications that "worked" 25 years ago.) At any rate, changes in classroom practice tend to leave such parents at least curious, if not uneasy or openly critical.

On the other hand, some parents remember their school experiences with loathing, feeling that their school years were a demoralizing time of not measuring up to their own or others' expectations. Parents whose school memories are primarily negative or painful may try to compensate by vigorously supporting their children's educational experiences. If school seems positive for their offspring, they tend to remain pleased and not overly concerned with what happens at school day by day. However, problems of any kind at school may remind them of their own negative experiences and lead them to react either by trying to prevent the same thing happening to their own children or by retreating into a belief that problems at school are inevitable.

Still other parents remember their school experiences somewhat more neutrally, as a boring set of hoops to jump through, or even as a blend of loathed and loved experiences. It is helpful to try to understand the motivations and the methods of individual parent protesters and especially to distinguish individual concerns about a particular student's school experience from those who want to take on the system. As most teachers realize, such circumstances require different responses.

While individual parent protesters often go unnoticed, those whose protests lead to court cases or state-level challenges often get national attention. For example, Peg Luksik, a Pennsylvania mother of five children, received considerable media attention as she led a statewide revolt against outcomes-based education (OBE). A former second-grade teacher whose own children attended Catholic schools, Luksik had previously gained political experience by establishing a nonprofit center for single mothers and by protesting the state's sex education curriculum (Harp, 1993, p. 1). Her fight with the State Board of Education over mandated outcomes-based education strengthened the network of supporters she had established as she moved from project to project. Eventually, what started out as a curriculum protest led to filing as a gubernatorial candidate and surprising everyone by garnering 46 percent of the primary vote (Harp, 1993, p. 20).

It is important that we, as teachers, recognize the commitment and skill that some parent protesters bring to major challenges of the system. Although Luksik described herself as "just a mommy who makes sandwiches for five little kids" (Harp, 1993, p. 19), she was articulate and politically astute in expressing her opinions about the flaws of outcomes-based education. Publicly downplaying her political skill and experience, she attributed part of her success in challenging the system to her ability to speak for "Sally Average" and "John Q. Lunchbox" (p. 21).

With admirable drive and passion, she made fighting OBE a priority issue in her life, devoting her own time freely to researching the subject and gathering ammunition: "She gathered news stories and reports on the topic, read the theories of its main proponents, and reviewed the state's background materials" (Harp, 1993, p. 20). Emboldened by her study, when she appeared in public forums she "held up the state's own paperwork and outside research to throw doubts on the program" (p. 19).

Whether or not we agree with the stance protest leaders take on particular issues, we can learn from Luksik's example and from the insight and advice she offered to her fellow protesters: "Politics is a game of pressure and perseverance, and you have to not buy into the rhetoric that it's a done deal. . . . You have to not believe that you can't stand up against people like the NEA . . . and then you go in and do it, and, if you continue to talk and continue to build your grassroots constituency, you can beat them" (Harp, 1993, p. 19).

Peg Luksik may well have devoted more time, energy, and commitment to her research on OBE than did many of the Pennsylvania legislators or State Department of Education staff. Too often, legislators and state-level employees depend on a quick review of the issues with the result that they may not develop a solid case that would stand up to the hard questions that Peg Luksik raised—questions about the "valid research base" for OBE, about budget cuts in other areas to implement OBE, and even what the mission of public education is and who has control. Relentlessly, Luksik held state bureaucrats' feet to the fire: "We started asking questions and didn't get reasonable answers or consistent answers, and sometimes we didn't get any answers. We need to quit guessing" (Harp, 1993, p. 21).

We can learn from the persistent strategies that protesters use but must also try to discover their underlying concerns and perspectives. Luksik revealed clues about her own educational philosophy as she described how she had taught second grade: "I didn't get into the touchy-feely programs because there were so many facts . . . we had to cram in as much as we could. I really felt my focus was to fill their minds and give them the tools to live their lives" (Harp, 1993, p. 21). Perhaps unaware of constructivist approaches to teaching and learning, she saw herself as one who transmitted facts to passive student-receivers and assumed that what was taught was learned, thus reflecting an educational philosophy that may have sounded reasonable to her audience of legislators and parents but that seems outdated and ineffective to many of today's educators (see Chapter 2).

Peg Luksik teaches us not to underestimate parent protesters. Some may appear simply uninformed or dogmatic, but most are intelligent, articulate, persuasive, energetic, and fearless—and they know how to use their passion and research skills to get results. As parents weigh what they hear against what they know about their children's school experience and against their own school memories, they are often easily influenced by another parent protester who taps into their uncertainties or misgivings about their children's education. Teachers, of course, can be as intelligent, articulate, persuasive, energetic, and bold as individual protesters. But once challenged, we must be just as ready to marshal all our evidence and resources individually and collectively as we interact with parents and address challenges and potential censorship.

First Signs and Impulses

When a complaint is registered, it is likely that throughout that school day and for several days to follow the teacher or teachers involved will do a lot of thinking about the complaint. In such circumstances, a teacher cannot help but try to sort out what, if anything, someone might legitimately consider objectionable, what might have been done differently, how to respond, and whether or how to rethink classroom practices in order to reduce the likelihood of future challenges. Sometimes this soul searching is accompanied by a flurry of discussions with administrators, phone calls from colleagues, grocery-aisle chats with neighbors, and even newspaper headlines. If so, the incident often becomes a life-changing teacher experience.

Ignoring or Minimizing Signals

Sometimes teachers ignore early signs of potential protest. For instance, if a student asks, "Why are we studying this stuff?" or comments, "I don't think we ought to be reading this book," the question or comment may mean the student (1) genuinely questions the purpose and value of an assignment and deserves a thoughtful response or (2) is not interested in the topic, does not like to read, or feels unable to handle the material and thinks that complaining will nudge the teacher to reconsider the assignment. On the other hand, the "Why are we studying this stuff?" question may mean the student (3) has complained at home to parents, who have responded by examining the materials and deciding they're objectionable or (4) is comfortable with the materials but has heard concerns expressed by parents who have scrutinized reading materials and homework assignments.

Not wanting to overreact, many reasonable teachers do not get alarmed in such circumstances. With so many demands on our time and thoughts, we simply often hope for the best. But too often in the past, teachers and administrators have been sorry later that they responded in a minimal way. Instead, we need to take careful note of controversy in neighboring districts and stay alert so that we can sense when organized protest may be brewing in our own community.

When a parent complains or expresses concern about an issue, teachers know that a single conversation can often dispel the parent's concerns and demonstrate the value of the challenged materials or classroom experiences. Such thinking depends, however, on the belief that the parent has good intentions but simply misunderstands the "real" situation—that is, it is a matter that should be easily settled. This approach often works, for example, when the teacher explains the rationale for a classroom experience of which, once understood, the parents will approve. Of course, the single session intended to offer reassurance occasionally backfires. Parents are not always convinced by teachers' explanations and reassurance, and teachers who are convinced that the matter is a simple misunderstanding are amazed if parents continue to object. Individual complaints and concerns can grow into major challenges and controversies, and when they do, teachers are once again caught off guard.

Making Concessions

When an individual teacher is challenged or is faced with potential censorship, that teacher's first impulse is often to feel shocked and alienated. Brown and Stephens (1994), in fact, reported that sometimes "teachers actually feel that the challenge is an assault on them personally; they are ashamed and embarrassed and don't talk about what has happened to them" (p. 125).

As teachers, we sometimes publicly underreact by trying to show the protesters how reasonable we are by seeking a quick compromise. The trick is to be reasonable and to make only the concessions that will maintain or improve conditions and learning without "caving" under pressure. Unfortunately, in case after case, teachers have responded to protests by saying, "We can handle this...we'll simply adjust a little." And too often, administrators have assured teachers that the integrity of the curriculum will remain intact and have insisted that a few "minor" adjustments will not jeopardize the entire program. For example, when a school superintendent met with parents who were protesting against whole language, he offered partial accommodation to their requests as a sign of goodwill. However, his plan to include "just a little more phonics" resulted in next-day headlines that misrepresented the current curriculum and that seemed to make more than minor concessions: "Parents Receive Promise of Return to Phonics" (Westaby, 1994).

Unfortunately, this less-is-more attitude means operating out of a naive belief that the protesters will appreciate a fair-minded approach and feel compelled to reciprocate in kind, looking for ways to conciliate with the teacher or school district. Teachers and administrators have learned the hard way that some protesters interpret willingness to compromise as weakness and consequently move aggressively to gain even more ground.

Launching an Aggressive Counterattack

If underreacting does not work once a protest occurs, neither do overreacting counterattacks. In the midst of chaos, it is natural to respond first with shock. Even a teacher with long experience can be shaken if it is the first time he or she has been challenged openly or threatened with censorship. In a flash, one's censorship-won't-happen-here attitude disappears and panic sets in. But in many schools, censors can count on and use to advantage the immediate panic (Donelson, 1994, p. 237) that leads teachers to counterattack too aggressively.

Increasingly, protesters register complaints about an entire curriculum or an entire approach to education. In these cases, *groups* of teachers tend to react differently from *individual* teachers whose practices are challenged. A whole staff of teachers can become emboldened when classroom practices are questioned. Of course, it is much easier to be bold if all our colleagues are being challenged along with us. Teachers in such situations often feel less vulnerable and are less likely to engage in self-doubts, at least initially. Instead, these groups of teachers are more likely to launch a quick self-defensive counterattack on their challengers.

Groups of teachers are also more likely to respond with anger and aggression. Having read alarming accounts of occurrences in other school districts, and emboldened by the safety of their numbers, they dig in their heels and try to defeat the protesters by rallying support within the community. Such was the case when a community priest wrote a well-intentioned letter to the editor in support of his local school district that was being criticized for promoting outcomes-based education, cooperative learning, whole language, multiculturalism, and so forth (Reckker, 1994). The letter was very effective in that it helped bring hundreds of people from the community to the next school board meeting.

The priest's letter, nevertheless, had the unintended effect of simultaneously generating allies for the protesters, since the contents of the letter included a barrage of undocumented accusations against the local protesters and the national groups that influenced them. The inflammatory letter compared the protesters' tactics to those of Joseph McCarthy and the Salem witch trials and listed—without documentation—what the priest believed to be the protesters' targets, including the Catholic Church, Pope John XXIII, Mother Teresa, Chrysler, *Reader's Digest,* and others (Reckker, 1994).

Thus, we are wise to beware of overkill. Understandably, the teachers in the priest's district were encouraged by the strong support of the local priest and benefited from the community support that his letter generated. Such support is especially important when, as in this case, the protesters were aligned with national organizations. But teachers and school communities must weigh carefully the value of such support. Sometimes we pay a high price for support that leads to rigid battle lines between "us" and "them." Sometimes we also pay a high price for responses that sound condescending: "If we do that," Donelson (1994) warned, "objectors almost invariably come back to haunt us, and they should" (p. 239).

Searching for Appropriate Action

Sometimes school districts have reacted to curricular challenges in ways that are simply inappropriate or wrong. In the suburban school district where I live, for example, administrators with the best intentions rushed too quickly to address concerns expressed by a small group of African American parents about the teaching of *The Adventures of Huckleberry Finn*. The parents did not ask that the book be withdrawn from the curriculum but expressed concern that racial issues were not being handled with sensitivity in class settings where each of their children was the only African American student. My daughter reported that in her own class, the *Huckleberry Finn* texts were simply collected from students. On the next day, her teacher distributed and introduced *A Connecticut Yankee in King Arthur's Court,* apparently with little explanation about why the *Huckleberry Finn* texts were removed. When the copies were eventually returned, the semester schedule left no time for students to finish reading it. Caught off guard, this district's inappropriate reaction to parents' concerns far exceeded the parents' request and consequently ended up as school-sponsored censorship.

Living in a "Heads-Up" School World

Virtually everyone who writes about school censorship and controversy agrees that no community, no school district, no teacher, and no area of the curriculum is off limits for those who challenge curricula and classroom experiences. Jenkinson (1990) identified challengers' targets that range from mythology to the swimwear issue of *Sports Illustrated* (pp. 16–17) and reported that teachers' most unrealistic belief is that censorship "can't happen here" (p. 60). PFAW's list for challenged materials for just one year included "literature anthologies, biology textbooks, novels and films used in the classroom; books and magazines available in libraries; material on optional, supplemental and summer reading lists; school newspapers and literary magazines; self-esteem curricula; student-performed plays; and health and sex education curricula" (PFAW, 1994).

Potentially even more frightening than the threat of increased school district censorship are proposed "religious freedom" and "parents' rights" legislation intended to "clarify" the First Amendment and to place burdensome restrictions on information available for use in classrooms (see Chapter 11). Such legislation is being carefully crafted with innocuous-sounding language that hides the truth from unsuspecting voters, who may learn too late that they have prevented teachers and students from discussing an article from yesterday's local newspaper unless the school board first approves it or that they have approved using public money to pay for tuition at religious schools.

Teaching in a changing and controversial classroom world demands that we learn to live in a "heads-up" environment, as alert as athletes watching to see which direction the ball might come from next. This means:

- It is not a matter of *if* we will be faced with challenges but rather a matter of *when*.

■ From the moment we first decide to teach to the day we retire, we need to pay attention to issues of intellectual freedom and censorship.

■ One of our most important responsibilities is being ready day by day to explain and defend our classroom decisions, which is the only way to prevent the "never-in-our community" syndrome that has left so many teachers blindsided.

If we are well prepared to defend our curriculum and classroom experiences, we can stop thinking that challenges reflect our own poor decision making or our inability to adequately "sell" a program or text to parents and community members. We can stop thinking that anyone who protests is a loser or an antiintellectual bigot. We can stop thinking that there is nothing worse than parent protests.

Are There Other Possibilities?

Being *caught off guard* means being caught unaware, not knowing, not seeing. High school teachers Lynda Kapron and Rita Paye learned the hard way. With the help of a small grant, they set about producing a literary magazine. Lots of commitment and hard work by the two teachers and their students eventually paid off as they proudly began selling the $2 copies at school and sending complimentary copies to school administrators and board members. As luck would have it, a parent objected to the Satanism thought to be suggested by a picture of a dragon. The superintendent then complained that the champagne bottle in one of the illustrations encouraged drinking, and soon a few other readers noticed words and illustrations that they did not like either. When Kapron and Paye refused to censor the already printed copies of the magazine, they received written reprimands.

Over three years later, their case was heard by a federal judge who ruled that school administrators could censor the literary magazine since it had not been designated as an "open forum" (Kapron & Paye, 1994, p. 190). The reprimand letters were removed from their files, but Kapron and Paye lost their battle, and their students lost their right to publish an uncensored literary magazine. In hindsight, these teachers explained, "Belatedly, we educated ourselves on the history of censorship. Like many Americans, we had naively ignored the gradual restriction of speech and publication rights in this country during the 1980s" (p. 186). In the midst of their very busy teaching schedules, they just didn't think censorship would happen to them.

In that moment of discovering that one has been caught off guard, the very first impulse is understandably defensive, but in many cases, there is the possibility of a positive outcome. Such moments often become a turning point. Most of us believe—intellectually, at least—that crises are also times of opportunity. Wise teachers, such as Kapron and Paye and the one who shared the multiple versions of the Cinderella story, will develop the courage to face potential controversy in a positive way. For such teachers, an official complaint *can* become a time to hold on to what is worth defending and to consider new classroom possibilities.

What might have happened in my daughter's classroom? Her *Huckleberry Finn* experience could have become an occasion for her, her classmates, and her teachers to talk about and to learn about how and why intellectual freedom works. Controversial materials *can* lead to positive discussions about intellectual freedom, as happened with the students who encountered the online poem, "inborn consent," cited earlier in the chapter. The process of composing a response to the poet taught these students to weigh their own reactions, to take a position, and to articulate a reasonable response to the poet and the poem.

Our thinking should be ongoing and evolving about what materials we use in the classroom and how we use those materials. For example, if the elementary teacher continues to use the Cinderella stories, at some future point she may modify this unit, possibly in response to a query from a feminist parent concerned about the gender-role messages in stories about damsels in distress being rescued by princes.

Teachers can learn that "disagreement and conflict are central ingredients of a democracy and are not fatal to progress" (Goldstein, 1989, p. 31). It is tragic to censor controversy from public school classrooms. A People for the American Way study of history and civics texts revealed that the one missing component was controversy. The lifeless texts ignored or barely mentioned the "fierce debates, colorful characters, triumphs and tragedies" that students need in order to understand and to remember the lessons of the past (Carroll et al., 1987).

How we teachers think of ourselves personally and professionally is what matters most as we decide how to handle controversy. Teachers who are reflective practitioners are already in the habit of carefully examining classroom materials and experiences and therefore are arguably the best prepared to face challenges. Unlike teachers in the past who relied on the "authority" of prepackaged programs to defend their classroom practices, reflective practitioners today grow professionally self-confident from knowing and being able to articulate the reasons for their curricular decisions.

Many of us learn to pay attention to who our students are and what values and experiences they bring with them to school. As we consider new possibilities, we can examine our own attitudes toward our students' parents and their lifestyles and world views. We can learn to defend what we teach and why we teach it. And we can stay alert to potential protest and controversy, work toward building bridges to those whose views may be very different, and resist organized attacks intended to destroy public education.

HELPFUL RESOURCES

1. *Newsletter on Intellectual Freedom.* Chicago: Intellectual Freedom Committee, American Library Association. This bimonthly publication provides detailed information about censorship and intellectual freedom issues and controversy. Contact: Office for Intellectual Freedom, 50 East Huron Street, Chicago, IL 60611.

2. *Attacks on the Freedom to Learn.* Washington, DC: People for the American Way. Published annually, this report documents state-by-state challenges to instructional materials in public schools. Its "Executive Summary and Introduction" provides a concise analysis of current trends in school-based censorship challenges and in broad-based incidents involving protests of school reform efforts, and so forth. Contact: People for the American Way, 2000 M Street, N.W., Suite 400, Washington, DC 20036.

3. Local newspapers. Because school controversy makes national news, local newspapers often offer at least brief articles mentioning particular materials that have been challenged. Local and regional challenges to school materials or experiences often get much greater news attention. It is worth clipping all such news articles in your local paper(s) to monitor attention-getting issues, especially so that you can be ready to respond to questions that may well be asked about similar issues in your own district.

4. Professional periodicals. In addition to broad educational publications such as *Education Week*, *Educational Leadership*, and *Phi Delta Kappan*, professional content area organizations have publications that report on censorship and school controversy issues. For example, the National Council of Teachers of English publishes the *SLATE (Support for the Learning and Teaching of English) Newsletter* three times a year to report on national issues that affect teachers.

REFERENCES

American Library Association. (n.d.) *Challenges to school and school library materials.* Unpublished document.

American Library Association. (1995). Library challenges rose in 1994. *Newsletter on Intellectual Freedom, 44,* p. 123.

Associated Press. (1995, Dec. 25). Parents object to school's segregation of sect's children. *Kalamazoo [MI] Gazette,* p. A6.

Brown, J. E., and E. Stephens. (1994). Being proactive, not waiting for the censor. In J. E. Brown (Ed.), *Preserving intellectual freedom: Fighting censorship in our schools* (pp. 125–132). Urbana, IL: National Council of Teachers of English.

Carroll, J. D., W. D. Broadnax, G. Contreras, T. E. Mann, N. J. Ornstein, and J. Stiehm. (1987). *We the people: A review of U.S. government and civics textbooks.* Washington, DC: People for the American Way.

Donelson, K. (1994). Ten steps toward the freedom to read. In J. S. Simmons (Ed.), *Censorship: A threat to reading, learning, thinking* (pp. 231–242). Newark, DE: International Reading Association.

Feldman, C. (1994, Aug. 22). Teachers censor selves as conservatives watch. *Kalamazoo [MI] Gazette.*

Goldstein, W. (1989). *Controversial issues in schools: Dealing with the inevitable.* Bloomington: Phi Delta Kappa Educational Foundation.

Harp, L. (1993, Sept. 22). Pa. parent becomes a mother of "outcomes" revolt. *Education Week, 13* (3), 1, 19–21.

Jenkinson, E. B. (1985). Protecting Holden Caulfield and his friends from the censors. *English Journal, 74* (1), 26–33.

Jenkinson, E. B. (1990). Child abuse in the hate factory. In A. S. Ochoa (Ed.), *Academic freedom to teach and to learn: Every teacher's issue* (pp. 10–20). Washington, DC: National Education Association.

Kapron, L. K., and R. E. Paye. (1994). Who's protecting whom and from what? In J. E. Brown (Ed.), *Preserving intellectual freedom: Fighting censorship in our schools* (pp. 178–191). Urbana, IL: National Council of Teachers of English.

May, A. C., and P. Slayton. (1994). Keeping abreast in the trenches: Inservice censorship education. In J. E. Brown (Ed.), *Preserving intellectual freedom: Fighting censorship in our schools* (pp. 143–150). Urbana, IL: National Council of Teachers of English.

Meade, J. (1990). A war of words. *Teacher, 2* (3), 37–45.

Mizner, D. (1995, Fall). The next battleground—Your local library. *People for the American Way News, 2* (1), 6.

Owen, T. (1995). Poems that change the world: Canada's wired writers. *English Journal, 84* (6), 48–52.

People for the American Way. (1996, 1995, 1994, 1993, 1992, 1991, 1990). *Attacks on the freedom to learn.* Washington, DC.

Reckker, S. (1994, Jan. 12). [Letter to the editor]. *The Romeo [MI] Observer,* p. 6A.

Rohter, L. (1994, May 30). Florida town debates fundamentalist influence on schools. *Kalamazoo [MI] Gazette,* p. A4.

Shanahan, M. (1994, Aug. 11). When cultures collide. *Kalamazoo [MI] Gazette,* p. B1.

Westaby, J. (1994, Feb. 24). Parents receive promise of return to phonics. *Grand Rapids [MI] Press.*

2 Rethinking Classroom Censorship and Decision Making

Regardless of specific motives, all would-be censors share one belief—that they can recognize "evil" and that other people must be protected from it. Censors do not necessarily believe their own morals should be protected, but they do feel compelled to save their fellows.

—American Library Association,
Intellectual Freedom Manual

Censorship is not easy to define or describe. So much depends on who is speaking about whom. But censors do exist, which is to say that I can make a judgment about the actions of persons or groups and proclaim them to be censors. The censors I identify, however, probably would not accept my label. The word *censorship* carries such negative connotations that almost no one uses the first-person term to describe himself or herself. If one were to ask teaching colleagues about censorship, they almost invariably would say they disapprove—so do parents, administrators, and legislators, at least to hear them tell it. This chapter studies a worst-case scenario and then explores definitions of terms and examines views toward school censorship that determine how individuals and groups define their own actions.

Worst-Case Censorship Scenario

Recent history provides a practical, true story for classroom teachers who want to understand the roots of current classroom censorship and controversy. The 1974 landmark Kanawha County (West Virginia) conflict over textbooks provides a worst-case scenario that is unmatched, an actual case history appropriately described as "war." Sadly, it is a story with parallels to some of our more recent cases of school censorship and school controversy.

Like many later conflicts, the original discontent can be traced back to the 1962 and 1963 Supreme Court decisions that removed school-sponsored prayer and devotional Bible reading from public school classrooms. When the textbooks were challenged in 1974, the residents of the small coal-mining towns around my hometown of Charleston, West Virginia, did not hesitate to use the protest strategies of the 1960s—sit-ins, demonstrations, and marches—that had generated support for liberal causes.

The furor involved a language arts and reading series for elementary and secondary students adopted by the Kanawha County Public Schools, a large countywide district. James Moffett, senior author/editor of the series, explained: "The program was conspicuous for its unusually rich array of diverse subjects, media, and methods. The point of this multiplicity was to ensure that any learner of any background, level of development, temperament, or interest could find plenty of ways to engage with and develop language. . . . We took a strong stand for pluralism and multicultural expression" (1988, p. 6). At the time, West Virginia law required that textbook selection committees be comprised only of professional educators. No citizen advice was provided for, although there was a nonfunctioning Curriculum Advisory Council comprised of lay and school people (Moffett, 1988, p. 11).

This landmark textbook challenge, described in detail in *Storm in the Mountains* (Moffett, 1988), was led by outspoken Alice Moore, a Kanawha County school board member and wife of a fundamentalist minister. As Moore spoke to rural church and community groups, always sharing excerpts from the offending textbooks, she quickly gathered supporters by charging that the books were "filthy, trashy, disgusting, one-sidedly in favor of blacks, and unpatriotic" (p. 14). Although county leaders spoke out in support of the texts, many residents of the small communities around Charleston joined Moore to fight the system. The textbook censorship battle soon became a lightning rod that attracted protesters with a variety of social and political agendas. Before the "war" was over, thousands of area coal miners and local city bus drivers had gone on strike, two men were wounded by gunfire at picket points (p. 19), protesters marched in the streets and boycotted schools, and school buildings and the board of education building were bombed (p. 22).

The protesters eventually brought suit against the school board on the grounds that the textbooks were so offensive they violated the First Amendment guarantee of religious rights. A U.S. District judge, however, dismissed the suit, explaining that religious rights are constitutionally guaranteed by the First Amendment, but "the Amendment does not guarantee that . . . nothing offensive to any religion will be taught in the schools" (Moffett, 1988, p. 24). In the end, most of the controversial textbooks were approved for classroom use in Kanawha County, but rigid textbook selection policies were put into place and protesters began organizing to create private Christian schools (p. 24).

The protesters' version of the controversy is partially represented in a song, "Textbook War—Hills of West Virginia," composed by some of the protest leaders and included in a record album. Like many ballads and country and western songs, this was a somebody-done-somebody-wrong song that celebrated the fiercely independent, antiintellectual response to trouble, much in keeping with West Virginia's Appalachian tradition and folklore. The songwriters defended the protest leaders and mocked their critics, assuming that the challengers had been falsely accused of stirring up trouble when they were actually acting on behalf of God, the punisher of evil deeds. Believing their children's very souls were in danger, they were determined to fight the ungodly promoters of "dirty books" and a "one-world plan"—perceived as parts of a conspiracy theory still held by some Christian fundamentalists whereby the United Nations would participate in a global takeover by communists.

The song identifies those who supported the protesters' opponents—the arrogant National Education Association (NEA) and American Civil Liberties Union (ACLU)—and ridicules them for their faulty assumptions—that is, that the protesters were backward hillbillies who should defer to the professionals. The song also recounts one of the violent incidents that marked the Kanawha County textbook controversy and implies approval of vigilante behavior if it could accomplish a desirable goal.

Finally, the songwriters positioned the textbook protesters in opposition to the Supreme Court, which—like all the opponents mentioned previously—were clearly *not* on God's side but "committed treason for the shape our nation's in." A listing of 1960s and 1970s "treasonous" decisions, according to the protesters, included removing public prayer from public schools, legalizing abortion, and busing public school students to eliminate segregation. As further indication of the morally upside-down world they found themselves in, the songwriters called attention to the Vietnam War and the unpatriotic citizens who refused to fight. They encouraged support among "believers" (only those whose theological views closely matched their own) and reminded listeners of the battle's spiritual significance (Moffett, 1988, pp. 48–49).

Lessons for Today

At the time, the Kanawha County textbook war attracted enormous attention and is still frequently cited today as a landmark case that demonstrates the worst outcome when individuals or groups protest curricular materials. Unfortunately, many of the same issues that generated conflict in 1974 still create conflict today, and protesters today use many of the same strategies. Initially, the protesters had no idea how far their protest would go. They simply reacted to unfamiliar and seemingly offensive texts ("dirty books") and believed they were carrying out God's will. One zealous protester carried great influence by speaking up and passionately devoting herself to the fight to "save" children from what she perceived as harmful. She easily built her support among those who shared a feeling of being ignored or dismissed by school authorities and used alliances with other groups. Complaints about a single school board action spread to encompass other past incidents and issues, so that a full-blown conspiracy seemed likely. Some of the objections to the multicultural textbooks revealed blatant racism. Extremists were among those attracted to the protest and used the incident as an opportunity to lash out against authority and to break the law.

What Is Censorship?

Fortunately, many years later, no school-based censorship challenge has matched the 1974 Kanawha County worst-case scenario. Equally as fortunate, many teachers have learned (from this case) about censorship and about school and classroom strategies that can prevent a recurrence. Teachers today still can use the Kanawha County case as a cautionary tale and can resolve to learn enough about school-based censorship to be better prepared for whatever challenges may occur.

As a place to begin, we can think of *censorship* as action taken by a person or group of persons who feel able to decide what information or experiences other persons should not have access to. Almost everyone agrees, in theory at least, that most acts of censorship are undesirable or wrong. But some conservatives argue that what is presented to the public as censorship really is not. Syndicated columnist and former vice president of the Moral Majority, Cal Thomas, for example, objects to any attempt to broaden a definition of censorship to include "challenges." In fact, he has called banned books "a liberal fantasy" and opposes the American Library Association's annual observation of "Banned Books Week" (Thomas, 1995). Citing a report produced by Focus on the Family, a national organization headed by psychologist James Dobson, Thomas argued that in 1994 no books were "literally banned" from public libraries.

Former Dobson colleague, Gary Bauer, offered a similar response to People for the American Way's annual report that describes "attacks on learning." Bauer, who now heads the Family Research Council, defended "a parent's right to comment" on their children's education and criticizes school personnel for ignoring parents who are "merely trying to have input into the education of their children" (cited in Mincberg, 1995). He aimed his criticism at People for the American Way, which he said "still doesn't get it." Not content with PFAW's distinction between attempted censorship and broad-based challenges, Bauer insisted that, "when a government restricts what its citizens can read—that's censorship. But when parents have input on what local officials do in the schools—that's democracy" (cited in Mincberg, 1995, p. 179). Robert Simonds, president of Citizens for Excellence in Education, did not claim the "censor" label either but instead characterized himself as "one who prevents society from being debauched by immorality" (cited in Martin, 1990). From a more liberal perspective, when the Council on Interracial Books for Children (CIBC) calls for racially biased books not to be used, its actions also are not described as censorship but rather as "public interest criticisms" (cited in Shannon, 1992, p. 68).

Censorship Perspectives

Would-be censors take a variety of positions that can be plotted on a continuum anchored by the most radical and most reactionary perspectives:

Radical Censorship	Liberal Censorship	Conservative Censorship	Totalitarian Censorship

1. *Radical Censorship:* Extremely liberal progressives sometimes become so zealous in promoting justice and equity for underrepresented groups that they try to censor materials that portray any individual or group in a disempowered position. For example, in an attempt to eradicate traditional stereotypes, radical feminists sometimes try to censor children's books that portray any woman in a domestic role.

2. *Liberal Censorship:* Liberal censorship occurs when parents or organized groups attempt to remove or restrict materials that reflect politically conservative views and/or prejudicial racial and gender stereotypes. Like their conservative counterparts, often such persons hope to protect children by not infecting them with the biases that they see institutionalized in society.

3. *Conservative Censorship:* By far, teachers face more instances of conservative censorship than any other category. Many conservatives seek to protect students from ideas or experiences that they believe children and/or adolescents are not ready for or seek to prevent exposure to ideas and concepts with which they disagree. Parents in this category want to "prevent vice, promote virtue, or combat immorality" (People for the American Way, 1995–96, p. 6). Most parent protesters from Kanawha County were conservative censors.

4. *Totalitarian Censorship:* With the demise of the Soviet Union and the end of the Cold War, many people hoped that totalitarian thinking would decline. The spread of militia and hate groups, however, means that the possibility of totalitarian censorship still exists. Extremists who see their mission as "ridding the world of *all* members of the 'inferior' group as well as its symbols" (Levin & McDevitt, 1995, p. 8) are apt to seek absolute and complete control of ideas and experiences encountered by children. The links being developed between White supremacists and militia "patriots" (Roy, 1996) could conceivably drive parent protests and school controversy in a violent direction.

Testing Ourselves

Too often, classroom teachers hold unexamined or simplistic views about censorship, as Robert Small has noticed when he works with preservice and practicing teachers. Typically, new teachers' discussions of censorship consist of hesitant oversimplifications, such as, "Censorship is bad, right? Freedom is good, right? Censorship is un-American, right? Censors are kooks, right? I have the right to lead my life the way I want to, right?" (Small, 1994, p. 196). If we smile when we hear these ambivalent statement/questions, maybe it is because we recognize how little most of us know and can articulate about such complex issues as classroom censorship and intellectual freedom. Especially in a volatile climate (see Chapter 3) teachers need a deeper understanding of censorship to address the issues that surround censorship and controversy and to make wise classroom decisions. The "Teacher's Self-Test #2" will help you clarify what you already know about curricular censorship.

FIGURE 2.1   Teacher's Self-Test #2: Knowing about Censorship

1. What is *censorship?*

   _____
   _____
   _____

2. What is *selection* of classroom materials and experiences?

   _____
   _____
   _____

3. Name a school censorship case that you know about.

   _____
   _____
   _____

4. List up to three texts or classroom experiences that have been frequent targets of potential censors. Beside each, list the main objection if you know it.

   _____
   _____
   _____

5. List two groups (general or specific) that are frequently considered potential censors or curriculum challengers.

   _____
   _____

6. How does the First Amendment to the Constitution of the United States apply to curriculum protests and censorship?

   _____
   _____
   _____

7. What help is available to aid teachers who encounter curriculum protests and censorship?

   _____
   _____
   _____

Source: Adapted with permission from Anne Sherrill. (1991). "Educating Future Teachers about Censorship." *Focus: Teaching English Language Arts, 18* (1), 69–74.

Note: May be photocopied for use; source must be cited: Ellen Brinkley, *Caught off Guard: Teachers Rethinking Censorship and Controversy* (Boston: Allyn and Bacon, 1999).

Responses to Teacher's Self-Test #2

Earlier in this chapter, a tentative definition of *censorship* was presented. Later in the chapter, distinctions between *censorship* and *selection* will be discussed. The Kanawha County case and censorship targets have been described throughout Chapters 1 and 2. Chapter 3 describes pressure groups that are current or potential challengers of curriculum. Chapters 8 and 9 address First Amendment issues that apply to protests and censorship. Every chapter—especially Chapter 10—provides information and ideas that can help teachers who encounter curricular protests and censorship.

Librarians and Censorship

A lot of what teachers have learned about censorship has been learned from librarians. *Censorship* is "the removal, suppression, or restricted circulation of literary, artistic, or educational materials—of images, ideas, and information—on the grounds that these are morally or otherwise objectionable in light of standards applied by the censor" (Reichman, 1988, p. 2). Those who censor, according to the *American Heritage College Dictionary* (1993), are those "authorized to examine books, films, or other material and suppress what is considered objectionable." We can say, then, that library censorship involves an *action*—examination, removal, suppression, or restriction— and an *agent*—the censor, who has the authority to act on someone else's behalf. Such definitions raise many theoretical questions: (1) Why is there an apparent need for censorship? (2) Who decides what is morally or otherwise objectionable—that is, who sets the standards? (3) Who can appoint and authorize censors and censorship? (4) What qualifications does the role of censor carry? and (5) Do those who authorize censorship limit their own access to ideas, information, or experiences, or do their decisions affect only others?

At one time, librarians thought of censorship as part of their professional responsibility, as revealed in a speech given by the president of the American Library Association: "It is in this way that the librarian has become a censor of literature. . . . Books that distinctly commend what is wrong, that teach how to sin and how pleasant sin is, sometimes with and sometimes without the added sauce of impropriety, are increasingly popular, tempting the author to imitate them, the publishers to produce, the bookseller to exploit. Thank Heaven they do not tempt the librarian" (Bostwick, 1908). Librarians have since taken a strong anticensorship stand. Focusing on the censorship of specific publications, the American Library Association (ALA) provides a clarification of censorship that is useful for classroom teachers: *Censorship* is "not only deletion or excision of parts of published materials, but also efforts to ban, prohibit, suppress, proscribe, remove, label, or restrict materials" (ALA *Intellectual Freedom Manual,* p. xiv).

Acts of Censorship

In 1986, the ALA's Intellectual Freedom Committee identified five "levels of incidents" that may or may not lead to censorship:

1. Expression of Concern	An inquiry that has judgmental overtones.
2. Oral Complaint	An oral challenge to the presence and/or appropriateness of the material in question.
3. Written Complaint	A formal, written complaint filed with the institution (library, school, etc.) challenging the presence and/or appropriateness of specific material.
4. Public Attack	A publicly disseminated statement challenging the value of the material, presented to the media and/or others outside the institutional organization in order to gain public support for further action.
5. Censorship	A change in the access status of material, made by a governing authority or its representatives. Such changes include: exclusion, restriction, removal, or age/grade level changes. (Doyle, 1996, p. 88)

Such distinctions are especially helpful for classroom teachers if adapted to include curricular materials and classroom experiences. An earlier version of the levels-of-incidents document also includes *inquiry* as a preliminary, nonjudgmental level (Marsh, 1991, p. 1). I have drawn on both the 1984 and the 1986 documents to create the "What's Going On?" sheet (see Figure 2.2) that can be used by teachers and administrators to clarify specific situations that might be considered censorship. When challenges brought by individual or organized protesters suddenly catch teachers off balance, it is essential to understand exactly what is happening in order to know how to proceed. Marsh asserted that "none of these conditions is desirable" and insisted—erroneously, I believe—that "all infringe upon First Amendment rights of freedom of speech and of the press" (p. 1). An inquiry or an expression of concern, for example, as defined in Figure 2.2, is within parents' rights and may even prove to be a positive opportunity for teachers to inform parents about best practice.

Others identify acts of censorship in a variety of ways. The descriptors that define the PFAW categories of "attacks" on learning can be used to weigh variables to further clarify and characterize a particular situation. When is a challenge "attempted censorship" and when is it a "broad challenge"? People for the American Way (1995–1996) suggests that a challenge is probably *not* an act of *attempted censorship* if:

- It involves an attempt to prevent just one child's use of materials or participation in a program.
- It involves a request for removal that is withdrawn promptly once school officials offer to remove the protesters' children from the activities in question.
- It raises clear issues of pedagogy, as opposed to issues of religion or ideology.
- It does not unduly restrict students' legitimate freedom of expression.

A challenge probably *is* an act of *attempted censorship* if:

- It involves efforts to remove from a classroom library or curriculum, books or other materials or programs for ideological or sectarian reasons.
- It involves an attempt to prevent more than the protesters' own children from using materials or participating in a program.

FIGURE 2.2   What's Going On? Challenges to Classroom Materials and Experiences

Briefly describe the incident:

Given the circumstances described above, which of the following seems best to describe the incident?

Inquiry	Expression of Concern	Complaint	Attack	Censorship

1. ___ Is it an *inquiry?* An informational request, usually informal, which seeks to determine the rationale behind the presence of a particular item in the curriculum or a particular classroom experience.

2. ___ Is it an *expression of concern?* An inquiry that has judgmental overtones. The inquirer has already made a value judgment on the materials or classroom experience in question.

3. ___ Is it a *complaint?* A formal written complaint filed with the school administration, questioning the presence of and/or the appropriateness of specific materials or classroom experiences.

4. ___ Is it an *attack?* A publicly worded statement questioning the value of the material or experience, presented to the media and/or others outside the school district, in order to gain public support for further action.

5. ___ Is it *censorship?* The removal of material or classroom experience from the classroom by the school board.

Source: Adapted from *50 Ways to Fight Censorship* (p. 1) by D. Marsh, 1991, New York: Thunder's Mouth Press, cited from a 1984 American Library Association Statement.

Note: May be photocopied for use; source must be cited: Ellen Brinkley, *Caught off Guard: Teachers Rethinking Censorship and Controversy* (Boston: Allyn and Bacon, 1999).

■ It involves a request for removal that is not withdrawn promptly once school officials offer to remove the protesters' children from the activities in question.
■ It unduly restricts students' legitimate freedom of expression.

A challenge is more likely a *broad-based challenge* if:

■ It includes attempts by individuals or organizations to inject their own ideological or sectarian agenda into the educational process.
■ It includes efforts to distort textbook selection processes by bringing ideological or sectarian pressure, or advancing legislation or other initiatives that would inject such considerations.

These descriptors, with one exception, seem particularly helpful in further identifying exactly what kind of challenge is occurring so that teachers and administrators can plan a response. The descriptors recognize parents' right to challenge materials and to remove their own children from particular experiences. I am concerned, however, that pedagogical issues do not fall into PFAW's category of attempted censorship but that issues of religion and ideology do. When issues of religion and ideology are involved, it *is* more likely that protesters want to censor something that is perceived as antithetical to their views. I am convinced that the same is true today for pedagogy. Today's would-be censors do not just target classroom content and materials but protest specific teaching practices, as well. Protesters have never, to my knowledge, asked that spelling be removed from the curriculum, but they have asked that spelling not be taught by a strategy that encourages beginning writers to "invent" spellings. Such protests clearly intend to censor—that is, to suppress, remove, or restrict—this particular classroom practice.

How we name a situation can make a big difference in whether we cool tempers or inflame passions. The key is to be accurate—selecting terms so carefully that the challengers will agree with our characterization. Clearly, it is in everyone's best interest not to overreact to individual parents' genuine concerns about their children's education. By carefully defining each situation, we will have a better start in deciding what kind of response is appropriate and what kind of resolution might be most effective.

The Power of Reading

Many teachers find it easy to take a hard theoretical stand against censorship, to advocate curricular freedom based on their own professional decisions. It is easy, for example, for teachers to criticize overprotective parents who worry that reading a particular book or participating in a particular classroom experience may lead students morally astray. Frequently, parent protesters believe that reading books—fiction or nonfiction—will influence real-world attitudes and behavior. And the truth is, they are right. Reading is a "risky activity" (Bosmajian, 1987). As teachers, we know that reading a particular book *can* make a significant difference in a student's life: "We recognize the power of information and ideas to inspire justice, to restore freedom and dignity to the oppressed, and to change the hearts and minds of the oppressors" (American Library Association, 1992, p. 93).

What teachers and librarians sometimes do not always admit is that information and ideas can also negatively inspire *injustice,* can *destroy* freedom and dignity, and can *incite* oppression. This contradiction is acknowledged in comments about a National Library Week theme: "We reject the accusation that books in our libraries will change people into rapists, child molesters and pornography addicts, but we choose a National Library Week theme—LIBRARIES CHANGE LIVES!—and highlight stories of how books and information in libraries pull people out of poverty, get them jobs and turn radical hate into respect. . . . We cannot have it both ways" (Morgan, 1993). Although Morgan warns that slogans such as "Libraries Change Lives" feed the fears of "people who oppose access to diverse ideas" (p. 3), I do not believe this means library slogans should be changed. Instead, it means we should acknowledge to students and to parents that reading can and does make a difference. We *can* be influenced by what we read.

Clearly, reading is risky. Columnist Molly Ivins reported that the family and friends of Timothy McVeigh, convicted Oklahoma City bomber, attributed his extremism to his reading of *The Turner Diaries* by Andrew Macdonald (Hillsboro, WV: National Vanguard Books). When Ivins asserted that "reading is dangerous," it was not to defend book banning but to offer a tongue-in-cheek indictment of Timothy McVeigh's teachers: "Didn't anyone ever tell the poor boy the difference between a good book and a bad one?" (Ivins, 1995).

Margaret Sacco, who has over the last several years developed rationales for hundreds of adolescent novels, knows that "one of the great values of asking students to read widely and critically is that young adults can gain vicarious experiences and discover the universality of adolescent experiences safely between the covers of a book with a teacher's guidance" (Sacco, 1994, p. 69). This is not to say that young readers should read only adolescent literature—a genre that addresses realistically such issues as racial bias, rape, and homosexuality—but that vicarious experience allows young readers to evaluate actions and situations without suffering actual consequences. And there is a place for "a teacher's guidance" as students make reading choices and as they consider a range of themes and issues in their reading.

Is it possible that as a student Timothy McVeigh was never expected or taught to question what he read? If so, the nation may have witnessed a worst-case scenario as to what can happen when students are not taught to be critical readers.

Given the power of reading, students need strategies for examining ideas, weighing evidence, and taking and defending positions. Offering students more choices about what they read and providing classroom lessons focused on selection and critical reading strategies will help students learn that "suppression of ideas is fatal to a democratic society" and the answer to a bad book is another book, a good one (American Library Association, 1992, p. 111).

Daily Classroom Judgment Calls

Classroom censorship touches on issues that go well beyond reading particular texts. As teachers, we make daily decisions about curricular materials and about classroom experiences, and we make daily value judgments about our own and students' classroom behavior and language. For example, a friend of mine makes a value judgment when she asks her middle school students not to use the expression *That sucks* in her classroom. Some readers may think this request harsh, given a "sucks"-or-"cool" mentality that seems comfortable to Beavis and Butthead fans. My friend explains to her middle school students that such language is not a schoolwide punishable offense but rather it is a matter of her dislike for it. She encourages those who use the expression to check dictionary definitions, since "most don't have a clue about what it means." When they do, she reports, many respond with disgust and thereafter honor her request not to use the expression.

I once sent a high school senior to the office because of the tie he very uncharacteristically wore to school one day. On closer scrutiny, I noticed the word *fuck* printed all over it. In retrospect, I think that sending him to the office probably accomplished his primary purpose—to get attention and to try to get away with it. If it happened today, I am not sure I would handle the situation in the same way, but at the time, I remember wondering what he might do next if his tie went unchallenged.

Although we operate within a variety of guidelines and constraints, we are the primary decision makers about what happens daily in our classrooms. Many of these decisions are based on personal judgments—that is, on our understandings of policy and/or on our own individual sense of what is and is not appropriate. Such decisions are arguably questions of classroom censorship—in that they represent potential restrictions or prohibitions on expression and free speech. As we have encouraged students to be more active as learners and to make more classroom decisions for themselves—sometimes actually negotiating parts of the curriculum—we can also expect more parental concern and controversy focused on students' classroom language and behavior.

Censorship and Selection

How teachers make decisions about classroom experiences has led to ongoing discussions about the need to distinguish between *selection* and *censorship* of materials. If one takes the time to shake loose the details, such discussions can lead to a richer understanding of censorship as it occurs in classrooms. But these are slippery terms, indeed. As teachers, we tend to characterize our own decisions as *selection* and the decisions made by those outside the classroom as *censorship*. Thus, the perspective of the speaker often determines a rhetorical stance in which "we" favor selection while "they" want to censor.

Professional and Personal Selection Purposes

Several professional organizations and individual writers have tried to sharpen the distinctions between censorship and selection, with partial success. Reichman (1988), writing for the American Library Association and the American Association of School Administrators, explained that those who *select* operate positively from the perspective of a body of trained professionals who are familiar with a wide variety of available choices and guided by a "clear grasp of the educational purposes to be fulfilled." In contrast, those who *censor* operate negatively by making individual judgments that are most frequently based on "criteria that are inherently personal and often intolerant" (p. 5). Thus, Reichman tips the balance toward *selection* by valuing the professional knowledge of the teacher, who makes selections for educational reasons, not because of nonprofessional personal preferences, especially those that might be intolerant. These descriptions strike me as generally accurate, though they seem based on somewhat exaggerated assumptions about insiders and outsiders that could create divisions and conflict.

Choosing and Excluding

John Rich (1987) uses language that protesters and teachers alike might be willing to accept: *Selection* is defined as "the process of choosing materials for a course or a curriculum that will help fulfill objectives and be appropriate to learners," with an emphasis on decisions based on *choosing* (p. 446). *Censorship,* on the other hand, is defined as the "deliberate attempt to *exclude* materials that may damage the young, harm society, or offend the censor," with an emphasis on decisions based on *exclusion* (p. 445). But even Rich's description of harmful materials includes a playfully ironic twist. That is, censorship is a virtuous way to protect those who are vulnerable, but such judgments can also occur based on the mere whim of what one person considers offensive.

Frances McDonald (1991) attempted to explain the distinctions between *censor* and *selector* more from a classroom teacher's perspective. Creating a chart of the descriptors will help you to notice overall distinctions and to reflect on your own classroom practices (see Figure 2.3).

FIGURE 2.3   Defining the Roles of Selector and Censor

When I choose books and materials for my students, do I act as selector or censor?

Selector	*Censor*
____ May use any title that meets curriculum objectives or helps to teach a skill, idea, or concept.	____ Begins with specific titles that may never be used.
____ Looks at the whole and makes judgments based on the whole.	____ Makes judgments based on words, paragraphs, or pictures taken out of context.
____ Considers how a title could make an educational contribution.	____ Looks for reasons why a book or film should not be used.
____ Introduces additional ideas and concepts.	____ Seeks to limit the ideas and language to which children have access.
____ Approaches the process from a perspective of expanding the horizons of young people.	____ Approaches the process from the stance of protecting the young.
____ Is confident in the ability of readers to form their own judgments about the content of what they read.	____ Knows what will harm readers.

Source: Adapted from *Teaching Literature in the Secondary School* by Richard W. Beach and James D. Marshall, copyright © 1991 by Harcourt Brace & Company, reprinted by permission of the publisher.

Free Thought and Thought Control

Lester Asheim contrasted sociopolitical views about reading and thinking to distinguish between censorship and selection:

> Selection begins with a presumption in favor of liberty of thought; censorship with a presumption in favor of thought control. Selection's approach to the book is positive, seeking its values in the book as a book, and in the book as a whole. Censorship's approach is negative, seeking for vulnerable characteristics wherever they can be found anywhere within the book, or even outside it. Selection seeks to protect the right of the reader to read; censorship seeks to protect not the right—but the reader himself from the fancied effects of his reading. The selector has faith in the intelligence of the reader; the censor has faith only in his own.
>
> In other words, selection is democratic while censorship is authoritarian, and in our democracy we have traditionally tended to put our trust in the selector rather than in the censor. (Asheim, 1953)

In Figure 2.4, I have visually separated Asheim's helpful descriptions to allow you to read across or down the columns to construct more holistic definitions and to reflect on your own selection process.

Thinking for Ourselves

McDonald (1991) and others are right to suggest that the distinction between censorship and selection lies in the motivation or intent of the decision maker. If the decision-

---

FIGURE 2.4   Defining the Border Between Selection and Censorship

When I choose books and materials for my students, do I . . .

Select?

____ Begin with presumption in favor of liberty of thought?

____ Take a positive approach, seeking values in the materials as a whole?

____ Seek to protect the right of the student to read and view?

____ Have faith in the intelligence of the student?

____ Act democratically?

Censor?

____ Begin with presumption in favor of thought control?

____ Take a negative approach, seeking vulnerable characteristics wherever they can be found anywhere within the materials, or even outside them?

____ Seek to protect students from the "fancied effects" of their reading or viewing?

____ Have faith in my own intelligence?

____ Act in an authoritarian way?

Source: Adapted from "Not Censorship but Selection" by L. Asheim, 1953, *Wilson Library Bulletin, 28* (1), pp. 63–67.

making teacher works from an educational perspective and focuses primarily on educational suitability, the eventual decision will reflect a *selection* stance. If instead the teacher focuses primarily on how much trouble the decision might cause or on whether the underlying ideas and beliefs might conflict with those of the teacher or others, the eventual decision will reflect a *censorship* position (pp. 553–554).

Moving beyond the more hypothetical selection criteria offered by Asheim and by McDonald, to the more practical dimensions of my own application of selection criteria, I know that I frequently take into consideration a range of additional factors: How expensive will the books be for my students? Are useful examples and illustrations included? How visually appealing are they? How might a particular text complement or contradict other texts I am using or considering? How engaging and lively are the texts to read? How easy are they to carry around? Most educators would agree that all of these questions, in addition to more content-focused concerns, constitute appropriate "selection" criteria.

Self- and School-Sponsored Censorship

Clearly, selection decisions are opportunities for self-censorship, the most common form of censorship. Inevitably all of us—teachers, parents, librarians, or school administrators—on some occasions self-censor. *Self-censorship* is censoring action that a person consciously or unconsciously decides to take without consulting others or going through channels. It may involve the person censoring his or her own actions or access, but more frequently it involves a person's decision to restrict the actions or access of someone else. For example, a school librarian objected to the word *bastard* that appeared in Thomas Rockwell's *How to Eat Fried Worms,* and inserted the word *bum* in its place in the school's copies of the text. In this case, the librarian rationalized her actions by passing the buck: "Censorship is tricky territory, but it could be prevented by responsible editorship" (Donelson, 1987, p. 210). In another setting, a principal sent a confusing message to his school librarian: "Don't worry about censorship. I'll support you in anything you do, unless, of course, the book is truly *controversial*" (p. 210). In these examples, whether they realized it or not, the librarian was guilty of self-censoring and the principal was guilty of encouraging teachers to self-censor. Both seemed sincerely convinced that their stance toward censorship was just. But that is the problem. Almost everyone who censors believes they are acting in everyone else's best interests.

Those who take strong anticensorship positions would not cut the librarian or principal any slack. They apply the "censor" label not only to those who ban books or mark out words but also to teachers who skip words when reading a text aloud or who skip parts of an in-class showing of a video (McDonald, 1991, p. 554). By this measure, I may have been guilty of self-censorship when my ninth-graders read and discussed Steinbeck's *Of Mice and Men.* We freely discussed the text in class and occasionally read passages aloud. But I had decided ahead of time that unless there was a particular need to do so, I would not read aloud passages that included four-lettered words, in part because my administrators already questioned whether Steinbeck's novel was a good curricular choice and permitted only honors students to read it. As it turned out, my students followed my example without being told to do so. They had their own copies of the text, and we talked in class about the language of the novel without using the four-lettered words and without resorting to references to the "*s*-word" or the "*f*-word." (In this case, I believe it was my administrators who acted as censors, since they prevented the other ninth-graders from reading this important text.)

In many cases, self-censorship is intentional. Vigilantes act individually or as a group, marking out words in texts, tearing out pages, and "permanently" checking out school library books. It is not just parents, administrators, or librarians who are guilty of such deeds. Sometimes classroom teachers fall into this trap, as well, when their need to preserve the self or the status quo seems to override the need for intellectual freedom. In such cases, it is too easy to rationalize our self-censoring actions with the claim that we simply don't have time or energy to deal with challenges: "If a librarian or a teacher has a particularly unpleasant run-in with a censor, it sometimes hardly matters who wins the battle. The nagging fear of another encounter may make that librarian or teacher gun-shy" (Donelson, 1987, p. 212).

Self-censorship manifests itself whenever we feel intimidated by parents. We fear saying the wrong thing, being misunderstood, or appearing to be biased or outdated. Self-censorship also occurs when opposing groups are extremely aggressive in promoting their causes and when administrators or parents excessively monitor teachers' classroom decisions. Frequently, such actions serve as unspoken warnings to teachers to make only conservative, relatively "safe" curricular decisions.

In spite of being warned not to self-censor, in the real world of classroom decision making, teachers whose primary consideration is educational suitability often consider *to some extent* how problematic a choice might be. Also, we often consider *to some extent* how materials agree or conflict with our own ideas and beliefs and/or those of the school and local community. Yes, we must base decisions first of all on educational suitability and resist heavily weighing choices on the basis of potential conflict. But it is not necessarily true that considering the possibility of conflict means we are censoring. The lines between censorship and selection in real life are seldom that distinct.

It is not self-censorship if another equally good curricular choice exists that can accomplish the same educational goal as effectively without the controversy. The key, then, is to be honest with yourself and others and to avoid rationalizing your decisions to the point of making only what you believe will be strictly safe choices. As a further safeguard against self-censorship, when the decisions are yours to make, it is wise to seek advice from trusted colleagues.

Teachers who are determined not to permit censorship of their own curriculum sometimes question the extent to which they should be encouraged or required to include and teach from texts with which they may be personally uncomfortable. Some of the teachers I know say they purposely decide to teach materials occasionally that fall into this category in order not to limit students to the teacher's comfort level. I especially recommend this practice for teachers who notice that other teachers in their building or district seem to take more curricular risks than they do. Another benefit to this practice is that it allows the teacher to demonstrate to students the teacher's own critical responses to texts—that is, posing questions of the texts and arguing with their premises and views.

Another defense against self-censoring is to encourage students to use unlimited, or almost unlimited (depending on what schools decide to do with V-chips), access to materials and information through library collections and through Internet and World Wide Web connections. Such access should, of course, be accompanied by thoughtfully prepared lessons about how to make intelligent choices, formulate hypotheses, weigh evidence, and consider all points of view on controversial issues (see Chapter 9).

Thus, in terms of real-world selection of materials and experiences, I share the belief held by many teachers that no ideas or information should be forbidden. Yet, I am also convinced that all materials and experiences are not equally appropriate or beneficial for all students. I remember, for example, a reading assignment I gave college freshmen several years ago in a research and composition class that was thematically organized. My class focused thematically on literature and nonfiction discussions of death. It was a popular class, and Anne Sexton's poetry worked well as we considered a seductive fascination with death. One weekend, however, a student called me at home to express her concern that her roommate, my student, was talking a lot about the poetry we had been reading and saying things like, "I know just exactly how Sexton felt. I feel that way, too." After a long conversation and an immediate referral to the campus counseling center, I found myself reexamining the curricular questions about appropriateness, and in this case, individualizing the question: What is appropriate for this student at this time?

Unfortunately, there are no easy answers to such questions. I did not stop teaching Sexton's poems in later semesters, but I did learn from my experience to be aware that the class did not linger too long and too admiringly in our discussion of "For Mr. Death Who Stands with his Door Open" (Sexton, 1974). Also, the students and I talked frankly about the appeal of the poems and their possible effects on readers. The key for classroom teachers is to try to know students on a personal as well as an academic basis. That is the best way to be sensitive enough to be able to suggest individually "appropriate" texts. Then, too, in an interactive classroom community, such choices can be supported by class discussion, individual conferences, and/or dialogue journal conversations between teacher and students.

Often, many decisions about texts and materials used in classrooms are made through a formal process involving a school or district curriculum committee and approval by parents and school board members. We need to resolve to find ways to explain to parents and to administrators our rationale for using particular texts, materials, and experiences. This is especially true for materials and classroom experiences that are unique to our classroom and especially when some individuals might otherwise erroneously assume that we *endorse* all of the ideas and perspectives included in materials we select. Preparing such rationales carefully but briefly and clearly (i.e., without educational jargon) will force us to think through our own motives and to identify educational objectives that the materials or experience will help achieve (see Chapter 10).

Ironically, learning can be self- or school-censored not only by what is omitted but also by what is added. Conflict about curricular choices sometimes focuses on *including* something that does not appear in the curriculum. I protested when my daughter's middle school language arts teacher decided that she would *supplement* the official curriculum by adding sentence diagramming. My concern was that the time spent on sentence diagramming displaced almost entirely the time and attention that should have been devoted to writing—the more important part of the curriculum. I believe the teacher, in this case, perhaps unintentionally, self-censored the curriculum.

Censorship of Learning

The National PTA calls censorship dangerous because it "denies students the right to explore ideas and to make informed, rational judgments. In the long run, it also reduces their capacity to adjust to a changing world" (n.d.). Indeed, censorship short-circuits learning and thinking, and students are its victims. If one thinks of censorship in broad terms, one recognizes that learning is censored whenever teachers adhere strictly to a transmission model of teaching and learning that assumes that knowledge is directly transmitted from teacher or text to unquestioning, passive students. Learning is censored when teachers ask all the questions, and all questions have a single right answer. Learning is censored when students are fed a steady diet of textbooks and materials that are poorly written, unengaging, and visually unappealing.

Although students are usually not aware at the time that they are victims of censorship, sometimes students self-censor their own learning by refusing to learn. For one reason or another, sometimes students decide that learning is not in their best interest (Kohl, 1994; Krogness, 1995). Some students do not value learning for its own sake. Some never seem to buy the idea that school is worth their time or energy. Some do not learn much from textbooks that do not include illustrations portraying children who look like them. Some shut down when they feel invisible or silenced in classrooms in which they sense their home culture is not valued or included in the classroom community. For too many students, self-censored learning manifests itself as resistance and eventually results in a censorship of hope and spirit.

Unintended or *covert* censorship of learning occurs when students or their teachers unconsciously exclude alternative points of view and alternative perspectives, when the alternatives don't occur to authors or publishers (Shannon, 1992, p. 68). Covert censorship "actually strips students of their abilities to reason and to act because it leads them to behave as if the world is static and they are powerless to change it" (p. 70). Thus, the effect of unintended censorship can be a distorted and misrepresented reality, if readers and students encounter just one side of an issue or one part of the truth—for example, if history is unknowingly distorted by omitting the perspective of underrepresented groups, if religion or race or any other potentially controversial subject is unintentionally left out rather than addressed, or if a one-sided sociopolitical perspective is unconsciously adopted regarding controversial issues. As the slogan on a T-shirt I once saw captured so well, especially in the case of unintended covert censorship:

CENSORSHIP
HAS BEEN KNOWN
TO CAUSE BLINDNESS
IN   CHILDREN

Rethinking Censorship

Many teachers' experiences with censorship since the Kanawha County controversy have continued to drain public school districts' energy and financial resources. Perhaps it is also true, though, that censorship attempts or other controversy surrounding curricula *can* provide a spark to revisit old debates and to test old visions and ideas against new ones. Because parents and organized groups have become increasingly aggressive about efforts to shape curricula, it is to our advantage to rethink the likelihood that we can eliminate censorship "threats." Parents have the right to question what happens in classrooms. It is to our advantage in the long run to reconsider how to "cope with" controversy and to reconceptualize the challenges brought forward by individual parents and by organized groups.

Ultimately, many issues of censorship and selection focus on these questions: What should the curriculum consist of? How should it be taught? I know of no teachers who, if given a choice, would invite a parental protest of their curriculum and classroom experiences. As educators, we still consider censorship and controversy "bad" because they consume a lot of time and energy to address. Yet, some of the discussions and some of the controversy about what happens in classrooms are signs that people care about public education. Therein lies hope.

WHAT CAN YOU DO ABOUT CLASSROOM CENSORSHIP?

1. *Think through your own classroom decision-making processes, not just about text choices but about classroom experiences, as well.* Writing your thoughts down will give you the chance to analyze the factors that influence your decisions and to notice the possible censorship and selection dimensions of your own thinking. Sharing and comparing what you have written with your teaching colleagues can spark lively discussion—and eventual consensus—about classroom decision making.

2. *Give students access to primary sources.* As an undergraduate in a Black History class, I was amazed by how little I knew about prejudice and racism. After reading and discussing four or five books, such as *Soul on Ice, The Autobiography of Malcolm X,* and *Look Out, Whitey! Black Power's Gon' Get Your Mama!,* I was assigned a memorable research project that involved reviewing popular magazines and newspaper articles for a particular year (I was randomly assigned 1939) to create a collection of primary-source records of racism. By reviewing these primary documents, I was able to piece together a context for what I had been learning from the in-class texts and discussions. Eventually through this assignment, I became a vicarious witness to racism as I studied the assumptions about race revealed in old news columns, ads, and cartoons. I am convinced that all students need the lessons that primary sources can teach, especially as a measure to offset the possibility of covert censorship.

3. *Work hard to get the professional time needed to review materials carefully, prepare rationales, and so on.* I once showed high school students a film that I had not previewed. It was about Shakespeare's sonnets; how controversial could that be? I have repressed the details, but I remember that the film focused on a couple walking outdoors hand in hand, then moving inside where they started shedding their clothes in a burst of passion—all with a voice-over of sonnets. As I recall, it led to an interesting discussion, but not one that I had planned for that class session. The point is, classroom teachers need adequate time outside of class to prepare and preview materials to prevent unnecessary criticism and controversy.

4. *Seek creative responses to unrealistic challenges.* When bad things happen even in good school districts, a variety of creative positive outcomes are possible. For example, a social studies teacher reported that his local school board passed a motion that required "any material that included Russia in it" be approved by the board (Nelson, 1994, p. 128). Rather than try to fight the motion, the social studies teacher went out of his way to comply by sending the board a list of all world maps and all textbooks that included Russia in the index and by explaining that he and his colleagues could not teach "until it was all cleared." When confronted in this way with the absurdity of their motion, the board quickly rescinded its policy (pp. 128–129).

5. *Allow students access to materials and evidence so they can become independent thinkers and educated persons.* John Stuart Mill argued that freedom to express one's thoughts and opinions is essential in order to determine truth, that "suppressing opinion may blot out truth" and that "even when an opinion is false, it should be aired since truth is served by refuting error" (cited in Rich, 1987, p. 446). Mill further insisted that "an unconventional opinion may be useful because it contains some partial truth" (p. 446). Such arguments highlight the need for school guidelines to protect classroom intellectual freedom so that students can have more opportunities to learn to examine facts, ideas, opinions, and thoughts, and to make judgments based on information from a wide range of perspectives.

6. *Begin thinking of challenges as part of the expected, ongoing process of renegotiating curriculum.* In retrospect, the teachers of Vista, California, a district rocked by a new conservative school board, can look back and consider the positive outcomes to the turmoil that turned their district upside down. When I asked the president of the Vista Teachers Association if there were any positive outcomes to the Vista experience, he spoke about dramatic change in the schools and in the community: Vista teachers, he said, have learned to reclaim a voice within the public dialogue about education so that teachers do not simply react to the issues as they are framed by protesters. They have also learned to become public school advocates—standing in front of grocery stores, raising money, gathering signatures to recall school board members. This community, which had been labeled "apathetic" is now characterized as "very knowledgeable." Many have "become better people" as a result of the Vista experience. And even more significantly, "The schools feel the public believes in them. People don't sit on the sidelines anymore. People vote now. They realize that the last item on the ballot, which lists school board candidates, will have a more direct impact than who you vote for president" (Conry, 1995).

HELPFUL RESOURCES

1. *Banned Books Resource Guide.* This annual publication of the American Library Association lists books challenged or banned during the previous year and suggests a broad range of activities that librarians and teachers can use—especially during Banned Book Week—to call attention to censorship and to promote intellectual freedom. Contact: Office for Intellectual Freedom, American Library Association, 50 E. Huron Street, Chicago, IL 60611.

2. DelFattore, Joan. (1992). *What Johnny Shouldn't Read: Textbook Censorship in America.* New Haven: Yale University Press. This book focuses on the textbook adoption process and lawsuits involving attempts to ban or rewrite textbooks. It describes the powerful impact that conservative and liberal groups have on U.S. textbook publishers.

3. Jones, Janet L. (1993). *No Right Turn: Assuring the Forward Progress of Public Education.* This practical resource manual is for educators facing challenges by ultraconservative groups. Contact: Washington Education Association, Instruction/Human Relations, Eighth Avenue South, Federal Way, WA 98003.

4. National Council against Censorship. This alliance of national noncommercial organizations includes religious, educational, professional, artistic, labor, and civil rights groups. They are united by a conviction that freedom of thought, inquiry, and expression must be defended. They work to educate their own members about the dangers of censorship and how to oppose it. The coalition strives to create a climate of opinion hospitable to First Amendment freedoms in the broader community. Contact: 275 Seventh Avenue, New York, NY 10001.

5. Simmons, John S. (Ed.). (1994). *Censorship: A Threat to Reading, Learning, Thinking.* Newark, DE: International Reading Association, 1994. This book describes methods used by protesters to remove books and materials from classrooms and libraries and offers plans for taking action against censorship.

REFERENCES

American Heritage College Dictionary (1993). (3rd ed.). Boston: Houghton Mifflin.
American Library Association. (1992). *Intellectual freedom manual.* Chicago: American Library Association.

Asheim, L. (1953). Not censorship but selection. *Wilson Library Bulletin, 28* (1), 63–67.

Bosmajian, H. (1987). Tricks of the text and acts of reading by censors and adolescents. *Children's Literature in Education, 18* (Summer), 89–96.

Bostwick, A. E. (1908). The librarian as censor. *Library Journal, 33,* 257–264.

Conry, T. (1995, Nov.). S.L.A.T.E. Workshop, National Council of Teachers of English Annual Convention, San Diego.

Donelson, K. (1987). Six statements/questions from the censors. *Phi Delta Kappan, 69* (3), 208–214.

Doyle, R. P. (1996). *Banned books 1996 resource guide.* Chicago: American Library Association.

Ivins, M. (1995, Aug. 23). *Kalamazoo [MI] Gazette,* p. A3.

Kohl, H. (1994). I won't learn from you! Confronting student resistance. In B. Bigelow et al. (Eds.), *Rethinking our classrooms: Teaching for equity and justice* (pp. 134–135). Milwaukee: Rethinking Schools.

Krogness, M. M. (1995). *Just teach me, Mrs. K.: Talking, reading, and writing with resistant adolescent learners.* Portsmouth, NH: Heinemann.

Levin, J., & McDevitt, J. (1995, Aug.). Landmark study reveals hate crimes vary significantly by offender motivation. *Klanwatch Intelligence Report,* pp. 7–9.

Marsh, D. (1991). *50 ways to fight censorship.* New York: Thunder's Mouth Press.

Martin, J. (1990, Sept. 23). Kit urges religious cast to schools. *St. Petersburg [FL] Times.*

McDonald, F. B. (1991). Freedom to read: A professional responsibility. In R. W. Beach & J. D. Marshall (Eds.), *Teaching literature in the secondary school* (pp. 548–558). San Diego: Harcourt Brace Jovanovich.

Mincberg, E. (1995, Nov. 5). Annual report issued August 30. *ALA Newsletter on Intellectual Freedom, 44,* 179.

Moffett, J. (1988). *Storm in the mountains: A case study of censorship, conflict, and consciousness.* Carbondale: Southern Illinois University Press.

Morgan, C. D. (1993). Intellectual freedom on the line. *Media Spectrum* [Michigan Association for Media in Education], *20* (3), 3.

Nelson, J. L. (1994). Social studies and critical thinking skills versus censorship. In J. S. Simmons (Ed.), *Censorship: A threat to reading, learning, thinking* (pp. 123–133). Newark, DE: International Reading Association.

People for the American Way. (1995–1996). *Attacks on the freedom to learn.* Washington, DC: Author.

Reichman, H. (1988). *Censorship and selection: Issues and answers for schools.* Chicago: American Library Association, and Arlington, VA: American Association of School Administrators.

Rich, J. M. (1987, Oct.). Censorship and freedom to learn. *Social Education,* 445–447.

Roy, J. (1996, Feb.). Tracking the terror. *Klanwatch Intelligence Report,* p. 3.

Sacco, M. (1994). Using media to combat censorship. In J. E. Brown (Ed.), *Preserving intellectual freedom: Fighting censorship in our school* (pp. 192–197). Urbana, IL: National Council of Teachers of English.

Sexton, A. (1974). *The death notebooks.* Boston: Houghton Mifflin.

Shannon, P. (Ed.). (1992). *Becoming political: Readings and writings in the politics of literacy education.* Portsmouth, NH: Heinemann.

Sherrill, A. (1991). Educating future teachers about censorship. *Focus: Teaching English Language Arts, 18* (1), 69–74.

Small, R. (1994). Preparing the new English teacher to deal with censorship, or will I have to face it alone? In J. S. Simmons (Ed.), *Censorship: A threat to reading, learning, thinking* (pp. 190–197). Newark, DE: International Reading Association.

Thomas, C. (1995, Sept. 22). Banned books a liberal fantasy. *Kalamazoo [MI] Gazette.*

3 Facing Classroom and Community Controversy

Free societies . . . are societies in motion, and with motion comes tension, dissent, friction. Free people strike sparks, and those sparks are the best evidence of freedom's existence.

—Salman Rushdie, 1991
(cited in Doyle [1996])

As teachers, we are often baffled by attacks on teachers and curriculum and amazed that public education itself is threatened. When we talk about education with friends who are not teachers, it is often difficult to help them realize the complexity of school-related issues seldom reflected in simplistic headlines. This chapter examines basic assumptions and a variety of perspectives, pressures, and agendas that have created controversies and a quicksand environment for classroom teachers. Thus, this chapter lays the groundwork for considering classroom implications of the controversies that occur in frequently challenged content areas.

Schools today are often blamed for violence in society, for unemployment, and for a decline in morals. Politicians, corporate executives, and the media regularly pronounce the failure of public schools. When William Bennett became U.S. Secretary of Education, he targeted "the entire mediocre education enterprise in America" and explained that what schools needed was "on the order of a demolition squad" (1992, p. 47). On the other hand, David Berliner and Bruce Biddle have persuasively argued that much of the crisis in education has been "manufactured," often to achieve political goals (1995, p. 4). Meanwhile real crises arise when municipalities exempt local corporations from tax responsibilities, which reduces local funds for schools; when politicians mandate policies with little understanding of the likely consequences; and when so-called pro-family groups advocate school curricula that alienate and disenfranchise students whose heritage and perspectives differ from the majority. Unfortunately, too many of the real crises go unresolved, and the rhetoric of fear and divisiveness continues to threaten teaching and learning for all students.

Source: Reprinted by permission of Mark Antonuccio.

The "Good Old Days"

Many people remember their own school days as the "good old days." Especially when they hear media reports about problems in public education, they hark back to a mythical past when education "worked"—that is, all teachers knew what and how to teach, and all students learned what was taught. Such nostalgia assumes that there is or was a single best way to teach and to learn and that all schools in the past followed such practices. For many students, however, the good old days of education were not very good.

Many people who complain about public schools do not take into account that in the "old days" far fewer students were served for very long in the nation's public schools. Certainly in the good old days of the 1800s the country's educational expectations were much less ambitious, and relatively few students stayed in school very long. My great-grandmother (born in the mid-1850s) had finished her formal education after just eight years of school and was *teaching* school at age 14. Her children's generation (the oldest born in 1873, the youngest born 20 years later), however, saw educational opportunities expand and grow. Although her oldest child always resented not being able to attend high school since none existed in her West Virginia hometown, three of the younger children finished college and one went on to Harvard Medical School.

Still, a generation or two later, when the United States entered World War II, only half of the country's students in fifth grade would finish high school and only 20 percent would enter college. By 1960, however, three-fourths of the fifth-graders would graduate from high school and 45 percent would enter college (Berliner & Biddle, 1995, p. 270). As the nation has placed greater value on education as a gateway to higher income and opportunity, society has required more and more students to stay in school longer and expected public schools to meet the learning needs of *all* children.

Historically, the United States has had faith in public education, often unrealistically identifying it as a solution to national problems. But citizens have started blaming education when their expectations are not met. Corporations complain about students who are ill equipped for work; taxpayer groups complain that too much money is spent on education; liberal and progressive groups complain that the curriculum is too narrow; and religious, conservative parents complain that the curriculum is immoral and biased against religion. Politicians and the media feed on the controversy. Parents, religious groups, minority groups, and political advocacy groups have all battled over schools. Classrooms reflect sharp divisions within society, and teachers often get caught in the crossfire of conflicting pressures and agendas. A publication by Phi Delta Kappa and the Center on National Education Policy raises a question that much of society has considered unthinkable: *Do we still need public schools?*

Perceptions about Public Schools

Do we still need public schools? is now raised as a question worth serious discussion. As teachers and as citizens, it should shake us awake and set us on a course to seek and develop solid answers. We can begin to find answers by trying to understand the issues and the conflicts that have led the public to question the value of public education. Survey data collected by three different groups reflect a range of opinions about public education.

USA Today Poll

A 1996 *USA Today* poll (Kelly, 1996) showed, despite the antischool rhetoric, that 75 percent of parents are satisfied with their schools' academic standards and 83 percent would recommend their schools to others. Using an A–F standard scale, *USA Today* reported "grades"—all within the positive B+ to B range—given by more than 1,000 public school students and their parents for the following categories: teachers, principal/administration, equipment and facilities, school bus, the way students treat each other, and atmosphere. Only the parents responded to the following categories, giving them all grades in the B+ to B– range: communication/involvement, curriculum, superintendent, board of education, and budget/budget process (Kelly, 1996).

Parents of secondary students held more negative perceptions than parents of elementary students, as indicated by the following:

- 20 percent of elementary students' parents and 40 percent of secondary students' parents say they don't get enough feedback on their child's performance;
- 16 percent of elementary students' parents and 38 percent of secondary students' parents say schools don't adequately prepare students for college;
- 16 percent of elementary students' parents and 42 percent of secondary students' parents say schools don't adequately prepare students for the work world;
- 28 percent of elementary students' parents and 45 percent of secondary students' parents say schools don't teach ethical and moral values consistent with those of the student's family; and
- 17 percent of elementary students' parents and 32 percent of secondary students' parents say teachers don't challenge their child to learn. (Kelly, 1996)

Even phrased negatively, however, these statistics do not reveal massive dissatisfaction with public schools. The most negative of these figures indicates that over half (55 percent) of the parents of secondary students say that schools teach ethics and moral values consistent with those of students' families (Kelly, 1996).

Citizens for Excellence in Education Survey

Citizens for Excellence in Education (CEE), a group that frequently criticizes public education, reported the results of a 1994 survey conducted among their members to identify the problems of U.S. public schools. CEE president Robert Simonds reported that respondents provided 48 responses, with the top 10 being:

- Schools are not requiring the "basics" anymore. The new teaching methods produce poor learning. Classroom time is wasted on nonessentials;
- Government intrusion has robbed school districts of local control through "mandates," "guidelines," and funding;
- OBE [Outcomes Based Education]/Restructuring and psychological education formulas have robbed schools of time to teach academics and have slanted education toward political and anti-religious "correctness";
- Lack of moral teaching and character education has produced a nation of juvenile offenders and illiterates;
- Humanism (non-theism) has invaded public education with an a-theistic philosophy, damaging all children's faith in their Creator God;
- The National Education Association (teachers' union) has brainwashed otherwise wonderful teachers and encouraged faith-damaging curricula; and
- God has been excluded from schools, speech, school papers, literature, history, social discourse, readings and learning (listed in that order). (Simonds, 1994)

These responses highlight views commonly expressed by politically and religious conservative groups about education.

Public Agenda Report

Results of a survey conducted by Public Agenda, a New York-based research organization, were published in a report titled *First Things First: What Americans Expect*

Source: Ramirez; reprinted by permission of Copley News Service.

from the Public Schools (Willis, 1995). This telephone survey of 1,200 persons is reported to have found a "real consensus" among the public about education issues:

- *Safety and Order:* Seventy-two percent of respondents believe drugs and violence are a serious problem in their own community's schools, and 54 percent say teachers are doing only a "fair" or "poor" job dealing with discipline.
- *Back to Basics:* Sixty percent say education experts give short shrift to basics—skipping over them to stress the importance of critical thinking skills.
- *Higher Standards:* Eighty-eight percent support requiring students to demonstrate they can speak and write English well before being graduated from high school, and 76 percent support tougher grading and failing high school students who do not learn.
- *Traditional Teaching:* Eighty-six percent say students should memorize multiplication tables before they use calculators, and 60 percent reject encouraging children to write creatively and express themselves first without much attention to spelling and grammar.

As a teacher, I am struck by the similar responses in groups that we might assume would hold different views. Some common complaints echo across the surveys, expressing skepticism about innovative curriculum and distrust of teachers as well as citing a lack of the "basics," academic rigor, and moral values.

Good News about Public Schools

At the heart of the question Do we still need public schools? is the assumption that it is questionable whether public schools continue to fulfill the purposes for which they were designed. Despite public media reports, there is considerable research evidence that public schools have performed much better than many thought. Some of that research is discussed next.

National Science Foundation Report

A National Science Foundation (NSF) report explains that a comprehensive assessment of science and mathematics education, from elementary to graduate levels, found significant progress in test scores, curriculum, and academic preparation (*Chicago Tribune,* 1996). From 1977 to 1993, the NSF researchers compiled figures on tests, graduation rates, curriculum changes, and other assessments, including international studies and national tests such as the National Assessment of Educational Progress (NAEP). The researchers also made a particular effort to gauge recent progress in curriculum and standards. Their results show that elementary schools now devote more time to math and science, that more high school students take advanced science courses, and that student achievement for all ethnic groups has improved over the last 15 years on standardized tests, though achievement varies from state to state and from region to region.

Sandia National Laboratories Report

In 1991, the Sandia National Laboratories, Albuquerque, New Mexico, prepared a report "to provide a foundation for Sandia's future activities in education" and to underscore "the most pressing issues in American education" (Lathrop, Otto, & Raths, 1993, p. 259). The study includes "detailed analyses of dropout statistics, standardized tests, postsecondary studies, educational funding, international comparisons, and educator status" and also addresses "future workforce requirements, the changing demographics, and the education goals proposed by former President Bush and the nation's Governors" (p. 259). The Sandia researchers came to a striking overall conclusion: "To our surprise, on nearly every measure we found steady or slightly improving trends" (p. 259).

The Sandia researchers also explained some often-baffling statistics. The high dropout rate of Hispanic students is frequently cited as cause for alarm, but the figures do not tell the complete story: "We believe that roughly 50 percent of the reported Hispanic status dropouts are first-generation immigrants, the majority of whom have never enrolled in school in the United States" (p. 263). Thus, when 18- to 25-year-old immigrants arrive in the United States, many will never enroll in U.S. schools but will be counted among the dropout figures cited as evidence of the failure of public schools (p. 263).

When the Sandia group examined standardized test scores, they found more surprising evidence: The much publicized "decline" in average SAT scores misrepresents the facts about students' performance. The reason for the decline in overall scores is that more students "in the bottom half of the class" are taking the SAT today than in the past (Lathrop, Otto, & Raths, 1993, p. 272). The Sandia researchers also challenged the common belief that businesses have to provide remedial basic skills training because public schools are not doing their job. In fact, the researchers found that two-thirds of the money businesses spend on training goes to college-educated employees for "white-collar training of managers, professionals, supervisors, and salespeople" (p. 296).

The Manufactured Crisis

Berliner and Biddle, authors of *The Manufactured Crisis* (1995), have cited the Sandia findings and a host of other quantitative studies to refute often-cited earlier reports, such as *A Nation at Risk* (National Commission on Excellence in Education,1983), that paint a dismal picture of public education. Berliner and Biddle concluded that "on the whole, the American school system is in far better shape than the critics would have us believe," and "where American schools fail, those failures are largely caused by problems that are imposed on those schools, problems that the critics have been only too happy to ignore" (p. 12).

Classroom teachers can use such research results and analysis to help correct inaccurate perceptions held by parents and community groups. We can use statistics when they are available, but we also need more than hard numbers. We need the analysis and interpretation of the data that can help us and our friends outside education understand the "rest of the story" that often does not get told in local newspapers or half-hour television newscasts. Although many classroom teachers do not have time to read lengthy research reports, major studies, such as the Sandia Report, deserve a closer look because of the wealth of data they provide. It is helpful, for example, to know that 57 percent of U.S. students start postsecondary education. But that figure alone may not impress our friends. What will have greater impact is the fact that the 57 percent figure is about *twice* the number of Japanese students who start postsecondary programs. Similarly, it may not seem especially significant that approximately one in four people in the 25- to 29-year-old age group has completed at least a four-year college degree. But this rate seems profoundly significant when one learns that it is nearly the same as the rate of U.S. *high school* graduation in 1930 (Lathrop, Otto, & Raths, 1993, p. 274). Unfortunately, good news like this seldom grabs headlines today. Even more unfortunately, far too few teachers know enough about the data to hold their own in conversations about education.

Belief Systems That Put Pressure on Classroom Teachers

In spite of the good news about public education, parents and the general public continue to express doubts about the quality of public school education. Just one or two reports, even unfounded ones, of incompetent or lazy teachers or of violence at school can raise serious questions in the minds of parents and the public. Hearing reports about conflict and controversy in other school districts often creates fear that similar curricular problems may exist or will occur in their own children's schools. As teachers, it is natural for us to react defensively in such circumstances. Even so, we need to guard against adopting a dualistic "us-versus-them" stance, as we are so tempted to do when we feel that public education is threatened. "They" want to destroy public education, we are convinced, while "we" want to protect and strengthen it. Even if we are totally convinced that we are right and they are wrong, sooner or later we have to pay closer attention to what they are saying. Seldom within a public school context can we make unilateral decisions. We also must consider the collective values expressed by teaching colleagues, administrators, parents, school board and community members, as well as state and national lawmakers.

Trying to sort out the hopes and fears of so many stakeholders is a real challenge. One source that has been especially helpful to me is David Gerzon's *A House Divided: Six Belief Systems Struggling for America's Soul*. Based on 100 citizen interviews, Gerzon has described six "states" (adversarial belief systems and the pressure groups that embrace the beliefs) that he contends provide an overview of the hostility that has existed in the United States during the late twentieth century (Gerzon, 1996, p. 3): the governing state, the religious state, the disempowered state, the transformation state, the capitalist state, and the media. Although Gerzon has relatively little to say about public education and about school controversy, the pressure groups he has described can help educators understand major belief systems and the pressures they apply on classroom teachers and on public education itself. It has been helpful for me to think of public school classrooms in the center (at least of our professional world) and to consider the various pressure groups Gerzon has described as if they surrounded the classroom center, which in fact I believe they do. Although Gerzon has described the pressure groups in a neutral way, I discuss the pressures that I perceive each group to exert on teachers, classrooms, and school districts. I do not address the media as a separate category, since it is my perception that the media permeates all the other pressure groups and advances their agendas. They are a mighty force, to be sure, but one that seems not to exert a unique pressure on teachers, classrooms, and school districts.

Teachers can monitor personal reactions to the discussion of each pressure group and ask the following questions:

- Which of the pressure groups holds views most consistent with your own set of beliefs?
- Which group's beliefs make you feel most resistant?
- Which groups seem to reflect the views of other teachers you know?
- Which "states" do your students seem to live in? Their parents? Your school board members? Community leaders?
- Which groups play an explicit or implicit role in your curriculum and in the classroom experiences you provide?

Pressure from and within the "Governing State"

The pressure group teachers are most familiar with is the *governing state,* since, technically speaking, public school teachers represent the government. Our professional lives get shaped in part by government-sponsored reports, such as *A Nation at Risk* (1983), and by the ideas expressed and texts produced by leaders such as Ernest Boyer, John Goodlad, William Glasser, and a host of others who have described a range of enduring problems and offered a variety of promising visions and solutions. We who participate in content area professional organizations (such as the National Council of Teachers of Mathematics or the National Council for the Social Studies) and/or in school reform programs (such as the National Writing Project or the Quality Schools movement) often grow confident as professional leaders eager and willing to chart our own professional course inside the classroom and out.

Yet, teachers know that there is pressure within the profession and within the system. Curriculum committees meet continually, and curriculum always seems to be somewhat in flux. When school boards and administrators develop new policies, procedures, and schedules, everyone is expected to adapt and adjust. Beginning teachers struggle to learn the basics of the profession, and experienced teachers work hard to meet new challenges.

Teachers Feeling Pressure from the Public

As public employees, we also feel pressure from the public itself, which often takes a cynical and hostile view of anyone associated with government. In a time when almost everyone seems to think smaller government is better government, we feel the power of community taxpayer groups that do not want to spend more money to build or repair school buildings. We feel pressure from the public and the public media when we watch television newscasts that seem to start from the premise that public schools do not work and that incompetent teachers are a significant part of the problem.

From another perspective, we feel we are at the mercy of powerful legislators and other high-level governmental decision makers who decide how much money schools get, who mandate high-stakes tests and content standards, and who sometimes make decisions about methodology, as well. Increasingly, teachers as a group feel ignored by politicians who hold educational summit meetings, such as "Goals 2000," without teacher participation and who rush to take a stand on just about any education issue, whether it is sexuality education, phonics, or history standards. As public servants, teachers are accountable to all. The challenge is to bridge the gulf of misunderstanding and build the necessary partnership between educators and the general public for the common good (see Chapter 11).

Pressure from the "Religious State"

The title Gerzon (1996) gives this group sounds as if it might encompass a variety of religious beliefs, but his discussion of the *religious state* focuses entirely on the influence of politically and theologically conservative Christians, often referred to as the "religious right." From a theological standpoint, it is unclear whether Gerzon assumes that the conservative groups speak for all Christians or whether—more likely—he simply recognizes the political power by the religious right. Generally, the *religious right* refers to fundamentalists (who base their faith strictly on a literal reading of the Bible), evangelicals (who are somewhat less rigid than fundamentalists and focus on spreading the gospel), and pentecostals (who focus on being filled with the Holy Spirit, as manifested by the practice of speaking in tongues). Typically not included among the religious right are members of other faiths or progressive Christians or mainline Protestants and Catholics, though many mainline groups have strong subgroups that identify most with a religious conservative perspective.

I believe that the power and influence of the religious right—or more positively, "religious conservatives"—as a pressure group are often overstated. The Christian Coalition, for example, claims to speak for millions, possibly basing their claims on the number of names on their mailing list. The name of the organization implies that a "coalition" of Christians can speak for most or all Christians, and their former executive director, Ralph Reed, has claimed as much: "The liberals don't want Christians involved in the political process. But Christians are Americans, too, and we intend to make our voices heard" (Reed, n.d.). Thus, Reed confirms that the Christian Coalition speaks for Christians and that Christians are conservatives. We must be careful, however, not to dismiss the impact of real conservatives. Across the nation, this group, more than any other, has exerted the greatest pressure on our curricula and on public schools.

Teachers Feeling Pressure from Religious Conservatives

Classroom teachers, like many of the general public, have watched with interest and concern the growing prominence of religious conservatives in politics and in local, state, and national decisions about public school classrooms. Education is a top priority for leaders of conservative Christians (Christian Coalition, 1995). Consequently, public school teachers are prime subjects for conservative Christians' scrutiny and influence. This fact should nudge us to get beyond newspaper headlines and television sound-bites and to learn more about the groups and their issues so that we can use such information as we work with students, parents, and community groups.

We need to know, for example, that local churches whose members embrace conservative Christian political agendas provide both the fervor and the workers to achieve their goals. In these churches, even Sunday morning bulletins that include the day's litany and order of service sometimes include information about pending legislation, along with a note encouraging worshipers to ask their legislators to vote yes or no on particular bills.

We need to know what they most often criticize about public schools. For example, they look for hints that New Age or secular humanist beliefs are replacing Christianity and religion in the classroom. They complain that the absence of public prayer in school is a sign of a sinful, Godless society. They are concerned about (and sometimes pray for) their children's "unsaved, ungodly" teachers. They believe that public schools promote moral relativism and that innovative and untested teaching practices have replaced methods that "worked" in the past. Frills have replaced the basics, in their view, and multicultural literature and revisionist history have diminished patriotism. They tend to believe the worst, ultimately concluding that public schools are a failure.

We also need to know what they advocate instead. Christianity, some believe, should be taught and actually practiced in public school classrooms. Public schools should be forced to compete for students. Private corporations could do a better job of operating schools, and teachers should serve at the will of administrators. People with job experience outside of education probably would be better teachers. Moral absolutes should be directly taught as part of a curriculum focused on the "basics" and on tradition. The curriculum should emphasize classical, American and European-American literature, and pro-American history should be taught with uncritical praise for the government's actions.

The Christian Coalition

More than a dozen national organizations promote a conservative political agenda tied to conservative religious beliefs. Clearly, the Christian Coalition (Chesapeake, VA) is the largest and most influential group at the local, state, and national levels.

Christian Coalition members ostensibly care most about faith and family values, but their primary agenda is political. Former executive director Ralph Reed, for example, predicted, "We will be larger and more effective and will reach more people than the Democratic and Republican parties combined" (cited in Gerzon, 1996, p. 13). Part of the organization's success can be attributed to its "stealth" tactics, as indicated in the following analogy: "If you reveal your location, all it does is allow your opponent to improve his artillery bearings. It's better to move quietly, with stealth, under cover of night. . . . I want to be invisible, I do guerrilla warfare. . . . You don't know it's over until you're in a body bag" (cited in Goldin, 1993).

Although the Christian Coalition is a tax-exempt evangelical "Christian" organization, few people would believe such comments are about soul winning. They are about power and the desire to control other people against their will. Political power and control drive the Christian Coalition: It is political power that they use to pressure educators, and it is control of the curriculum, in part, that they seek. They work behind the scenes to elect school board candidates and to challenge classroom materials and experiences. Their legal organization, the American Center for Law and Justice (ACLJ), provides information and legal support for parents and groups involved in curricular protests and in school prayer court cases.

Citizens for Excellence in Education

Another group that has had significant influence on the public school classrooms is Citizens for Excellence in Education (CEE) in Costa Mesa, California. Its name sounds deceptively positive, but the organization constantly attacks public education and repeatedly recommends that religious parents select home-schooling or Christian schools for their children if at all possible: "The Lord has counseled me, and an impressive array of those associated in ministry have confirmed God's leading, that CHRISTIANS MUST EXIT THE PUBLIC SCHOOLS as soon as it is feasible and possible. The price in human loss, social depravity and the spiritual slaughter of our young Christian children is no longer acceptable (and certainly never was!)" (Simonds, 1998).

Like the Christian Coalition, the CEE organization gains its strength in part from state and local affiliates and claims to have over 1,000 such groups across the country. Citizens for Excellence in Education deserves teachers' careful scrutiny, since it is the only religious conservative organization I am aware of that focuses all of its attention on education issues. Its president, Robert Simonds, like leaders of the Christian Coalition, knows how to figure the statistics to motivate his followers to get out the voters for school board elections: "Most elections are won on 1 percent to 3 percent of the vote. If only 10,000 vote in your district, that means 100–300 voters could elect the entire new school board" (Hill, 1992, p. 19). Furthermore, he boldly enlists the help of church pastors to get members registered to vote: "There are 15,700 school districts in America. There are 155,000 evangelical churches alone, and if you take *all* the churches in, there are 265,000 of them. Well, think of that, when you only have 15,700 school districts! . . . We can vote who we want in and out" (cited in Hill, 1992, p. 21).

Time and again, educators have cited Simonds's words as proof of the disturbing national agendas of some religious conservative organizations. Simonds seldom hides his real intent: "The Bible, being the only true source on right and wrong, should be the guide of [school] board members. Only godly Christians can truly qualify for this critically important position" (cited in Hill, 1992, p. 18). When his candidates get elected, communities usually do not have to wait long to realize just how important local school board elections are. At a postelection open house, for example, one successful CEE-backed candidate asked, "Why do you teach honors classes and physical education to 14-year-old girls who should be learning to take care of babies?" This incredibly sexist question was probably followed at first by stunned silence on the part of teachers (Goldin, 1993). School board meetings soon became battlegrounds over procedures, such as opening meetings with prayer, and curriculum, such as adopting Creationism-based science texts.

Focus on the Family

Another notable group is Focus on the Family (FOF) (Colorado Springs), headed by psychologist James Dobson, a Reagan appointee who has become widely known for his syndicated radio program and newspaper advice column. Focus on the Family publishes Dobson's books and several magazines and newsletters, including *Citizen,* a public issues newsletter that carried a 1990 article on the *Impressions* reading series. This article spread like wildfire through churches and schools and no doubt played a key role in the widespread censorship of that multicultural whole language program (Mendenhall, 1990).

The Eagle Forum

Some of you will remember Phyllis Schlafly as a leader in the fight against the Equal Rights Amendment. She, too, was appointed by former President Reagan to a commission, and through the Eagle Forum (Alton, IL) she has supported a variety of causes, many focused on children. An attorney, Schlafly home-schooled her children to teach them to read and later developed her own phonics-intensive reading program, which she advertises in her mailings. She is the author of *Child Abuse in the Classroom* (1993), which she prepared from testimony at the Hatch Amendment hearings. The book frightened parents, who became convinced that their children's teachers and the government were intent on invading family privacy. Schlafly serves as a role model for religious-right women and almost surely has influenced other mothers, such as Peg Luksik (see Chapter 1) and Anita Hoge of Pennsylvania (Bates, 1993), not to be afraid to fight the system.

Other Groups

Other groups that sometimes play a role in promoting the Christian conservatives' education agenda are Beverly LaHaye's Concerned Women for America (Washington, DC), Gary Bauer's Family Research Council (Washington, DC), Donald Wildmon's American Family Association (Tupelo, MS), and Betsy DeVos's group, Of the People (Arlington, VA). Working behind the scenes are Mel and Norma Gabler's Education Research Analysts (Longview, TX), which has provided textbook analysis resulting in the direct censorship of hundreds of textbooks. The Gablers are known for their page-by-page, line-by-line hunt for any hint of *secular humanism* or *moral relativism* that might call into question a textbook being considered for adoption. Members of virtually all of these conservative Christian groups have used the Gablers' materials to challenge particular textbooks.

Pressure from the "Capitalist State"

As classroom teachers, we may not think of corporations as exerting pressure on our day-by-day classroom experiences, but they do—primarily because of their powerful influence in all sectors. Those who live in the "capitalist state," like those in the "religious state," tend to believe that public education is a failure. Often, local newspapers carry that message, as did an article in my local paper with the headline, "Ex-GM Exec Turns Focus to Education" describing a speech given by a former president of General Motors to the Michigan State Board of Education at a strategic planning session (Haglund, 1995). The former executive, who had been forced out of GM several years ago as it moved toward bankruptcy, expressed several complaints about public education and recommended publicly funded, for-profit schools as a partial solution. The conservative Michigan State Board of Education president liked the speech so much he ordered 5,000 copies printed and mailed to business, education, and media executives throughout the state.

Chief executive officers often recommend simplistic solutions for the complex problems within public education. Basically, they say to educators, "We know better than you do how to do your job—schools should be run like a business." These individuals do not hear the arrogance that such recommendations suggest, but they need to. The newspaper columnist who challenged the credibility of the former CEO of General Motors pointed out that "if [he] is going to suggest how to reform education, it's fair to examine his success in trying to reshape GM. It's not a pretty picture" (Haglund, 1995). Certainly, corporate executives have a stake in the education that their future employees will obtain, but multinational corporations usually have all they can do—and not always very successfully—to run their own businesses.

I admit that as a teacher it is hard not to feel defensive when corporations continually criticize public school teaching and the idea of public education. But sometimes those in the *capitalist state* seem as smugly superior to and intolerant of those of us who work in public institutions as religious conservatives seem toward those from other faiths. I once was shocked to hear a corporate trainer refer to public school teaching as corporate training's "dumber brother." Such comparisons suggest the corporate smugness that makes public educators despair, especially if they know that corporate trainers typically work directly with far fewer "trainees" for fewer hours a day while aided by support staff and technical equipment that most classroom teachers can only imagine.

Competition is the primary solution offered by corporate executives. It is based on the assumption that teachers, administrators, and students will never do their best work unless forced to compete with someone else. Some teachers do feel comfortable with competition, and most of us have occasionally used friendly rivalries among classroom teams or cooperative groups as positive incentives. But especially as we have become committed to meeting the diverse needs of all children, we have taken a new look at the classroom practices that pit students against each other. Many of us have learned as teachers and as parents that when individual children's lives are involved, there really are no level playing fields. Many of us find that the idea that competition "works" seems to appeal most to those who frequently "win." For many students, however, competition reduces or diminishes learning.

Business is generally portrayed by the media as a benefactor for public schools, buying ads for school yearbooks and newspapers, sponsoring local soccer teams, and providing guest speakers for career day programs. However, one needs to scratch the surface and weigh the evidence about corporations' bottom-line priorities. For example, former Secretary of Labor, Robert Reich, has pointed out that only 1.5 percent of corporate giving in the late 1980s went to public schools (Reich, 1995). Reich has explained that these contributions are often smaller than the amounts the corporations receive in tax abatements that companies negotiate when they threaten to move out of town. Reich also has pointed out that "the executives of General Motors . . . who have been among the loudest to proclaim the need for better schools, have also been among the most relentless in pursuing local tax abatements and in challenging their tax assessments" (p. 23).

Businesses operate with a narrow margin of profit, the public is told. They may not be able to stay in business unless their taxes are kept low. However, syndicated columnist Molly Ivins has pointed out, "If corporations currently paid taxes at the same rate they did in the 1950s, the U.S. Treasury would collect an extra $250 billion a year, two and a half times what they now pay (Ivins, 1995). Ivins has further reported that during the 1950s, individuals paid 49 percent of total taxes, whereas today they pay 73 percent. Also, individuals pay taxes on income *before* expenses, whereas corporations pay taxes on total income *after* expenses. According to Ivins, "Once corporations get through deducting expenses . . . many of them pay a rate of less than 0.1 percent."

Other lessons have been learned from corporate leveraged buyouts: Corporations themselves can be destroyed by corporate and investment predators, and companies sometimes abandon communities. When Youngstown Sheet and Tube moved out of Youngstown, Ohio, in the early 1980s, the local economy was soon devastated. The public has also learned that corporate downsizing increases short-term profits for stockholders *because* thousands of full-time employees lose jobs that included livable wages and adequate benefits.

Many people piece together two or three minimum-wage jobs, usually without health care coverage, and wonder what such things may mean for the next generation, who may never earn enough to support children, finance a home, and buy a car. I question corporate responsibility not only to shareholders but to society and democracy as well, especially when I hear that an AT&T vice president is promoting the idea of a "contingent" work force in a society that will become "jobless but not workless" (Leana, 1996). I question the civic responsibility and the long-term economic wisdom of the idea that typical U.S. firms now hope to become "free-floating" entities that try to "maximize profits, adding and dropping people as needed." I appreciate the perspective offered by one business professor who calls for corporations to remember their role as "social organizations" in the sense that they are a dominant institution in society, and they need to be held socially responsible (Leana, 1996).

Responding to Corporate Pressures

Based on current pressures felt at local, state, and national levels, I believe that corporate pressures on public education may represent as great a threat as those from religious conservatives. Often, the two groups share goals and work together, thus magnifying their combined power, although the views of corporate leaders often count more with the general public. Classroom teachers acknowledge, however, that business is to some extent a great benefactor, given that it provides the goods and services that all people need and given that business is the economic backbone of most local communities. And clearly, public schools need the best ideas that citizens from any sector can offer to support and strengthen public education. Some school-to-work initiatives and other school/business partnerships offer long-lasting mutual benefits for students and for corporations.

Part of the challenge, therefore, for businesses and for schools is to establish real partnerships where there is mutual benefit and a chance for real understanding. For some teachers, the only professional business connection classroom teachers have is to be grateful recipients of leftover carpet, paper, or wallpaper scraps local companies provide for classroom use. Other teachers work briefly with corporate representatives who come at lunch to read to and visit with young students. Everyone's intentions are good, and no doubt much actual good is accomplished, but these friendly, helpful donations of time and materials seldom lead to a mutual understanding or respect between teachers and corporate representatives. The nation needs other strategies to accomplish such a goal—strategies that involve, for example, dialogues and daylong exchange visits that pair teachers and corporate employees and that draw on the expertise of both to work on projects of mutual benefit.

Pressure from the "Transformation State"

Occasionally, teachers and curriculum are pressured by social activist parents who are especially concerned about the oppression of disempowered groups in society. These pressures often appear as charges of gender stereotyping or of racial insensitivity. Such challenges by parents and community members, however, are relatively rare and constitute just a fraction of curricular protests. More often, the pressure to incorporate social justice into the curricula and into teaching practices comes from classroom teachers who have adopted a critical stance toward teaching and learning. Many teachers and curricular leaders make a conscious effort to resist racism, sexism, and homophobia and to promote cultural diversity. Editors of professional journals regularly select themes focused on cultural diversity, critical pedagogy, and inquiry-based education.

But when progressive teachers face resistance from more traditional teachers and parents, divisive conflict often occurs. Thus, a middle or high school teacher may need to compose well-argued rationales (see Chapter 10) to convince administrators and parents of the educational value of using such texts as M. E. Kerr's novel *Deliver Us from Evie* about a lesbian teenager or Cynthia D. Grant's *Uncle Vampire* about rape and incest.

The message of social transformation is promoted by strong, visible social activists who boldly call attention to uneven school funding policies, substandard school buildings and equipment, and narrow curricular choices. Jonathan Kozol is a relentless critic of those who want to apply big business strategies to public schools. Responding to corporate leaders who argue for injecting competition into the funding of public education, Kozol stated, "I've never in my entire life seen any evidence that the competitive free market, unrestricted, without a strong counterpoise within the public sector, will ever dispense decent medical care, sanitation, transportation, or education to the people" (cited in Miner, 1995, p. 5).

To those who insist that the problems of public schools will not be solved by "throwing money" at them, Kozol recommended, "Let's tell the conservatives, 'You know, looking at your experience, it seems like you think you can buy a better car with more money, a better house with more money, a better holiday with more money, a better doctor with more money, a better psychiatrist for your children with more money, and you're paying $40,000 to send two kids to Andover or Exeter. So why not more money for public schools?'" (cited in Miner, 1995).

Progressive and critical educators have also been influenced to take a socially active, political classroom stand by the publications of Brazilian educator Paulo Freire and his student Ira Shor. As a teacher in Brazil, Freire taught impoverished adults to read and write and observed that his students passively accepted their life circumstances. To shake them awake to greater possibilities for themselves, he began a process of challenging and "transforming the consciousness" of his students (Shor & Freire, 1987, p. 174). Freire and Shor have argued that teachers do take a stand on social justice issues—a stand that is not neutral, whether or not that is the teacher's intention. Freire has encouraged teachers to become "dialogical educators" or "liberating teachers" who do not have the right to impose a position on students but who "can never stay silent on social questions" (Shor & Freire, 1987, pp. 174–175).

Putting Pressure to Work

Those who are critical of the status quo, who promote empowerment of the disempowered, raise the hard issues and propose tough solutions. For example, Enid Lee (1992) has addressed racism—the "hard stuff" as she refers to it—in new ways. She is impatient with "victim-blaming" discussions about students' low self-esteem and lack of motivation, violent and disruptive behavior by students, and the so-called problem of single-parent households. Lee insists that more attention should focus on "systems and the state that create the problem," and that teachers should uncover the politics in the "hidden" curriculum at work in such decisions as how texts are selected, who gets in the yearbook, or how parents are "allowed to get involved" (Lee, 1992).

For teachers who want to become more comfortable "living in" the *transformation state,* Bob Peterson (a fifth-grade teacher at La Escuela Fratney, a bilingual elementary school in Milwaukee, and coeditor of *Rethinking Schools*) offers some guidelines. For example, he points out the differences in ideological stance by imagining how three teachers might handle a November classroom food drive (Peterson, 1994):

- The *traditional* teacher affirms students' interest—"That's nice and I'm glad you care about other people"—but does not view the food drive as a potential classroom activity.
- The *progressive* teacher sees the food drive as an opportunity to build on "students' seemingly innate sympathy for the down-trodden" and asks students to count and categorize the cans and to write about how they feel about the experience.
- The *critical* teacher does the same as the progressive teacher but also uses the food drive as the basis for a discussion about poverty and hunger: "How much poverty and hunger is there is our neighborhood? Our country? Our world? Why is there poverty and hunger? What is the role of the government in making sure people have enough to eat? Why isn't it doing more? What can we do in addition to giving some food?"

Peterson explains that participating in the food drive is not enough to constitute critical teaching. Instead, the deciding factor is engaging children in "reflective dialogue." He identifies five characteristics that are essential for teaching critical/social justice (1994):

- A curriculum grounded in the lives of the students
- Dialogue
- A questioning/problem-posing approach
- An emphasis on critiquing bias and attitudes
- The teaching of activism for social justice

Patrick Shannon offers a helpful distinction for classroom teachers who want to evaluate their own political stance toward curricular issues. While a *politicized* education "indoctrinates students toward a specific political agenda," a *political* education "aims to teach students how to think and act in ways that cultivate the capacity for judgment" (Shannon, 1995, p. 115). Shannon rejects the argument that such plans impose a politicized agenda and justifies a political education by citing the more conservative "impositions" that students face from popular culture, the media, advertisements, and schools (p. 121). He suggests that we need to teach students to be critical examiners of texts and experiences to ask why things are the way they are, who benefits from these conditions, and how conditions can be made more equitable (p. 123).

The Influence of New Age Spiritualists

Just as many educators, to a greater or lesser degree, promote a progressive curriculum that emphasizes social justice, so also many teachers encourage positive thinking to develop strong student self-concepts. Many teachers also take a strong advocacy stance toward environmentalism. These are issues that some citizens, especially religious-conservative parents, associate with a New Age philosophy or worldview. Teachers, however, are often surprised when their classroom practices are criticized as reflecting "New Age" beliefs.

The writing of Marilyn Ferguson has influenced the public's understanding of "possibility" thinking or of expanded human potential. Ferguson's (1980) book, *The Aquarian Conspiracy,* discusses concepts such as "learning as process," "divergent thinking," "holistic learning," and "teacher as learner" that have influenced teachers since the 1970s. Teachers who have never heard of Marilyn Ferguson may find themselves accused of following a New Age philosophy when their students' parents have read religious conservative critiques of Ferguson's argument that "tens of thousands of classroom teachers, educational consultants and psychologists, counselors, administrators, researchers, and faculty members in colleges of education have been among the millions engaged in *personal transformation*" (Ferguson, 1980, p. 281). Such statements frighten religious conservative parents who worry that New Age teachers will influence their children to abandon their religious faith.

Teachers who use guided imagery and visualization strategies in the classroom will need to be ready to reassure parents that such activities serve an educational rather than a spiritual purpose. Frankly, many of the visualization exercises that I am most familiar with involve an imagined journey that eventually leads to seeking advice from a wise spirit guide figure. While I personally think such exercises are harmless, I believe they should be used with caution. Using a visualization exercise that involves a spirit guide leaves the teacher open to charges of inappropriate, devotional religious practice in the classroom.

Pressure from Extremists

Although Gerzon (1996) does not include a separate group for *extremists,* but no doubt there are extremists in all the groups that he describes. Although classroom teachers may not be fully aware of it, some of our students' parents may be extremists; and, in all truth, the odds are good that some teachers are extremists, as well. We must be cautious in using this label, however, so we do not mistakenly rachet up the emotional rhetoric and create barriers to real understanding and dialogue.

Extremists usually think that beliefs other than their own are immoral or un-American. They often seek to limit discussion of ideas with which they disagree and try to impose their own beliefs and lifestyles on others. In some cases, they believe that coercion and intimidation are acceptable to further their cause. By these measures, you might be inclined to think of one or more of the groups discussed in this chapter as extremist. Most people believe they have more to fear from militia groups than from the more exclusively political groups, but unless we read *Klanwatch* (Southern Poverty Law Center), we may not realize that some parents and some students believe that armed warfare is the only answer to society's problems. If we make a point to teach tolerance and to "celebrate" cultural diversity, we face the sobering prospect of having to defend tolerance and diversity when challenged by militia parents. Some of the teachers that I know face exactly that situation every day.

Extremists do not just exist among undereducated citizens. The Chalcedon organization (Vallecito, CA) is a think tank for extremists among conservative Christians. Chalcedon is led by R. J. Rushdoony, author of *The Institutes of Biblical Law* (1973), a book that lays out a plan for establishing the "dominion" of Christianity. A brochure describing the "ministry" of Chalcedon explains: "Our goal is to bring every area of life and thought into captivity to Jesus Christ. . . . It is not only our duty as persons, families, and churches to be Christian, but it is also the duty of the state, the school, our callings, the arts and sciences, law, economics, and every other sphere to be under Christ the King. Nothing is exempt from His dominion. . . . We believe in the necessity for the total surrender of our whole life and world to the dominion of Jesus Christ." Words such as *captivity, dominion,* and *surrender* may be innocent enough if used to express an individual's religious faith, but when applied to the state, school, law, economics, and "every other sphere," they exhibit religious and political extremism.

Is There Any Common Ground?

With so much potential conflict, it is no wonder that we teachers sometimes throw up our hands and become demoralized. It is important, however, that we focus on the hope that comes from knowing as much as we can about facts and realities. We need to find ways to build on the hope to create better teaching and learning in the future. In writing this chapter, I have not tried to present a neutral description of the pressure groups that influence public school classrooms. Some teachers will not share my biases, but most will favor some groups' views more than others. Identifying our own biases is an important step toward deciding how we might respond to each perspective. Reflecting on the questions posed earlier in this chapter will help you consider perspectives and pressures that exist in your own local and state areas:

- Which of the pressure groups hold views most consistent with your own set of beliefs?
- Which group's beliefs make you feel most resistant?
- Which groups seem to reflect the views of other teachers you know?
- Which "states" do your students seem to live in? Their parents? Your school board members? Community leaders?
- Which groups play an explicit or implicit role in your curriculum and in the classroom experiences you provide?

As public school teachers, we are reminded that our charge is to teach all children—and to work with all their parents. Given the possibility for serious conflict, surely the time to face current and potential classroom conflicts and controversies is now. Researchers from the Sandia National Laboratories have proposed that the first challenge that needs to be addressed is "forming a national consensus and finding leadership in education improvement" (Lathrop, Otto, & Raths, 1993, p. 309). I am afraid that national consensus is still a long way off, but we take an important first step in that direction by recognizing the complexity of the issues involved. There is a lot more at stake than "proving" that we are right and they are wrong.

The Center on National Education Policy (1996) reports that the founders of public education in the United States believed that schools should do more than teach children basic skills. They believed that public schools should:

- Prepare people to become responsible citizens.
- Improve social conditions.
- Promote cultural unity.
- Help people become economically self-sufficient.
- Enhance individual happiness and enrich individual lives.
- Dispel inequities in education.
- Ensure a basic level of quality among schools.

Given the great conflicts among the various pressure groups, it seems likely that many of their leaders and members have forgotten—or never realized—that such goals for public schools existed.

WHAT CAN YOU DO
ABOUT PRESSURES?

1. *Think about and write out your own views.* You may not have given much thought to articulating a philosophical or religious worldview or a view about human nature, but it is helpful, as you consider school controversy, to make your own views on key beliefs explicit. Write down your thoughts, then read back what you have written. You do not need to share your thoughts on this topic with others, but you will want to consider how your views intersect or conflict with those held by others in your school and local community.

2. *Consider more than just your own perspective and biases in terms of which of Gerzon's state(s) you live in.* Think through the perspectives and biases, as you understand them, of the students and parents in your community. Think also about the perspectives and agendas of local business leaders and clergy in your area. Consider the issues and concerns of racial and ethnic groups. With which state(s) might they be most likely to identify?

3. *Stay informed, especially noticing research reports, such as the Sandia Report, that attract the public's attention.* Stay informed about school issues that are broader, and especially those that are more controversial, than just the age-level or content-area concerns that affect your day-to-day decisions. You will not have time to study the detail of every issue, but you can subscribe to and read one professional publication, such as *Phi Delta Kappan* or *Educational Leadership,* that addresses broader educational issues.

4. *Do not just read what other educators have to say about perspectives and issues.* Make a point to read what those who hold very different perspectives have to say. To understand clearly what others are saying, you must hear the issues articulated by those who hold them (one reason this book includes so many direct quotations). We cannot really debate the issues unless we understand the perspectives of others well enough to articulate them in a way *they* would accept.

5. *Build personal, professional support with other teachers within your school district. If possible, get to know union representatives, local school board members, parent leaders, and community members.* Build support beyond your school district through state and national professional organizations and through grass-roots groups focused on public education. Try to locate groups and resources in your area that strive to bring together people to search for common ground. Be willing to listen—to actually *hear*—the arguments and positions of others.

6. *On the other hand, decide which, if any, perspectives you find intolerable—ones that you believe threaten your central values.* Some issues are worth fighting for, but you will want to choose your battles carefully. For me, my bottom-line issue is that genuine public education—that is, education that is free, accessible, effective, and public—is essential to a democratic society.

HELPFUL RESOURCES

A wealth of information is available for teachers who want to know more about national groups that have influenced or who seek to influence public education. Increasingly, professional journals, books, newsletters, and websites provide information about such groups. National advocacy groups that promote intellectual freedom provide additional publications and resources. To better understand diverse political perspectives on education issues, I have joined several organizations and read regularly the publications that articulate their agendas. The study of these materials has allowed me to weigh the positions taken and the rhetoric and strategies used by opposing groups. The information that follows identifies some of the most prominent groups that are concerned with education issues. We teachers need to know about these groups not only to know how to defend our curricula and public schools but also because some of our students and their families share the values and agendas associated with these groups.

1. Citizens for Excellence in Education (also the National Association of Christian Educators). Regular monthly or bimonthly publications include the *President's Report* and *Education Newsline,* available for a minimum donation of about $25. The organization also publishes books for parents and other materials. This is the single-best publication I know of to hear religious conservative critics of public education articulate their positions. If this organization has anywhere near as many local groups around the country as they claim, it is very likely there are CEE groups in your state, if not in your community. You need to know what they have to say about sexuality education, multicultural issues, and more. Contact: Box 3200, Costa Mesa, CA 92628.

2. Lewis, Barbara A. 1991. *The Kids' Guide to Social Action*. Minneapolis: Free Spirit Publishing. Available in many bookstores, this highly practical classroom resource is designed for children and teens to use on their own. It is filled with success stories, step-by-step advice, and examples that demonstrate ways to empower students and teachers alike to work for positive social change. Classroom teachers I know rave about this book.

3. *Rethinking Schools*. A newspaper published quarterly by Milwaukee-area teachers and educators with contributing writers from around the country, *Rethinking Schools* focuses on local and national reform and on issues of equity and social justice. One-year subscriptions cost $12.50, well worth the cost for hard-hitting articles that articulate educational issues from a transformational, critical pedagogy perspective. Contact: 1001 E. Keefe Avenue, Milwaukee, WI 53212.

4. *Teaching Tolerance*. Published twice a year, this magazine is distributed free to teachers. Each issue is packed with stories from real classrooms and schools that provide ideas and inspiration. Also included in each issue is information about a range of resources —books, award-winning videotapes, and organizations—that promote tolerance and social justice. No matter what subject or grade level you teach, this publication will serve you well. Contact: Southern Poverty Law Center, 400 Washington Avenue, Montgomery, AL 36104.

5. *SPLC Report* and *Klanwatch Intelligence Report.* To be sure, these quarterly newspaper reports are not pleasure reading, but they may be important, particularly if you teach in an area where extremist groups are active. Contact: Southern Poverty Law Center, 400 Washington Avenue, Montgomery, AL 36104.

REFERENCES

Bates, S. (1993). *Battleground: One mother's crusade, the religious right, and the struggle for our schools.* New York: Henry Holt.

Bennett, W. J. (1992). *The de-valuing of America: The fight for our culture and our children.* New York: A Touchstone Book, Simon and Schuster.

Berliner, D. C., & B. J. Biddle. (1995). *The manufactured crisis: Myths, fraud, and the attack on America's public schools.* Reading, MA: Addison-Wesley.

Center on National Education Policy. (1996). *Do we still need public schools?* Washington, DC: Center on National Education Policy.

Chicago Tribune. (1996). Overall, education in U.S. getting better, study says. April 28, section 1, p. 7.

Christian Coalition. (1995). *Christian action seminar manual.* Chesapeake, VA: Author.

Cox, H. (1995, Nov.). The warring visions of the religious right. *The Atlantic Monthly, 59–69.*

Doyle, R. P. (1996). *Banned books: 1996 resource guide.* Chicago: American Library Association.

Ferguson, M. (1980). *The Aquarian conspiracy: Personal and social transformation in our time.* New York: J. P. Tarcher.

Gerzon, M. (1996). *A house divided: Six belief systems struggling for America's soul.* New York: Jeremy P. Tarcher/Putnam Book.

Goldin, G. (1993, Apr. 6). The 15 percent solution: How the Christian right is building from below to take over from above. *Voice,* 19–22.

Haglund, R. (1995, June 29). Ex-GM exec turns focus to education. *Kalamazoo [MI] Gazette.*

Hill, D. (1992, Nov./Dec.). Christian soldier. *Teacher Magazine, 4* (3), 18–21.

Ivins, M. (1995, Nov. 30). Tax laws rip off middle class. *Kalamazoo [MI] Gazette.*

Kelly, D. (1996, May 13). Poll finds mix of good, bad and mediocre. *USA Today,* p. 8A.

Lathrop, R. L., W. Otto, & J. D. Raths (Sandia National Laboratories). (1993, May/June). Perspectives on education in America: An annotated briefing. *Journal of Educational Research, 86* (5), 259–310.

Leana, C. R. (1996, Apr. 14). Why downsizing won't work. *Chicago Tribune Magazine,* pp. 14–16, 18.

Lee, E. (1992, Autumn). The crisis in education: Forging an anti-racist response. *Rethinking Schools, 7* (1), 3–4.

Mendenhall, D. (1990, Sept. 17). Nightmarish textbooks await your kids. *Citizen, 4,* 9.

Miner, B. (1995). Savage inequalities–Four years later: An interview with Jonathan Kozol. *Rethinking Schools, 9* (4), 5.

Ministry of Chalcedon. (n.d.). [Brochure]. Vallecito, CA.

National Commission on Excellence in Education. (1983). *A nation at risk: The imperatives for educational reform.* Washington, DC: U.S. Department of Education.

Peterson, B. (1994, Spring). Teaching for social justice. *Rethinking Schools, 8* (3), 3, 10–12.

Reed, R. (n.d.). Cited in *The two faces of the Christian Coalition.* Washington, DC: People for the American Way.

Reich, R. (1995, July–Aug.). Secession of the successful. *The Other Side, 31* (4), 20–26.

Rushdoony, R. J. (1973). *The institutes of biblical law.* Vallecito, CA: Ross House Books.

Schlafly, P. (Ed.). (1993). *Child abuse in the classroom* (3rd ed.). Alton, IL: Pere Marquette Press.

Shannon, P. (1995). *Text, lies & videotape: Stories about life, literacy, & learning.* Portsmouth, NH: Heinemann.

Shor, I., & Freire, P. (1987). *A pedagogy for liberation*. New York: Bergin & Garvey.

Simonds, R. L. (1995, Sept.). *President's report*. Costa Mesa, CA: National Association of Christian Educators/Citizens for Excellence in Education.

Simonds, R. L. (1998, Feb.). *President's report*. Costa Mesa, CA: National Association of Christian Educators/Citizens for Excellence in Education.

Willis, S. (1995, June). What the public wants. *Education Update, 37* (5), 4–5. Alexandria, VA: Association for Supervision and Curriculum Development.

4 Reading, Writing, Research, and Expression

The freedom to study, learn, teach, and express ideas is the defining characteristic of the concept of academic freedom for teachers and students.
—J. L. Nelson (1990)

At the elementary level, a storm of controversy surrounds the teaching of reading, the role of phonics, the correction of spelling, and the fate of whole language. Secondary teachers struggle to decide appropriate classroom research topics and resources. Students' speech and writing at all K–12 levels are increasingly challenged as students actually compose meaning and speak out in their own voices about issues and ideas that are important to them.

This chapter discusses curricular issues that have attracted the potential censors' attention and explores the concerns and agendas that lie behind attacks on particular parts of the English language arts curriculum. Although the chapter includes stories of teachers whose curricula have been attacked, more importantly, it describes what teachers have done and can do to avoid needless mistakes, to make defensible curricular choices, and to use controversy and even "bad" books in positive ways to promote literacy learning.

Fighting about Phonics and Meaning Making

One of the most highly visible curricular controversies focuses on teaching young children to read. Part of the controversy is based on public misunderstandings about *phonics* (letter-sound relationships) and *whole language* (a philosophy of literacy learning that values keeping language whole and teaching reading and writing through authentic literacy experiences). Another part of the controversy is based on honest professional disagreements about research and pedagogy. It takes place within a social and theopolitical battle about who has the power to influence and control the reading curriculum. The conflict involves not just teachers and parents but also researchers, teacher educators, legislators, state departments of education, publishers, and other entrepeneurs.

All of the major stakeholders as well as the general public have been inundated with misinformation about phonics and whole language. For example, they have heard or read that whole language teachers do not teach phonics but simply encourage children to "guess" at words when they read. Or they have heard that whole language is not supported by research. Or they have read that research shows phonics to be a superior method of teaching children to read. Unfortunately, many people seem to have made up their minds about phonics and whole language on the basis of one radio talk show or magazine article.

The professional controversy about phonics exists partly because whole language teachers teach phonics in a different way than intensive, systematic phonics advocates do. Whole language teachers seldom teach isolated phonics drills but instead teach phonics and *phonemic awareness* (the ability to hear and differentiate between the various words, sounds, and syllables in speech [Routman & Butler, 1995]) within the context of reading and composing meaningful texts. The controversy exists partly because of professional disagreements about word-attack skills and about how children process information as they encounter it during the reading process. Whole language teachers do not teach beginning readers to *guess* at words. Rather, they help young readers learn to *predict*—to anticipate or to "think ahead"— and to "use context along with phonics knowledge to get difficult words, to notice when something they've read doesn't make sense, and to reread to solve the problem" (Weaver, 1997, p. 2).

Frequently, proponents of intensive phonics or of whole language try to argue the superiority of one philosophy over another. To the tiny segment of the general public willing to look at the research, the results seem to be inconclusive because the research methodologies are often so different (scientific vs. ethnographic), because the studies compare teaching methods that do not include whole language at all—as when phonics intensive programs (emphasis on sounds and parts of words) are compared to sight-word programs (emphasis on recognizing whole words)—or because the research uses only standardized tests rather than observational, classroom-based research to measure reading. The professional and public controversy leaves too many teachers uncomfortably unsure about what their own professional knowledge and experience tell them, but more and more elementary teachers are drawing the following conclusion:

> Studies using diverse measures of reading development suggest that, in comparison with children in classrooms where skills are taught in isolation, children in skill-in-context classrooms—including "at risk" children—typically have developed more strategies for dealing with problems in reading, made better use of phonics knowledge, could better retell what they had read, and were more confident and independent as readers. Typically the skills-in-context children also scored as well or very slightly better on standardized reading tests and even on subtests of phonics knowledge. (Weaver, 1997, p. 2)

Often, an overemphasis on matching letters and sounds can be seen most clearly in later grades, when teachers expect students to be focusing most on meaning. Middle school teacher Jeffrey Wilhelm noticed, for example, that a student read the following sentence from a baseball story: "Jack slid into second and kuh-nocked his kuh-nee," pronouncing both silent *k*s (Wilhelm, 1995, p. 96). Wilhelm explained that when he asked Marvin if he could "see" what was happening in the story, Marvin replied, "No," even though he acknowledged that he had both played and watched baseball games. Wilhelm later learned that Marvin had rarely read stories or been read to and that his reading instruction over the past several years had consisted almost entirely of exposure to DISTAR (Direct Instructional System for Teaching Reading), "a method in which students repetitively identify letters and words" (Engelman & Osborn, 1976, p. 98).

Money, Religion, and Politics

The fight about phonics and whole language is, however, about more than professional disagreements. It is also about time and money, power and politics. Districts often create their smallest classes at K–1 levels and provide Title I and Reading Recovery programs for at-risk and struggling readers. They typically spend the biggest chunk of their curriculum budget on published basal reader series, literature anthologies, teachers' manuals, and an array of consumable workbook and resource materials. Thus, within school districts, more time, staff resources, and money are devoted to teaching reading than to any other part of the curriculum. Beyond school districts, reading is a multimillion-dollar industry. Phonics programs and reading clinics operated by universities and private corporations sell their services to worried parents who fear that their children are not reading as well as they should. And a steady stream of radio commercials promise quick-and-easy phonics help and better grades for a small price.

On a deeper level, the phonics and whole language debate is rooted to some degree in conservative theological beliefs about the reading of sacred texts. These roots are revealed when national religious and family advocacy groups promote phonics-intensive curricula, and local church pastors encourage parents to teach their children phonics at home. One reason church groups focus so much on phonics is that they especially value reading "correctly" word for word, since they believe their children's eternal life depends on their relationship with God, who is "reliably known only through the Bible" (Boone, 1989, p. 13). Such groups believe that the truth of their own view of religion cancels out the truth or validity of all others, and they seem to hold views of reading instruction that are just as dogmatic: "This country was discovered and ordained to exist because of God. From its infancy phonics was the basis in reading. There is a connection. God the Creator knows us and how we work. He used phonics historically" (Thogmartin, 1994, p. 120). Pat Robertson, founder of the Christian Coalition, has expressed the belief that there is a Christian way of teaching reading, insisting that learning to read is easy "if reading is taught the way God made us to talk—by syllables, by what is called phonics, not by the 'look say' method forced on the schools by the behaviorist models" (Robertson, 1990).

Robertson's position on reading and the position of many national religious-conservative groups have become highly politicized. Phyllis Schlafly, author and conservative activist, cited California's low reading test scores as evidence that the "whole language method is a disaster" (1996), ignoring the fact that the majority of reading teachers have not had enough whole language training to put it into practice in their classrooms and failing to mention that California's reduction in reading scores coincides with a dramatic rise in its English as a second language (ESL) student population.

More disturbing, state and national legislators increasingly involve themselves in how reading is taught. A U.S. Senate Republican Policy (1989) document about reading instruction cited "overwhelming evidence" indicating that "the cure for the 'disease of illiteracy' is the restoration of the instructional practice of intensive, systematic phonics in every primary school in America!" Since 1990, state-level, phonics-related legislation has increased substantially (Patterson, 1996), often mandating the use of phonics-intensive programs to teach reading. During the 1996 political campaigns, some political party platforms included phonics planks, and presidential candidate Bob Dole "made his disdain for whole language part of his presidential campaign" (Duff, 1996, p. A1; see also Chapter 11).

Helping Others Make Sense of the Phonics Controversy

Those who polarize phonics and whole language create a false dichotomy that classroom teachers can help refute. Teachers can start by agreeing with protesting parents and with each other that beginning readers need to learn phonics and phonemic awareness. And teachers can demonstrate that beginning readers also need to encounter whole texts from the beginning—another issue about which there is broad agreement. We can help parents come to realize that phonics is important to the reading process but it cannot alone account for teaching children to read. In fact, phonics is just one cueing system—no more important in the reading process than *semantics* (meaning, context, and background knowledge) and *syntactics* (structure and grammar) (Routman & Butler, 1995).

Good teachers certainly do not focus on just one teaching strategy. In good whole language classrooms, teachers focus sufficiently on all the cueing systems—phonological, semantic, and syntactic—to help young children become proficient readers. Good teachers immerse children in reading a variety of engaging texts. Using big book texts that all the children can see, good teachers extend the reading by incorporating phonics instruction based on selected words, syllables, phonemes, and/or letters that students are ready to learn. And good teachers know how to take advantage of the texts their students read and write, teaching not only letter-sound relationships but also spelling patterns and sentence structure features that help beginning readers and writers anticipate what comes next and how to use the meaning and context of the whole text to support the reading and writing of individual words. Such lessons may appear to be spontaneous and unplanned to casual observers but are intentionally designed by teachers who use particular texts when they know their students are ready to learn about particular text features.

It is easy for good teachers to lose heart in the face of legislative mandates that dictate that particular curricula or methodologies be used and even prescribe rigid "scripting" of daily lessons. Such actions are as professionally insulting as they would be if legislators specified in law which procedures surgeons could use in removing tonsils. Most teachers know that the controversy about reading is much more complex than media accounts would have us believe.

"His parents just called. They want you to teach him only
15 letters of the alphabet."

Source: Beattie; reprinted by permission of Copley News Service.

My colleague, Constance Weaver, and I have discovered through our work developing a grass-roots group (see Chapter 11) that the general public—including parents, local and state school board members, and even legislators—often do not have basic facts about literacy issues that could help them make decisions that would better serve our students. Busy people, we have learned, do not take time to read long research studies; but many will take time to read brief statements, especially those that are highly targeted and presented in an easy-to-pinpoint format, such as the fact sheet, "What about Whole Language?" (reformatted to fit Figure 4.1).

Misunderstandings about Purposes for Reading

One fact is clear: All parents want their children to learn to read. However, parents hold different views about the broader purposes for reading and about the stance readers can or should take toward reading particular texts. All parents want their children to learn the skills needed to decode written texts. And all want their children to be able to take what Louise Rosenblatt has called an *efferent* stance toward reading—that is, reading primarily to retrieve information. When people read efferently, they tend to read quickly and selectively—skimming to find information that carries widely accepted

FIGURE 4.1   Whole Language Fact Sheet

What about Whole Language?

Myth: Whole language teaching is just the same as the whole word method of teaching children to read; it is widely used; and it's responsible for all the illiteracy in our country today.

Reality: Whole language teaching is very different from a whole word approach for teaching reading; even today, very few teachers are whole language teachers; and whole language could not be responsible for adult illiteracy because hardly any teachers practiced it before the late 1980s and early 90s.

• *Whole language is a research-based philosophy of learning and teaching, not a method of teaching reading.* Whole language teaching reflects the constructivist view of learning that underlies current methods of teaching in most disciplines today—most notably, math and science. Constructivism acknowledges that we learn best by doing—by trying things out for ourselves, with assistance as needed. Individual interest is recognized as an important stimulus to learning, and this leads to giving students many choices in what they read, write, and study. Furthermore, whole language teachers constantly assess children's learning and promote their development as learners, focusing on the processes that lead to superior quality products. Because they view all children as successful learners to some degree and reject the sorting and labeling of children according to arbitrary standards, whole language teachers are sometimes viewed as lacking in standards. However, nothing could be farther from the truth. Whole language teachers simply recognize that we do not all learn in the same way, at the same time. Their purpose is to help all children achieve their personal best, not to find ways of labeling some children as unsuccessful.

• *Whole language ways of teaching reading are very different from the whole word approach popular from the 1930s to about the mid-1960s.* Through repetition of words and sometimes the use of flash cards, a whole word approach emphasized learning words as wholes. In contrast, whole language instruction goes from whole texts to words and parts of words. For instance, a teacher might read to children a simple text: perhaps a song, poem, or patterned story. As she rereads the text, she points to each word and encourages the children to chime in. From repeated readings, the children learn to read many of the words—and learn phonics as well. In fact, some recent research studies suggest that knowing a lot of print words promotes phonics knowledge and the use of phonics better than instruction in phonics does. However, whole language teachers do not merely leave the learning of phonics to chance. Beginning with familiar texts, they focus children's attention on concepts of print (such as the fact that we read left-to-right in English), specific words, letter/sound patterns (phonics), and reading strategies. Reading skills and strategies are not only taught but assessed directly, as children actually read and write, which enables teachers to determine what additional instruction is needed. Of course, whole language teachers also read books to and discuss them with children, and these are often books more complex than the children could read or understand by themselves. In whole language classrooms, children become not only successfully but joyfully literate—connoisseurs of books and authors and illustrators.

Myth: Whole language educators think learning to read is just like learning to talk.

Reality: This is an exaggeration, though they see some parallels.

• *Whole language educators see at least two important parallels between learning to speak one's native language and learning to read the way many children have learned to read in the home and in school.* First, in both cases the child is most concerned with meaning; adult speech and adult accuracy in reading are mastered only gradually. In other words, children learning to talk begin with the "whole" of what they want to communicate, and only gradually master the parts. Similarly

FIGURE 4.1 Continued

with reading: it is easiest for most children to become familiar with and retell enjoyable and interesting texts, then learn more and more of the words and the letter/sound patterns within them. A second important point is that both learning to talk and learning to read are facilitated when adults treat children as meaning-makers and focus on meaning first.

Myth: Whole language teachers don't teach literacy skills, especially phonics. They just teach children to guess at words when they read.

Reality: Whole language teachers teach skills in the context of learning to read and write.

• *Whole language teachers know that children generally learn* and apply *skills best when the skills are taught in the context of what the children are trying to accomplish.* When children are reading, for example, whole language teachers will help them learn to predict (to "think ahead," not to guess), to use context along with phonics knowledge to get difficult words, to notice when something they've read doesn't make sense, and to reread to solve the problem. When children are ready to revise their writing, whole language teachers will help them learn punctuation and spelling. As writers gain more experience and skill, whole language teachers will also teach grammar in the context of writing—helping children rearrange, expand, or combine sentences, for instance, and helping them learn to edit for standard conventions. Of course various aspects of phonics, spelling, and grammar are also taught in focused lessons, but whole language teachers have found that guiding children in *using* language skills is often the most effective and efficient way of teaching them.

Myth: There's no research that supports whole language teaching.

Reality: There is a growing body of research that supports it.

• *Various lines of research support whole language teaching, including research on how children learn to read and write, plus research into the nature of the reading process. Since 1985, a new body of comparative research suggests that children get off to a better start as readers when they are taught to use reading skills and strategies as they are reading and writing whole, interesting texts: the primary way they are taught in whole language classrooms.* The seemingly contrary research typically uses only standardized tests to measure reading. But studies using diverse measures of reading development suggest that, in comparison with children in classrooms where skills are taught in isolation, children in skills-in-context classrooms—including "at risk" children—typically have developed more strategies for dealing with problems in reading, made better use of phonics knowledge, could better retell what they had read, and were more confident and independent as readers. Typically the skills-in-context children also scored as well or very slightly better on standardized reading tests and even on subtests of phonics knowledge. On the National Assessment of Educational Progress, children in whole language-like classrooms typically score better than children in classrooms that teach skills mainly in isolation.

Source: © 1996 Michigan for Public Education, <http://www.ashay.com/mpe>; relevant research is discussed in more detail in C. Weaver (Ed.), *Reconsidering a Balanced Approach to Reading* (National Council of Teachers of English, 1998). In C. Weaver, L. Gillmeister-Krause, & G. Vento-Zogby, *Creating Support for Effective Literacy Education* (Heinemann, 1996). Revised 7/97 and included in the second printing, 1997. May be copied.

"public meaning" (Rosenblatt, 1985, p. 70)—and then they lay the reading material aside once it has served its purpose. Almost all readers take a decidedly efferent stance when they "read" a telephone book or television schedule. Taking an efferent stance can, according to Rosenblatt, also mean reading for "conclusions to be drawn, solutions to be arrived at, analytic concepts to be applied, and positions to be tested" (p. 70). But even for these extended purposes—often associated with job-related reading tasks—the focus is primarily on efficiently extracting information and meaning to be used for a practical purpose.

Unfortunately, some parent protesters—with the best intentions—want teachers to encourage their children to adopt an efferent stance toward reading *all* of the texts they encounter at school. In addition, some teachers make the mistake of teaching reading skills as if all texts can be approached from an efferent stance. Such practices hold true both for elementary teachers who focus almost entirely on decoding skills and for secondary teachers who teach students simply to seek out the "facts" of literary texts.

Consequently, some parents—and some English language arts teachers—do not seem interested in encouraging student readers to take an *aesthetic* stance toward the texts they read at school—that is, to read to enjoy a text or to appreciate and learn from the text's language and insights (Rosenblatt, 1985). Most English language arts teachers at all levels want students to read fiction to appreciate the unfolding of a story, for vicarious experience and "imaginative flight." We want students to linger over a poem and reread favorite lines. In other words, we want students to focus primarily on "what is being lived through during the reading" (Rosenblatt, 1985, p. 70).

Once the idea of reading for different purposes is clear, some parent protesters can accept that students need to learn—depending on the text—to take an aesthetic stance as well as an efferent stance toward texts. But some parents who are comfortable with both an efferent and with an aesthetic stance are disturbed when we encourage student readers to take a *critical* stance toward a wide range of texts. That is, we challenge student readers not to accept texts uncritically at face value but to recognize the effects of their own attitudes, experiences, and values on their reactions to texts (Simmons, 1994, p. 6), to inquire about the author's background and historical context to gain a sense of the author's worldview, and to test the author's sociopolitical perspective or worldview against their own. Many teachers believe it is our responsibility to teach students to question and "talk back" to the author as they read, so that reading becomes a dialogue: "Critical reading consists of questioning a text, challenging it, and speculating on ways in which the world it creates can illuminate the one we live in" (Kohl, 1995, p. 22).

Many parents, community members, and legislators seem not to realize that the meaning readers make from texts may consist of more than the author's intended meaning. They believe simply that what is on the page is what the author said and meant, period. They often do not consider the varied, equally valid meanings that can emerge based on the knowledge, attitudes, and experiences that readers themselves bring to their reading. Many teachers, on the other hand, work from a constructivist perspective, believing that readers construct meaning through an interaction, or a *transaction* (Rosenblatt, 1978) between the reader and the text. Readers "make" meaning by fitting what they understand of texts into their worldviews.

We need to do a better job of explaining a constructivist view of reading. If we say that readers *construct* meaning from encounters with texts, we suggest that meaning and truth are not entirely contained in the texts children read. Some parents may resist that explanation as an attack on the "truth" of the Bible, around which their faith is built. Parents who want to understand how reading is taught can recognize that the idea of constructing meaning is not necessarily antithetical to their own theological beliefs (see Brinkley, 1994; 1995). For example, teachers can explain that those who believe that God speaks to them through the reading of the Bible or other sacred texts believe that the meaning of the text emerges from a "transaction" not just between the reader and the text but between the reader, the text, and God.

WHAT CAN YOU DO ABOUT READING CONTROVERSIES?

   1. *Reflect on and learn from your own past school-based memories so that you can know how to approach parents, since parents' protests about reading and phonics are based partly in their memories of early school reading experiences.* For many, the idea of reading as meaning making is what parents remember least about their own K–1 reading lessons. More likely, parents recall explicit phonics instruction and/or a steady diet of fill-in-the-blank workbook pages. Perhaps they remember *Dick and Jane*'s unnatural language, abbreviated plots, and flat characters whose dress and manner seemed so different from those of real families. Many will recall reading round-robin style in a group with the teacher listening so that she (almost always, it was a *she*) could correct the reader when he or she mispronounced a word. The goal, the students assumed, was to read without making any "mistakes."
   Parents who have these or similar memories usually do not recall an early emphasis on meaning and probably will not be aware of the role and value of beginning readers' miscues (saying *home,* for example, when the text says *house*). Thus, whenever we talk with parents—in parent conferences, evening literacy events, or hallway conversations—we need to look for chances to teach parents how their children learn to read. We can, for example, respond to sincerely concerned parents who ask questions about reading instruction by calling attention to the part that error plays in a variety of learning situations, such as learning to skate. There are always a number of falls, or failed attempts ("errors") that occur naturally on the way to success in learning any new skill. We can help parents realize that the only reason a young reader says *home* when the text says *house* is that the reader understands the meaning of the text. We can also demonstrate that fluent adult readers commonly make such miscues on a regular basis.

   2. *Become a critical "reader" yourself—ready to challenge public statements that are made by politicians and talk-show hosts about the teaching of reading.* We teachers have every right to ask the question: What do politicians know about teaching reading? We will be wise, however, to pay close attention to political positions being taken and the influences that motivate such positions. An editorial by Robert Holland (1994) is based on an interview with Robert Sweet, identified as "a former Education and Justice Department official who founded the non-profit Right to Read organization." It would be helpful if readers also knew that Sweet is frequently quoted as a whole language opponent and is listed as the staff contact on the U.S. Senate Republican Policy document mentioned earlier in this chapter. As teachers, we need to read even professional publications critically and challenge the basis for off-the-cuff opinions, such as those included in Holland's report: Sweet had told him that "greed" was the reason that schools prefer whole language and that the major publishing houses "have a lot to gain...from repackaging...the failed look-say programs as whole language." The very next sentence, ironically, included an 800-number for Sweet's Right to Read national help line that offered a phonics test "at a nominal cost."

3. *Stay professionally active and alert.* Be vigilant by reading not only the local newspaper but also professional publications—such as *Reading Today, Language Arts,* and WLU's (Whole Language Umbrella) *Talking Points*—that can provide vitally important information about research and about parent protesters and agendas. For legislative updates, check the following websites:
> http://www.house.gov/Legproc.html
> http://ncte.org/action/rea/
> http://reading.org/advocacy/

4. *Help parents and the public understand that even most of those who advocate the intensive and/or early teaching of phonics and phonemic awareness do not advocate phonics first.* Phonics advocate Marilyn Adams makes clear in her book *Beginning to Read: Thinking and Learning about Print* that children should have numerous and rich experiences with books before phonics is introduced. People need to know that hardly any researchers advocate phonics first in isolation—not even most intensive phonics advocates.

5. *Find appropriate ways to explain technical concepts and language (e.g., terms such as* semantic, syntactic, *and* phonological) *for parents and the general public.* This is a lesson learned by a group of New York teachers and their principal, Joanne Falinski. They worked hard to develop a whole language school, only to have public opinion turn against them. Falinski was suspended as principal and banned from her office because of her defense of whole language. A *New York Times* feature points out, "If there is one point on which the two sides sometimes converge, it is that perhaps Dr. Falinski should have worked harder at making parents more comfortable with her teaching theory" (Berger, 1993).

6. *Provide legislators with accurate, classroom-based information and recommendations.* Few legislators, parents, or political editorial writers know the reading research of Jeanne Chall (1967/1983), Marilyn Adams (1990), or Kenneth Goodman (1967), much less the work of lesser-known researchers. They make up their minds on most issues based on secondhand information and opinions. Send them succinctly but carefully worded information that explains what you support, based on research and on your classroom experience. They need to hear classroom teachers explain what works in real classrooms and why.

7. *Do not be too defensive or too quick to criticize those who express a preference for intensive phonics, especially those who do so for theologically based reasons.* Mark B. Thogmartin, who identified himself as adhering to a fundamentalist Christian worldview but sympathetic to a whole language philosophy (1994, p. 125), observed that many of the teachers in Fundamentalist Christian schools "admitted that they were somewhat unfamiliar with other methods besides phonics." At professional conferences for Christian educators, Thogmartin noticed that "every workshop having to do with reading instruction had 'phonics' somewhere in the title or description" (p. 117). He heard one teacher say, "I just have a 'gut' feeling that humanism may be tied in with whole language programs" (p. 121).

What seems sad is that these teachers and parents did not know what else they might try and are seldom encouraged to try something new. Thus, it is possible that many might be receptive to new ideas if they were presented in a nonthreatening, nonpolitical way. I take hope in the fact that some Christian educators—such as Arden Ruth Post, professor of education at Calvin College in Grand Rapids, Michigan—write convincingly to Christian teachers and parents that "the whole language philosophy gives teachers the opportunity to acknowledge the nature of God-given communication and the holistic nature of the child. It does not advocate omitting or neglecting skills" (1996, p. 14). If we keep our own rhetoric at a reasonable pitch, we may find parents of many faiths ready to hear us and recognize that whole language is just as consistent with the tenets of their faith, if not more so, than other teaching philosophies.

8. *Engage parents in literacy experiences that let them learn firsthand about the joys of literacy.* It is essential that we demonstrate for parents what it means to read for different purposes. This is especially important so that parents will not assume that all reading experiences should be approached with the same level of assent and belief. Carefully constructed, brief mini-lessons can be developed for use at such events as back-to-school parents' meetings.

9. *Do not let enthusiasm for whole language distort the message that gets to parents and the public.* Some teachers I have worked with have become so enthusiastic about engaging children's interest by reading real children's literature and by inviting them to write stories from their own experiences that they act as though they believe that engagement with reading and writing is the only thing that matters. Such teachers need to rethink this position and to add targeted direct instruction into their curriculum. New, eager young teachers especially need to remember that parents and the public do not really want to hear only about how much "fun" kids are having at school. Parents want to know—in language they can easily understand—enough about what and how children are being taught to assure them that (1) the teachers know what they are doing and (2) that the children are learning to read and write.

10. *Teach students about different stances they can take toward texts and about different purposes for their reading.* Help parents and the public understand the importance of this lesson. High school teacher Vicky Greenbaum explains to parents the value of "making meaning from texts instead of being possibly swayed by any 'message' the words might convey" (1997, p. 17). She invites students to choose what stance they take to particular texts, consciously deciding the level in which to involve themselves in the text or to distance themselves from it (p. 18).

11. *Recognize that some parents will teach their children to choose reading selections and to be critical readers based on whether the texts fit with the parents' theological worldview.* In one sense, all people self-censor to the extent that they make conscious decisions about not reading particular books. Amish children are taught to self-censor and to choose "faith-appropriate" texts, for example (Fishman, 1988, p. 134). Many religious-conservative parents want the same thing for their children: "A reader must be careful not to follow the ideas presented in a literary work to determine his beliefs or be the basis of his perception of truth; all ideas should be tested in the light of God's word" (Menendez, 1993, p. 96).

Controversy about Student Writing, Research, and Expression

Parents have challenged their children's curriculum because of reading far more often than because of writing. This is not surprising, given that many parents and teachers cannot recall very many occasions of being asked as students to compose meaning through writing. Instead, most remember penmanship practice, writing book report summaries, and piecing together paraphrases and quotes from encyclopedias and other library texts for major "research" papers. In place of writing, many adults spent large blocks of classroom time on grammar exercises and spelling lists and tests.

Unfortunately, a number of students who get early megadoses of penmanship and grammar exercises virtually never move on to writing for real purposes. That is, they never learn to write to compose and express original ideas that are important to them. Too often as English language arts teachers, we have censored students' writing ourselves, particularly if we have let other things get in the way of actual writing. We may unwittingly have encouraged students to do as little writing as possible and to self-censor their own writing for fear of making errors.

Sometimes we have lost sight of writing as a way of composing meaning and have focused more attention on form than on ideas. We have marched students through lessons about patterns of organization and asked them to fill in the blanks, so to speak, with ideas that will fit into whatever form is being taught. We have forgotten that professional writers do not get up in the morning saying, "Gee, I haven't written comparison/contrast in ages. Let's see, what could I compare?" Instead, research (Perl, 1980; Flower & Hayes, 1981) has taught us that professional and student writers usually start by having something important to say and then deciding how best to organize and shape the ideas and information. Thus, teachers who overteach and overemphasize paragraph structure, the five-paragraph theme, or patterns of organization are short-changing their students.

On the other hand, we also short-change student writers if we spend so much time on clever writing prompts that we never buckle down to writing for serious purposes. Also, we effectively silence young writers if we neglect to teach them to revise and edit their writing so they can self-confidently communicate ideas that are important to them.

Parents and the public, however, are sometimes led to believe that time not spent focused on correct spelling and grammatical usage means that teachers do not care about upholding standards. A couple of newspaper articles helped me understand how the public mistakenly views research-based classroom practices for the teaching of writing and writing skills. In an article titled "Supporters Defend 'Invented' Spelling," the unnamed Associated Press reporter seemed to approach the topic from a mildly skeptical point of view, pointing out that functional spelling is supposed to make students be more "comfortable and creative" and occurs when "children give their best guess of how a word is spelled." A first-grade teacher reportedly never tells a child a word is "wrong" and "doesn't believe young children should worry about correct spelling when writing" (Associated Press, 1995). Such statements almost guarantee a negative reaction from parents and the public. In another article on the same topic, the leader of a conservative family organization said, "We believe there is such a thing as truth and such a thing as non-truth. If a word is to be spelled in a certain way, then it should be spelled that way. . . . It won't hurt the child's psyche to teach them the right way now rather than let them practice the wrong way indefinitely" (Trimer-Hartley & Richardson, 1995).

Frustrated teachers who read such articles often suffer from "yes-but" anxieties, since there is so much more that should be said about functional spelling. One important concept not mentioned in these articles is that spelling for *polished* pieces of writing gets careful attention during the editing phase of the writing process. I wonder if the teacher being interviewed remembered to make this fact clear to the reporter? Another important point not mentioned is that in order to "invent" spelling, young writers have to think in a very strategic and complex way—focusing intensely on using all their phonemic awareness skills to produce letters in sequence that represent all the sounds of the words they want to write. It is possible that the teacher could have made a better case, not by discussing "invented" spelling but rather "sound" spelling or "phonetic" spelling, which more accurately suggest the cognitive processes used by beginning writers. I wonder if the teacher pointed out that students' effort to produce letters to match sounds results in more active and effective learning—not only of spelling but also of phonemic awareness skills that can be applied to reading and writing. Although it is difficult to know from reading a newspaper article, it appears that the teacher's comments unintentionally reinforced the suspicions of the reporter that "invented spelling" is simply a feel-good method used by incompetent teachers.

In discussing the issues of spelling and grammatical correctness, one of the most important things English language arts teachers can do is to help parents understand the part error plays in learning to write. Humans are not born with the ability to communicate in full sentences; babies are encouraged to experiment with language until they eventually get it right, certainly long before they learn subject-verb-object patterns. Similarly, children should not be denied the chance to write until they have mastered spelling and grammar. Too often, teachers have, perhaps unwittingly, self-censored the teaching of writing, as one of my daughter's teachers did when she delayed including writing until second semester. She explained, "Right now, I've got kids who don't know what a sentence is, and I'm not going to do writing with them until I get that taken care of." Both research and common sense demonstrate that young writers learn about sentence boundaries through targeted mini-lessons that are not taught in isolation but are linked to classroom writing workshops where they can learn about sentence boundaries within the context of their own attempts to make meaning (Calkins, 1994; Weaver, 1998).

Personal Writing in Journals and Writing for Social Action

Some parents object to journal and expressive writing that asks students to write about their own experiences. Parents usually object because they believe some of the topics teachers suggest are intrusive. Schlafly (1984) insists that classroom teachers use writing—especially journal writing—to pry into students' personal and family behaviors and beliefs. Wise English language arts teachers, therefore, will explain carefully the educational reasons for using journal writing. Teachers can show parents sample journal entries to reassure them that journal or notebook writing provides a place for writing practice, for experimenting with new forms, and for exploring new ideas—not a place to pry into family secrets. This may be done by wisely selecting writing topics, avoiding such unnecessarily problematic prompts as "Who has the last word in your family?" (Schlafly, 1984).

Public school teachers also need to think carefully before asking students to reveal particular cultural traditions or religious beliefs, as suggested in "essay questions that are sure to get kids' pens moving" provided in an ad for children's books about angels: "Do you believe in angels? Why or why not?—Have you ever had an experience where you felt an angel was watching over you?—Can people be angels? How could you act more angelic in your everyday life?" (Puffin Books, 1995). Although the topics sound innocent on the surface, to conservative Christian parents and others who take the idea of angels seriously, answers to such questions technically are not any of the school's business unless the student chooses voluntarily to reveal his or her thoughts.

We can preserve personal journal writing or writers' notebooks by developing and following reasonable guidelines and practices (e.g., asking students to fold over "private" journal entries). We can use or adapt journal guidelines by thinking through responses to the following questions:

- What educational objectives are being served by the questions, assignments, or activities?
- How do they add to the students' knowledge or understanding of the subject matter?
- Why must anyone know this particular information? How will it be treated? Who will have access to it?
- What harm might result to students or their families if other teachers, students, or administrators have access to the information? (Jenkinson, n.d.)

Conservative parents are not the only ones who object to a steady diet of personal journal or expressive writing. Progressive and critical educators object to an overemphasis on idealized personal experiences as a way of developing the voice of student writers (Macedo, 1994, p. 182). Critical teachers insist that voice should be "a process that turns experience into critical reflection and political action" (p. 182). Brenda Miller Power shares Donaldo Macedo's view of deeply personal writing but criticizes academic leftists for overselling a political agenda. Writing by itself has no transformative power, Power insists, but can become transformative if used as a political force to improve society (1995). Without sounding quite so political, Allison Wilson rejects "the exclusive use of personal writing topics requiring no knowledge of larger issues or contrasting viewpoints and therefore no outside reading or other research" (1994, p. 95). Such experiences, Wilson insists, produce an "intellectually sterile environment" (p. 95).

It seems unlikely that conservative parents who resist personal, expressivist writing will be eager for their children to use their writing for political purposes, especially progressive ones. Thus, I predict that writing will continue to attract the would-be censors' attention. Teachers who plan a curriculum for writing will want to be careful to provide writing for multiple purposes, including both personal, expressivist writing and writing to effect social change. As director of a National Writing Project site, I find that too many students today still have not had the chance to become passionately involved in writing even about their own experiences, and they need that chance. But I also believe that some of us have lingered too long with personal anecdotes and narratives. Students can and should be invited to write about enduring controversial issues, and they should be nudged to use writing to challenge established biases and ideas and to offer new ideas and possibilities.

Writing, Inquiry, and Research

Some parents favor censoring the topics that students can select for research and inquiry projects. They are right, of course, to believe that not every topic is appropriate for any research or inquiry occasion. To be defensible, research and inquiry topics should not only be of interest to students but should also serve educational purposes and, in many cases, especially for secondary students, involve critical examination of multiple perspectives. Teachers will therefore want to consider carefully what topics students should be permitted to choose and what topics, if any, should be off limits.

A high school English language arts teacher, Todd Goodson, understood the need to nudge students to examine sources to search for reliable information and truth. But one of his students began writing a research paper focused on witchcraft and satanism, a topic that Goodson admitted made him very uncomfortable (1994). Eventually, he asked the student to choose another topic. As he discussed the incident in retrospect, however, he wished that he had not forbidden the student from continuing her paper on a topic that clearly interested her. A better plan, he realized, would have required that she consult a variety of sources on the topic that could create a "dialogue of opinion" (p. 24).

Another teacher, Chris Davis, was faced with new research questions when four students in a high school class chose religion as a focus for their I-Search topics (1995). Two focused on Mormonism and evangelical Christianity, and two researched creationism versus evolution. When students posted Internet queries for information on these topics, they got over 20 e-mail responses and began a "heated discussion" online that generated over 60 pages of debate and discussion (p. 28). A major issue the teacher faced was how to help the students decide what to do with the confusing array of messages and perspectives among the e-mail responses. Students who were used to assuming that material in books is reliable found that the Internet "brings a world of divergent and complex ideas directly to you; it forces you to determine what is true; and it encourages you to think" (p. 29). In the end, one of the students reflected, "One reason my search was so interesting was that it really made me question my faith. I don't think I was questioning it in a bad way, but in a way that made it stronger" (p. 30). Some parents would be troubled by the testing of faith that might occur as students conduct Internet research. But, while we search for answers to questions that many of us could not have anticipated earlier in our careers, it becomes increasingly evident that our challenge is to teach students to "use their own intellect to find the truth" (p. 30).

Challenging Students' Freedom of Speech and Expression

Good English language arts teachers are lovers of language who schedule in-class readings of student writing so that students can share their work and learn from hearing their classmates' writing topics, genres, and styles. Often, we encourage students to enter writing contests and to publish and even perform their work. However, since the 1988 *Hazelwood School District v. Fuhlmeier* U.S. Supreme Court decision, English language arts teachers and students have faced increased restrictions on students' freedom of written and oral speech and expression.

All English language arts teachers, not just those who sponsor school newspapers or literary magazines, need to be familiar with the *Hazelwood* decision—specifically, the ruling that "gave school officials virtually unchecked power to censor any student expression that is school-sponsored or appears to have the school imprimatur" (Hentoff, 1992, p. 358). Only when expression occurs in a publication designated as a "public forum" is it protected, since the *Hazelwood* decision affects all "school-sponsored non-forum student activity that involves student expression" (*Hazelwood,* 1988, p. 38).

In Michigan, a group of middle school student writers learned a hard lesson about democracy when their award-winning school newspaper found its articles censored by school administrators. The superintendent admitted that the story about a shoplifting incident on a school field trip was well written but he censored the article because it "reflected poorly on the district" (Parker, 1997). The superintendent explained, "I view any piece of information that comes out of the schools as our opportunity to put our best foot forward." When school administrators met with the paper's sponsor, they decided that "the newspaper will now be used as a showcase of student writing about the positive aspects of the school" (p. A2). This case received heavy local news coverage that generated pressure on the administrators to reconsider their decision to tighten controls on the student newspaper, but to no avail. Instead, administrators at that point began to offer other explanations for their censorship, such as not wanting to call attention to the students (though unnamed) involved in the shoplifting incident.

At a high school in Texas, students and their teacher learned a different lesson from entering controversial territory. In one issue of their 32-page school newspaper, they included a 5-page section on gays, lesbians, and homophobia, with the goal of encouraging students to understand and accept diversity in their school. In subsequent issues they planned to feature racial, gender, religious, and ability differences. Recognizing the need to approach the topic from a variety of perspectives, the students included an interview with a gay student, a summary of religious objections to homosexuality, a graph showing the mixed results of a student poll on the topic, and an overview of the related battles over legal rights ("Whose News?" 1994).

As luck would have it, the newspaper issue was discussed on a local talk radio show, which sparked a number of calls of complaint to the school. Deanne Kunz, the teacher sponsor, explained that although her administrators had the power to intervene in the student publication, "our administration has been nothing but supportive, trusting that students will report with honesty, fairness and accuracy." Still, given all the controversy, she reported that the newspaper staff felt "a kind of nagging doubt about whether we had done the right thing" (Kunz, 1994). Eventually, a meeting between a parent and the student editor led both to rethink their positions: The parent asserted that he should decide at home what to teach his son about homosexuality, which is a reasonable assertion, but he went on to suggest a parallel between homosexuality and pedophilia. At that point, the student editor, no doubt drawing on his recent research of the topic, was able to respond by asserting, "Homosexuality and pedophilia are certainly not related. Homosexuality involves two consenting adults, while pedophilia is like rape, because one of the parties is too young to make a mature decision" (Flynn, 1994).

Later, the student editor observed that the newspaper staff had been shocked by the "vehemence of the reaction" and concluded, "We have had to follow our own advice and accept diversity: the diversity of opinions different from our own." From the responses of students and the community, Kunz and her students recognized that the student body and the community gained a better "understanding and appreciation for diversity" and that "controversy itself can be an educational experience" (Kunz, 1994).

Thus, within the constraints of the *Hazelwood* decision, teachers are working to create the most positive experience possible for students. In addition to learning what *Hazelwood* restricts, teachers need also to know that there are some limits on the scope of the *Hazelwood* decision, as explained by Mel Krutz, Nebraska teacher and NCTE leader in addressing censorship issues. Krutz (1994) warns teachers and journalism advisors not to self-censor and pull articles that may be controversial and not to try to guess what might be offensive to someone. She advises teachers who face censorship by administrators to appeal to the school board, since administrators can only censor if the school board permits. Teachers can also use public pressure by getting "parents, community, librarians, the press, other media, fellow faculty, and students to petition or take other public action, including debate." Teachers can take positive action by urging schools to adopt a protection policy for school publications and by establishing an award honoring "administrators and others who are committed to upholding and defending freedom of speech in the schools." Even more important for the long term,

Krutz recommends, is to promote state legislation to protect student First Amendment rights, as Iowa, Massachusetts, Colorado, California, and other states have already done (p. 225).

Students' Oral Expression in the Classroom

Unfortunately, we cannot assume that administrators will do what is right or that they will even do what is legal, as a Missouri high school creative writing teacher learned from painful experience when she tried to defend her students' written and videotaped work. The school district had in place a set of instructional policies that included a strong academic freedom statement for teachers and a discipline code for students. But Cissy Lacks (1997) was suspended by her principal and eventually fired by the school board because profanity was listed in an appendix to the student code.

When questioned about offensive language that appeared in students' poetry, veteran creative writing teacher Lacks showed her administrators three poems written by a student for whom writing had significant impact. Lacks explained that the resistant student had progressed from sitting in the back of the room with his head on the desk to composing angry, gang slang poems and then to writing a poem that won a district award. Lacks's administrators, however, ignored the circumstances and discarded the award-winning poem, focusing instead on the language of the student's two earlier poems as evidence of Lacks's incompetence. Also used against Lacks were videotaped scripts her students had written, which included street language. She explained that the videos were made to encourage students to use their authentic voices. Although Lacks had promised her students that the videos would be used only in the classroom, they were eventually shown in public, against her wishes and without the students' permission, even on national television.

Lacks was suspended and fired on the grounds that she had not honored one part of the appendix of the discipline code for students that listed profanity among "minor misbehaviors that might disrupt class or show disrespect." The media attention, however, ultimately worked in Lacks's favor by providing public support. With additional support from professional associations and National Education Association attorneys, Lacks fought her case in the courts. She explained: "I told my attorney the legacy you create for me and for all teachers must be the right one. I don't want my name to be associated with the case that struck fear in the hearts and minds of every teacher. And certainly, I don't want self-censorship to take place because teachers do it themselves out of fear. I want a strong statement to be made for academic freedom and teachers' rights to teach because those practices make for good education" (p. 29).

In 1996, Lacks won her case and was awarded $750,000 plus $76,000 in back pay—sending an important message that I hope administrators across the country will pay attention to. Hard questions emerge from such cases, however: What have students learned about freedom of—and the limits on—speech and expression? What have administrators learned from such occasions, and how might one decision affect administrative decisions made at a later time? And how will future decisions made by the teachers in the district be affected? Teachers and administrators will do well to work together to consider the implications of these incidents and the questions they raise before a crisis occurs.

WHAT CAN YOU DO ABOUT CONTROVERSIES ABOUT WRITING, RESEARCH, AND EXPRESSION?

1. *Work hard to help parents understand the writing development of young writers, especially spelling development (see Temple, Nathan, Temple, & Burris, 1993).* Use dated writing samples over the course of a school year to show parents the improvement that comes from regularly writing for a variety of purposes and audiences.

2. *Ask students to write or rubber stamp "DRAFT" and the date on written works in progress that get taken home so that parents will understand that drafts may include uncorrected spelling and other surface feature errors.*

3. *Respect students and protect their individual and family privacy rights.* Often, teachers can offer students a range of inquiry-based assignment topics and materials so that students do not need to reveal personal or family information. Parents are right to object to potentially embarrassing writing assignments, but students can voluntarily select personal and family topics. In their speech and writing, however, students should not be required against their will to share personal beliefs or family experiences with their classmates or their teacher.

Teachers need to explain carefully ahead of time how they will treat the information revealed in students' writing, especially in journals. At the beginning of the year, one high school teacher I know explains to her students that they should not tell her anything in their journals that they do not want her to know, because she will act on it. Thus, when she finds anything illegal discussed in a student's journal—such as selling drugs—she makes a copy for the school counselor. When she finds in the journals what appears to be a cry for help arising from possible abuse or suicidal feelings, she writes a note in the student's journal offering her support and sends a copy of the student's entry and her own response to the counselor.

4. *Explain the educational purposes of journal and expressive writing.* Describe the benefits that frequent journal, log, or notebook writing has for developing fluency and for generating ideas and insights that can be used in future pieces of writing. Also explain the value of informal, ungraded writing-to-learn pieces that actively engage students' thinking and thereby extend and enrich learning. The NCTE suggests that teachers explain that journals are not diaries but are tied to the content of courses; that teachers award points for journals but not grade them; and that teachers respond only to entries that pertain specifically to the class (Jenkinson, n.d.).

5. *Remember that students can research and write about faith issues.* Students can report their findings to the class, but those who share their work with classmates should not preach.

6. *Make a point to show parents the range of reading and writing experiences planned for their children, including informational texts (biography, inquiry reports,* *personal narrative, observation logs, letters, etc.).* Parents are probably right to complain if students read and/or write in a single genre.

7. *Help your district create a curriculum that serves all children well—that does not expect too little or short-change real reading and writing.* Sherry Guice and Greg Brooks (1995) found the following in their study contrasting classroom practice in a large urban district and a small rural school district: (a) children in the financially poor urban school district spent 10 times more time filling in worksheets than children in the more affluent rural district; (b) children in the urban school spent only half the time doing real composing than did their peers in the rural school; and (c) urban children spent half as much time in silent reading. *All* children need an effective English language arts curriculum that will provide needed skills but also challenge the intellect, capture the imagination, and encourage students to use their voices to speak out on issues that are important to them.

8. *Promote the adoption of a journalism curriculum that stresses the importance of freedom of the press.* School-sponsored publications that are established as public forums for public expression have far fewer restrictions on students' and teachers' speech. Organizations, such as the Student Press Law Center, can provide help for districts that want to establish new policies that create open-forum publications. (See "Helpful Resources" at the end of this chapter.) I am grateful to Dan Holt, teacher and sponsor of an award-winning school news magazine, for offering the following advice to journalism advisors and for describing a philosophical stance that advocates preserving an open forum for student publications.

Freedom of Press, the High School Newspaper, and Enlightened Administrators*

Dan Holt, St. Joseph High School, St. Joseph, Michigan

I almost never title any piece before I write it. I guess this is an old reporter habit: headlines are always composed in the editing process, after the story has been written. To come up with the headline first might produce a slanted story, so titles usually come after the story has been completed. Headlines are also usually written by someone else, an editor who can see the story with fresh eyes and perspective . . . there's that journalistic desire for objectivity again.

This time it's different. I know exactly what I want this story to say, and I've known it for years. And I don't care about objectivity. Freedom of the student press is something about which I am very subjective. I've taught high school journalism and have advised high school publications for nearly thirty years, and I can say my attitude toward the subject has not changed at all during that time. I started my teaching career believing that student journalists and high school publications need freedom of speech and the press, and I still believe that. I preach press freedom and the responsibilities that come with it to my students daily and have defended that freedom on numerous occasions.

*Printed by permission of Dan Holt.

First, I have to say that without freedom of expression, a high school newspaper is a lifeless exercise and bound to fail. The students who the paper is written for will know that the publication is censored and will refuse to support it and students won't want to write for it either. The few students who do write for the paper will constantly be looking over their shoulders for the censor, and their stories will consist of lifeless writing assignments meant to please adults who have all the power. I doubt that students can even learn to write in an atmosphere of censorship.

The high school newsmagazine, which I advise, services a student population of approximately 850 students, grades nine through twelve. We print 600 newsmagazines every time we publish and often sell out. If the old formula is followed that the circulation is the number of newspapers sold times three, our circulation is actually twice the size of the student population of our school, or approximately 1,800 readers. I think this is a pretty accurate figure, especially considering that after the newsmagazine is sold I seldom see copies in the hallway or in trash cans. Parents tell me that the students bring them home and the parents read them too.

This degree of support from our readers is essential. The *Wind-Up* (our publication) is self supporting; we get no budget from the administration to run the magazine, and we have even purchased our own cameras, computers, printers, light tables, and file cabinets over the years with the profits. Our revenues come from the money we made in sales and in the money we get from selling advertising space in addition to the profits from an occasional dance or other money-raising activity. If we fail to please our readers and they stop buying the magazine, we will go belly up. That's why it's important for our readers to know they are reading the real thing.

I recommend that all high school publications operate on a self-supporting basis. In addition to the feeling of independence the students will derive from being financially on their own, students will also learn that journalism is a business and that to stay in business they must give their readers what they want. And what our readers want is truth, at least the truth as student journalists see it. These financially independent students will take ownership of their publication and start to care about what it says and stands for. At least that's the way this has worked in my school.

Of course, for some time now, since the *Hazelwood* case at least, administrators have been given license by the courts to censor the school press. But I believe in most schools, administrators have always exercised censorship of the school press, either through official approval of potential stories or the more covert (but more effective) advisor pressure approach. In the latter, administrators get advisors to do their dirty work for them, knowing that censorship coming from a staff member who has established a rapport with the student journalists is less likely to produce a negative reaction from either students or parents. Advisors, who are overworked, underpaid, and underappreciated are often bullied into censoring their own students by principals who hold all the cards.

The first thing in dealing with administrators who would like to make you as advisor do the censoring is to establish that you believe in freedom of the press for your students. Once you establish this fact, you are at least operating from a position of conviction, installing yourself on the high ground. If your principal wants to keep a particular article out of the paper, make him or her make the decision. Administrators want advisors to take them off the hook, but don't do it. Of course, all of this depends on the fact that the article in question is in good taste, is not libelous, or potentially disruptive. If you support an article filled with four-letter words, humorous references to sex or drugs, or one that makes potentially libelous statements about students or staff members, you are contributing to the demise of student freedom of speech in your school. It is then your job to convince the editors that it is in their best interest to pull the article themselves to keep from getting censored. Remember, your students' freedom of speech should be tempered with good sense. You must select your battles over free speech carefully, making sure that the stories are sound.

I've generally avoided these situations by helping my editors carefully screen stories and by reminding administrators when the need arises that my official title is "advisor." That means I advise the editors but let them make the final decisions. I am not paid to be a censor. I further tell the administrators that I will be happy to change the publication, calling it an official high school newsletter with the goal of showing the school in a good light if that is what they (the administrators) want. If they want a public relations vehicle, I'm perfectly willing to help the students create one, but I'm not willing to lie to anyone, to make a PR publication seem to be a real newspaper. I have on occasion told administrators that the choice is theirs, and I have meant it. I've explained there is nothing wrong with a PR publication as long as everyone knows that's the purpose, but to produce a PR publication in the guise of a newspaper or newsmagazine is dishonest and violates my moral standards. (Remember the high ground?) Of course, I also tell them that the publication would have to be fully sponsored by the school, and that we'll probably have to give the thing away as the students are not likely to financially support what amounts to a school advertisement.

I have to say that I have very little problem with censorship in my school. Perhaps it's because I have established that I won't go along with censorship or maybe it's because our principals are intelligent and enlightened individuals who understand the importance of a free student press. Perhaps they realize that not only does the school newsmagazine provide a wonderful training ground for future journalists and an effective publishing opportunity for countless students (approximately sixty students have already published pieces in the *Wind-Up* so far this year), but it also helps the entire student body understand the role that a free press plays in a democratic society. If it is not true that my administrators are enlightened, I'd rather not know it. Of course, it's possible that our administrators only go along with a real newspaper because we've established a free press tradition, and they know the community would not now stand for a censored student press. But I would rather think that our administrators are indeed enlightened.

HELPFUL RESOURCES

1. Brown, J. E. (Ed.). (1994). *Preserving Intellectual Freedom: Fighting Censorship in Our Schools*. Urbana, IL: NCTE. This collection for English language arts teachers at all levels offers personal examples, discussion of philosophical and psychological considerations, and legal precedents that provide insight about how censorship can come about, its impact and repercussions, and the ways it can be fought.

2. DelFattore, J. (1992). *What Johnny Shouldn't Read: Textbook Censorship in America*. New Haven, CT: Yale University Press. This prize-winning book focuses on the textbook adoption process and on lawsuits involving attempts to ban or rewrite textbooks. It provides a carefully researched look at key cases and the self-censoring effects on U.S. textbook publishers.

3. International Reading Association. Professional journals for teachers focus on improving reading instruction and promoting the life-time reading habit. Journals include *The Reading Teacher* (for teachers of children ages 1–12), the *Journal of Adolescent & Adult Literacy,* and the *Reading Research Quarterly*. IRA also publishes professional books for teachers, sponsors professional conferences, and provides international leadership in taking stands in support of literacy education. Contact: 800 Barksdale Road, P.O. Box 8139, Newark, DE 19714-8139, (302) 731-1600, http://www.reading.org

4. Meade, J. (1990, Nov./Dec.). A war on words. *Teacher Magazine,* 36–45. This article tells the shocking story that jolted elementary language arts teachers awake to the fact that censorship and controversy is a reality. What happened in one community's fight over the *Impressions* reading series has been repeated in countless others, teaching painful lessons for elementary language arts teachers caught off guard.

5. National Council of Teachers of English. NCTE publishes a range of professional journals that address literacy issues at all levels: *Primary Voices K–6* focuses on practical, real-classroom stories; *Language Arts* includes discussion of research and classroom issues for K–8 teachers; *Voices from the Middle* addresses issues unique to middle school language arts teachers; *English Journal* addresses research and classroom issues for secondary teachers of English language arts; and *Research in the Teaching of English* publishes original research and scholarly essays on the relationship between language teaching and learning at all levels. Contact: 1111 W. Kenyon Road, Urbana, IL 61801-1096, (217) 328-3870, http://www.ncte.org

6. NCTE/SLATE and the NCTE Standing Committee against Censorship. *Guidelines for Selection of Materials in English Language Arts Programs.* This is a simple brochure that is packed with clearly articulated explanation of how and why to think through and develop selection policies and procedures. Single copies available free from NCTE. Contact: 1111 W. Kenyon Road, Urbana, IL 61801-1096, (217) 328-3870, http://www.ncte.org

7. Routman, R. (1996). *Literacy at the Crossroads: Crucial Talk about Reading, Writing, and Other Teaching Dilemmas*. Portsmouth, NH: Heinemann. Routman takes a close look at the "hits" that literacy educators have taken by those who promote a back-to-basics agenda. This book provides a detailed examination of controversies in several states involving phonics and whole language, spelling, and handwriting.

8. Simmons, J. S. (Ed.). (1994). *Censorship: A Threat to Reading, Learning, Thinking*. Newark, DE: International Reading Association. This collection of articles focuses on censorship of literacy and critical reading; curricular complaints and challenges to literacy best practices; and information and suggestions to help teachers fight censorship and stop the threat to students' right to read, learn, and think.

9. SLATE (Support for the Learning and Teaching of English). This organization seeks to influence public attitudes and policy decisions affecting the teaching of English language arts and serves as NCTE's intellectual freedom network. SLATE members worked through the NCTE/IRA Joint Task Force on Intellectual Freedom to publish *Common Ground,* a practical brochure filled with nuts-and-bolts ideas, action plan/strategies, and resources to jog your thinking and nudge you to do something to protect intellectual freedom. Single copies available free from NCTE. Contact: 1111 W. Kenyon Road, Urbana, IL 61801-1096, (217) 328-3870, http://www.ncte.org

10. Student Press Law Center. This organization provides information and support for students whose publications are challenged. Contact: 1101 Wilson Boulevard, Suite 1910, Arlington, VA 22209, (703) 807-1904, e-mail: <spic@cap.access.org>

11. Weaver, C., L. Gillmeister-Krause, & G. Vento-Zogby (1996). *Creating Support for Effective Literacy Education: Workshop Materials and Handouts.* Portsmouth, NH: Heinemann. This book addresses the need to help parents, administrators, and other teachers understand the nature of learning and the processes of language and literacy development. It includes materials that can be copied, such as fliers, letters, brochures, and fact sheets on various topics relating to emergent literacy and teaching practice.

12. The Whole Language Umbrella (WLU). This organization is now an assembly of the National Council of Teachers of English. WLU promotes literacy research and the use of whole language instruction in classrooms, publishes *Talking Points: Conversations in the Whole Language Community,* and sponsors lively professional conferences where whole language teachers learn from each other. Contact: 1111 W. Kenyon Road, Urbana, IL 61801-1096, (217) 328-3870, http://www.ncte.org

REFERENCES

Adams, M. J. (1990). *Beginning to read: Thinking and learning about print.* Cambridge, MA: Harvard University Press.

Associated Press. (1995, Mar. 6). Supporters defend "invented" spelling. *Kalamazoo [MI] Gazette,* p. A4.

Berger, J. (1993, Nov. 17). Fighting over reading. *New York Times,* pp. B1, B6.

Boone, K. C. (1989). *The Bible tells them so: The discourse of Protestant Fundamentalism.* Albany, NY: State University of New York Press.

Brinkley, E. H. (1994). Intellectual freedom and the theological dimensions of whole language. In J. E. Brown (Ed.), *Preserving intellectual freedom: Fighting censorship in our schools* (pp. 111–122). Urbana, IL: National Council of Teachers of English.

Brinkley, E. H. (1995). Faith in the word: Examining Religious Right attitudes about texts. *English Journal, 84* (5), 91–98.

Calkins, L. M. (1994). *The art of teaching writing.* Portsmouth, NH: Heinemann.

Chall, J. (1967/1983). *Learning to read: The great debate.* New York: McGraw-Hill.

Davis, C. (1995). The I-search paper goes global: Using the Internet as a research tool. *English Journal, 84* (6), 27–33.

Duff, C. (1996, Oct. 30). How whole language became a hot potato in and out of academia. *Wall Street Journal,* pp. A1, A11.

Engelman, S., & J. Osborn. (1976). *DISTAR language: An instructional system.* Chicago: Science Research Associates.

Fishman, A. (1988). *Amish literacy: What and how it means.* Portsmouth, NH: Heinemann.

Flower, L. S., & J. R. Hayes. (1981). A cognitive process theory of writing. *College Composition and Communication, 32,* 365–387.

Flynn, C. (1994, Fall). Embracing controversy. *Teaching Tolerance, 3* (2), 27.

Goodman, K. S. (1967). Reading: A psycholinguistic guessing game. *Journal of the Reading Specialist, 6,* 126–135.

Goodson, F. T. (1994). Culture wars and the rules of the English classroom. *English Journal, 83* (5), 21–24.

Greenbaum, V. (1997). Censorship and the myth of appropriateness: Reflections on teaching reading in high school. *English Journal, 86* (2), 16–20.

Guice, S., & Brooks, G. (1995, Fall). *Literacy instruction in schools serving poor children. Literature Update.* Albany: National Research Center on Literature Teaching & Learning.

Hazelwood: A complete guide to the Supreme Court Decision. (1988, Spring). *Student Press Law Center Report.* Washington, DC: Student Press Law Center.

Hentoff, N. (1992). *Free speech for me—But not for thee.* New York: HarperCollins.

Holland, R. (1994, Apr. 6). Phonics to teach reading is politically incorrect. . . . *Richmond Times-Dispatch,* p. A11.

Jenkinson, E. (n.d.). *Writing assignments, journals, and student privacy.* ERIC Digest Clearinghouse on Reading, English, and Communication, EDO-CS-94-01.

Kohl, H. (1995). *Should we burn Babar? Essays on children's literature and the power of stories.* New York: The New Press.

Krutz, M. (1994). *Hazelwood:* Results and realities. In J. E. Brown (Ed.), *Preserving intellectual freedom: Fighting censorship in our schools* (pp. 216–227). Urbana, IL: National Council of Teachers of English.

Kunz, D. (1994). What are we teaching the children? *Teaching Tolerance, 3* (2), 26.

Lacks, C. (1997). The teacher's nightmare: Getting fired for good teaching. *English Journal, 86* (2), 29–33.

Macedo, D. (1994). *Literacies of power: What Americans are not allowed to know.* Boulder, CO: Westview Press.

Menendez, A. J. (1993). *Visions of reality: What Fundamentalist schools teach.* Buffalo, NY: Prometheus Books.

Nelson, J. L. (1990). The significance of and rationale for academic freedom. In A. S. Ochoa (Ed.), *Academic freedom to teach and to learn: Every teacher's issue.* Washington, DC: National Education Association.

Parker, R. (1997, Feb. 8). Decision to yank story upsets Otsego student editor. *Kalamazoo [MI] Gazette,* pp. A1–2.

Patterson, F. R. A. (1996). *Mandating methodology: Promoting the use of phonics through state statute.* University of Oklahoma, Department of Educational Leadership and Policy Studies.

Perl, S. (1980). Understanding composing. *College Composition and Communication, 31,* 363–369.

Post, A. R. (1996). The whole language debate. *Christian Home & School, 74* (2), 11–14.

Power, B. M. (1995, Nov.). Bearing walls and writing workshops. *Language Arts, 72* (7), 482–488.

Puffin Books. (1995). The guardian angels. *Puffin Papers* [publisher's newsletter]. New York.

Robertson, P. (1990). *The new millennium: Ten trends that will impact you and your family by the year 2000.* Dallas: Word Publishing.

Rosenblatt, L. M. (1978). *The reader, the text, the poem.* Carbondale: Southern Illinois University Press.

Rosenblatt, L. M. (1985). Language, literature, and values. In S. N. Tchudi (Ed.), *Language, schooling, and society* (pp. 64–80). Portsmouth, NH: Boynton/Cook.

Routman, R., & Butler, A. (1995). Why talk about phonics? *School Talk, 1* (4).

Schlafly, P. (1984). *Child abuse in the classroom.* Westchester, IL: Crossway Books.

Schlafly, P. (1996, July). Phonics vs. whole language. *The Phyllis Schlafly Report, 29* (12).

Simmons, J. S. (1994). Dimensions of critical reading: Focus on censorship elements. In J. S. Simmons (Ed.), *Censorship: A threat to reading, learning, thinking* (pp. 3–12). Newark, DE: International Reading Association.

Temple, C., R. Nathan, F. Temple, & N. A. Burris. (1993). *The beginnings of writing* (3rd ed.). Boston: Allyn and Bacon.

Thogmartin, M. B. (1994). The prevalence of phonics instruction in fundamentalist Christian schools. *Journal of Research on Christian Education, 3* (1), 103–130.

Trimer-Hartley, M., & Richardson, J. (1995, Mar. 16). Debate over how to teach turns ugly. *Detroit Free Press*, pp. 1A, 10A–11A.

U.S. Senate Republican Policy Committee. (1989, Sept. 13). William L. Armstrong, Chairman. *Illiteracy: An incurable disease or education malpractice?* Unpublished document.

Weaver, C. (1997). What about whole language? [Fact sheet.] Portage, MI: Michigan for Public Education.

Weaver, C. (Ed.). (1998). *Lessons to share: On teaching grammar in context.* Portsmouth, NH: Boynton/Cook.

"Whose News?" *Teaching Tolerance, 3* (2), 24–25.

Wilhelm, J. (1995). *You gotta BE the book: Teaching engaged and reflective reading with adolescents.* Urbana, IL: National Council of Teachers of English.

Wilson, A. (1994). Censorship and the teaching of composition. In J. E. Brown (Ed.), *Preserving intellectual freedom: Fighting censorship in our schools* (pp. 91–99). Urbana, IL: National Council of Teachers of English.

5 Censorship in Science and Science Education

RONALD G. GOOD
Louisiana State University

JAMES A. SHYMANSKY
University of Missouri

LARRY D. YORE
University of Victoria, British Columbia

Recently an inexperienced teacher in a conservative Christian community was suspended for several days by the superintendent of schools based on a parental complaint about the use of an innovative teaching strategy—mind mapping (a combination of guided imagery and concept mapping). An elementary student had described this exciting new activity in a science class that involved visualization, mental images, ideas, maps, memory, and the brain. The child's recount of the activity led the parent to conclude that some form of "brain washing," "values manipulation," or "occult" was taking place in the public school. The protective parent, motivated by a set of values representative of the community's standards, sought swift action by the quickest means: political pressure on the public interface of the schools—the superintendent!

Here is a clear example of the contemporary censorship caused by misunderstandings and jealous actions. The inexperienced teacher did not fully understand the community standards and did not attempt to inform the parents about the science curriculum and instruction. The jealous parent (afraid of possibly "losing a child to Satan") did not fully investigate or verify the implications and was quick to find fault and take decisive punitive action. The superintendent did not safeguard professional freedom and yielded to political pressure.

Many such incidents—though certainly not all—could be avoided through better planning and a careful examination of the issues. Ultimately, studying science issues leads one to the following question: What is the "science" in science education? This chapter describes contemporary views of science and knowledge that open science education to new, more subtle attempts at censorship. Furthermore, it provides a historical perspective of censorship in science, illustrates examples of current attempts to censor science through direct and indirect means, and suggests strategies that science teachers can use to deal with the various faces of censorship in the classroom. The chapter is intended to stimulate discussion, reflection, and action on the issues of censorship.

The nature of science, contemporary views of knowledge, constructivist models of learning, and conventions of scientific evidence, warrants, and claims influence both what should be taught in science education and how it should be taught (American Association for the Advancement of Science [AAAS], 1990, 1993; National Research Council [NRC] 1996). However, this dynamic context of science and science education has provided fertile fields for divergent points of view and a growing potential for censorship.

What Is Science?

Science is people's attempts to search out, describe, and explain in natural terms generalizable patterns of events in the natural world. This definition describes the context, content, universals, and constraints of science. It emphasizes that science is made by people—both women and men—and involves disciplined inquiry that can produce descriptions and explanations while constantly seeking to produce causal relationships that are applicable in the natural world. The scientific enterprise is based on and ultimately verified by nature.

Nussbaum (1989) described the change in epistemologies (ways of knowing) of science from the inductive, sensory-oriented empiricism of Bacon, to the deductive, intellect-oriented rationalism of Descartes, to the hypothetico-deductive, sociocultural-oriented constructivism of Lakatos (see Figure 5.1).

Induction (specific to general) is a systematic reasoning process in which common regularities (specific attributes, relationships, or procedures) are identified and synthesized into an umbrella category or label (generalizable concept, law, principle, or theory). People focus on exemplars to eliminate noncritical features and to emphasize necessary and essential characteristics by comparing and contrasting examples and nonexamples. *Deduction* (general to specific) is a systematic reasoning process in which a general rule is used to predict or explain the occurrence of specific observations and events. People combine generalizations to promote or prove the existence of new relationships and ideas. Traditional "chalk and talk" science instruction used a deductive sequence of concept introduction lectures followed by "I told you so" laboratory activities to illustrate the concept. *Hypothetico-deduction* (hypothesis-driven deduction) is a systematic reasoning process that presents a plausible hypothesis (a blueprint of potential causality between independent and dependent variables), predicts outcomes based on both the likelihood that the hypothesis is true and the likelihood that the hypothesis is false, and collects valid data in an attempt to disconfirm or to support the hypothesis. People focus on if-then scenarios to stress the predictive nature of statements. Unfortunately, many people believe concurrence of predictions and outcomes constitutes "proof" without realizing that it takes an infinite number of

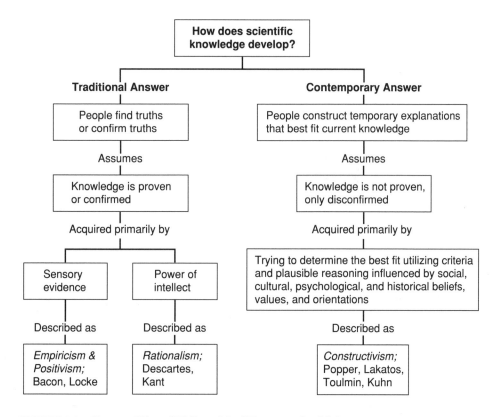

FIGURE 5.1   Concept Map of Philosophical Framework of Science

Source: Adapted from "Classroom Conceptual Change: A Philosophical Perspective" by J. Nussbaum, 1989, *International Journal of Science Education, 11.*

concurrences to justify such a claim. A more efficient approach is to seek disconfirmation that takes only a single case of nonconcurrence.

Throughout these changes in the epistemology of science, the importance of observations, quality of evidence and argument, logic, imagination, and critical thinking remained central to science. Clearly, the scientific enterprise is not accurately described by one, rigidly applied scientific method (i.e., problem statement, hypothesis, data collection, data analysis, and conclusion.) Science is not a linear process but rather a cyclic, recursive process that speculates, tests, verifies, and speculates again (see Figure 5.2).

The *National Science Education Standards* (NRC, 1996) promote a holistic perspective of science as inquiry: "Scientific inquiry refers to the diverse ways in which scientists study the natural world and propose explanations based on the evidence derived from their work.... Inquiry is a multifaceted activity that involves making observations; posing questions; examining books and other sources of information to see what is already known in the light of experimental evidence; using tools to gather,

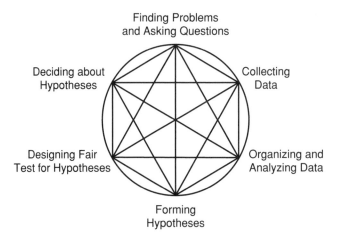

FIGURE 5.2   Scientific Inquiry

analyze, and interpret data; proposing answers; explanations, and predictions; and communicating the results" (p. 23).

This process does not conclude with finality but produces current *best fit* conceptions and overarching mega-concepts (theories). Furthermore, contrary to popular belief, scientific theories are no less tentative than scientific laws and principles; rather, they attempt to unify and integrate previously disconnected concepts, laws, and principles. The term *theory,* as used in the natural sciences, is very different from the way theory is used in casual conversation (i.e., as a hunch or guess). The confusion of the meaning of theory in science is a source of many disagreements and misuses of the term, which will be discussed later in the chapter.

Three Views of Knowledge

Parallel to the changes in the scientific enterprise were changes in the views of scientific knowledge (Kuhn, 1991; Kurfiss, 1988; Perry, 1968). The traditional, *absolutist view* of knowledge assumes that there is a *right* answer and that disciplined inquiry can *discover* the laws. People holding this view insist "that knowledge consists of absolute truths and meanings that cannot be questioned" (Whitson, 1994, p. 17). Different religious and academic groups attribute to various sources the ultimate authority over these absolutes (e.g., Supreme Being, God, Allah, Grand Architect of the Universe, Nature, etc.).

The contemporary *evaluative view* suggests that knowledge is constructed by people and that different people construct different understandings of the same information because they have different conceptual backgrounds and "lived experiences," ask different questions, or perceive the information through different lenses. People holding this view assume that different constructed understandings must be verified and assessed for support or disconfirmed for lack of support or negative evidence leading to a hierarchy based on merit.

Then there is a third, postmodern *relativistic view* that also suggests knowledge is constructed but that the alternative explanations of the same phenomena constructed by different groups are of equal merit. People holding this view insist that alternative conceptions must not be questioned and to do so suppresses the authoring group's individuality, rights, and academic freedom.

The *science* promoted in *National Science Education Standards* (NRC, 1996) and *Science for All Americans* (AAAS, 1989) is based on an *evaluative view* of knowledge. Science literacy, according to authors of these science education reforms, is characterized by a sound conceptual understanding of big ideas in science, technology, mathematics, and society. Science literacy is undergirded by "habits of mind" that recognize the value of evidence, logic, uncertainty, and critical thinking and the communicative abilities to persuade others of the veracity of these informed perspectives and opinions. In short, "science literacy is the knowledge and understanding of science concepts and processes required for making personal decisions, participation in civic and cultural affairs, and economic productivity" (NRC, 1996, p. 22). The science education promoted in the *National Science Education Standards* and *Science for All Americans* is based on a constructivist perspective of teaching and learning. Teaching involves a variety of instructional strategies designed to access and engage prior knowledge, delineate problems, predict outcomes, set and clarify goals, address personal and societal issues, provide hands-on/minds-on experiences, and apply knowledge to real situations. Learning involves critical thinking, brainstorming ideas, exploring alternative ideas, monitoring progress, and self-regulated action. Teaching is viewed as a social event, but learning is viewed as a private act (Hennessey, 1994).

The Changing Complexion of Censorship

The common meaning of censorship involves suppression of books and other materials that are deemed objectionable by individuals or organizations. In literature, censorship has been practiced on such classics as *Antigone, Brave New World, The Diary of a Young Girl, A Farewell to Arms, The Grapes of Wrath, The Merchant of Venice, Slaughterhouse-Five,* and *To Kill a Mockingbird* (Gallo, 1994, p. 115). Censors believe that ideas and their expression, values, and actions must be monitored carefully to save an unthinking, illiterate populace from subversive influences. The reasons for censorship in the nation's schools are as varied as the offending books, ideas, values, and actions, but censorship involves more than banning or burning books. It involves repressing specific concepts, promoting questionable views of knowledge, emphasizing politically correct agendas, deemphasizing certain educational goals, and disallowing innovative instructional strategies—anything that a philosophical, ethnic, cultural, religious, or political group believes disagrees with their dogma and wants suppressed (Whitson, 1994).

Censorship and suppression of ideas, views, goals, and approaches in science and science education is still alive and active! Book burning has decreased, but other, more subtle approaches have become popular. Special-interest representatives on governing boards, editorial panels, and administrative committees attempt to suppress specific ideas and issues by using equity principles (gender equity, civil rights, political correctness, etc.) to confuse people's thinking, developing hidden agendas to divert reasoned judgment, using uncertainty to distort or stall actions, and using technical vocabulary and epistemology improperly to confound the argument. The targets of censorship have included the structure of the universe, evolution, human reproduction, and environmental science; the epistemology of science and the structure of scientific knowledge; and instructional strategies such as guided imagery, mind mapping, values clarification, and critical thinking.

A Brief History of Censorship in Science

Since the time of Copernicus, Kepler, Galileo, and Newton in the sixteenth and seventeenth centuries, science has been the object of censors' wrath. It is helpful to know the history of science censorship in trying to understand its current meaning and implications. Much early censorship was based on the apparent conflict between literal interpretations of religious documents and new ideas in science. These conflicts were viewed as a *win-lose* situation. The perception that a religious document was not only a philosophical document but a historical account and a scientific treatise frequently led to problematic situations and open conflict. Beliefs about Heaven, Earth, and Hell were basic sources of conflict with the early heliocentric (sun-centered) alternative to the geocentric (earth-centered) model of the solar system/universe.

Giordano Bruno (1548–1600) was burned at the stake on February 17, 1600, by agents of the Roman Inquisition. What was Bruno's crime? He received the ultimate form of censorship for promoting ideas such as Earth is not at the center of all things and our universe is infinite in size, with many worlds not unlike our own. For speaking out and promoting such blasphemous ideas, Bruno was silenced. However, these ideas, which can be traced in part to Aristarchus (220–150 B.C.) and Copernicus (1473–1543), survived Bruno's death and influenced many people. Johannes Kepler (1571–1630) used the forbidden idea of a heliocentric solar system to derive his famous three laws of orbital motion, and Galileo Galilei (1564–1642) shattered Aristotelian physics, which had become the accepted doctrine of Thomas Aquinas (1225–1274) and other Christian scholars, by showing experimentally that all moving objects follow the same laws of nature. Regardless of the decrees of Aristotle, Thomas Aquinas, and the Roman Inquisition, uniform motion was found by Galileo (and of course, a bit later by Isaac Newton) to be the natural motion of the new physics. Nature was undeterred by the censors!

It is well known that the Catholic Church disliked Galileo's support of Copernicus's heliocentric model of the solar system because it seemed to reduce Earth and its inhabitants to a far less lofty place in the universe. After warnings from officials of the

Roman Catholic Church, beginning in 1615, to discontinue speaking out on Copernican "doctrine," Galileo maintained silence on the issue until 1627, when he published *Il Saggiatore,* in which he supported the sun-centered Copernican system once again.

By cleverly avoiding direct criticism of the Roman Catholic Church, Galileo was able to continue his work and in 1632 published *Dialogue of the Two Principal Systems of the World*. This time, the Holy Office charged that Galileo had taught Copernican ideas as truth rather than hypothesis and he was ordered to Rome by the Inquisition. Although in poor health, and after a few months' delay, Galileo was taken on a litter to Rome, arriving February 13, 1633. The trial of Galileo occurred in April and although his inquisitors were unable to offer solid evidence against him on the charge of heresy, Galileo was ordered by Pope Urban VIII to imprisonment for an indefinite term at the pleasure of the Holy Office. For the remainder of his life (d. January 8, 1642) Galileo was to remain under house arrest. Ironically, it was during the years following his trial in Rome that Galileo published his best-known work, *Two New Sciences* (1638), in which he showed the fallacies of Aristotelian physics.

The next major focus of the censors' wrath was provided by Charles Darwin when, in 1859, he published *On the Origin of Species,* the book that many scholars have seen as the most influential science text ever published. By showing that natural selection is the primary mechanism by which species evolve, it was interpreted that Darwin removed the need for supernatural oversight and purposeful design of life. The outstanding British biologist and science author, Richard Dawkins (1986), has written in a nontechnical way on how the theory of evolution by natural selection effectively eliminates the need for a purposeful design argument.

The attack on evolution peaked in 1925 when censors used a Tennessee law banning evolution from schools to prosecute a biology teacher named John Scopes. Though ridiculed as "ignorant and anachronistic" (Scharmann, 1994, p. 152), antievolution laws stayed on the books of many southern states and effectively kept evolution theory out of public school classrooms and textbooks until the late 1960s when the laws were declared unconstitutional. But even today, antievolution groups continue their assault on evolution theory, as Scharmann (1994) and Numbers (1993) have documented.

Recently some Tennessee lawmakers were looking to repeat history. A proposed ban on the teaching of evolution as "fact" was under consideration in the state capitol in Nashville (LoLordo, 1996). Once again, the debate pits scientific theory against religious theory, civil liberations against fundamentalist Christians. The central issues are almost the same as in 1925, and the clarity of debate has not improved in 71 years! Biblical proponents, representing the religious conservatives, focus on evolution as a scientific "theory" in their attack—"to my knowledge it's never been proven" (LoLordo, 1996, p. F15). Religious conservatives receive support from creationists such as Professor Kurt Wise (Bryan College, Dayton, OH), a 36-year-old Harvard-educated paleontologist who believes "the earth is only thousands of years old . . . what the Bible constrains the age of the world to be." He supports the development and use of teaching materials from a literal Biblical version: "What would benefit us all would be to move toward something our Founding Fathers wanted—a free exchange of ideas" (LoLordo,

1996, p. F15). His request for a balanced perspective, equal time, and open discussion sounds reasonable but dilutes science with a mix of pseudoscience and nonscience ideas.

Still other policy makers are forcing a head-to-head conflict utilizing disclaimers that equate scientific and religious theories. Louisiana teachers in Tangipahoa Parish will present the following disclaimer whenever the scientific theory of evolution is studied if their school board's efforts are successful:

> It is hereby recognized by the Tangipahoa Parish Board of Education, that the lesson to be presented, regarding the origin of life and matter, is known as the Scientific Theory of Evolution and should be presented to inform students of the scientific concept and not intended to influence or dissuade the Biblical version of Creation or any other concept.
>
> It is further recognized by the Board of Education that it is the basic right and privilege of each student to inform his/her own opinion or maintain beliefs taught by parents on this very important matter of the origin of life and matter. Students are urged to exercise critical thinking and gather all information possible and closely examine each alternative toward forming an opinion.

The disclaimer approach is the latest in a long list of attempts by groups with political or religious agendas to suppress ideas that are seen as a threat to their belief system(s). Giving students an advance warning that the information they are about to read or hear may be hazardous to their (and their parents') belief systems is both absurd and deviously clever. Dressed in critical thinking garb, this disclaimer tells both teacher and student to beware of certain arguments because they could have the effect of causing them to challenge their current ideas or beliefs. Under the guise of critical thinking, critical thinking (i.e., scientific thinking) is suppressed.

Unnecessary Conflicts

It is easy to see why Darwin's theory so threatened religious groups when it was first published and why it continues to do so today. Arguments comparing scientific theories with religious laws are futile and can never be reconciled—it is a classic case of comparing apples and oranges. But is this head-to-head, win-lose conflict necessary? Most scientists with religious beliefs have personally resolved the conflict by realizing that their science is based on reason and evidence from the natural world, whereas their religion is based on scriptures and faith. Evolution—with its mechanisms of mutation, natural selection, and so on—for many scientists with religious beliefs is simply part of their Creator's divine plan.

Censorship in science can usually be traced to misconceptions about the speculative nature of science and confusion over terminology associated with absolutist views of knowledge. The epistemologies of the natural sciences and theology are clearly different. The patterns of argumentation, the quality of evidence, warrants, and claims, and the values and beliefs are different for the two domains. Science is grounded in nature, whereas theology is grounded in faith. Comparisons of positions on the same questions derived across the domains cannot and should not be made.

Another major source of confusion lies in the use of terminology. The precise use of terminology in science differs from other disciplines or common usage. *Theory* does not mean an idea that is more or less tentative than law, principle, or concept. Rather, the term *theory* is reserved in science for unifying mega-ideas that integrate other laws, principles, and concepts. Unlike "laws" in religious scripture that are provided by a Creator and, according to some religious leaders, not to be questioned, theories and laws in science are not viewed as ultimate truth about nature; they are constantly questioned and tested and they stand until a more valid idea replaces or expands them.

Two Sides of Science

As historians and news reporters know, what is missing from a story is often as informative as the actual account. However, by omitting certain information, an author can misinform even though what is included in the story is accurate. When science is portrayed only as facts and laws of nature, and the personal, discovery side is omitted, the result is a biased picture that misrepresents the whole, complex enterprise as an absolute body of knowledge with little substantive justification.

Harvard science historian Gerald Holton (1988) explained the dilemma created by using the single term *science* in reference to two very different activities—private science and public science: "[Private science] refers to the speculative, creative element, the continual flow of contributions by separate individuals, . . . [Public science] in contrast, is science as the evolving compromise, as the growing network synthesized from these individual contributions by the general acceptance of those ideas which do indeed prove meaningful and useful to generations of scientists" (p. 406). Science textbooks and teachers often portray public science reasonably well, but private science is not well represented, resulting in a biased picture of the nature of science. Science is portrayed and taught as a set of truths to be accepted unquestionably. This image casts school science as dogma which then must compete with all other dogmas.

An additional example of the personal side of scientific discovery should help convey this important "other side" of science:

> The use of logic and the close examination of evidence are necessary but not usually sufficient for the advancement of science. Scientific concepts do not emerge automatically from data or from any amount of analysis alone. Inventing hypotheses or theories to imagine how the world works and then figuring out how they can be put to the test of reality is as creative as writing poetry, composing music, or designing skyscrapers. Sometimes discoveries in science are made unexpectedly, even by accident. But knowledge and creative insight are usually required to recognize the meaning of the unexpected. Aspects of data that have been ignored by one scientist may lead to new discoveries by another. (Holton, 1988, p. 27)

Further complicating the problem of misrepresenting science is what Wolpert (1992) calls the *unnatural* nature of science. Science provides explanations about nature that are often abstract and counterintuitive. This makes the image of school science appear mystical and without basis in the natural world, which, in turn, alarms political groups and religious conservatives and clouds the distinctions between science and pseudoscience. The *National Science Education Standards* clarifies this distinction by describing science as inquiry:

> Students at all grade levels and in every domain of science should have the opportunity to use scientific inquiry and develop the ability to think and act in ways associated with inquiry, including asking questions, planning and conducting investigations, using appropriate tools and techniques to gather data, thinking critically and logically about relationships between evidence and explanations, constructing and analyzing alternative explanations, and communicating scientific arguments. (NRC, 1996, p. 105)

The direct coupling of science with hands-on/minds-on inquiry exposes endeavors that mimic science and produce pseudoscience based on authority and unquestionable absolutes.

New Forms of Censorship

Equal Time Arguments

During the second half of the twentieth century, Christian fundamentalists started the Creation Research Society (CRS), trying to make it appear that creationism is science not religion. Created in June 1963 (Numbers, 1993, p. 229) by a few fundamentalists with marginal scientific credentials, the CRS published texts promoting "scientific creationism" as an alternative "theory" to Darwin's theory of evolution. They argued that scientific creationism should receive equal time in biology classrooms where Darwin's theory was taught, and by 1981, 20 states had introduced equal time bills (Scharmann, 1994). Only two states, Arkansas and Louisiana, passed state laws requiring equal time, and those laws were eventually ruled unconstitutional.

Creation science advocates lost in the courts, but they were successful once again in influencing textbook publishers—who abhor controversy because it can negatively affect sales—to reduce or eliminate coverage of legitimate biological evolutionary theory in high school biology texts. The "*e*-word" had become too risky for many publishers and for many teachers, especially those in communities where religious fundamentalism was a significant force. As Scharmann (1994) noted, the overt censorship efforts in the courts were unsuccessful but covert censorship continued: "Thus, although many individual biology teachers either dismiss or actively resist such creationist tactics, others, either through self-persuasion or pressure from their principal, avoid the potential controversy by simply not teaching evolution" (p. 157).

Censorship efforts by religious conservatives continued into the 1990s. Buoyed by President Ronald Reagan's support of creationism in the 1980s and the success of fundamentalist-friendly politics in the 1990s, the creationists continue to work hard at the local school system level to elect school board members who are willing to promote censorship as a way of protecting children from offensive ideas in literature, science, and elsewhere.

The equal time battles for creation science and evolution are not reserved for the South. In 1995, the Abbotsford School District in British Columbia was in open conflict with the B.C. Ministry of Education over the school board's policy of requiring equal time for creation as evolution. Gopaul (1995), an experienced biology teacher, stated: "Creation science . . . claims to know the final truth on the origins of earth and all life forms. [This pseudoscience] cannot be construed as science. Science never claims to have the final truth and any scientific idea must invoke naturalistic explanations for phenomena" (p. 3). Gopaul pointed out that the deliberate ploy of mislabeling pseudoscience as science, undermines science, sets up false conflicts between religion and science, misleads students, and strips people of the power to distinguish between natural events and supernatural articles of faith. Niles Eldredge (1982), in *The Monkey Business: A Scientist Looks at Creationism*, suggests that if pseudoscience is provided *equal time,* it may give the impression that the scientific community is equally divided on the creation-evolution issue, an impression that is both false and dishonest. Whitson (1994) emphasized, "What is at stake here is the ability to teach to any kind of scientific literacy at all. . . . Scientific thought and understanding are preempted by the practice of acquiescing to . . . authority" (p. 16).

The Abbotsford situation continued in the media for eight months involving the CBS television and radio, CTV, major newspapers, local weeklies, and small newsletters. Early headlines declared "Creationism Evolving into a Chaotic Subject," "School Balancing Act Defies Science," "Weird Science," "Faith and Fact," "If There Are Dinosaurs, It Must Be Abbotsford," and "Abbotsford Teachers Want Genesis out of Biology 11 Class." The conflict was finally addressed by the Minister of Education, Art Charbonneau, declaring a prohibition on teaching creation theory in science classes. A September 7, 1995, news release was required to clarify the Minister's earlier statement that creationism or any religious belief or dogma are outside the mandate of Biology 11 and 12.

CONTENT OF BIOLOGY 11/12 COURSE CLEARLY DEFINED

VICTORIA—The curriculum guide for biology and a series of ministerial orders have been revised to make it clear to school boards that teaching creationism as part of a science course is not permissible in B.C. schools, Education Minister Art Charbonneau said today. "The science classroom is not the place to provide instruction or require discussion of religious dogma or religious belief systems," said Charbonneau. "It is my expectation that all school boards will comply with the law and ensure that biology courses are offered in accordance with the curriculum guide and ministerial orders. The only place where instruction on religious belief systems may occur is in a locally developed comparative religions course." (Ministry of Education, 1995)

The Minister's strong, straightforward position on the side of science and against pseudoscience did not pass without negative reactions from the religious right. The sentiments were captured in later headlines: "Parents Want Creationism in Schools," "Students Need Choice," "A Flood of Ideas Is Good for the Mind," "Truth by Law Heavy Handed," "Government's Atheistic Agenda," "Province's Stand on Creationism Is Hypocritical" and "Creation Stance Will Cost." Several of these articles stress the importance of a balanced perspective and the need to allow students to decide between alternatives that are reasonable, as long as they involve science alternatives and allow critical thinking and reasonable judgment. The last headline implies that taking a strong stand can have political consequences.

Multicultural Arguments

People behind the push for "multicultural science" do not necessarily disagree with the current content of biology, chemistry, physics, and so on; they simply want to add "a few well-chosen examples of sciences from other cultures" (Stanley & Brickhouse, 1994, p. 396). Multicultural critics of science charge that the traditional white, European, male science found in textbooks does not adequately represent the various cultures that might be represented in the classrooms of the country's schools. To be fair, they argue, traditional non-Western, *alternative* sciences from other cultures must become a part of the school science curriculum. On the surface, this may sound like a good idea on political grounds, but is it on scientific and pedagogical grounds?

An example of an effort to introduce alternative "sciences" into the school science curriculum is the Portland, Oregon, Schools *African-American Baseline Essays*. The Superintendent of Portland Schools explained the purpose of the *Essays:*

> The *African-American Baseline Essays* are but one part of a larger product to fulfill the Board of Education's goal: . . . to develop in all students a better understanding and appreciation of the history, culture, and contributions to society of different ethnic groups and cultures. The *Baseline Essays* provide information about the history, culture, and contributions of Africans and African-Americans in the disciplines of Art, Language Arts, Mathematics, Science, Social Studies, and Music and should be used by teachers and other District staff as a reference and resource just as adopted textbooks and other resources are used. (Prophet, 1990, p. ii)

The science part of the *Essays* describes a set of fundamental principles of African and African American science:

> This concept called Maat represents the first set of scientific paradigms: A set of general principles which serve as the basis from which the ancient Egyptians did all types of scientific investigations. Let us take a cursory examination of a few of the most fundamental ones.
>
> 1. Acknowledgment of a supreme consciousness or creative force.
> The Egyptians notwithstanding, most Africans' lives were and are, even today despite the influence of secular materialism or Marxism, ritualized about the adoration and service of some Supreme Consciousness or Creative Force.

2. Existence via divine self-organization.

From being co-conscious with Nature, they readily saw the relationship between all living things. Creation is a dynamic ongoing process, yet God is the evolver of all things, not chance. As Einstein said, "God doesn't play dice with the universe."

3. A living universe.

To the Egyptians, the entire cosmos is a unity, a living entity, and as such, everything is alive. All things are related either directly or indirectly, and furthermore, everything is affected by everything else.

4. Man/life itself is a mystery.

African people see life as the Creator's supreme mystery: they accepted the fact that their knowledge was limited, and would always be so (eons before Kant). (pp. 5–12)

The list continues with four more "general principles of Maat."

In the name of science and apparently with good intentions, as suggested in Prophet's earlier quote, mysticism and pseudoscience are injected into the science curriculum of a major U.S. school system. Furthermore, Ortiz de Montellano (1992) stated the Portland Public Schools are not alone; the *Baseline Essays* in science "have been or are being seriously considered by school districts as diverse as Fort Lauderdale, Detroit, Atlanta, Chicago, and Washington, D.C." (p. 2).

This is not a simple case of urging teachers to be more sensitive to the values and ethnic backgrounds of students. The Portland Public Schools experience is an example of what can occur when science is misunderstood or simply not taken seriously by school personnel. The feeling of being right in trying to be sensitive to students' perceived multicultural needs by administrators and school board members apparently dominated the decision making regarding the nature of science and evaluative aspects of scientific knowledge.

Some science educators are calling for the inclusion of alternative, ethnic sciences into the school science curriculum. They appear to embrace relativistic views of science knowledge and, of course, deny the view of universal science knowledge (i.e., knowledge that explains and generalizes, is self-regulated, and is verified by evidence from nature). Proponents of alternative "sciences" suggest that other cultures have generated reliable knowledge about natural phenomena, therefore principles of fairness and reason invite exploration of the possibility that other cultures may have different sciences (Pomeroy, 1992, p. 257). Others suggest:

> There is a need to struggle to assert the equal validity of Maori knowledge and frameworks and conversely to critically engage ideologies which reify Western knowledge (science) as being superior, more scientific, and therefore more legitimate. (Smith, 1992, p. 7)

> Concern with multiculturalism and antiracism demands that we question the image of science presented in school: its purpose, its methods, the role and status of scientific knowledge and theory, the Nature of evidence, the criteria of validity employed by its practitioners, and the ways in which scientific knowledge is recorded and reported—in fact, a critical scrutiny of everything that characterizes the western perception of science. (Hodson, 1993, p. 702)

> If students can also learn how the purposes of scientific activity have varied in different cultures and historical times, and how other cultures have developed sciences to meet these purposes, then they can also learn that the contemporary Western science is not universal, inevitable, or unchangeable. This kind of understanding is needed to encourage the critical thinking about the purposes Western science has served, and how these could be changed to create future sciences that better meet the needs of the diverse societies that support them. (Stanley & Brickhouse, 1994, p. 396)

The apparent good intentions of these science educators to find ways of reducing racism and achieving other humanitarian goals cannot be realized by denying the universal character of nature's laws and the natural sciences. The critical question and test is whether these alternatives, like European or Native American folklore, are science or activities that do not attempt to explain and generalize but simply describe.

Censorship can include efforts to change a message that is objectionable. Is the multicultural sciences proponents' appeal to humanitarian ideals to include local/ethnic "sciences" in the school science curriculum without danger? The knowledge base of the natural sciences is what it is regardless of what some persons or organizations might want it to be. Trying to delete or add information to science's knowledge base about nature for humanitarian goals or for other nonscience purposes is just as clearly a form of censorship as book banning and burning.

Some confuse science, the process of finding out about nature, with technology, the application of science's findings to human goals. This confusion is seen in the prior quote by Stanley and Brickhouse (1994, p. 396) and by their frequently quoted colleague, feminist philosopher Sandra Harding (1991): "What kinds of knowledge about the empirical world do we need in order to live at all, and to live more reasonably with one another on this planet from this moment on? Should improving the lives of the few or of the many take priority in answering this question?" (p. 102).

Confusing technology and applied science with the efforts of biologists, geologists, physicists, and so on, to find out about nature ensures arguments with scientists and others knowledgeable about science, regarding what is and what is not science. Or, as Harding says, conflating science with society's judgments about how to allocate its resources will inevitably lead to arguments over what is and what is not science.

Although the reasons for producing and using the *Baseline Essays'* ethnic science and technology in school science may be different, there is a disturbing similarity to the "creation science" advocates' efforts to promote equal time for creationism in biology classrooms when biological evolution is taught. In each case, pseudoscience or mysticism is promoted in the name of science. Science is thus censored by including nonscience into the curriculum because valuable instructional time is taken from the study of the natural sciences. If the domain of science can be broadened to include any belief system about nature, science education will be rendered ineffective. In the world of philosophy, this situation is called *relativism*. The universal knowledge of science becomes many local or ethnic knowledge claims that are considered equally valuable or viable. Gross and Levitt (1994) provided an in-depth critique of the various postmodern approaches to local sciences that is required reading for persons interested in the science part of science education.

Nature as the Ultimate Censor

Unlike other forms of knowledge, the knowledge base of nature built by the natural sciences must answer to the ultimate test—nature itself. Matthews (1994) has stated: "The core universalist idea is that the material world ultimately judges the adequacy of our accounts of it. Scientists propose, but ultimately, after debate, negotiation and all the rest, it is the world that disposes it" (p. 182). The authors of the *National Science Education Standards* (National Research Council, 1996) described how scientists test their ideas against nature: "Science distinguishes itself from other ways of knowing and from other bodies of knowledge through the use of empirical standards, logical arguments, and skepticism, as scientists strive for certainty of their proposed explanations" (p. 201).

Unlike other ways of knowing, the natural sciences of biology, chemistry, physics, and so on must answer to nature itself. Problems are embedded in nature and solutions are verified by nature. Science must attempt to explain and to generalize. This universalist position is supported by countless scientists and other individuals who study the nature of science, in addition to scientific organizations such as the AAAS and the NRC/National Academy of Sciences. With such overwhelming support by those who study science (e.g., historians and philosophers of science), it is curious that the universalist idea would be brought into question at all.

The earlier discussion of the nature of science and multiculturalism revealed the philosophical differences such as the feminist critique of science and the relativistic view of science. Most, if not all, scientists of any gender and nationality would agree that science involves an *evaluative view* of knowledge. They might suggest that scientists of different gender or cultural background might approach some phases of scientific inquiry differently, but there would be far greater commonalities than differences. The differences would be in the early imaginative phases of problem finding, question asking, and hypothesizing. The later phases of data analyses, hypotheses evaluation, and decision making would be basically the same (McDonald, 1995). Furthermore, the evidence, other than in socio-biology, is not compelling that there is any significant difference in the resulting science (Gross & Levitt, 1994). Neither women nor men would disagree that science needs to be firmly grounded in nature for both the source of problems and verification of ideas.

Censoring Critical Thinking

Simmons (1994) identified Hayakawa's (1972) classic *Language in Thought and Action* as a foundation to critical judgment about what to believe and what to do. Simmons suggested that critical thinkers need to discriminate among inferences, judgments, and reports and become aware of persuasive linguistic tricks used to falsely convince people. Many progressive educational innovations include critical thinking as their central focus and promote the development of self-regulated critical thinking by addressing real disputes in the specific disciplines. This means that critical thinking is associated with the progressive education controversy and current problematic issues. Jenkinson (1994) found critical thinking at the top of the censors' overt hit-list in a survey conducted in 1990, and Nelson (1994) reported covert censorship of critical thinking in which teachers are encouraged not to consider controversial issues in social studies.

A fundamental principle of reforms in science education is the requirement that *all* ideas and explanations in science be critically examined. The *Benchmarks* (AAAS, 1993) refer to these critical examination skills as *habits of mind*. These include such things as:

- Asking "How do you know?" in appropriate situations and attempting reasonable answers when others ask them the same question.
- Questioning claims based on vague attributions (such as "leading doctors," celebrities, non-experts).
- Knowing why curiosity, honesty, openness, and skepticism are so highly regarded in science and how they are incorporated into the way science is carried out; exhibit those traits in their own lives and value them in others.
- Using and correctly interpreting relational terms such as *if . . . then . . . , and, or, sufficient, necessary, some, every, not, correlates with,* and *causes.*
- Suggesting alternative ways of explaining data and criticizing arguments in which data, explanations, or conclusions are represented as the only ones worth consideration, with no mention of other possibilities. Similarly, suggesting alternative trade-offs in decisions and designs and criticizing those in which major trade-offs are not acknowledged. (pp. 284–300)

Instructional strategies encouraged in recent science reforms that promote reasoned judgment and clarification of descriptive claims, values, and logical relations have become the target of some censors. The use of guided imagery (mind mapping) to improve access to prior knowledge has been viewed as "brain washing"; issues analysis in science-technology-society-environment (STSE) problems has been represented as "value tampering"; and critical challenges that require deliberation, conjecture, and explanation are condemned as "subversive."

But should any group with a political, economic, religious, or social agenda be allowed to skew topic coverage, strategy development, or instructional techniques in science classrooms? Science teachers' academic freedom and professional responsibility must ensure that suppression is met and that fair, balanced scientific coverage is afforded all legitimate science topics and issues.

The irony of censoring critical thinking is survival as well as salvation. All of the most pressing STSE issues and technological innovations require critical thought. Literate citizens must make informed decisions about energy, population, and lifestyle.

Furthermore, it is impossible with the evolution of the Internet to censor information, leaving critical thinking as the sole defense to misinformation. Blockading the library doors and burning books will not work in the twenty-first century. Every computer and modem is an entrance to a wide-open electronic library.

WHAT CAN YOU DO ABOUT CENSORSHIP IN SCIENCE?

As a science teacher (or scientist, science teacher educator, etc.), you need to be proactive regarding censorship and have at hand an array of controlled reaction strategies when the best of proactive plans fail. Spicola and Stephens (1989) stated: "[The] best defense against censorship comes from developing procedures for dealing with challenges before the challenges actually occur" (p. 2). Although they were focusing the attention on procedures for selecting print materials for a language arts program, their advice applies equally well to selecting topics, issues, and instructional approaches in science. The success of any action depends on anticipating the unknown. Be prepared!

Proactive Strategies

The following five guidelines describe a proactive framework for meeting challenges by groups or individuals who would attempt to suppress, confuse, or dilute topics or instructional strategies you have chosen. The strategies will also help to ensure that you will not be accused of censoring ideas in your classroom.

1. *Be aware of censors' tactics.* Censors use petitions, trial by newspaper and other media, single-issue organizations, lawsuits, and bills of particulars and errors in textbooks to remove books and courses from schools (Jenkinson, 1994). Petitions, letters to the editor, and talkshows are common, inexpensive strategies suggested by national, state, and local organizations to initiate censorship actions. Legal actions such as lawsuits, grass-roots policy changes, and curriculum studies by experts are censorship strategies used by well-funded committees, groups, and organizations. Also gaining popularity among censors is the election process. Special-interest, single-issue candidates running for school boards and government offices count on strong turnouts of supporters and voter apathy in groups opposed to or at least neutral to censorship to force policies on censorship.

2. *Become informed about controversial topics, issues, and instructional approaches.* Science teacher organizations (e.g., National Science Teachers Association [NSTA] and National Association of Biology Teachers [NABT]) and professional journals (e.g., *Phi Delta Kappan, Science and Children, Science Scope, The Science Teacher,* and *Educational Leadership*) frequently alert science teachers to pending, potential, or actual censorship problems. Specialized organizations such as the National Center for Science Education (P.O. Box 9477, Berkeley, CA 94709) keep a watchful eye on censorship activities of creationist groups. The National Academy of Sciences (1998) has recently produced an understandable, well-documented resource for teachers on evolution and the nature of science that addresses evolution as a unifying concept (Natural Research Council, 1996), the equal time arguments, and multicultural science issues.

3. *Develop a working definition of* science *to guide your professional decisions and actions.* Science teachers need to be critical consumers of science and be able to differentiate among science, pseudoscience, prescience, and antiscience. Current science reform publications such as *Benchmarks for Science Literacy* (AAAS, 1993) and the *National Standards for Science Education* (NRC, 1996) provide a sound foundation on which to develop a personal understanding of the nature of science. Statements from these documents or your personal formal statement defining science should be drafted and made available to students, colleagues, administrators, and parents.

4. *Build a professional justification for topics, issues, and instructional approaches used in your science classroom.* Professional research journals (e.g., *The Journal of Research in Science Teaching* and *Science Education*) provide substantive evidence for curricular and instructional decisions. You should also consider conducting "action research" in your own classroom to provide evidence and rationale for your science program. Do not rely on undocumented, popular suggestions about band-wagon topics, issues, or instructional approaches. Even the infusion of reasonably well-received or well-documented ideas from another curricular area (e.g., whole language) need clarification and justification for use in a science classroom.

5. *Be aware of your community's standards and sensitivities; present balanced perspectives on controversial issues; and do not unnecessarily introduce red-flags.* Science teachers must be aware of their local community when addressing controversial issues. This does not mean that you should avoid these issues, but you should anticipate reactions and have a plan to address them: "We must be willing to check our facts to avoid misrepresentations, and we must be willing to present in a fair and unbiased manner, all sides of an issue about which there is conflicting scientific evidence" (Creager, 1975, p. 11). The National Science Teachers Association's 1985 position on creationism, for example, provides insights for handling sensitive issues:

> I. Respect the right of any person to learn the history and content of all systems and to decide what can contribute to an individual understanding of our universe and our place in it.
> II. In explaining natural phenomena, science instruction should only include those theories that can properly be called science.
> III. To ascertain whether a particular theory is properly in the realm of science, apply the criteria stated above, that is:
>   1. The theory can explain what is observed.
>   2. The theory can predict that which has not yet been observed.
>   3. The theory can be tested by further experimentation and be modified as new data are acquired.

IV. Oppose any action that attempts to legislate, mandate, or coerce the inclusion in the body of science education, including textbooks, any tenets which cannot meet the above criteria. (National Science Teachers Association, 1995, p. 5).

The National Association of Biology Teachers issued a 1995 *Statement on Teaching Evolution* that includes 20 tenets of science, evolution, and biology education. Three of the tenets are particularly useful in meeting potential challenges by censors:

- Students can maintain their religious beliefs and learn the scientific foundation of evolution. Teachers should respect diverse beliefs, but contrasting science with religion, such as belief in creationism, is not a role of science.
- Science teachers can, and often do, hold devout religious beliefs, accept evolution as a valid scientific theory, and teach the theory's mechanisms and principles.
- Science and religion differ in significant ways that make it inappropriate to teach any of the different beliefs in the science classroom. (p. 23)

Reaction Strategies

What options do science teachers have to actual instances of censorship? The Abbotsford case in British Columbia (Gopaul, 1995) provides some clear hints at what a teacher can do when proactive strategies fail. The high school biology teachers in the Abbotsford School District resisted the school board policy of *equal time* by taking legal action and conducting a well-articulated media campaign. They finally convinced the Minister of Education to enforce the spirit of the biology curriculum and the ministry's own School Act. The Minister of Education directed the school board to stop requiring that *creation science* be placed in biology, maintaining that creation science is religion, not science.

Teaching Science in a Context of Change

At a recent science education research meeting, a discussion on writing in science surfaced some startling insights into the religion and science controversy. A biology professor using journaling to personalize and enhance science learning discovered the dilemma of several young female teacher education students. The college was affiliated with a centralist Christian religion, but these students still expressed the misconception that to accept a scientific view of the world required them to refute their religious view of the world. Follow-up interviews with these students indicated that they viewed science and religion as competing dogmas and they were not ready to sacrifice their souls for a passing mark in biology. Clearly their school science experiences and their religious training were so similar that they believed science and theology used the same epistemology!

The 1990s have been a good time for science education. Many exciting changes are suggested by the current science reforms. Some changes may be misinterpreted; some will be misunderstood; and others will be taken farther than intended. This context of innovation and change will raise anxiety levels, rekindle old conflicts, and initiate new debates.

Well-intentioned, well-informed professional science teachers are key in the defense against and fair resolution of censorship conflicts. Articulated and strategic responses to any censorship will increase the probability of supportive action by politicians and other leaders.

And controversial issues must be addressed in a fair and sensitive manner. Just as an effective science teacher would not dismiss or "put down" student ideas in a classroom, issues of religion and science, pseudoscience, and alternative sciences cannot be dismissed out of hand. These controversial issues must be analyzed and evaluated with the best critical response skills that can be brought to bear. Science teachers need to rehearse these challenges in readiness for some that may actually arise. They need to be prepared—no, be *overly* prepared—to address any censorship challenges and be sensitive to the motivations behind those who may sincerely believe that students must be "protected" from science that appears to threaten belief systems.

REFERENCES

American Association for the Advancement of Science. (1989). *Science for all Americans.* New York: Author.

American Association for the Advancement of Science. (1990, 1993). *Benchmarks for science literacy.* New York: Author.

Creager, J. G. (1975). Freedom in science teaching. *American Biology Teacher, 37* (1), 11.

Dawkins, R. (1986). *The blind watchmaker: Why the evidence of evolution reveals a universe without design.* New York: Norton.

Eldredge, N. (1982). *The monkey business: A scientist looks at creationism.* New York: Washington Square Press.

Gallo, D. (1994). Censorship of young adult literature. In J. Simmons (Ed.), *Censorship: A threat to reading, learning, thinking* (pp. 115–122). Newark, DE: International Reading Association.

Gopaul, H. (1995). "Creation Science" is not science and why the teaching of evolution science makes sense in grade 12. *Catalyst, 38* (6), 3–4.

Gross, P., & Levitt, N. (1994). *Higher superstition: The academic left and its quarrels with science.* Baltimore, MD: Johns Hopkins University Press.

Harding, S. (1991). *Whose science? Whose knowledge?* Ithaca, NY: Cornell University Press.

Hayakawa, S. I. (1972). *Language in thought and action.* New York: Harcourt Brace.

Hennessey, M. G. (1994, May). *Alternative perspectives of teaching, learning, and assessment: Desired images—A conceptual change perspective.* Paper presented at the annual meeting of the National Association for Research in Science Teaching, Anaheim, CA.

Hodson, D. (1993). In search of a rationale for multicultural science education. *Science Education, 77,* 685–711.

Holton, G. (1988). *Thematic origins of scientific thought: Kepler to Einstein.* Cambridge, MA: Harvard University Press.

Jenkinson, E. B. (1994). Tactics used to remove books and courses from schools. In J. Simmons (Ed.), *Censorship: A threat to reading, learning, thinking* (pp. 29–36). Newark, DE: International Reading Association.

Kuhn, D. (1991). *The skills of argument.* New York: Cambridge University Press.

Kurfiss, J. G. (1988). *Critical thinking: Theory, research, practice, and possibilities* (ASHE-ERIC Higher Education Report No. 2). Washington, DC: Association for the Study of Higher Education.

LoLordo, A. (1996, March 9). Ban-evolution debate heats up. *Times Colonist,* p. F15.

Matthews, M. (1994). *Science teaching: The role of history and philosophy of science.* New York: Routledge.

McDonald, B. (1995, September). *Quirks and quarks—Feminist critique of science: An interview with Paul Gross, Ruth Hubbard, and Sarah Blafer-Hurdy.* Toronto, Ontario, Canadian Broadcasting Corporation.

Ministry of Education. (1995, September 7). *Content of biology 11/12 course clearly defined.* (News release #NR24-95). Victoria, BC Canada: Province of British Columbia.

National Academy of Sciences. (1998). *Teaching about evolution and the nature of science.* Washington, DC: National Academy Press.

National Association of Biology Teachers. (1995). *Statement on teaching evolution* (Position Statement). Reston, VA: Author.

National Research Council. (1996, November). *National science education standards.* Washington, DC: National Academy Press.

National Science Teachers Association. (1995). Are you under pressure to teach Creationism in your classroom? *NSTA Reports,* October/November, p. 5.

Nelson, J. W. (1994). Social studies and critical thinking skills versus censorship. In J. S. Simmons (Ed.), *Censorship: A threat to reading, learning, thinking* (pp. 123–133). Newark, DE: International Reading Association.

Numbers, R. (1993). *The creationists: The evolution of scientific creationism.* Berkeley, CA: University of California Press.

Nussbaum, J. (1989). Classroom conceptual change: A philosophical perspective. *International Journal of Science Education, 11,* 530–540.

Ortiz de Montellano, B. (1992, Feb. 11). *A critique of the Portland schools baseline essay on African-American science.* Paper presented at the American Association for the Advancement of Science meeting, Chicago, IL.

Perry, W. G., Jr. (1968). *Forms of intellectual and ethical development in the college years: A scheme.* New York: Holt, Rinehart and Winston.

Pomeroy, D. (1992). Science across cultures: Building bridges between traditional Western and Alaskan native cultures. In S. Hills (Ed.), *History and philosophy of science in science education, Vol. 2* (pp. 257–267). Kingston, Ontario: Queens University.

Prophet, M. (1990). *African-American baseline essays.* Portland, OR: Portland Public School District.

Scharmann, L. (1994). Teaching evolution: Past and present. In J. Simmons (Ed.), *Censorship: A threat to reading, learning, thinking* (pp. 148–165). Newark, DE: International Reading Association.

Simmons, J. S. (1994). Dimensions of critical reading: Focus on censorship elements. In J. S. Simmons (Ed.), *Censorship: A threat to reading, learning, thinking* (pp. 3–12). Newark, DE: International Reading Association.

Smith, G. (1992). *Kura Kaupapa Maori schooling: Implications for the teaching of science in New Zealand.* Unpublished paper, Education Department, University of Auckland.

Spicola, R., & Stephens, C. (1989). Intellectual freedom: The censorship war continues. *Texas Reading Report, 11* (4), 7–8.

Stanley, W., & Brickhouse, N. (1994). Multiculturalism, universalism, and science education. *Science Education, 28,* 387–398.

Whitson, J. A. (1994). Critical literacy versus censorship across the curriculum. In J. S. Simmons (Ed.), *Censorship: A threat to reading, learning, thinking* (pp. 13–28). Newark, DE: International Reading Association.

Wolpert, L. (1992). *The unnatural nature of science: Why science does not make (common) sense.* Cambridge, MA: Harvard University Press.

6 Literature and the Imagination

I could never have dreamt that there were such goings-on in the world between the covers of books, such sand-storms and ice blasts of words, such slashing of humbug, and humbug too, such staggering peace, such enormous laughter, such and so many blinding bright lights breaking across the just-awaking wits and splashing all over the pages in a million bits and pieces all of which were words, words, words, and each of which was alive forever in its own delight and glory and oddity and light.

—D. Thomas (1951)

When English language arts teachers think about censorship, we think first about literature, and when local newspapers run stories of books being censored, more often than not it is literature they are writing about—*The Adventures of Huckleberry Finn, Catcher in the Rye,* or anything written by Judy Blume. All 10 of People for the American Way's top 10 most-often challenged books during 1982–1996 are works of literature. Clearly, teaching literature—and using literature to teach other content areas—is problematic.

Secondary English language arts teachers have learned to keep the threat of censorship in the back of their minds as they make classroom literature selections. They know that even if the only literature that students read comes from a district-approved literature anthology, there is still plenty of room for parents to object to particular selections. And once teachers supplement the anthology with class sets or individual copies of trade books, every single title is challengeable.

Since the mid-1980s, elementary teachers have begun to learn the same lessons. They have faced increasing numbers of challenges as they build a curriculum around the reading of authentic, whole works of literature instead of texts and materials prepackaged by publishers of basal reader series. They are learning that some parent protesters worry about the influence of "real" books, especially imaginative literature, on their children. They are also learning that they need to keep parents well informed about the literature that is used in the classroom.

Questioning the Value of Literature

Not all parents value the teaching of literature. To some, literature is an unnecessary frill that will not help students as adults on the job. Others seem uncomfortable with the imaginative nature of literature, as if nonfiction were enough. Thus, we need to decide and be able to articulate why we believe students should read and study literature. A group of English teachers has generated the following answers to that question—some that most parents would affirm and some that staunchly conservative parents would resist:

- Literature gives pleasure. All students love stories. Some students even love words;
- Literature challenges and clarifies students' values. It forces them to examine their beliefs, attitudes, and values;
- Literature informs students about other cultures and times and about varieties of human experience;
- Literature provides students new ways of looking at familiar things and, as well, confirms the way they already look at things;
- Literature, like all the arts, provides students with an experience to share, a common experience to describe, savor, and debate...."Remember what happened in the story when...?";
- Literature gives students language and forms to express their feelings;
- Literature is one of the arts. It has its own special characteristics which students should experience and analyze;
- Literature provides students experience with a disinterested use of language, a use of language to amuse and inform without manipulating them for others' ends;
- Reading American literature from all historical periods and from America's diverse cultural groups acquaints students with their American heritage; and
- Reading literature fosters students' general reading development. (Perry, 1991)

We who teach English language arts usually say we want most to pass on our love of literature to our students. Too often, however, we have turned literature study into a litany of, "Here's the story, here are the study questions, be sure you know the 'facts' of the plot, be sure to learn the vocabulary, be sure to know the facts of the author's life, and now I'll explain what's probably too difficult for you to grasp on your own—the theme, the symbolism, and the significance." Eventually, after plodding through all the scope and sequence matrix of suggested lessons and activities, we test students about what they have read by requiring them to identify characters, match poets with the titles of their poems, and so forth. Such plans might be called a "Trivial Pursuit" approach to literature study since they are filled with isolated, testable bits of knowledge.

Maybe we have taken the Trivial Pursuit approach because we are expected to grade students on literature. But we need to remind ourselves—and to teach our students—that we do not read most literary texts primarily for facts or practical information. Instead, we read novels, short stories, and poems for the pleasure of the experience. We need to convince parents and the public that literature—and pleasure— serve educational purposes. Literature challenges one's assumptions, teaches one about human experience, makes one a better reader, extends one's use of language, and more.

Even when parents and the public value literature, many people disagree about which literary texts should be taught. Several years ago, I tacked a magazine ad on my high school classroom bulletin board. The picture in the ad showed an old man sitting and reading a book in the middle of a big room with tall stacks of books piled on the tables and floor around him. Tall bookshelves, overflowing with books, lined the walls of the large room. The caption read: "Read the best books first. You may not have time to read them all." I remember hoping that the ad would help my students realize the value of reading "good" books. I assumed, of course, that there was general agreement about which books are the "best"—or at least that I as an English language arts teacher could select them. Today, I still value the classics—those canonical texts generally considered the "best"—but I value and teach a broader range of literary texts, as well.

When parents or community groups object to specific works of literature, they often reveal the "best books" logic in their thinking, explaining that, "There are so many good books to choose from. Why is it important for our children to read this particular book? Why this one instead of the good books I read as a child?" We hear such comments not only from parents but from administrators, as well: "With all the good literature available, it would be my hope we could accentuate the best and leave a lot of the questionable stuff off the shelves and the reading lists" (Reichman, 1988, p. 13).

Sometimes I too have been lulled into thinking there is always another book that could be used if someone objects to a particular text. Literature is, after all, about experience, about art, about human nature, and about views of life and the world. Many different books can teach these lessons. So why not just teach the books that everyone agrees are the best? Most English language arts teachers answer this question by agreeing that we need to teach some common texts, and some of these should be the classics—the "best" books so that students can learn how to read a challenging text, learn about their own and other groups' literary heritage, and share their responses to literature. But we need to offer at least some choices of texts because of readers' diverse interests, tastes, and skill levels, and because we want to teach students to make independent literary choices.

How Literature Is Censored

Many censors operate without ever touching a book. A newspaper ad, for example, reprinted several lines from Robert Cormier's popular novels *The Chocolate War* and *I Am the Cheese* with the so-called dirty words left blank and accompanied by the following statement: "If you object to this type of material being taught to your children, write to me" (Cormier, 1988, p. 38). Cormier expressed a feeling of helplessness in trying to respond to this mass media form of censorship: "It's hard to counter such an ad. I feel like taking out an ad and saying, 'Read the whole book.' But it wouldn't work. It's much easier to get people to read nine words with a blank space in the middle than it is to get them to read 75,000 words" (p. 38).

Charles Suhor, former Deputy Executive Director of the National Council of Teachers of English (NCTE), described the more typical censorship process in English language arts, explaining that protesters cite particular, decontextualized passages they find offensive, and they make and distribute copies of the contested passages. Suhor said that protesters often assume that anything that is used in the classroom is *endorsed* by teachers and/or the school. Frequently, the protesters seek a total ban of the work for all students, not just their own child (1997, p. 26).

Suhor has worked on behalf of NCTE to defend curricular choices of English language arts teachers across the country, but he insists that there are unsound choices and that he has never defended an anything-goes approach. Suhor cited the following as examples of unsound choices: a high school teacher's decision to distribute a reading list acquired from a gay and lesbian group but not intended as a resource for students, and a seventh-grade teacher's decision to have students read John Steinbeck's *Of Mice and Men* aloud, "profanities and all, to their obvious discomfort" (p. 28).

Such was not the case for a Virginia teacher who was personally attacked on a radio talk show for teaching Clyde Edgerton's novel, *The Floatplane Notebooks,* a text that had been approved by the teacher's vice principal and principal (Goldwasser, 1997). When Marion McAdoo Goldwasser decided to publicly defend herself and the contested book, the community erupted. Some supported Goldwasser, but the radio listeners planned a public demonstration to protest the book and those who had approved it. Interestingly, the superintendent met with three families in the community and "agreed to never let the book be taught again if they agreed to cancel their demonstration" (p. 37). The superintendent then issued a statement that implied that the teacher, rather than the superintendent, had not followed district policy. Goldwasser asked NCTE for help, and they conducted an investigation. The administrators responded by intimidating other teachers who had supported Goldwasser, suggesting that teachers' pay raises might be jeopardized because of her actions. In the end, Goldwasser did not lose her job. The book was reviewed by a committee that withheld approval for teaching the novel at eleventh grade but approved its use for twelfth-grade honors students (p. 41).

Issues That Spark Literature Challenges

The major issues that spark literature challenges are undergirded by an assumption—either explicit or implicit—that literary texts are not just imaginatively true but literally true, as well. More often than not, parents object to works of literature because they—and presumably their children—read literature as truth. Fishman (1988) noticed that when Amish people read fiction, they referred to fictional characters as the "people" in books and stories. For Amish readers and perhaps for some of our students as well, "Anything written about people...requires vicariously experiencing the events recounted, appreciating the circumstances of the people involved, and applying the explicitly or implicitly drawn morals to one's own life" (p. 135).

DelFattore (1992) similarly found as she studied censorship cases that many parent protesters "did not distinguish between what a fictional character says and what the story is 'officially' promoting, nor did they see any difference between asking *whether* something is true and teaching that it *is* true" (p. 47). Consequently, many English language arts teachers have learned to be careful not to assume that students can and do distinguish between fact and fiction but to teach students explicitly about the art of literature and what it means to suspend disbelief while reading literary texts.

Offensive Language

Profanity and/or offensive language is one of the most common reasons parents and others protest particular works of literature. Cormier (1988) reasoned that words carry more authority when they appear in print: "They might complain about television, but it's the books that they burn" (p. 34).

Paterson reported that *The Great Gilly Hopkins* is often the focus of protests because of offensive language: "Gilly, the angry foster child who lies, steals, fights, bullies the weak and handicapped, and displays a particular tasteless variety of racial prejudice, is also caught with the occasional profanity upon her lips" (1992, p. 57). When a child asked Paterson why Gilly "had to cuss," Paterson responded, "Well . . . a child who lies, steals, fights, bullies, and ferociously acts out her racial prejudice, is not usually a child who says 'fiddlesticks' when frustrated."

In an exchange that followed, the child responded, "But . . . if you put it into a book, we might think it's okay of us kids to talk like that"—a comment that I suspect echoes concerns first expressed by the child's parents. Paterson wisely replied, "Then, of course . . . you would also think it's okay to lie, steal, fight, bully emotionally disturbed children, and make ugly racist remarks," to which the child responded, "Oh, no . . . of course not."

Paterson said that she is disturbed that "as often as the book has been challenged, not once has anyone objected to the rest of Gilly's rather awful behavior, only to her language" (p. 57). Offensive language, she insists, is a red flag that becomes an easily identifiable target but misses the point. Occasional profanity is important to the development of the character Gilly, whose "inappropriate behavior, including her language, is an angry defense against the world which has labeled her disposable" (p. 57).

Clearly, teachers can and should weigh the part offensive language plays. The language that readers sometimes find offensive in literature selections (and in the writing done by students) should serve a literary and/or an educational purpose and not be included to titillate or call attention to itself. Teachers can and should be explicit in discussing the language of the literature with students and parents, explaining the part the language plays in creating an imagined world. If the language of a particular text is likely to be an issue parents are concerned about, teachers can send a letter to parents, explaining the book's merits and reasons it is important to the curriculum, and explaining the purpose the language serves.

Sexuality

Sexuality in literature is another prime censorship target that is easy to identify in texts. Parents worry that their children's attitudes and sexual behavior may be influenced by the fiction they read. They are right. Young readers, who understandably have questions about sex anyway, have been well served by Judy Blume books, such as *Are You There God? It's Me, Margaret,* that inform them about subjects—such as, menstruation, masturbation, and intercourse—that no adult may have explained to them.

Admittedly, most young teens can locate the "good parts" of popular novels in their classroom or school library. Julian Thompson humorously described his own book searches when he was starting high school: "Like convicts in a prison yard, we'd mutter authors' names and titles to each other. Then, in the privacy of the library, sitting at a table near the open stacks, we "test" each book. . . . The method was simplicity itself: squeeze the book between both hands and set it on its spine, then take the hands away and let it open . . . naturally. If the book had been around a while and if our information was correct, it would always open to the "good parts" (as we called them)" (1991, p. 3).

It is true that the "good parts" sometimes get more attention than the rest of the story. Many people, especially those who grew up immersed in literature, discovered at least some of what they learned about sex in the novels they read or partially read at school, in the library, or in the aisles of neighborhood bookstores. But most English language arts teachers insist—and many parents recognize—that it is *normal* and *appropriate* for curious young adolescents to want to seek information about sexual activity in books.

Yes, sex in literature should be there for a reason, and we should call students' attention to the author's use of sexual behavior in creating the story. What role does sex play? How is it important to the characters and to the story? Again, we are expected to be able to explain the educational and/or literary value of each text. Less easy to address are views held by many parents who accept some sexuality in literature but protest the inclusion of texts that portray sexual behavior outside of heterosexual marriage—especially if there seem to be no negative consequences, as in *Heather Has Two Mommies* (Willhoite) and *Daddy's Roommate* (Newman).

Violence

Violence in literature must, like offensive language and sexuality, serve an educational and/or a literary purpose. Dahl explained that he includes some violence in his books, but always undercuts it with humor: "Children know that the violence in my stories is only make-believe. It's much like the violence in the old fairy tales, especially the Grimms' tales. These tales are pretty rough, but the violence is confined to a magical time and place. When violence is tied to fantasy and humor, children find it more amusing than threatening" (1988, p. 75). But some educators question whether even "amusing" violence is appropriate. While it might not horrify, it conveys a message that condones violence as a way of negotiating differences. However, violence is a part of the human condition, and some violence—even in children's literature—is justified, especially if it portrays historical events or current social conditions (Tomlinson, 1995, p. 40).

A more serious problem exists if older students choose to read literary texts that carry a heavier violent message. How can we, as English language arts teachers, best serve students who might choose to read *The Turner Diaries*—the text that apparently influenced Timothy McVeigh's thinking? Or *The Vigilantes of Christendom*—a text based on a literal reading of a Bible passage (Numbers 25) that is used by the militant revolutionary group Phineas Priest to justify violent means to accomplish their purposes (Southern Poverty Law Center, 1996)? My impulse is to draw the line against such texts, to censor them from the classroom as inappropriate, not because of violence per se as much as the hatred that generates the violence. On the other hand, I recognize the possibility of using such texts—or excerpts from them—to teach students not to fear particular texts but to challenge, critique, and weigh the message and the values expressed.

Racial Stereotypes

Dahl was surprised when *Charlie and the Chocolate Factory* was criticized as portraying Africans unfavorably. The NAACP and others, however, noticed and pointed out that the fantasy creatures called "Oompa-Loompas" were pygmies from Africa. Dahl said, "I saw them as charming creatures, whereas the white kids in the book were, with the exception of Charlie, most unpleasant. It didn't occur to me that my depiction of the Oompa-Loompas was racist" (1988, p. 72). Dahl listened to and learned from the criticisms. He found himself sympathizing with the protesters, and he subsequently revised the book (p. 72).

Most of us would argue that protests on racial sensitivity grounds are more justified than those in which parents object to an occasional four-lettered word. How groups of people are portrayed is a more important issue and a valid reason that parents or community members might protest against a text. I am especially sympathetic to parents' charges that stem from concern about their own child—who may be the only African American student in a class—and about how a European-American White teacher might insensitively handle particular texts. We need to remember that if race is an issue in a text read by the whole class, it will affect the classroom relationships among racially diverse students, whether or not it is officially addressed. Especially difficult to teach are texts like *The Adventures of Huckleberry Finn,* which portrays racial bias that is pervasive throughout a whole society. Less difficult to teach are texts where author's stereotypes are merely inaccurate and can easily be explained: *Jake and Honeybunch,* for example, is criticized for depicting African Americans as those who eat barbecued ribs and chicken, and for portraying objects in heaven (everyday clothes and a jazz band) in ways that contradict African folklore (white and gold clothing and choirs) (Banfield & Wilson, 1983, cited by McClure, 1995, p. 10).

Gender Stereotypes

At one extreme, some protesters challenge every traditional presentation of women, insisting that such ingrained roles must not be perpetuated by being portrayed in textbooks (DelFattore, 1992, p. 161). They call for more portrayals of women in "leadership roles, construction work, sports, and other activities that have tended to be dominated by men" (p. 161). At the other extreme, Norma Gabler, ultraconservative critic of textbooks, has devised a formula for figuring out the percentage of women in traditional roles that should, she insists, appear in elementary textbooks: "She estimated that about 50 percent of all mothers work, and that at least 75 percent of them consider motherhood more important than a career. Adding the women who do not go out to work to those who work but give priority to motherhood, Gabler concluded that 88 percent of all women should be classified primarily as wives and mothers" (DelFattore, pp. 159–160).

To English language arts teachers, both positions are indefensible. A much better plan is to be conscious of an overall balance, not precisely calculated, among texts assigned and provided in a classroom library. Even more important is discussing gender issues and roles as they occur naturally within classroom literature discussions (see Whaley & Dodge, 1993).

Witchcraft and Satanism

These days, even witches must be treated with respect. Wicca, an organization of witches, has objected to *Hansel and Gretel* because it allegedly teaches that it is okay to burn witches and steal their property (McClure, 1995, p. 5). The U.S. Constitution prohibits persecution based on religious beliefs, even those of religions that the majority of people reject. Thus, in English language arts classes, we cannot ridicule Wiccan beliefs, but many people in the United States do not believe witches are real, and many English language arts teachers are not ready to "celebrate" the practice of witchcraft, since we believe it personifies evil.

Given so much objection to the appearance of witches and satanic figures in literature, I was amazed to discover "devil" tales recommended as a focus for elementary school literature study. Moss articulated well the positive rationale for this unusual plan: "Devils come in all shapes and sizes and vary widely in their personality traits and behaviors. Because of this interesting diversity and the wide array of traditional and modern devil tales available in collections and single illustrated editions, the study of devil characters was chosen as the focus of a literature unit which would activate the spirit of curiosity and invite inquiry" (Moss, 1990, pp. 63–64).

It is especially interesting to notice that this literature study did *not* have the effect of increasing students' beliefs in the existence of devils, as some might have predicted. Moss reported that the focus of the study was on story motifs, such as pattern of three, transformation, magic objects, impossible tasks, unfavorable prophesies, rewards and punishment, and reversal of fortune (p. 71). Thus, children studied the stories as literature and learned to test one tale against another and to compare the morality of various characters and the strategies used to resolve moral dilemmas.

Elementary language arts teachers learned from the 1980s censorship of the *Impressions* series that parent protesters take the study of devils very seriously (see Mendenhall, 1990). Conservative parents' fear of devil worship or Satanism has played a key role in reducing or eliminating the celebration of Halloween. One parent explained, "People make fun of the fact that a child is dressing up as a cute witch or devil, but I can't laugh at it. . . . They're making fun of something that's evil and wrong.

There ARE witches, there ARE demons . . . and the devil is someone we battle daily" (Miron, 1995). Teachers interested in a deeper understanding of the appeal of Satanism and the exaggeration of Satanism for a variety of purposes will want to read *The Satanisn Scare* (Richardson, Best, & Bromley, 1991) along with other sources, such as Fine and Victor (1994).

New Age and the Imagination

The fears of religious-conservative parents are expressed in even broader objections to anything that might be described as reflecting a New Age worldview. Parents may have been warned by their local church pastor to watch out for a range of topics and teaching methods sometimes used in English language arts classrooms that some parents believe might corrupt their children (Cumbey, 1985; Martin, 1989: Rowe, 1985):

holism, whole	human potential
multicultural education	self-esteem
intuition	possibility thinking
self-awareness	unity
guided visualization	global studies

Parents especially protest against any classroom activity that might suggest relying primarily on self or on a spiritual guide. Like *secular humanism*—a charge used frequently during the 1980s against textbooks—the term *New Age* applies to just about anything that protesters object to that does not carry a more specific label.

Ultimately, what seems to be at the heart of curricular challenges involving New Age beliefs and practices is a fear of—and a challenge to—the imagination itself. What English language arts teachers especially value about the imagination is exactly what some parents fear most: "It makes a person bigger than her or his experience and is the strongest manifestation of the idea of freedom that we know on an intimate level. . . . The imagination is the power to go beyond experience and, in the mind, to break or change the rules of all the games we are forced to play. . . . It is a source of new rules as well, of thinking the as-yet-unthought-of as we experiment with the development of felt values" (Kohl, 1995, p. 65).

Parents are advised to warn their children against imaginative classroom experiences, such as guided imagery: "Make a game of discovering examples of humanism and New Age spirituality. . . . Warn your child that meditation, guided imagery, ESP, and other spiritual or psychic techniques are not neutral exercises. They can bring him [sic] in contact with dangerous supernatural forces" (Kjos, 1990, pp. 35–36). We can expect some students, therefore, to resist what they have been led to believe are dangerous activities: "Explain the significance of God's armor. Practice putting it on together. Assure your child that this armor will keep him [sic] spiritually safe, no matter what spiritual forces surround him. Remind him that if coerced into being physically present during meditation, seances, or guided imagery, he need not be afraid or participate mentally. Instead, he should thank God for keeping him safe in the armor" (p. 36).

We may be troubled by such heavy-handed objection to the world of the imagination, but we must nevertheless respect parents' prerogative to influence their children in spiritual matters. Asking students to close their eyes and to imagine situations is defensible if the activity has an educational purpose. Many English language arts teachers, however, decide not to use guided imagery exercises, especially those that invoke a spiritual guide figure.

Defending Literature Study

As we make literature choices, and especially when we wonder about the wisdom of a particular choice, we are wise to (1) read the text in question, (2) find out what others have said and written about it, (3) weigh our own strengths and weaknesses as a teacher of literature, (4) consult trusted colleagues, and (5) ask for school-based professional development focused on ways of teaching literature and of addressing particular issues.

Moss especially defends the use of fairy tales for children aged 5 to 8, based on evidence that children of those ages are most engaged by fairy tales, an interest that declines in most children by the age of 10 or 11 (Favat, cited in Moss, 1990). Children are attracted to fairy tales because of their predictability and because "these tales reaffirm the child's conception of the world as a stable and gratifying universe" (Moss, 1990, pp. 6–7). Thus, fairy tales present a positive worldview. Although Moss's curricular plan could elicit knee-jerk reactions from parent protesters—who sometimes focus on the violence of particular fairy tales—Moss is able to articulate a clear rationale that describes the richness of literature study by pointing out that children read literature and enjoy it; they enjoy the intellectual challenges of "studying traditional literature as an art form, as a cultural mirror, and as a basis for understanding all literature"; they enjoy discovering "recurring patterns and motifs, similarities and differences between variants of the same tale, and connections between traditional and modern tales"; they focus on "universal themes and structures, language patterns, art of storytelling, and nature of the oral tradition"; and they learn "to read like writers and to think like folklorists" (p. 7).

Even for children, however, life does not always provide happy endings. Author Stephanie Tolan insists that we betray students if we provide only literature that ends happily. Of course, students should read some literature with happy endings, but not all. Tolan insists that her stories that do not have a happy ending offer *hope* but not a *promise* that life will be what they want it to be (Tolan, 1992, p. 63).

As children learn from experience about the complexities of living, they often seek literature that reflects a real world that is less stable than that portrayed in fairy tales. They still read literature for enjoyment, for aesthetic experience, and for intellectual challenges, but they also read to learn how to face real dangers in the safety of vicarious experiences. Parents of young teens, however, protest adolescent fiction for this very reason—that it deals with more complex, real-life issues that require more than absolutist responses. Teachers who defend adolescent literature, then, need to assume responsibility not only for teaching the literature but for helping students recognize why they are drawn to it. The students can, in turn, help their parents value its potential to help young readers face "the mischief and danger that exists in our world" (Reed, 1989) and to consider their own ethical responses and choices.

Defending Multicultural Literature

A major target for would-be censors is literature that portrays other cultures, other lifestyles, and/or other religions in a positive light. Clearly, the bias against multicultural literature reflects broader cultural biases. Some protesters believe that although other cultures may be interesting and may be respected to a point, everything about those cultures must be rejected if their citizens embrace a non-Christian religion. As I grew up, I was taught about other cultures in Sunday school so that I would know how to "witness" to "unsaved" people—that is, to teach others the error of their ways so that they could embrace my faith, the only true faith, without which they might be eternally condemned. Religious-conservative parents today continue to be warned to reject and to fear multiculturalism and religious pluralism. They "grieve for the Hindu, the Buddhist, the atheist, the Satan worshiper and men and women of all religions and all creeds who have not yet accepted Jesus Christ as their personal Lord and savior" (Marrs, 1989, p. 127).

Some critics, such as Mel Gabler, have more political reasons for rejecting multicultural literature: "One thing that we have to consider in the American history [books] is that so much emphasis is put upon so many of the minorities. The great majority of Americans are being short-shrifted throughout American history.... And then Mrs. Rosa Parks, now I believe this was put in to get the woman mentioned. I think to resurrect people that were hardly known and give them predominant space is not fair to the great men who did accomplish something in this country" (Gabler, cited by Hulsizer, 1989, p. 13). A Michigan lawmaker would agree: "The emphasis on multicultural diversity is a bunch of garbage.... We're a Western civilization. Lots of times with this multicultural stuff, they try to bring out an isolated society and make it look like the norm" (Hornbeck, 1994).

Such views have led to school board mandates of cultural intolerance, as occurred in a Florida county where teachers were ordered to teach that American culture is superior ("U.S. Superiority," 1994). Critical educator Donaldo Macedo (1994) explained, however, that "only those who have power can generalize and decree their group characteristics as representative of the national culture. With this decree, the dominant group necessarily depreciates all characteristics belonging to subordinated groups, characteristics that deviate from the decreed patterns" (p. 101).

Some have even blamed social unrest and violence on a multicultural focus in public school curricula: In 1992, Robert Simonds, Citizens for Excellence in Education President, asserted that "multiculturalism emphasizes diversity among races rather than our commonalities...and thus breeds prejudice.... Parents have begged our schools to stop multiculturalism before it breeds racial violence—only to be called 'elitist bigots'" (1992, p. 1). Four years later, Simonds concluded that, "the L.A. riots, three years after multiculturalism was taught in L.A. schools, was the result" (1996, p. 2).

High school and middle school English teachers have especially felt the effects of such attitudes of cultural intolerance as they try precariously to balance canonical and culturally diverse texts and as they self-consciously monitor the literature included in their classroom libraries. English language arts teachers need to develop strong rationales for multicultural literature choices, knowing that political protesters can blame school or community unrest—even the Los Angeles riots—on school-based multiculturalism.

Teachers who use multicultural literature and need to defend these literature choices can learn from negative and positive models identified by Fishman. The *Tribal Approach* to multicultural literature, for example, leaves English language arts teachers' vulnerable to criticism, since it emphasizes differences and an us-versus-them stance in order to demonstrate that we are superior (Fishman, 1995, p. 76). Another approach that leaves English language arts teachers vulnerable is the *Disney/Coca-Cola Approach,* which reduces differences to "details of skin color, clothes, houses, food, and holiday celebrations" and thus suggests that diversity is superficial (p. 76). As a positive alternative, Fishman advocates a *Pluralist Perspective* that emphasizes the legitimacy of multiple cultures and the acceptance and celebration of difference (p. 76).

Defending Critical Literacy for All Students

If we do not teach critical literacy, we create citizens who cannot act independently or who cannot intellectually stand their ground. In a computerized world of virtually unlimited, uncensored sources of information and ideas, we have no choice but to teach all children to be critical, discerning readers of literature.

Many English language arts teachers at all grade levels are integrating curriculum, teaching in teams, and experimenting with curricular connections. When selecting literature, especially for cross-curricular programs, English language arts teachers will want to consider the sociopolitical messages conveyed to young readers either explicitly or tacitly. A review of genre types among children's favorite books conducted by critical educators Abrahamson and Shannon revealed that "the authors promoted concern for self-development, personal emotions, self-reliance, privacy, and competition rather than concern for social development, service to community, cooperation toward shared goals, community, and mutual prosperity" (Abrahamson & Shannon, cited in Shannon, 1992, p. 69). Thus, we need to notice and discuss with students the social values expressed in various works of literature.

Kohl (1995) has expressed concern about the perspectives that are revealed in children's and adolescent literature. By studying his own childhood favorite, the stories of Babar, Kohl was troubled by "the triumph of the strong and the mocking of the weak...the glorification of wealth and the sanction of 'deserved' poverty" (p. 4). Young readers, Kohl insists, learn from the Babar stories that "there are different classes of people and the Rich Lady is of the better (that is richer) class and that elephants are not as good as people, but might be if they imitate people" (p. 7). Kohl's study of adolescent novels revealed stories about incest, racism, AIDS, and domestic violence, but again he found almost no texts that questioned the economic and social structure of society (1995, p. 59).

When Kohl studied historical texts for young readers, he focused especially on the Rosa Parks story, since there are several books that tell the story of the role she played in the 1960s civil rights movement. Most of the texts, he noticed, featured variations on a "Rosa the Tired" theme, with an emphasis on the brave act of an individual woman who decided not to give up her bus seat primarily because she was too tired. Kohl criticizes such texts for distorting the truth, for leaving out the fact that Parks was a community activist who worked with others in her community to carry out planned resistance to segregation (p. 43). Such treatment, as emphasizing "Rosa the Tired," Kohl insists, gives young readers the false impression that only a hero or heroine acting alone can create change—something most people would not want to attempt: "Not every child can be a Rosa Parks, but everyone can imagine her- or himself as a participant in the boycott" (p. 47).

Those who advocate teaching young readers to be critically literate generally do not recommend censoring texts that convey messages of which they disapprove. Instead, they urge teachers to teach students to think and act: "Children quickly come to understand that critical sensibility strengthens them. It allows them to stand their ground, to develop opinions that are consistent with deeply held values, and, when conscience requires it, to act against consensus or the crowd" (Kohl, 1995, p. 16). Although we may be challenged by parents who fear the consequences of critical literacy, we can demonstrate to parents of many different perspectives the value of questioning a text and of "speculating on ways in which the world it creates can illuminate the one we live in" (Kohl, 1995).

WHAT CAN YOU DO ABOUT LITERATURE CONTROVERSIES?

1. *As a reader and a teacher of literature and reading who values prior knowledge and experience, recognize and identify the various "cultures" (ethnicity, economic level, religion, etc.) you come from and the perspectives that influence your own understanding of literary texts* (see Fishman, 1995). Help your students understand their own perspectives and affiliations by discussing or plotting on a web the overlapping communities and affiliations that shape their views and experiences.

2. *Prepare to work with parents from a variety of pressure group perspectives.* Recognize the possibility that parents may have more say in the future about particular classroom experiences than they do now. Therefore, anticipate parental challenges of the literature studied in your classroom and be prepared to offer alternative selections within a structure that will minimize or eliminate individual students' discomfort. Individualize some literature study so that students can make individual and small group choices. Use literature circles (see Daniels, 1994) to allow for more active student response to literature and to provide for a range of literature choices.

3. *Take the time to establish district, school, or even personal rationales and policies for literature choices.* The study of literature needs to be supported by the strongest justification, especially since literature is more often challenged by parents than any other part of the curriculum and since many of the protesters do not especially value literary experience. Always focus on educational purposes (see Chapter 10). Use or adapt resolutions and statements prepared by national professional associations (e.g., see Figure 6.1) that support students' rights to read and teachers' rights to teach a wide range of literary texts:

4. *Be careful in setting up English language arts classroom libraries, which often function somewhat like a public library when the works of literature are used for individual free-choice selection and reading.* Classroom libraries need to be developed on the basis of thoughtful guidelines, not just on what teachers can find in storage rooms and at home. Not every item needs to have a written rationale but you should be able to articulate a reason why each text is appropriate to the reading instruction and literature study that occurs in the classroom. For classroom libraries, probably more so than for school libraries, you need to be able to defend the educational suitability of each text.

5. *Work with colleagues at a variety of grade levels to establish a district plan for reading particular works of literature at particular grade levels, but avoid rigid literature lists.* I agree with Susan Ohanian, who said, "I've never met a required-book list I liked. Such lists are always prescriptive and retrospective.... Once you let a core list into your life, it's very hard to dislodge it" (Ohanian, 1992). I know, too, that would-be censors sometimes use such lists as a focal point for public scrutiny, criticism, and protest. Still, while few of us want a lock-step program, many of us value the identification of a few works that are earmarked for particular grades while preserving lots of individual choices.

6. *Do not use "literary merit" as the sole criteria for defending a work of literature because "for almost any title that you can name, there are going to be people who feel it is of high literary quality and others who feel it is trash"* (McClure, 1988, p. 158). Stronger support comes from a carefully prepared rationale based on educational purpose and suitability.

7. *Plan how you will handle mature subject matter in literary texts.* Usually it is the teacher's modeling that sets the tone. Teachers should be calm, serious, and casual but expect students to act as sophisticated readers (Greenbaum, 1997, p. 19). Prepare young readers for what they will encounter in the literature they read, warning them about four-lettered words or violent incidents and discussing the significance of the language or violence to the story.

8. *Do not rule out literature about religion, especially for classroom libraries and free choices.* Dara Gay Shaw reported that the "independent investigation of spiritual truth" is a recurring theme in adolescent fiction (1995, p. 20). Literary texts run the gamut in taking a perspective toward religion—some very negative (such as *The Choc-*

FIGURE 6.1   Censorship Statement

INTERNATIONAL READING ASSOCIATION
Censorship Statement

The following statement was prepared by the Intellectual Freedom Committee of the International Reading Association and was adopted by the International Reading Association Board of Directors at its winter Board Meeting in January, 1985. It was originally published in the October, 1985 issue of the Association's journal The Reading Teacher.

The International Reading Association supports freedom of speech, thought and inquiry as guaranteed in the First Amendment of the Constitution of the United States. Censorship infringes upon that freedom by denying individuals the right to select what they read and by limiting access to alternative points of view. Free inquiry is necessary to a democratic society.

In the spirit of freedom, members of the International Reading Association are committed to advancing reading comprehension and literacy at all ages and stages. Reading comprehension must go beyond literal understanding, to interpretation and evaluation of what is read. The First Amendment makes this critical perspective possible by permitting the publication of materials which represent diverse points of view. Helping students develop this critical perspective, however, requires an enlightened educational program, with curricula that provide for: (1) freedom to choose from a rich choice of classroom and library materials dealing objectively with many facets of a diverse society; (2) freedom to discuss issues identified by such reading; and (3) freedom to defend collective and individual positions against challenges from groups and individuals with different points of view.

IRA supports the rights of parents to monitor the materials that their children are required to read, and IRA believes that no student should be forced to read materials which he or she finds morally offensive. IRA further believes, however, that formal channels should be established for handling criticisms of school materials, and that parents and others should use these channels when filing a complaint.

Many communities and institutions have found that the best defense against censorship comes from developing procedures for dealing with challenges before challenges actually occur. The use of standard procedures for text selection is essential for answering challenges of materials and for maintaining the right of students to select what they read. Such standard procedures should set forth policies for book selection in academic libraries and classrooms. The determination of normal procedures for text selection should include development of the following:

(1) There should be policies for the selection of printed materials. These policies should be developed from community groups, including teachers, students, parents, and civic leaders. Policies must be written and approved by appropriate governing bodies (board of directors, trustees, etc.).

(2) There should be written guidelines for identifying and handling complaints.

(3) There should be a system for openly communicating with civic, religious, educational and political bodies in the community.

(4) There should be systematic methods for disseminating positive information about intellectual freedom through newspapers, radio and television.

(continued)

FIGURE 6.1   Continued

Members of the International Reading Association must determine whether guidelines and procedures for selecting materials and answering challenges exist in their agencies and schools. If such guidelines do not exist, members should push for their adoption. These guidelines and procedures allow the school system to respond in a careful, considered manner to challenges against materials used in the schools. This can provide insurance against incidents which may inflame a community and endanger academic freedom.

Association members are encouraged to reproduce this statement to share with educators in their communities.

Source: International Reading Association Censorship Statement. © The International Reading Association. Reprinted by permission.

olate War, in which "Cormier's imagery suggests a negation of religion") and some very positive (such as *N.I.K.: Now I Know,* in which Nik falls in love with but is rejected by a young woman who believes a romantic relationship will interfere with her spiritual mission) (Shaw, 1995). Some adolescent novels, such as Kathryn Lasky's *Memoirs of a Bookbat* and Richard Peck's *The Last Safe Place on Earth,* focus on the personal and social implications of mixing religion and politics. None of these texts should be excluded because of their religious content. The key is not to weight one perspective for or against religion too heavily and to provide overall religious neutrality across the selections provided.

9. *Teach students to make informed, critical judgments about the books they read.* Read and compare different versions of the same story told and retold in different ways. Ask students to read about the same theme across genres and authors, testing one text against another to notice parallels and differences.

10. *Do not be afraid to teach what you can defend.* Knowing the literature well and being able to explain carefully how a particular work is important to the curricular goals will give you the assurance you need to make a selection; to explain why to students, parents, and administrators; and to avoid initial panic if the selection is challenged. Susan Hepler and Susan Steinberg (1993) use what they know about books and about children and the effects of stories on children to make a case for the books about dragons they selected. They can explain that while picture books for older children often depict dragons "in their full, awesome power," modern picture books for young children often ignore the more "evil aspects and treat dragons more lightly, making them into humorous creatures, declawed pets, guardians, companions, or family members" (p. 5).

11. *Ask students to write responses to the books they read and save a sampling of the responses.* These will demonstrate the range of student reactions to particular texts and will provide evidence in students' own words that they have not focused on violence or offensive language but on larger themes and issues and on the literary characteristics that made the work a pleasure to read.

12. *Find appropriate ways to handle controversial language.* Controversial language in fiction can lead to a deeper understanding of sensitive topics. One fifth-grade class (including four Asian American, three African Americans, and two first-generation European Americans) discussed the banning of the novel *The Cay* because of the "*n*-word" (Knecht, 1996). When the discussion turned to the descriptor *Negro* for one of the main characters, the teacher used the occasion to address the issue of racist terms. As a homework assignment, students and their teacher asked parents and friends what they thought the word *Negro* meant and then reported their findings in class the next day. The teacher, for example, learned from an African American friend that, "although Negro is not a derogatory term, her family and other people whom she knows from the South don't like it, saying, 'It's just another term that white people put on us. . . . We didn't give it to ourselves" (p. 18). This discussion gave them the chance to consider the effects of racial slurs and name calling. An African American student insisted that, "if someone calls me Negro, I'll get mad," to which a Japanese American student, responded, "There are words they call people from Japan, but I won't.say them." At this point, the teacher stepped in: "Some words are considered crude and inappropriate everywhere. . . . But out of respect, you should never call anyone what they don't like to be called." On a later occasion with an historical novel, the group decided to use the term *Negro* for historical accuracy in place of *nigger,* which they preferred not to hear read out loud. Excluding the offensive terms from classroom conversation, in this case, created a more respectful atmosphere, but the teacher insisted that it would have been a mistake to exclude the *literature* that contained the words, which would have deprived students of "the greatest springboard for thought and discussion" (p. 18).

13. *Do not leave parent and public opinions to chance.* Unless you explain, parents often do not know why their children are reading contemporary fiction and keeping personal journals. Send occasional letters home to parents, including a brief but carefully written explanation of some part of the curriculum. High school English teacher Jim Burke works hard to keep his parents informed. He and his Burlingame (CA) High School English Department colleagues produce and distribute *The English Paper,* a double-sided, one-page newsletter that includes brief articles about English Department curriculum decisions. Burke also sends letters home to parents prior to teaching a potentially controversial work of literature (see Figure 6.2). Writing such letters takes a lot of time and effort, but clearly it is time and thought well spent.

14. *Recognize and accept the fact that you can never cover all the bases.* Whether the issue is portrayals of women in careers, strict parental authority, or junk food, from time to time parent and community protesters will still complain. These examples are not cause for despair but for facing reality. Very likely, parents will at least occasionally question the literature you select for your students.

FIGURE 6.2   Sample Letter to Parents

Dear Freshman Honors English Parent:

I conclude each year by having students in the freshman honors class evaluate the books we read, the projects we did, and the way I taught. In the first few years the novel *Nectar in a Sieve* has consistently come in dead last in this evaluation and number one in the category of "if I were to change one book which one would it be?" The book has served our purposes in the integrated English-History program, but as a serious reader I find it lacking in some important areas. It does not challenge the students as readers or thinkers, really; the language is simple, the story predicable after a certain point, the characters of limited depth. Its scope is also, and perhaps most importantly, too narrow. While Mr. Firpo spends the entire quarter studying India and its culture, I like to take advantage of the opportunity to build a bridge between India and our own country, a place where more and more Indians have come to make their home and exert their own cultural influence. I am interested in the way literature allows us to examine not only what it is like to be traditional (or non-traditional) Indian/Hindu/Muslin.

No other book accomplishes all this as well as Bharati Mukherjee's novel *Jasmine.* A professor of literature over at Berkeley, Mukherjee has written some impressive novels and collections of short stories, one of which—*The Middleman and Other Stories*—won the National Book Award a few years ago. She does a better job of examining the interplay between generations and cultures and countries specific to America and India than any other Indian writer, though Chitra Divakaruni (a professor down at Foothill College) has come out with a brilliant new collection of short stories called *Arranged Marriage* which explores some of this same terrain.

In the past I have required students to read one Indian novel outside of class in addition to *Nectar in a Sieve,* and *Jasmine* consistently comes out on top when I survey kids. It was on the summer reading list and I have spoken to several kids and, more importantly, their parents, who read the book and discussed it with their children. I bring this up because the book presents several emotionally difficult scenes that are appropriate to the story and the discussion of the culture. Parents I spoke with about these scenes did find them strong but effective in helping their freshman to better appreciate the strength of the young girl's character and her ability to overcome such adversity on the way to being accepted into American society.

The book presents a very rich range of issues and experiences to discuss. It would significantly challenge the students and raise the level of our discussion—to say nothing of the student's interest in the book. But I feel it is important to ask your support to use the book for two reasons. One, the nature of the story merits your attention and needs your consent. Two, given that it is not available to us in the district, I would have to ask you to purchase it. I can arrange to buy the book for $4.00 per student through a local distributor.

My hope is you will not only support the use of this new book—Mr. Firpo has read it and also thinks it will bring some new blood to our program—but consider reading it (and all other books throughout the year) so you can discuss it with your son or daughter. Given that I must order the book, I would need to have the money by early next week; if you are willing, I will take cash or check (whichever is more convenient to you) made out to Jim Burke, as it would be to reimburse me for the books I will buy with my own money.

FIGURE 6.2   Continued

If you have any questions at all I encourage you to call me during my prep period (1:00–2:00) at [school phone number]. Thank you for your time and involvement in your child's education; I respect and appreciate it.

Sincerely,
Jim Burke

Source: Reprinted by permission of Jim Burke. A version of this letter appears in *An English Teacher's Companion* by Jim Burke (Boyton/Cook, 1999).

15. *Create a plan of action to take if and when you and/or your English language arts curriculum are challenged.* Use the information cited in the Helpful Resources listings at the end of this chapter. Work with colleagues and administrators—or on your own if you need to—to establish a course of action based on sound professional advice. Mark Figure 10.7 in Chapter 10 so that you may easily refer to or photocopy NCTE's "Reconsideration Request" form when needed.

In one striking case, discussed in Chapter 4, Cissy Lacks, a high school English language arts teacher from Missouri, worked with leaders from NCTE and People for the American Way (PFAW) and was awarded $750,000 after losing her job because her administrators so badly mishandled a challenge involving her English language arts curriculum. NCTE leaders also provide help on a smaller scale, often sending the right letter to the right person at the right time to make a positive difference (see Figure 6.3).

HELPFUL RESOURCES

1. Assembly on Literature for Adolescents, National Council of Teachers of English (ALAN). For some teachers I know, membership in ALAN is the most exciting spark to their professional growth and enthusiasm for teaching literature. ALAN publishes a journal focused entirely on literature, authors, and classroom ideas, and they sponsor a two-day conference held in conjunction with NCTE's fall convention. For membership, contact: NCTE, 1111 W. Kenyon Road, Urbana, IL 61801-1096, (217) 328-3870.

2. Dr. Margaret Sacco, teacher education professor, works with ALAN to help teachers make a case for teaching adolescent literature and to defend particular books. When she gets a request from a teacher, she sends a rationale, if available, from a large database created by practicing and preservice teachers; relevant literature on censorship; a bibliography of information about censorship; and names and addresses of anti-censorship organizations and contact persons. NCTE will soon offer a CD-ROM pro-

FIGURE 6.3   Letter in Defense of a Challenged Book

National Council of Teachers of English
1111 W. Kenyon Road, Urbana, Illinois 61801-1096
Telephone (217) 328-3870
Fax (217) 328-9645

Matthew N. Darliss, President
Board of Education
Harrison Unified School District
Harrison, IL 61801

Dear Dr. Darliss:

The situation concerning the removal of the book *Go Ask Alice* from a classroom in your district prompts this letter of deep concern.

By way of background, allow me to describe briefly how the National Council of Teachers of English sees its mission in relation to controversies related to instructional materials and methods. The Council is a professional organization of 130,000 members and subscribers. Our members are dedicated to improving the quality instruction in the English language arts at all educational levels. We have more than 130 regional, state, and local affiliates whose membership totals 50,000, including the Illinois Association of Teachers of English with over 2,000 members.

NCTE supports students' right to read and teachers's professional judgment in the selection of books and methods of instruction. NCTE opposes censorship because it "leaves students with an inadequate and distorted picture of the ideals, values, and problems of their culture" *(The Students' Right to Read)*. In two resolutions NCTE has stood for the selection of books that "represent a large segment of the community and not the vested interest of a few vocal members," and for the rights of students to have "access to a wide range of books and other learning materials under the guidance of qualified teachers and librarians."

Although I deal with book challenges quite frequently, I must say that the events related to the removal of *Go Ask Alice* from the classroom of Shana Stimpson are shocking. The book, which is widely read in high schools throughout the country, has apparently been in Ms. Stimpson's program for 15 years. As I understand it, students were given the option of reading an alternate work if they desired, a procedure that is surely fair to students and parents and consistent with democratic principles. However, one student's parents' complaint was the basis for action in which the superintendent's office summarily ordered the immediate removal of the book from Ms. Stimpson's classroom, without a conference with her, during a day on which she was absent. Let us be candid about what has occurred here: the parents of a single student, having declined the opportunity to opt for an alternate book for their child, were permitted to foreclose on other parents' rights to guide their children's reading. The protesting parents in effect have dictated program content to the teacher and the entire district.

NCTE is also alarmed that the judgement about *Go Ask Alice* was made without respect to the entire book. A common technique of censors is to quote or photocopy snippets of texts, taking them out of context. An author's broad moral vision, total treatment of theme, and commitment to realistic portrayal of characters and dialogue are ignored when protestors focus only on bits and pieces that are offensive to them.

FIGURE 6.3   Continued

Reducing the literature program to works which contain no isolated phrases offensive to any parent or special interest group in the community would lead to massive book-banning, and perhaps ultimately to no literature study at all. Forcing teachers to provide a written synopsis and rationale for every book in their program (as is apparently the current requirement for Ms. Stimpson) would be punitive and would have a high chilling effect on the selection of appropriate materials.

NCTE supports teacher selection of literary works within professionally sound guidelines, and we support the notion of district-wide procedures for handling protests of classroom materials. I understand that the School Improvement Council in your district endorsed these principles and procedures as well. We earnestly urge the Harrison Board of Education and administration, then, to restore *Go Ask Alice* to Ms. Stimpson's classroom and to establish a district policy for processing complaints about materials. NCTE's *Students' Right to Read* (excerpt enclosed) is a model that has been successfully used or adapted by hundred of districts in setting such policies. NCTE or its affiliate in Illinois would be pleased to work with you in drafting a clear and even-handed document for dealing with protest of books and other materials.

Please call me at 1/217/328-3870 if I can be of assistance. I hope that the Harrison Unified School District will move towards a democratic, policy-based approach to dealing with censorship problems.

Yours truly,

Charles Suhor
Deputy Executive Director

Source: Copyright 1982 by the National Council of Teachers of English. Reprinted with permission.

gram that includes rationales for hundreds of works of literature. Contact: Dr. Margaret Sacco, 301 McGuffey Hall, Miami University, Oxford, OH 45056, (513) 529-6686.

3. Lehr, S. (Ed.). (1995). *Battling Dragons: Issues and Controversy in Children's Literature*. Portsmouth, NH: Heinemann. This thoughtful and detailed book addresses attacks on children's literature selections and examines particular themes—gender roles and family values, freedom and oppression, good and evil—that have generated protests.

4. Kohl, H. (1995). *Should We Burn Babar? Essays on Children's Literature and the Power of Stories*. New York: The New Press. Written by a progressive educator, this powerful book provides a new perspective on well-known children's stories and highlights instances of racism, sexism, and condescension that detract from the tales being told. Kohl's insights are all ultimately hopeful, but they will help you—and, in turn, your students—detect bias and become critical readers. Although Kohl focuses on children's literature, this book can help teachers at all grade levels take a new look at all literature choices.

5. Kaywell, J. F. (Ed.). (1993, 1995, 1997). *Adolescent Literature as a Complement to the Classics.* 3 vols. Norwood, MA: Christopher-Gordon Publishers. These practical books offer specific classroom suggestions for linking canonical literature—which is often distant from students' experiences or difficult to read—with more accessible young adult literature. Kaywell's texts provide ideas that are useful not only to enrich the literature curriculum but also to help teachers know how to defend young adult selections that support the teaching of the classics.

6. An NCTE/IRA Joint Task Force on Intellectual freedom has published *Common Ground,* a practical brochure filled with nuts-and-bolts ideas, action plan/strategies, and resources to jog your thinking and nudge you to do something to protect intellectual freedom in English language arts classrooms. Single copies are available free from NCTE and from IRA. Contact: NCTE, 1111 W. Kenyon Road, Urbana, IL 61801-1096, (217) 328-3870, or IRA, 800 Barksdale Road, P.O. Box 8139, Newark, DE 19714-8139, (302) 731-1600.

REFERENCES

Cormier, R. (1988). The authors speak. In M. I. West (Ed.), *Trust your children: Voices against censorship in children's literature* (pp. 29–39). New York: Neal-Schuman Publishers.

Cumbey, C. E. (1985). *A planned deception.* East Detroit: Pointe Publishers.

Dahl, R. (1988). The authors speak. In M. I. West (Ed.), *Trust your children: Voices against censorship in children's literature* (pp. 71–76). New York: Neal-Schuman Publishers.

Daniels, H. (1994). *Literature circles: Voice and choice in the student-centered classroom.* York, ME: Stenhouse Publishers.

DelFattore, J. (1992). *What Johnny shouldn't read: Textbook censorship in America.* New Haven, CT: Yale University Press.

Fine, G. A., & Victor, J. (1994). Satanism tourism: Adolescent dabblers and identity work. *Phi Delta Kappan, 76* (1), 70–72.

Fishman, A. (1988). *Amish literacy: What and how it means.* Portsmouth, NH: Heinemann.

Fishman, A. (1995). Finding ways in: Redefining multicultural literature. *English Journal, 84* (6), 73–79.

Goldwasser, M. M. (1997). Censorship: It happened to me in southwest Virginia—It could happen to you. *English Journal, 86* (2), 34–42.

Greenbaum, V. (1997). Censorship and the myth of appropriateness: Reflections on teaching reading in high school. *English Journal, 86* (2), 16–20.

Hepler, S., & S. Steinberg. (1993). Here there be dragons! *Book Links, 3* (2), 5–9.

Hornbeck, M. (1994, Nov. 20). Multicultural curriculum in hands of GOP. *Detroit News,* pp. 1A–3A.

Hulsizer, D. (1989). *Protecting the freedom to learn: A citizen's guide.* Washington, DC: People for the American Way.

Kjos, B. (1990). *Your child and the New Age.* Wheaton, IL: Victor Books.

Knecht, K. (1996). Facing the "N-word." *Teaching Tolerance, 5* (1), 16–18.

Kohl, H. (1995). *Should we burn Babar? Essays on children's literature and the power of stories.* New York: The New Press.

Macedo, D. (1994). *Literacies of power: What Americans are not allowed to know.* Boulder, CO: Westview Press.

Marrs, T. (1989). *Ravaged by the New Age: Satan's plan to destroy our kids.* Austin, TX: Living Truth Publishers.

Martin, W. (1989). *The New Age cult.* Minneapolis: Bethany House.

McClure, A. (1988). The anticensorship activists speak. In M. I. West (Ed.), *Trust your children: Voices against censorship in children's literature* (pp. 155–163). New York: Neal-Schuman Publishers.

McClure, A. (1995). Censorship of children's books. In S. Lehr (Ed.), *Battling dragons: Issues and controversy in children's literature* (pp. 3–30). Portsmouth, NH: Heinemann.

Mendenhall, D. (1990). Nightmarish textbooks await your kids. *Citizen* [newsletter of Focus on the Family], *4* (9) 1–7.

Miron, M. (1995, Oct. 28). Debate continues: Should Halloween be shunned? *Kalamazoo [MI] Gazette,* p. A4.

Moss, J. (1990). *Focus on literature: A context for literacy learning.* Katonah, NY: Richard C. Owen Publishers.

Ohanian, S. (1992). Classroom structures that really count. *Education Week, XII* (13), 18, 20.

Paterson, K. (1992). Tale of a reluctant dragon. In P. Shannon (Ed.), *Becoming political: Readings and writings in the politics of literacy education* (pp. 53–59). Portsmouth, NH: Heinemann.

Perry, J. (1991). The power of literature: Equipment for life in a multi-ethnic society. *Focus: Teaching English Language Arts* [Southeastern Ohio Council of Teachers of English], *18* (1), 28–38.

Reed, C. (1989). The back door: Are we censoring adolescence? *ALAN Review, 16* (2), 47–48.

Reichman, H. (1988). *Censorship and selection: Issues and answers for schools.* Chicago: American Library Association, and Arlington, VA: American Association of School Administrators.

Richardson, J. T., Best, J., & Bromley, D. G. (Eds.). (1991). *The Satanism scare.* New York: Aldine De Gruyter.

Rowe, E. (1985). *New Age globalism.* Herndon, VA: Growth.

Shannon, P. (1992). Overt and covert censorship of children's books. In P. Shannon (Ed.), *Becoming political: Readings and writings in the politics of literacy education* (pp. 65–71). Portsmouth, NH: Heinemann.

Shaw, D. G. (1995). The treatment of religion and the independent investigation of spiritual truth in fiction for adolescents. *ALAN Review, 22* (2), 20–22.

Simonds, R. (1992, June). *President's Report.* National Association of Christian Educators/Citizens for Excellence in Education.

Simonds, R. (1996, Feb.). *President's Report.* National Association of Christian Educators/Citizens for Excellence in Education.

Southern Poverty Law Center. (1996). Terrorists in the name of God and race. *Klanwatch Intelligence Report, 83,* 1–5.

Suhor, C. (1997). Censorship—When things get hazy. *English Journal, 86* (2), 26–28.

Thomas, D. (1951). Notes on the Art of Poetry.

Thompson, J. (1991). Is it worth the trouble? *ALAN Review, 18* (2), 2–5.

Tolan, S. S. (1992). Happily ever after. In P. Shannon (Ed.), *Becoming political: Readings and writings in the politics of literacy education* (pp. 60–64). Portsmouth, NH: Heinemann.

Tomlinson, C. (1995). Justifying violence in children's literature. In S. Lehr (Ed.), *Battling dragons: Issues and controversy in children's literature* (pp. 39–50). Portsmouth, NH: Heinemann.

U.S. superiority ordered taught. (1994, May 25). *Kalamazoo [MI] Gazette,* p. A2.

Whaley, L., & L. Dodge. (1993). *Weaving in the women: Transforming the high school English curriculum.* Portsmouth, NH: Boyton/Cook.

7 Censorship in Sexuality Education

JODI BROOKINS-FISHER

Central Michigan University

Sexually active students who are ignorant about protection become victims of cruel and misguided censorship. A responsible protective program must stress abstinence first and foremost, but also must reach out to students who choose not to abstain to avoid sending the message of "I told you so!" to any who fall victims to AIDS, other sexually transmitted diseases or premature parenthood.

I ask those who oppose sex education: How could education ever be wrong? How could ignorance ever be right? What good is reading, writing, and arithmetic to a student who will die of AIDS because he or she was denied education by our schools? There are many reasons why schools must educate students on life issues like protective sex education. Ignorance is not bliss.

—Travis Lund Moon, *Los Angeles Times,* February 28, 1994

A continual concern in public school curricula is sexuality education. In fact, it has been said that "no issue concerning public schools may be more divisive than teaching children about sex" (Cozic, 1995, p. 176). Yet, as adults debate the issue of sexuality education, the rates of teenage pregnancy and sexually transmitted diseases among young people continue to soar. Studies show more than half of U.S. teens have had sexual intercourse (Center for Disease Control and Prevention [CDC], 1995). This statistic equates to millions of U.S. adolescents, or approximately 61 percent of male youth and 48 percent of female youth (Planned Parenthood Federation of America [PPFA], 1995).

Should sexuality education be taught? What should be included? How do we give students accurate and adequate information to make healthy decisions, without stepping on parents' rights and responsibilities? What will be done with the few, yet vocal, community citizens who will fight us no matter what is covered in a sexuality curriculum? These concerns, as well as solutions, will be considered in this chapter.

Comprehensive Sexuality Education

Many health professionals would agree that sexuality education is best presented as part of a comprehensive school health curriculum. Since sexuality is only one part of a person's life, be it an important component, it should be associated with other issues and topics related to health and the whole person. As part of a comprehensive school health curriculum, however, sexuality education should also be comprehensive in nature.

What is *comprehensive sexuality education?* It can be defined as a sexuality education curriculum throughout grades K–12, that is extensive, sequential, and age and developmentally appropriate for students. This curriculum should include components in four areas: (1) accurate information; (2) attitudes, value, and insight exploration and development; (3) relationship and interpersonal skill building; and (4) responsibility for one's sexuality (Haffner, 1994).

Sexuality education should include more than fragmented lessons on HIV/AIDS or growth and development during puberty. According to Fetro (in Ogletree et al., 1994), to be successful at imparting knowledge, building decision-making skills, and helping behavior change a sexuality program should include the following elements: (1) accurate information about the short- and long- term consequences or risks (physical, psychological, social, and legal) of sexually related decisions; (2) internal and external factors influencing personal health practices and peer group impact; (3) strategies to heighten self-esteem; (4) opportunities to build personal and social skills; (5) a peer education component; and (6) parent/guardian involvement (Ogletree et al., 1994).

Sexuality education may have different names, depending on the school district and the community. "Family life education" may include components of a sexuality curriculum, as might "AIDS education." However, these programs are usually not comprehensive in nature and do not take into account the broad domain of human sexuality. In fact, contrary to critics' beliefs, very few states have mandated comprehensive sexuality education (Delaware, Florida, Georgia, Iowa, Illinois, Kansas, Maryland, New Jersey, Nevada, Rhode Island, South Carolina, Vermont, Virginia, and Washington, DC), and in those that do, there are great discrepancies within district programs (PPFA, 1995). There is also great need to evaluate existing programs to get better information on long-term benefits.

For too long, we have taught under the auspices of "sex ed," which suggests only the behavior of human sexuality, and not the many other important, natural components that make people sexual human beings. Perhaps this strategy has landed sexuality education in the predicament it is in today.

Regardless of the particular curriculum, or what it may be called, all parties agree on one concept: Sexuality education should occur in partnership with parents. Parents are the ultimate educators of their children, and have the right to help make decisions about what information is to be included in the sexuality curriculum. The school must supplement parental education with a sexuality education curriculum of factual information that can be taken into the home and put within the context of parental and other value systems. Most parents who express concern over materials within the sexuality curriculum are just that—concerned parents. Their issues may resolve themselves once school personnel give them adequate attention. However, a few parents and community members will never be content with any sexuality curriculum. This minority can be a potential problem. It is important to decipher who is a concerned parent and who is an extremist, as concerned parents will make a comprehensive sexuality education curriculum more solid, more in tune with community values, and better equipped to meet diverse student needs.

Areas of Controversy

Since the early 1980s, health education controversies have often focused on mental health, sexual morality, and sexually transmitted diseases (STDs). Anspaugh and Ezell (1994) cited sexuality, family life, AIDS, and drugs as the most controversial topics within a school health curriculum. If topics such as abortion and homosexuality are included within the sexuality component of a comprehensive school health education curriculum, they will generate the most concern and opposition. Often, a few topics will lead to scrutiny and ridicule of an entire comprehensive curriculum, but careful planning with community involvement will allow a school to provide a comprehensive curriculum without later backlash. This is not to say a curriculum should exclude topics, but rather that including adversarial groups in the planning stages can lead to understanding and possibly compromise *before* implementation.

   Not surprisingly, certain issues within the contents of a sexuality curriculum continue to receive pressure from the outside community. People have a variety of personal reasons why they might be concerned or even opposed. For example, those with strong religious beliefs may oppose the discussion of abortion and/or homosexuality, as these topics may be at odds with the beliefs they are helping their children develop. Others may oppose parts of a sexuality curriculum to maintain privacy in family matters. However, when the public was surveyed about their beliefs regarding school health education in general, 88 percent of adults stated that school health education could reduce problems plaguing adolescents (Torabi & Crowe, 1995). Torabi and Crowe also found that 90 percent of these adults felt school health education to be as important as, or more important than, other subjects taught in school. Furthermore, these adults perceived two of the biggest problems young people face to be STDs/AIDS and inadequate sexuality education. Clearly, this random sample showed there is support among the public for sexuality education. Earlier U.S. surveys have found similar results. A 1985 Harris Poll, for example, found that 90 percent of parents want their children to receive sexuality education within the schools (PPFA, 1995).

   These parents are not alone. In 1991, the National Coalition to Support Sexuality Education was founded and now includes close to 60 affiliates and organizations. The coalition's goal is for all U.S. schoolchildren to receive comprehensive sexuality education by the year 2000. Coalition members include the National Education Association, the American School Health Association, the Children's Defense Fund, the American Medical Association, the YMCA of the USA, and the National Urban League (Haffner, 1994). The health objectives for the year 2000, *Healthy People 2000*

(Public Health Service [PHS], 1991), included the following objectives that support sexuality education within the schools:

> 5.8: Increase to at least 85% the proportion of people ages 10–18 who have discussed human sexuality, including values surrounding sexuality, with their parents and/or have received information through another parentally endorsed source, such as youth, school, or religious programs
>
> 18.10: Increase to at least 95% the proportion of schools that have age-appropriate HIV education curricula for students in grades 4–12, preferably as part of quality school health education
>
> 19.12: Increase instruction in sexually transmitted disease transmission prevention in the curricula of all middle and secondary schools, preferably as part of quality school health instruction

Religious organizations have also supported sexuality education, including the following Protestant denominations: the Episcopal Church, the Lutheran Church of America, the Southern Baptist Convention, the United Church of Christ in the USA, the United Methodist Church, the Lutheran Church—Missouri Synod, the Presbyterian Church, and the United Presbyterian Church (Haffner, 1995). Additionally, the National Council of Churches, the Synagogue of America, and the United States Catholic Conference have developed a statement of guidelines for "family life education" programs developed by other agencies (see Figure 7.1). Consulting information from these and other church groups will ensure that the belief systems of community members have been recognized and incorporated in the district/school curriculum.

FIGURE 7.1   Guidelines for Family-Life Education

To those groups responsible for developing school and community programs in family life, we suggest the following guidelines:

1. Such education should strive to create understanding and conviction that decisions about sexual behavior must be based on moral and ethical values, as well as on considerations of physical and emotional health, fear, pleasure, practical consequences, or concepts of personality development.
2. Such education must respect the cultural, familial and religious background and beliefs of individuals and must teach that the sexual development and behavior of each individual cannot take place in a vacuum, but are instead related to the other aspects of his life and to his moral, ethical and religious codes.
3. It should point out how sex is distorted and exploited in our society and how this places responsibility upon the individual, the family and institutions to cope in a constructive manner with the problems thus created.
4. It must recognize that in school, family life, insofar as it relates to moral and religious beliefs and values, complements the education conveyed through the family, the church or the synagogue. Family life in the schools must proceed constructively with understanding, tolerance and acceptance of differences.

FIGURE 7.1 Continued

5. It must stress the many points of harmony between moral values and beliefs about what is right and wrong that are held in common by the major religions on the one hand and generally accepted legal, social, psychological, medical and other values held in common by service professions and society generally.

6. Where strong differences of opinion exist on what is right and wrong sexual behavior, objective, informed and dignified discussion on both sides of such questions should be encouraged. However, in such cases, neither the sponsors of an educational program nor the teachers should attempt to give definite answers or to represent their personal, moral, and religious beliefs as the consensus of the major religions or of society generally.

7. Throughout such education human values and human dignity must be stressed as major bases for right and wrong; attitudes that build such respect should be encouraged as right, and those that tear down such respect should be condemned as wrong.

8. Such education should teach that sexuality is a part of the whole person and an aspect of his dignity as a human being.

9. It should teach that people who love each other try not to do anything that will hurt each other.

10. It should teach that sexual intercourse within marriage offers the greatest possibility for personal fulfillment and social growth.

11. Finally, such a program of education must be based on sound content and must employ sound methods; it must be conducted by teachers and leaders qualified to do so by training and temperament.

Source: From a statement by the National Council of Churches, the Synagogue of America, and the United States Catholic Conference. Reprinted by permission.

Why the Controversy?

Why does the United States continue to have a problem in presenting factual information to young people about sexuality-related issues? European countries have been teaching comprehensive sexuality education for years with proven track records of fewer cases of teenage pregnancies and sexually transmitted diseases among young people than in the United States. Americans, on the other hand, shelter young people from this same information yet continue to have the highest teenage pregnancy and sexually transmitted disease rates among young people of any industrialized nation.

The controversy stems in part from the approach to sexuality from the beginning of time. Sexuality has never been a "public" issue to discuss, but one that is talked about (or more likely ignored) within the family. Some do not understand why it is important now to arm adolescents with correct information to make healthy decisions within the schools versus simply "handling it" within the family. Perhaps the following statement by Randy Engel from *The New American* (January 27, 1992) sums up this sentiment:

> Group sex education amounts to a perversion of nature. It makes public and open that which is naturally private and intimate. Any teaching about sex in a public setting violates privacy

and intimacy. Sex education in the classroom is an insidious and unnatural invitation to sexual activity; it is erotic seduction; and it is even a form of child molestation, violating the natural latency and post-latency periods of child development, periods which are crucial for normal development of the whole person (in Mack, 1994, p. 136).

Another contributing factor is that parents, other community members, and even teachers and administrators believe that their value system is the "right" system, and they bring this personal perspective into the curriculum. Maneuvering through the curricular process with so many personal belief systems about "right" and "wrong" becomes difficult. These beliefs are often, though not always, tied to religious or political beliefs. Many religious denominations have doctrines about issues such as birth control, abortion, and homosexuality. Those following these doctrines will be against most, if not all, lessons that include these particular concepts.

These beliefs are part of a general bias in U.S. society. This is not a society that welcomes difference. In the case of sexuality education, welcoming difference would involve discussion about homosexuality. Homophobia is a learned behavior passed through generations, which leads to hate and fear. Some fear that discussing homosexuality in a factual manner within the classroom would translate into same-gender sexual practices among young people. This fear is sometimes tied to religious beliefs about the "wrongness" of this kind of relationship. Along these same lines, many feel that discussing any sexuality education will lead to premature sexual behavior, which has clearly been proven not to be the case. Instead, studies indicate that sexuality education increases knowledge (Adame, 1985). Although studies are inconclusive on the delay of sexual intercourse due to sexuality education, it most certainly does not lead to teenage sexual activity.

Some parents and community members spark controversy in order to control the curriculum process. And some organizations, often with a religious-conservative perspective, work through the legislative process by providing largely propagandized material to legislators to make them fearful about what is and is not discussed in sexuality programs. During the 1996 Utah legislative session, one group, the Eagle Forum, distributed copies of an anti-gay video to certain legislators. The videos were sent to "educate" the legislators before they voted on the inclusion of gay/straight alliances in public high schools. These videos are laden with misinformation about gay and lesbian youth and their issues. Without correct information about gay/lesbian issues, these videos would impart fear—exactly the Forum's purpose.

Such groups often use similar approaches in scaring community members. In the past, these large-scale, highly organized efforts have been staged to discredit public education. During the same Utah legislative session, many involved believed the purpose of fighting gay/straight alliances was to bruise public education in order to acquire funding for home schooling. Some of those in greatest opposition to sexuality education in public schools do not even have children within the public school system, as they home-school. Organizations such as the American Family Association, American Life League, Citizens for Excellence in Education, Concerned Women for America, Eagle Forum, Focus on the Family, and the National Organization for Abstinence Education have been very active in trying to control what is taught within sexuality education curricula (PPFA, 1995).

Many opponents of comprehensive sexuality education, regardless of their affiliation with any particular group, believe these curricula are misguided. They feel that sexuality education does not instill strong moral values in children and young people (criticizing what they call "value-neutral education") and too quickly offers alternatives to sex within marriage.

We as teachers must realize that controversy will continue to surround comprehensive sexuality education. Spalt (1996) has called controversy the "professional epidemic of the Nineties" (p. 339). It is like a "chronic disease which necessitates some changes in our professional behavior" (p. 339). However, controversy is not always negative. It enables comprehensive sexuality education to remain in the limelight, which will help ensure its accuracy. But as stated earlier, educators must distinguish between concerned parents and those trying to sabotage the sexuality curriculum. We must realize that educators and parents become polarized when teachers are defensive when approached about a concern. Polarization does nothing to further the importance of including sexuality education in a comprehensive school health curriculum, nor does it help those for whom the sexuality curriculum was designed—the community's young people. Figure 7.2 provides responses to sexuality education critics.

FIGURE 7.2   Opposition Arguments and Possible Responses

Argument: Sex education causes friction between parents and children, opposes parents' values, and is an invasion of privacy. Parents have the sole right to be their children's sex educator. In addition, most parents do not want sex education in the schools.

Response: Sex education supplements, not supplants, parents.

- Sex education increases parent-child communication (i.e., parents have a greater chance to communicate their values).
- Eighty percent of adults favor sex education, and parents of children under age 18 are even more likely to be in favor.
- Curricula encourage teachers and students to discuss moral issues with parents.
- Programs are offered for parents.
- In communities where parents are most involved, programs are more, not less, comprehensive.

Argument: Sex education is value-free and immoral, teaches children how to have sex, and uses role play to brainwash children into having sex. Sex education is the cause of teenage sexual activity and pregnancy. Besides, children in latency (between the ages of five and puberty) are not interested in sex.

Response: Sexuality education teaches children to make difficult decisions and resist peer pressure.

- Sex education is based on fundamental values, including the advantages of knowledge as compared to ignorance; the importance of self-esteem in resisting exploitation; and the principle of relating to others in ways that increase and support dignity, worth, and equality.

(continued)

FIGURE 7.2   Continued

- Rather than brainwashing, roleplays are actually rehearsals for how to behave under pressure, a more responsible approach than letting young people learn through trial and error.
- Both psychiatric opinion and the number and range of questions children of all ages seek about sex show the "latency" period to be an invalid concept. If parents think it will harm children, they can remove them from instruction.
- Research shows that education does not cause sexual activity, but that it does increase knowledge and tolerance for others whose values are different. If contraceptive information is included, programs can reduce unplanned pregnancy. Education also increases parent-child communication about sex.

Source: Adapted and reprinted from *The Front Lines of Sexuality Education: A Guide to Building and Maintaining Community Support* (pp. 77–78) by Peter Scales, ETR Associates, Santa Cruz, CA.

New Movements: Abstinence-Based versus Abstinence-Only Curricula

Amazingly enough, abstinence-based and abstinence-only curricular materials rarely mention what a teen should abstain from. For the purposes of this discussion, *abstinence* is implied as "leading a healthy lifestyle by avoiding risky behaviors, including sexual activity, and the use of alcohol, tobacco, and other drugs" (Michigan Abstinence Partnership, 1993).

The 1990s saw an increase in the development of abstinence-based and abstinence-only curricula from a variety of organizations throughout the United States. Abstinence-*based* curricula stress abstinence as the best choice for a healthy life, but also include information for the 53 percent of U.S. teenagers who have already engaged in sexual intercourse. Abstinence-*only* curricula discuss abstinence as the only healthy option in a teenager's life. Both curricula inherently assume that due to the physical, emotional, and social consequences of a sexual relationship, a teen is best advised to wait for sexual intercourse. However, how these curricula go about educating this issue is very different.

Abstinence-only advocates of programs such as "Free Teens," "FACTS," "Sex Respect," and "Teen Aid" state that theirs is a values-based approach to sexuality education. This contention implies that parents want a "just say no" message only, and that schools should enforce this belief. It also implies that there are moral rights and wrongs for everyone to follow. These advocates feel that other sexuality curricula have hidden values about homosexuality, abortion, and contraception, which are "wrong." They also believe that an abstinence-only message will offer support to the many young people today who choose not to engage in sexual intercourse.

Abstinence-based proponents believe young people have the right to accurate information about sexuality to incorporate into their own belief systems—with parents and others helping to determine its value. Some of these programs are "Postponing Sexual Involvement: An Educational Series for Young Teens," "Human Sexuality: Values and Choices," and "Reducing the Risk: Building Skills to Prevent Pregnancy,

HIV and STD" (Ogletree et al., 1994). These programs are not "value-free," but sensitive to the many value systems in this diverse society. They encourage abstinence, but respond to the majority of parents who want sexuality information accompanied by information about topics such as HIV/AIDS and birth control (Haffner, 1994). Abstinence-based curricula supporters believe that many abstinence-only curricula are fundamentally religious, and provide (mis)information in a format that elicits guilt and shame in teenagers. Kantor (1994) stated: "The focus on abstinence (in these curricula) is not the issue; rather, the abstinence-only curricula are problematic because of their reliance on instilling fear and shame in adolescents in order to discourage premarital sexual behavior" (p. 159). Abstinence-based supporters believe that abstinence-only curricula are in direct opposition to achieving a healthy sexuality in teens, and that the scare tactics do not help teens postpone sexual behaviors.

The trend for some type of abstinence curricula within a comprehensive sexuality education curriculum will continue. In order to serve the needs of this country's diverse young people, many states, counties, and cities have established coalitions, with conservative and liberal organizations alike, to address problematic curricular areas. Some, like the Michigan Abstinence Partnership, have developed guidelines for districts considering some kind of abstinence initiative (see Figure 7.3). This particular partnership recognizes that young people are facing difficult decisions and must be

---

FIGURE 7.3   Abstinence Program Principles

The following basic principles must be met to make abstinence programs successful:

1. The program must be broadly supported by the community as a whole. If consensus as to the importance of the message and methods of the program is not attainable, the program cannot succeed.
2. All segments of the community must be committed to working together to give consistent messages.
3. Programs must focus on increasing knowledge and skill building, so that young people not only know the reasons for abstinence, but also how to deal with pressure.
4. Young people must be motivated to build self-confidence, so that they can effectively choose to abstain despite pressure from peers, the media, and themselves to engage in risky behaviors.
5. Programs should be long-term. Short-term solutions such as one-time presentations with no community involvement are ineffective. Instead, ongoing educational opportunities about abstinence, goal setting, and skill-building for young people and their parents are needed.
6. Structured recreational opportunities and programs where supervision and "free-time" are provided.
7. Programs must have an evaluation component to learn what works and what doesn't.
8. Children themselves must be a part of the program development and evaluation. It is often surprising to learn what young people really think about what may actually happen to them.
9. Programs should be based on sound health education principles.

Source: Michigan Abstinence Partnership. (1993). Promoting healthy behaviors for Michigan's children: An action primer for families, schools and communities. Michigan Department of Community Health. Reprinted by permission.

supported by families, schools, and communities. The Partnership (1993) stated that young people must be helped to (1) learn what abstinence means, and why it is important to their health; (2) face societal, peer, and media pressures; (3) understand their sexuality and how to express it safely and appropriately; (4) create alternatives to unhealthy behavior; and (5) be hopeful of their futures.

When a community considers which types of program to implement, the Partnership (1993) suggested that any program initiated should:

- Provide individual attention for youth.
- Identify young people who are at high risk and provide assistance/referrals.
- Promote parental responsibility.
- Link families with schools and the community.
- Have community programs support and reinforce school efforts.
- Deal with relationships and peer pressure.
- Teach future aspects of their lives, like career development.
- Help train others in the community on abstinence messages.
- Ensure all community groups are working together for young people.

WHAT CAN YOU DO ABOUT CENSORSHIP IN SEXUALITY EDUCATION?

Since there will probably never be a time when all parents give their children accurate information about sexuality, the school will continue to be a partner in relaying the information necessary to help young people make healthy decisions. In fact, fewer than 15 percent of those students questioned in a national survey in a period of 12 years felt their parents presented them with adequate sexuality information (Gordon, 1994). Given this, a teacher should be prepared to teach controversial sexuality topics in the classroom, and to do so in an appropriate manner.

1. *Teachers need adequate training in teaching health education.* Training is the most crucial step in the preparation process. The nation has consistently placed health at the bottom of the pile of all of the topics taught within the school setting, and those teaching health have often been the least trained to do so. The scenario is easy to picture—the tenured gym teacher getting "stuck" with health one class period per day. Many have assumed that those teaching physical education know everything needed to address topics like sexuality, which is usually not the case. School administrators would seldom assume that the English teacher could teach math, so why might they assume that the physical education teacher can teach health? Schools need to own this particular dilemma in the controversy of sexuality education, since many teachers are not qualified, which understandably leads to problems.

Appropriate training would include a degree in education with a school health emphasis. This training may also include certification in teaching health education, if the state has such a process. Additionally, all health educators (including school health educators) should be competent in seven areas upon graduation from a university with an approved health education program: (1) determining the appropriate focus for health education, (2) planning health education programs based on identified community needs, (3) implementing these planned programs, (4) evaluating program effectiveness, (5) coordinating health education efforts, (6) acting as a resource for health education, and (7) communicating health education needs, concerns, and resources (National Commission for Health Education Credentialing [NCHEC], 1996). Although these competencies focus on health education, professionals realize the need to identify more explicit competencies for those within the classroom environment. Teachers assessing their own skills and finding they might not be adequately prepared in these seven competencies might gain valuable information through professional conferences (e.g., American School Health Association), in-service training, and continuing education courses.

2. *Along with meeting general health education competencies, teachers must be knowledgeable on topics within a comprehensive sexuality education curriculum.* Few students have questions about anatomy and physiology (Gordon, 1994), but many students raise questions about relationships, body changes, and sexual behavior (see Figure 7.4). These are questions that teachers should know how to address, as deemed appropriate in the classroom according to school district policy.

3. *A good teacher will use appropriate terminology when referring to body parts.* Teachers should replace the slang terms used by students with appropriate words. Doing so sets up what is to be expected and helps young people to become aware of correct terminology but does not remove the feeling of an open environment.

4. *When necessary, teachers need to help develop a sexuality curriculum.* Once the curriculum is in place, teachers can provide pertinent and appropriate information within the curriculum confines, without having to chart unknown territory. While curricula do exist, many districts develop and adopt their own curriculum.

Of the sexuality curricula that currently exist, 23 were found to be comprehensive in nature by Ogletree and colleagues (1995). These curricula were rated in the following areas to determine their potential classroom effectiveness: comprehensiveness, breadth and depth, compliance with SIECUS (Sexuality Information and Education Counsel of the United States) Guidelines for Comprehensive Sexuality Education (SIECUS, 1991), content accuracy/currency, skill-building variety, methods variety, developmental appropriateness, cultural sensitivity, ease of implementation, evaluation, appearance/production quality, and overall quality. Even though comprehensive, many programs lacked important components such as an umbrella philosophy statement, which is necessary to establish a program's goals and objectives as well as to provide content justification to potential critics.

5. *Teachers should also have a certain comfort level with the information to be presented.* This does not simply mean being well versed in sexuality information, but also being comfortable with our own sexuality. The more comfortable teachers are with themselves, the less likely they are to project value judgments onto others. It is also

FIGURE 7.4 Questions Students Ask

Grades 7 and 8

How do boys feel when they find out their girlfriend is pregnant?

Why are girls always to blame for pregnancy?

How can you prevent hurt from divorce?

Why do some families fight a lot?

How can you prevent child abuse?

How do pregnant teenagers cope with their problems?

What makes a strong, loving family?

What are ways of solving family problems?

Why do we have sexual urges?

I would like to learn a lot more about sex, more than we do learn, not just about reproduction but about feelings between boys and girls.

Grades 9 and 10

How can the guy be made to take more responsibility in a teenage pregnancy?

How does sex affect you after it's over?

When you get a check-up and discuss birth control with your doctor what occurs in this medical check-up?

How can you tell if you are going to marry the right person?

How can you say "no" to a partner?

How do you keep your values when you are in a car with a girl?

How do you know when you are mature enough for sexual activity?

Do contraceptives really work; are they harmful?

What makes people have sexual feelings towards the opposite sex?

How do you know the difference between caring for a person and being actually in love?

Grades 11 and 12

Why does society somewhat set a time period when sexual activity is O.K., such as when a girl is over 21?

What risks are taken using birth control?

What makes you want to have sex?

Do most teenage marriages fail?

What causes people to abuse their children?

How does a child deal with being abused?

When is the right time to have sex?

How does teenage pregnancy affect future lifestyle?

What are the different choices of birthing processes and what is involved in each?

In choosing a mate, how can you tell if you have anything in common?

How can I be sure about marriage so it won't end in divorce?

What changes may arise in a person or persons after getting married?

What makes people get upset over things that don't have to do with them?

How can you value your own ideas so you won't be influenced so much by peers to do something you really would not have done by your own standards?

Source: Permission to include information from *Students Speak—A Survey of Health Interests and Concerns: Kindergarten through Twelfth Grade* © 1984 was granted from Comprehensive Health Education Foundation (C.H.E.F.®), Seattle, WA. Additional use or duplication is prohibited without written permission from C.H.E.F.® All rights reserved.

important to be comfortable with adolescent sexuality. Our students need teachers who are honest, open, and nonjudgmental. Last but not least, we must show comfort with the information to be presented. Young people will see right through any discomfort, so it is best to be familiar with the material, and to let students know if we feel uncomfortable with the information. This openness adds humanness and honesty to the discussion.

   6. *Teachers need to pay attention to school district- or state-level policy and procedures when teaching such potentially controversial subjects.* Some states have developed a policy regarding the instruction of sexuality education within the schools, but many states have left this up to individual school districts. Those teaching sexuality education should be aware of any district policy about such issues as the depth and breadth allowed when discussing certain topics (e.g., abortion or homosexuality), handling student questions in the classroom, consulting with students on an individual basis, what information is considered confidential, what must be shared with parents/guardians, and referral processes. Most teachers are not criticized for making a conscious effort to stay within guidelines, but rather when there is blatant disregard for policy. Most policies still leave room for teacher creativity, openness, and the dissemination of appropriate and accurate information within the classroom.

   7. *Teachers and those involved in developing comprehensive sexuality curricula should be aware of community values.* These programs should acknowledge the diversity in communities and should teach respect for all families. They should also allow for the presentation of factual information without denouncing or promoting any particular secular or religious belief system (PPFA, 1995).

OTHER CONSIDERATIONS

Gaining Support

To develop and implement a comprehensive sexuality education curriculum within a district or school, the community should be highly involved. A community advisory committee consisting of key players in the area (i.e., clergy, school administrators and board members, etc.), as well as teachers, parents, and students is highly recommended. Public forums on curricular content and/or information dissemination at parent/teacher association meetings may also be helpful. Enlisting organizations such as the local PTA and gaining parents' support of the curriculum ahead of time will help to counter community resistance. The following suggestions by Schiller (1973) still hold true when trying to gain support for a sexuality education curriculum:

   1. A proposed program must first gain support from the highest authority within the school organization. Administrators and parent leaders alike must provide backing.
   2. A small committee is then formed to determine the receptiveness of parents and other appropriate individuals. If strong opposition is likely from some individu-

als, informed professionals should meet with these individuals to answer questions and lessen anxieties.

3. An advisory committee representative of appropriate community components should be formed. Chaired by an influential leader, this committee should advise and support professional personnel on overall policy concerning the nature of the program and its philosophy, concepts, and approaches.

4. The advisory committee spearheads parent meetings to describe what "family life" education is and why it should be taught. Such meetings should give attendees a chance to meet in small groups to discuss their feelings.

5. After the meetings, parents should answer a questionnaire to determine their feelings about family-life education. They should be asked about content, approaches, and desired qualifications for those running the program.

6. Technical experts should help in developing a curriculum for "family life" education.

7. Educators should be trained through in-service programs, workshops, college courses, or other practical means.

8. Educators ought to be volunteers and should be carefully screened for their attitudes, values, and ability to relate to students, parents, and other involved individuals.

9. The initial program should be small to allow for pilot testing and evaluation. The school should meet with the advisory committee frequently and consultants should be used.

10. If the program is successful, it should be revised and broadened to improve it. This helps keep everyone involved and facilitates program understanding. If the program is unsuccessful, alternate approaches should be considered.

11. Parallel to the basic program should be parent education or education for other significant groups.

W H A T   E L S E   C A N   Y O U   D O ?

1. Besides having appropriate training in health education and content knowledge, teachers must also provide a climate of learning that is open and trusting. Since many activities currently used in sexuality education are values clarification exercises, teachers must be good facilitators. These activities often list statements about values issues. Students must decide—without value references from the teacher, and based on their own belief system—if they agree or disagree with the statement. Although opponents of sexuality education scoff at values activities, these are instrumental in helping a young person to clarify his or her own belief system, as well as to understand and tolerate those that are different. A good teacher will allow students to state values and opinions but not allow attacks from other students with differing value systems. These activities also allow for the transfer of knowledge without value judgments.

2. Good sexuality education teachers will not only provide factual information but will also allow for skill building through roleplaying, scenarios, and other activities.

Educators realize knowledge alone will not influence behavior. By providing activities that influence attitudes and skills, chances increase that adolescents will be equipped to make healthy decisions about their lives. Movement toward outcomes-based education (testing competencies before moving on to another unit) means that the old lecture to separate groups of boys and girls about the changes they will encounter during puberty is not adequate to meet student needs. We must be open to new teaching ideas and strategies.

No teacher training programs currently offer courses on sexuality education teaching methods (Rodriguez et al., 1995/96), although pieces of these methods may be offered elsewhere. Thus, finding creative approaches to sexuality education may be cumbersome. Although survey results found teachers to be comfortable in teaching sexuality education, despite student religious beliefs, parental protest, and lack of administration support, they were relatively uncomfortable at taking sexuality education to the skill-building level (Haignere et al., 1996). Barriers most cited for teaching these methods were a lack of materials and time (Haignere et al., 1996). Therefore, school districts and schools that provide comprehensive sexuality education must have materials budgeted for the courses and have ideas and plans for classroom lessons and experiences. Teacher training in facilitating skill-based activities would also help teachers acquire the comfort level they need.

The goal of providing a variety of activities for sexuality education in a positive classroom climate is to equip students with the knowledge and skills they need to make healthy decisions in the future. Teachers with the appropriate training, materials, and comfort level will be more likely to provide this positive, learning environment.

REFERENCES

Adame, D. (1985). On the effects of sex education: A response to those who say it promotes teenage pregnancy. *Health Education, 16* (6), 8–10.

Anspaugh, D. J., & Ezell, G. (1994). *Teaching today's health in middle and secondary schools.* New York: Merrill.

Bensley, L. B., & Bensley, R. J. (1996). *Implementing and evaluating sex and HIV/AIDS education in Michigan schools.* Kalamazoo, MI: Balance Group Publishers.

Centers for Disease Control and Prevention. (1995). Trends in sexual risk behavior among high school students—United States, 1990, 1991, and 1993. *Morbidity and Mortality Weekly Report, 4,* 124–126.

Cozic, C. P. (1995). *Sexual values: Opposing viewpoints.* San Diego, CA: Greenhaven Press.

Gordon, S. (1994). Sex education is necessary. In Karin L. Swisher (Ed.), *Teenage sexuality: Opposing viewpoints* (pp. 127–132). San Diego, CA: Greenhaven Press.

Haffner, D. W. (1994). Schools should provide candid education on sexuality topics. In Karin L. Swisher (Ed.), *Teenage sexuality: Opposing viewpoints* (pp. 141–145). San Diego, CA: Greenhaven Press.

Haignere, C. S., Culhane, J. F., Balsley, C. M., & Legos, P. (1996). Teachers' receptiveness and comfort teaching sexuality education and using non-traditional teaching strategies. *Journal of School Health, 66,* 140–144.

Kantor, L. M. (1994). Many abstinence-based programs are harmful. In Karin L. Swisher (Ed.), *Teenage sexuality: Opposing viewpoints* (pp. 158–166). San Diego, CA: Greenhaven Press.

Mack, D. (1994). Sex education is harmful. In Karin L. Swisher (Ed.), *Teenage sexuality: Opposing viewpoints* (pp. 133–140). San Diego, CA: Greenhaven Press.

Michigan Abstinence Partnership. (1993). *Promoting health behaviors for Michigan's children: An action primer for families, schools and communities.* Michigan Department of Community Health.

National Commission for Health Education Credentialing. (1996). *A competency-based framework for professional development of certified health education specialists.* Allentown, PA: Author.

Ogletree, R. J., Fetro, J. V., Drolet, J. C., & Rienzo, B. A. (1994). *Sexuality education curricula: The consumer's guide.* Santa Cruz, CA: ETR Associates.

Ogletree, R. J., Rienzo, B. A., Drolet, J. C., & Fetro, J. V. (1995). An assessment of 23 selected school-based sexuality education curricula. *Journal of School Health, 65,* 186–191.

Planned Parenthood Federation of America. (1995). Children should receive comprehensive sex education. In Charles P. Cozic (Ed.), *Sexual values: Opposing viewpoints* (pp. 177–185). San Diego, CA: Greenhaven Press.

Public Health Service. (1991). *Healthy People 2000: National health promotion and disease prevention objectives—Full report with commentary.* Washington, DC: U.S. Department of Health and Human Services.

Rodriquez, M., Young, R., Renfro, S., Arencio, M., & Haffner, D. W. (1995/1996). Teaching our teachers to teach: A SIECUS study on training and preparation for HIV/AIDS prevention and sexuality education. *SIECUS Reports, 24,* 15–23.

Schiller, P. (1973). *Creative approach to sex education and counseling.* New York: Association Press.

Sexuality Information and Education Council of the United States. (1991). *Guidelines for comprehensive sexuality education: Kindergarten–12th grade.* New York: Author.

Spalt, W. S. (1996). Coping with controversy: The professional epidemic of the nineties. *Journal of School Health, 66* (9), 339–340.

Torabi, M. R., & Crowe, J. W. (1995). National public opinion on school health education: Implications for the health care reform initiatives. *Journal of Health Education, 26,* 260–266.

8 Making a Place for Religion

Students who know how humankind has struggled with the great religious questions are not so vulnerable to the nonsense and dangerous ideas spouted by certain groups and movements.

—Charles Haynes (cited in Ruenzel, 1996)

The job of educators is to educate, not to instill religious devotion . . . a person cannot be fully educated without understanding the role of religion in history, culture, and politics. And the law, constitutional or otherwise, is no impediment to the realization of this aim.

—Supreme Court Justice Clark,
Abington School District v. Schempp (1963)

Religion, moral and social values, and intellectual freedom all play important roles in the search for longer-term solutions to school- and community-based controversies and censorship. But there are no easy answers. These are highly charged issues fraught with potential danger. But as we take a new look at these complex and challenging issues teachers can begin to respond to the deepest concerns of parents and community protesters and thereby begin to reduce conflict and to resolve controversies.

The most volatile topic of all—religion in the classroom—has generated more rhetoric, more misunderstanding, more parental protests, and more court cases than any other issue. Teachers need accurate information and practical advice and suggestions about making an appropriate place for religion in the classroom while maintaining First Amendment mandates for separation of church and state. It is not enough to develop materials selection policies and procedures for handling complaints, important as those measures are (see Chapter 10). This chapter provides a discussion of the First Amendment and its implications so that educators can more clearly understand what is appropriate for the classroom and how to avoid self-censorship. This chapter also considers specific strategies for handling school-based protests and conflict with respect for a variety of strongly held religious perspectives.

Religion and the Role of Schooling

Parents and community members who hold contrasting views about religion often also hold different views about the role of schooling as preparation for future personal and social responsibilities. Many believe that school is primarily preparation for work, that students need to *learn* so they will be able to *earn*. Others focus on schooling primarily for citizenship, emphasizing the importance of an educated public, upon which democracy depends. We may not consciously focus daily on the extent to which our classroom practices are driven by one view or the other, but many educators and parents believe that we have a responsibility to prepare students for work and for citizenship but also for personal growth and family responsibilities.

Another way to look at the question of the role of schooling is to consider legal definitions about the intellectual atmosphere of the classroom and the relationship between the teacher's role and that of the student. School can be described as primarily a place for *indoctrination* (teaching a set of principles, often imbued with an ideological point of view), a place for *inculcation* (teaching ideas through frequent instruction but without an intentional ideological point of view), or a place for the exchange of ideas or even as a "marketplace" of ideas. Over the years, unfortunately, courts have taken varying positions on this issue, sometimes leaving teachers uncertain as to how to proceed in the classroom.

David Moshman, author of *Children, Education, and the First Amendment* (1989) provides insightful definitions and discussion of these complex issues, especially as they apply to contestable ideas and information. It may be helpful to mentally plot the terms he discusses on a continuum:

| Indoctrination | Inculcation | Noninculcative teaching |

Indoctrination—generally considered unacceptable for public schools—occurs when "reasons and alternatives are omitted because the school (or other indoctrinator) does not want the views it favors to be subjected to critical analysis or rational evaluation. Viewpoints are presented, for example, as if no alternative could possibly be defensible, with the intention that students not only will adopt certain beliefs but will continue to believe them regardless of relevant evidence" (Moshman, 1989, pp. 45–46).

Inculcation carries more innocent motives than *indoctrination,* since "the teacher does not present students with a full range of reasons for believing something or a full range of alternative ideas because the time available is limited or because the students' cognitive abilities are too immature for them to grasp certain justifications or to grapple with competing points of view" (Moshman, 1989, p. 45). Inculcation, then, can be legitimate based on evidence about "how many views and how much information students of a given age are capable of comprehending" (p. 131).

Unlike *indoctrination* and *inculcation,* Moshman insists, *noninculcative teaching* occurs when "a wide diversity of views and a range of information resources are presented. Students are encouraged to pursue their interests and ideas and to express and justify their opinions" (1989, pp. 45–46). Figure 8.1 nudges you to use definitions

FIGURE 8.1   Teacher's Self-Test #3: Roles of Schooling

As a teacher, you will want to consider the roles of schooling that are reflected in your teaching. Actually writing out responses will help you articulate what may otherwise remain fuzzy and vague. Encourage your teaching colleagues to respond, as well. Then compare notes with each other.

1. Which roles of schooling seem most reflected in my teaching?

_____

_____

_____

_____

2. Which roles of schooling best characterize what I seek for my students?

_____

_____

_____

_____

3. Which roles of schooling are reflected in the materials and resources my students work with?

_____

_____

_____

_____

4. What roles of schooling do my colleagues, administrators, parents, and school board members want?

_____

_____

_____

_____

5. Do different parts of my curriculum and some of my students' classroom experiences require different roles of schooling? Do they need to be handled in different ways?

_____

_____

_____

_____

Note: May be photocopied for use; source must be cited: Ellen Brinkley, *Caught off Guard: Teachers Rethinking Censorship and Controversy* (Boston: Allyn and Bacon, 1999).

Moshman provides by considering which roles of schooling are reflected in your own classroom practices and in your school community.

Upon reflection, many of us discover that we inculcate some ideas and values even if we provide an inquiry-based curriculum in which students read widely, discuss freely, and negotiate at least part of the curriculum. Like conservative educators, we may especially agree that although the public school operates as a marketplace of ideas, it is a "special" marketplace—that is, subject to restrictions (see Whitehead, 1994). And like progressive educators, we may recognize the need for inculcating basic facts and uncontested ideas but take the position that many widely accepted, prevailing ideas need to be challenged and alternatives considered. As we begin to tackle the toughest topics—religion in this chapter and moral and social values and intellectual freedom in Chapter 9—it is helpful to weigh what we inculcate, indoctrinate, and/or encourage.

A Place for Religion

Teachers are learning to be inclusive, to celebrate cultural diversity, and to honor multiple ways of knowing. Nevertheless, there is widespread agreement that in most classrooms what is generally omitted from the curriculum is information about the role of religion and religions in society and throughout history. Teachers and parents alike are afraid of religion in the classroom, and consequently classroom discussion of religious ideas seldom takes place. Most teachers, with little sense of what is and what is not appropriate on this issue, simply operate in default mode: When in doubt, leave it out. But real resolutions to conflict and controversy about teaching and learning and about public education involve acknowledging the role religion plays in the lives of many citizens and teaching about the role religions have played in history and in the arts.

Nationally organized groups have for years complained about the omission of religion from the classroom. Christian Coalition publications, for example, regularly cite cases that demonstrate "intolerance toward public expression of faith" (Thomas, 1996, p. 12). A publication of the Traditional Values Coalition itemizes typical complaints from religious conservatives involving students' expression of their faith: high school cheerleaders who were stopped from saying prayers at pep rallies; a second-grade girl who was told by her teacher that she could not discuss God with a friend on the playground; and a high school principal who prohibited a student from wearing a T-shirt imprinted with a Bible passage (Traditional Values Coalition, n.d.). Although many people can decide who they think may be at fault in each case, most would want to seek more information before passing judgment in any of these circumstances.

Professional education organizations have also come to recognize that religions and religious and nonreligious beliefs are too often omitted or are invisible in the classroom. They have found, for example, that publishers are sometimes guilty of "editing works of literature to remove references to God" and even "removing any mention of evolution from biology texts" (Association of Supervision and Curriculum Development, 1987). Scholarly research and opinions conclude that matters of religious faith are generally not handled appropriately and that religion is widely invisible in the classroom. A 1987 study of U.S. government and civics textbooks, conducted by People for the American Way, found that the texts often ignored "questions of belief and value at the heart of people's 'lives and fortunes and sacred honor'" (Carroll et al., 1987).

Warren A. Nord, philosophy professor at the University of North Carolina, contends that "in American public schools and universities students can—and most do—earn high school diplomas, college degrees, M.B.A.s, J.D.s, M.D.s, and Ph.D.s without ever confronting a live religious idea" (1995, p. 1). Similarly, in *The Culture of Disbelief* (1993), Stephen Carter, a Yale law professor, describes a pervasive "trivialization" of religious beliefs and practices and explains the problem teachers face, saying, "The concern to avoid even a hint of forbidden *endorsement* of religion has led to a climate in which teachers are loath to *mention* religion" (p. 206).

Clearly, the prevailing opinion is that religion in the classroom is absent or invisible. My own school experience supports this conclusion. As I grew up, I did not expect my public school teachers to understand or respect my religious beliefs and practices. In retrospect, I believe the reason is partly because I heard at church and at home how godless the rest of society was. It was possible that some of my teachers shared my religious perspective, but day by day in the classroom, discussion of religion and of life's biggest questions just did not happen. Thus, I can identify with students in public schools today who find almost no recognition of their religious ways of knowing, and

" YOU MAY WRITE A REPORT ON ANY INSECT YOU'D LIKE ... EXCEPT, OF COURSE, THE PRAYING MANTIS ! "

I understand what drives some religious conservative parents to lash out in frustration (Brinkley, 1994, 1995).

One way to reduce the attacks on teaching and learning—and perhaps to begin resolving the broader conflicts about public education, as well—is to find a place *within* classrooms for religion. The First Amendment establishes religion as a "legitimate, legally protected form of difference in American society," and students get short-changed when teachers act as though it does not matter (Green, 1996, p. 27). Teachers who have learned to promote classroom tolerance—or even celebration—of diversity of race, ethnicity, and sexual orientation now need to adopt an inclusive stance toward religious and nonreligious views held by students from a variety of faith perspectives. The First Amendment does not call for "celebrating" religion or religious views, of course, but it does require that we be tolerant of them. Thus, as long as we ignore religious views in the classroom, we do not meet our First Amendment obligation to promote tolerance.

The idea of making a place for religion raises many questions in classroom teachers' minds, especially the question: How to accomplish it? We have trouble knowing how to begin thinking about religion in the classroom, since our own past experiences as students and as preservice teachers may have led us to believe that scant, if any, classroom attention should be given to religion. But again, there is remarkable consensus, officially at least, among scholars within the profession. The omission of religion can be addressed by (1) acknowledging religion as an important part of many people's day-by-day experiences and (2) teaching about religions and the role they have played and continue to play in such fields as social studies, literature, and the arts (see Nord, 1995; Carter, 1993; Noddings, 1993; Haynes & Thomas, 1994).

It is important to clarify, however, that acknowledging the role of religion in many people's lives and teaching about religions are not in any way linked to calls from religious conservatives for reinstating school-sponsored prayer and devotional classroom Bible reading or for teaching creationism in science classes. I support neither. But I do believe that there are ways to make a place for religion and religions without jeopardizing the separation of church and state.

Making a place for religion may begin to address the deepest, sometimes unspoken fears, especially those of genuinely concerned religious parents, regardless of their politics. It may reduce some of the explosive tension between parents and schools and reassure parent protesters that their concerns are not disregarded but are taken seriously. If so, individual families, schools, and society will all benefit. To be sure, however, there are some risks involved: Discussing religion and honoring religious pluralism may, of course, frighten or anger extremists from both the political right and left. But the vast majority of parents and citizens will approve and support educators' intention to make a place for religion in the classroom in these ways.

Teaching about Religions

Nord, author of *Religion and American Education: Rethinking a National Dilemma* (1995), has proposed what many would see as a radical idea—that high school students be *required* to take an introductory course in religion. He persuasively argues this controversial position on the grounds that "(1) religion is a tremendously important aspect of human experience; (2) religion is too complex a subject to be handled adequately by natural inclusion (by teachers not educated to teach about it); and (3) religion must be granted at least one required course to offset or balance the conventional secular wisdom so that indoctrination can be avoided" (p. 212). Including religion in the curriculum, Nord has insisted, would ultimately prove to be less controversial than other proposals, since it could help settle the controversy that has been created by the absence of religion (p. 232).

Another proponent of including religion in the curriculum is Nel Noddings, author of *Educating for Intelligent Belief or Unbelief* (1993), who argues that public schools should play a "major role" in teaching about religion. She is careful, however, to explain the need to respect students' rights to "unbelief" as well as to religious belief and to call for balanced presentations and discussions of religious claims and religious "critiques" (p. xv). Making a place for religion in the curriculum is legal and desirable, so long as religious pluralism is the focus and so long as course materials and classroom experiences reflect a clear understanding of the First Amendment and the need for fair treatment for all points of view.

Elective courses in religion are, many believe, a more realistic possibility for public schools than a required religion course. Teachers at St. Louis Park High School (a suburb of Minneapolis) designed a religion curriculum, *Religion in Human Culture,* when they realized how uneasy they felt about the Christmas trees, caroling, and gift exchange that took place in a school in which one-third of the students were Jewish (Carnes, 1994). The teachers first helped develop a policy that banned religious observances in school but then encouraged "descriptive, balanced inclusion of religious subject matter in the curriculum" (Carnes, 1994, p. 31) and developed the World Religions class to help achieve this goal.

The World Religions course begins by working with secular ideas and experiences students bring with them to the class. Students look first at secular symbols—such as the flag, a dollar sign, a heart, and so on. They are asked to think about something that is important to them and to find a physical embodiment of it to share with the class. Each student presents his or her symbol and applies a "three-part model" to it—observing, describing, and interpreting—as a way to realize that expression of abstract ideas is tricky and calls for developing symbols (Carnes, 1994, p. 30). By the end of the course, students report that they gain "a broader understanding of diverse religions and their expression in individual lives" (p. 32).

Other teachers in the same school district have begun exploring religious elements within a variety of content areas. A history teacher, for example, includes primary sources and discussion of the spiritual dimensions of the Native American Ghost Dance so that it does not appear as simply a "weird thing that just happened" (Carnes, 1994, p. 32). Students understand the religious and the historical context when they learn about the boarding schools Native American children were placed in and the effects of Christian denominations dividing reservations into missionary "territories" (p. 32). Students from India have drawn on their religious experience when they tell their classmates about the philosophical traditions that influenced Transcendentalist writers of nineteenth-century New England, and Cambodian students have explained views about the Vietnam War from a Buddhist perspective. "The basic idea," teachers report, "is that different cultures are supposed to learn from each other" (p. 33).

In other parts of the country, new resources and professional development programs are helping teachers who are at a loss to know how to discuss religious issues in ways that are both enlightening and impartial (Ruenzel, 1996). For example, the 3Rs Project—which focuses on rights, responsibilities, and respect—provides workshops where teachers can learn about appropriate, noncoercive discussions of religion in the classroom. Such discussions may focus on the negative as well as the positive historical influences of religion. Charles Haynes, a founder and leader of the 3Rs Project, has said, "It's dangerous for kids not to understand religion. After all, how can you defend the rights of people you disagree with if you don't have at least some understanding of who they are and what they believe?" (Ruenzel, 1996, p. 33).

Teaching about religion can, of course, go wrong. A high school social studies teacher in New York has been accused of improperly bringing his beliefs into class (Hill, 1997). The teacher claimed to heal people with his shamanic powers, a skill he apparently learned at school district expense. He admits that he sometimes mentions shamanism in class, such as when he teaches Native American culture. And he does not deny that he went into "a light trance one day, shaking rattles and drumming to heal an athlete's afflicted knee." Clearly, such classroom experiences are *not* consistent with guidelines for teaching about religion that have been established by the National Council for Social Studies (see Figure 8.2).

Separation of Church and State

The First Amendment to the U.S. Constitution is:

> Congress shall make no law respecting an establishment of religion, or prohibiting the free exercise thereof; or abridging the freedom of speech or of the press; or the right of the people to assemble, and to petition the Government for a redress of grievances.

Finding an appropriate place for religious and nonreligious views in public schools is not easy. Many suggestions are offered later in this chapter to help you begin that process. It is just as important, however, to know how to *eliminate* religious expression and activities that are not appropriate for public schools. Consider, for example, three recent cases:

- In a high school hallway, a Warner Sallman "Head of Christ" portrait of Jesus hung for 30 years. A student protested that the picture should not be there (Mah, 1994).
- A parent protested when a prayer was used in her child's Thanksgiving program. School officials insisted that what the parent protested was a song rather than a prayer. The words of the "song": "Thank you for the world so sweet, thank you for the food we eat, thank you for the birds that sing, thank you God for everything" (Reen, 1993).

FIGURE 8.2   National Council for the Social Studies Guidelines for Teaching about Religion

1. Study about religions should strive for awareness and understanding of the diversity of religions, religious experiences, religious expressions, and the reasons for particular expressions of religious beliefs within a society or culture.
2. Study about religions should stress the influence of religions on history, culture, the arts, and contemporary issues.
3. Study about religions should permit and encourage a comprehensive and balanced examination of the entire spectrum of ideas and attitudes pertaining to religion as a component of human culture.
4. Study about religions should investigate a broad range, both geographic and chronological, of religious beliefs, practices, and values.
5. Study about religions should examine the religious dimension of human existence in its broader cultural context, including its relation to economic, political, and social institutions as well as its relation to the arts, language, and literature.
6. Study about religions should deal with the world's religions from the same perspective (that is, beginnings, historical development, sacred writings, beliefs, practices, values, and impact on history, culture, contemporary issues, and the arts).
7. Study about religions should be objective.
8. Study about religions should be academic in nature, stressing student awareness and understanding, not acceptance and/or conformity.
9. Study about religions should emphasize the necessity and importance of tolerance, respect, and mutual understanding in a nation and world of diversity.
10. Study about religions should be descriptive, nonconfessional, and conducted in an environment free of advocacy.
11. Study about religions should seek to develop and utilize the various skills, attitudes, and abilities that are essential to history and the social sciences (that is, locating, classifying, interpreting data; keen observation; critical reading, listening, and thinking; questioning; and effective communication.)
12. Study about religions should be academically responsible and pedagogically sound, utilizing accepted methods and materials of the social sciences, history, and literature.
13. Study about religions should involve a range of materials that provide a balanced and fair treatment of the subject and distinguish between confessional and historical fact.
14. Study about religions should be conducted by qualified and certified teachers selected for their academic knowledge, their sensitivity and empathy for differing religious points of view, and their understanding of the Supreme Court's decision pertaining to religious practices and study about religions in the public schools.

Source: Gaddy et al., 1996. © National Council for the Social Studies. Reprinted by permission.

- A mother of six protested against the intercom and classroom prayers and religious Bible classes in her children's public schools, saying, "I simply do not want the school telling my children how and when to pray." Most of the local residents in her new community did not support her efforts, and she reported that her children were ridiculed by classmates. Her son, for example, was called "football head" after a teacher made him wear headphones to drown out the prayers broadcast on the school's intercom (Holland, 1994).

Each case involves the separation of church and state—a key issue as important today as it has been in the past but one about which many classroom teachers know little. Most of us were taught as preservice teachers that such distinctions are important, but too many of us paid too little attention to those undergraduate lectures and textbook chapters, since we did not plan to ask our students to pray or read the Bible in class anyway. Now caught up in the hectic schedule and daily demands of school life, many teachers know only what is in the local newspaper about court decisions that have the potential to change dramatically what we can and cannot do in the classroom.

Prayer and Bible Reading

An important place to begin, especially as we work with conservative Christian parents and community members, is to develop a clear understanding of the facts and the implications of the 1962 and 1963 cases banning school-sponsored prayer and devotional Bible reading in the classroom:

- In 1962, the Supreme Court struck down the daily recitation of a generic prayer that had been adopted in the 1950s by the New York State Board of Regents: "Almighty God, we acknowledge our dependence upon Thee, and we beg Thy blessings upon us, our parents, our teacher, and our Country" (*Engel v. Vitale,* 370 U.S. 421 [1962]).
- In 1963, the Court ruled as unconstitutional the practices of reciting the Lord's Prayer and reading aloud sections of the Bible for religious purposes in school (*Abington School District v. Schempp,* 374 U.S. 203 [1963]). The Court found that these school exercises had the effect of "sponsoring" a religion and declared that the First Amendment "requires the state to be neutral in its relations with groups of religious believers and nonbelievers."

It is especially important that teachers know that the 1962 and 1963 decisions did *not* have many of the effects attributed to them by some religious conservatives and by some who hold nonreligious and antireligious viewpoints. There is a common misconception that the 1962 prayer decision banned religion from public schools. But the Supreme Court, in fact, warned that its decision should not be read as hostility to religion. The judge endorsing the majority decision wrote that the Court was *protecting* religion from governmental interference, not protecting government—in this case, public schools—from religion. In 1963, Justice William Brennan made clear the intent of the Court:

> The holding of the Court today plainly does not foreclose teaching about the Holy Scriptures or about the differences between religious sects in classes in literature or history. Indeed, whether or not the Bible is involved, it would be impossible to teach meaningfully many subjects in the social sciences or the humanities without some mention of religion. To what extent, and at what points in the curriculum, religious materials should be cited are matters which the courts ought to entrust very largely to the experienced officials who superintend our Nation's public schools.... Any attempt to impose rigid limits upon the mention of God

or references to the Bible in the classroom would be fraught with dangers. (Justice William Brennan, *Abington School District v. Schempp,* 374 U.S. 203, 300-01 [1963])

Just from Justice Brennan's statement, we can learn that:

- Schools are not supposed to be hostile to religion.
- It is okay to teach about the Bible and other sacred texts as appropriate within the curriculum.
- It is okay to teach about religious groups as appropriate within the curriculum.
- The 1962 and 1963 decisions do not at all mean that social studies and humanities classes should omit teaching about religion.
- Local school district leaders should be responsible for decisions about using religious materials in the curriculum. Notice, however, that the statement does not say that individual classroom teachers can make such decisions arbitrarily on their own.
- It is not necessarily wrong to talk about a supreme being or about a sacred text in the classroom.

The misconception about the intent of the 1962 and 1963 decisions has been used to the advantage of those from both extremes: Religious conservatives have used the misconception to promote religious-rights amendments or prayer-in-schools amendments (see Chapter 11). And those who are personally nonreligious or who are antireligious—that is, who view religious belief as a hindrance to human development and/or society—use the misconception as an excuse not to include religion at all in the classroom. On this issue, those in the middle—that is, those who oppose new constitutional amendments but favor acknowledging religion and teaching about religions—are taking a radical but realistic position that could lead to dramatic resolution to longstanding conflict.

Continued Debate

In spite of the clarity of Justice Brennan's 1960s explanation, the debate continues over the church-and-state issues of prayer and Bible reading. Many religious conservatives favor student-led prayer, with a teacher present, or even favor teacher-led prayers. By contrast, many others who argue in favor of finding a place for religion in public schools *resist* a return to public prayer and devotional Bible reading to the classroom (Nord, 1995; Gaddy, Hall, & Marzano, 1996; Carter, 1993). Charles Haynes has called the drive for public school prayer "the wrong solution to a real and urgent problem: confusion about the proper role of religion in public education" (cited in Gaddy, Hall, & Marzano, 1996, p. 193). What we need, then, is not a constitutional amendment that would eliminate separation of church and state nor an amendment that would permit school-sponsored or endorsed public prayer. Haynes has maintained that the push for school prayer constitutional amendments may disappear "when freedom of conscience is truly protected in American public life and when education about religion is returned to the curriculum" (Gaddy, Hall, & Marzano, 1996, p. 193).

Sorting Out the Historical Facts

Disagreements about separation of church and state almost always focus at some point on the intent of the United State founders. Religious conservatives often build their arguments on what they have learned from a popular video series titled "The Foundations of American Government." The videos feature historical lectures by David Barton (1992), who argued that the founders never considered the possibility that the country would be led by anyone with a faith other than Protestant Christianity or by a nonreligious person. Therefore, Barton has insisted, freedom of religion does not mean that religion should be separate from the state. According to this argument, when the founders used the word *religion* in writing the Constitution and the Bill of Rights, what they really meant was religious *denomination,* in which case the founders assumed a link between the Christian religion and government—which would mean a link between Christian religion and public schools. What the founders were concerned primarily about, in Barton's view, was being sure that a particular Protestant denomination, such as the Episcopal Church, could not be established as a state religion. Barton says that because modern courts misunderstand the founders' intentions, they have mistakenly ruled against the practice of religion in government.

Barton's arguments are refuted by Robert S. Alley (1996) who conceded that there was controversy among the founders over whether a particular denomination should become the national, established church. However, the bigger issue at stake was, according to Alley, whether *any* church should be "established" (pp. 16–17). Alley also admitted that James Madison did at one time publicly support the establishment of the Anglican Church in Virginia (which included what is now West Virginia, Kentucky, and land over to the Mississippi River). But the reason for Madison's support for this establishment, according to Alley, is that Madison felt sure that dissenting groups—Methodists, Baptists, and Presbyterians—would resist the establishment of the Anglican Church, a single denomination, which in turn would eventually lead to a religious liberty law, which Madison strongly supported.

In 1777, two competing plans were proposed for Virginia: Jefferson's plan "rejected any civil authority in matters of religion" and affirmed complete freedom of belief and worship, thus expressing concern about protecting religion from government interference (Peterson, 1994, p. 119). The other plan authorized taxation in support of a "plural establishment" of the *Christian* religion regardless of denomination (p. 119). After years of debate, Madison argued persuasively in 1785, "Who does not see that the same authority which can establish Christianity, in exclusion of all other religions, may establish with the same ease any particular sect of Christians, in exclusion of all other sects?" (p. 120). Jefferson's bill favoring religious liberty, supported by Madison, became law in 1786.

The historical review Barton has offered in his video series is designed ultimately to challenge the 1962 and 1963 rulings on public prayer and devotional Bible reading in public schools. Barton's lectures use graphs and charts to portray a cause-effect relationship between the 1962 and 1963 Supreme Court rulings on prayer and Bible reading and subsequent increases in divorce rates, teen pregnancy, and violent crimes. These arguments and the motives of those who offer them have been challenged by

Stephen Carter, who pointed out fallacies of Barton's arguments and insisted there are no reliable data to support the theory that prayer in school or a moment of silence in the future would have a positive effect. Removing prayer, Carter has explained, did not *cause* increases in teen pregnancy, youth violence, and drug use, just as school-sponsored prayer prior to 1962 didn't *prevent* such atrocities as "slavery, Jim Crow, lynchings, child labor, the oppression of women, and much more" (Carter, 1994, p. 64).

Alley has insisted that the efforts to change the First Amendment to eliminate the concept of separation of church and state would not achieve the effect their advocates seek, but such efforts would instead threaten the "fundamental principles of religious non-establishment and freedom" that the First Amendment founders provided, would promote a "degradation of the nation's public schools," and would diminish "any sense of national identity that transcends narrow sectarian divisions" (Alley, 1996, p. 5).

Treating Religious and Nonreligious Beliefs in a Neutral Way

The First Amendment, still in place and unamended, dictates that government—including public schools—must neither promote nor inhibit religious beliefs and practices. The courts have made it clear that religion is a special case that should be handled neutrally by governmental agencies. Classroom teachers know that neutrality is difficult indeed to achieve, but in the case of religion, by law, neutrality must be our goal and we must find ways to achieve it.

The appearance of neutrality may have been easier to achieve in past generations. When more teachers routinely adopted a transmission model of teaching and learning, they designed or followed a prescribed curricular plan, often using just one comprehensive textbook for each subject area. So long as many classroom teachers stuck to publishers' lesson plans and used single texts, focusing on inculcating the information therein, the burden for achieving neutrality fell primarily on the publisher of the curricular materials.

When teachers adopt a constructivist model of teaching and learning, they depend less on a single adopted textbook and more on a variety of sources and resources. More important, they rely on their own ability to design classroom learning experiences so that they can tailor the curriculum at least to some extent to the needs and interests of particular students. While many teachers strive to achieve classrooms that are built substantially on an "exchange of ideas" view of the role of schooling, one of their most difficult tasks in such an environment is to create a classroom community that is characterized by neutrality toward religion and other controversial issues. Some educators argue that neutrality—not only about religion but about morality and politics and virtually any subject—is in fact impossible (Shor & Freire, 1987, p. 174). From this perspective, even when we think we are being neutral, we are actually working from a set of assumptions that constitutes taking a position.

Nord and others contend that few teachers currently manage to establish classroom communities that provide genuine neutrality. Classroom discussions and textbooks that ignore, omit, or trivialize religious perspectives are not neutral. To be religiously neutral, according to Nord, textbooks must meet the following criteria:

- Take seriously religious and nonreligious ways of understanding any question that is religiously contested;
- Characterize each alternative fairly, from "the inside," that is, as advocates of that point of view would characterize it;
- Give sufficient space in the text (and time in the classroom) to a position so that students can make sense of it in the context of supporting evidence and assumptions; and
- Not take one side. (Nord, 1995, p. 167)

Nord later argued that fairness and neutrality should characterize the curriculum as a *whole,* assuming a class uses multiple texts, rather than to apply necessarily to individual texts or experiences (1995, p. 237).

Rethinking Secular Humanism

A generation of school protesters has charged public schools of not being neutral because they teach secular humanism. Over the years, educators and the courts have grown weary and impatient with this overused charge, especially when it has been applied to anything that is not perceived as consistent with the protesters' belief system. Today's protesters sometimes substitute the "New Age" label to describe whatever seems at odds with their own beliefs, but the effect is essentially the same.

Haig A. Bosmajian, editor of the *First Amendment in the Classroom Series,* explains that protesters who have become plaintiffs in court cases contend that anything that is considered "secular" or "humanist" can be considered "anti-religious" (1987, p. 180). Using the terms in this way would allow protesters to divide all classroom texts, ideas, and experiences according to whether they are consistent with the protesters' religion or whether they reflect "anti-religion" (i.e., secular humanism) (p. 180). However, Supreme Court Justice Jackson explained in 1948 that there are "256 separate and substantial religious bodies" in the United States. He warned, "If we are to eliminate everything that is objectionable to any of these warring sects or inconsistent with any of their doctrines, we will leave public education in shreds. Nothing but educational confusion and a discrediting of the public school system can result" (Bosmajian, 1987, p. 184).

Bosmajian has rejected the protesters' dualistic thinking that allows them to label everything either *religious* or *antireligious.* He has insisted that many "secular" materials and concepts are instead *nonreligious* and thus carry a more neutral label. He has warned, "If the [First Amendment] establishment clause ["Congress shall make no law respecting an establishment of religion"] is to have any meaning, distinction must be drawn to recognize not simply 'religious' and 'anti-religious,' but 'non-religious' government civility as well" (p. 181).

These are helpful distinctions for teachers to remember in accurately character-izing the overall effect of curricular materials and classroom experiences. Bosmajian explained further that, in light of a case fought over the novel *The Learning Tree,* a text as a whole must be examined to determine if it should be characterized as *secular human-ist* or *anti-Christian* and that individual works must be considered within the context of the course as a whole or of the school curriculum. Objectivity must be determined in terms of how "partisan, subjective material is presented, handled, and integrated into the school curriculum" (p. 183).

Thus, we need to explain carefully to parents and to students that, as Bosmajian explains, the study of Greek mythology does not *advance* pantheism. And teaching about the divine right of kings "does not endorse a particular dogma, although one is neces-sarily explored" (p. 183). The issue is not whether a particular work "disapproves of any particular religious vision," Bosmajian explained, but whether its "inclusion in the public school curriculum indicates, intentionally or not, that the government joins in that disapproval" (p. 183).

The key to establishing neutrality is to apply the neutrality test to the content of a course or of a class as a whole. We cannot—and would not want to—teach in class-rooms where there is an attempt to provide only neutral information and ideas. Doing so would censor learning. Our central focus, then, should be on examining the overall effect of the curriculum and on being sure that the overall curriculum, not necessarily individual sources, is characterized as neutral in terms of religion.

This is not to say that curricular neutrality is easy to achieve. I have been struck by recent discussion of the secular humanism issue that gives more credence to pro-testers' arguments that the curriculum as a whole has not been neutral. Nord has argued that the overall effect of public school curricula can, often unintentionally, promote an "underlying worldview of modern education" that reflects what some have called the "religion of secular humanism" (1995, p. 160). Admitting that public education "does not indoctrinate students against religion by overtly attacking it or by promoting a militant secularism," Nord has asserted that often the effect of an under-lying worldview of modern education "removes the awareness of religious possibili-ties; it makes religious accounts of the world seem implausible, even inconceivable" (p. 188).

Moshman similarly has asserted that "the systematic exclusion of religion from public school textbooks may not be intended to inculcate secular humanism but it nevertheless constitutes a significant deviation from government neutrality toward religion" (1989, p. 149). He further explained that nonreligious ideologies such as secular humanism "may nonetheless serve the same role" as religious ones and insisted that, "If the First Amendment is to prevent government intrusion into peo-ple's lives, it must require government neutrality not only among religions (narrowly defined) but between religion and anything that serves as an alternative to religion" (p. 145).

Since 1971, neutrality has been determined on the basis of the three-part test that was established in the *Lemon v. Kurtzman* case. To be considered neutral, a text or classroom experience needs to:

1. Be adopted with a secular purpose
2. Have a principal or primary effect that neither advances nor inhibits religion
3. Not result in an "excessive entanglement of government with religion" (*Lemon v. Kurtzman,* 403, U.S. 602 [1971])

Some say that the *Lemon* test has resulted in illogical rulings, however, and has generated considerable confusion in deciding what constitutes secular purpose, primary effect, and "excessive entanglement." They recommend that the "endorsement test" formulated by Justice Sandra Day O'Connor be used instead. The endorsement test asks whether a government action (such as a classroom resource or practice) is invalid if it creates the perception that government (i.e., a school) is endorsing or disapproving a religion. It specifically asks whether the activity conveys a "message to non-adherents that they are outsiders, not full members of the political community, and an accompanying message to adherents that they are insiders, favored members of the political community" (Whitehead, 1994, p. 221).

Unfortunately, neither the *Lemon* test nor the O'Connor alternative provide enough clarity to serve as a definitive guide for classroom decisions. Achieving neutrality is an elusive task at best, and we need to think through carefully the ways that we can establish and maintain classrooms that are genuinely neutral in regard to religion. Nord (1995) has offered what can be arranged as a continuum of eight markers to help teachers weigh the religious neutrality of a range of positions that might be taken in terms of curricula, texts, and approaches to topics (see Figure 8.3). The following are my comments regarding these eight items:

Commentary

1. Many teachers would agree that religion can be ignored in some circumstances. Being sure religion is not ignored when the subject matter is contested is a bigger challenge.
2. For teachers who are personally hostile to religion, sometimes the biggest challenge is to avoid treating religion in a hostile way or reducing it to an insignificant irrelevancy.
3. A bare mention is appropriate when religion is just one of several equally important factors or influences. When religion plays a bigger role, the key is to provide enough context and detail from the perspective of the religious persons involved.
4. **4, 5,** and **6.** Generally, teachers feel most comfortable adopting one or more of these neutral positions as they decide how to approach specific topics, materials, and classroom circumstances.
7. Teachers who take strong stands on peace and social justice issues often take this position about selected issues. The key is to be careful *not* to take such stands about religious beliefs in the classroom.
8. This position is appropriate, if at all, only in religious or private schools.

FIGURE 8.3   Gauging Religious Neutrality: Teachers, Texts, and Courses

____ 1. Religion might be *ignored*. In some texts and courses—say in arithmetic or drivers' education, where the subject matter is not religiously contested—this is not a problem. But if the claims or theories or methods of a subject are religiously contested and the text or the teacher ignores religion, then neutrality and fairness have been violated.

____ 2. Religion might be discussed, but only *reductively*... in terms of some worldview hostile to religion. This might happen, for example, if Freudian categories (ego, superego, id) are used to explain religion in a psychology class or if a historian explains only in fully secular terms why certain events happened. If the text or teacher fails to provide students with the alternative religious account(s), they are neither neutral nor fair.

____ 3. Religion might receive *bare mention*, in which case it is neither ignored nor explained reductively, but it is taken seriously (from the inside, as a contender for truth). The text or teacher might mention some fairly straightforward facts relating to religion (such as, that ancient Hebrews were monotheists). But if students are given little, if any, sense of why this is the case, and the text or the teacher uses a secular worldview to explain the subject at hand, then neutrality is violated.

____ 4. The text or teacher might convey to students an understanding of religion(s) *from the inside*, that is, as described by those who practice the religion(s).

____ 5. The text or teacher might consider religious ways of understanding the world as live contenders for the truth, to be argued about and critically assessed. If the text or teacher refrains from drawing conclusions, both fairness and neutrality have been achieved.

____ 6. A teacher might offer his or her own *personal conclusion* about the truth or significance of religious claims, perhaps in response to a student's question, but not argue for it, and certainly not insist that students accept it as an official conclusion of the course.

____ 7. The teacher or textbook author might actively *argue* for particular conclusions after all the relevant views have been taken seriously but stop short of making them the official view. In effect, the teacher's voice is added to the conversation. This is certainly more than the expression of a personal view: it is the argument of someone with some authority in the subject, citing evidence and building a coherent case. In this case neutrality is not defined by the teacher's or author's arguments or conclusions but by the structure of the complete course or text—by its fairness, its openness to conclusions other than the teacher's or author's, and by the weight and priority given the teacher's or author's reasoning and conclusions.

____ 8. The teacher or textbook author might consider all points of view fairly, argue for the truth of a particular point of view, and make that the final and *official conclusion* of the course or text. Now neutrality is clearly dropped.

Source: From *Religion and American Education: Rethinking an American Dilemma* by Warren A. Nord (pp. 249–251). Copyright © 1995 by the University of North Carolina Press. Used by permission of the publisher.

Parents and Community Members

When parent or community protesters challenge curriculum on the basis of theologically based concerns, we need to respond thoughtfully and carefully. As *citizens,* we might be tempted to criticize protesters' theological views, but as teachers we should not—no matter how attacked we feel—respond by counterattacking parents' religious views. Religious beliefs and practices are constitutionally protected in almost every case, even when worshippers handle poisonous snakes as an expression of their faith. Legally, we must respect the right of parents to hold whatever religious beliefs they like. Sometimes teachers freeze up when parent protesters link curricular challenges to religious beliefs. But we need to think ahead of time how to handle such occasions. We can explain—possibly drawing on the language of this chapter—the ways that our curricula are not antireligious but are appropriately neutral toward religious beliefs and practices.

When working with religious-conservative parents who are genuinely concerned about their individual child's classroom experience, sometimes teachers who profess a religious faith can call attention to the fact that their teaching practices may be consistent with, and in some cases even embody, Christian theology. I have rejected much of the fundamentalist Christian orthodoxy I grew up with, but I have thought a lot about the theological dimensions of what I do in the classroom and find no inconsistency between the Christian faith and best classroom practices as I understand them. Both value respect for individual students as people with needs, interests, and talents. Both value the promise of each student. Both value reading as a means to personally engage with written texts and ideas, and both value writing and oral language as a means to express what is important.

But one thing is clear: As teachers, we can do a better job of acknowledging the possibility of religion in our students' lives, and we can do a better job of teaching about religion. We can learn to be sensitive to the religious insights that students express. For example, child psychiatrist Robert Coles described a 10-year-old Hopi girl who talked to him about how the sky watches people. Apparently, she had been told by her teacher that God lived in the sky. But when her teacher asked her where *her* God lived, she responded, "I don't know." She explained her answer to Coles by pointing out that "her own God *is* the sky ... *is* the sun" (Coles, 1990, p. 25). When Coles asked her if she had offered this explanation to her teacher, she said, "No ... because she thinks God is a person. If I'd told her, she'd give us that smile ... the smile that says to us, 'You kids are cute, you're dumb; you're different—and you're all wrong!'" (p. 25).

Teachers do not pretend to be able to solve all the controversial issues that must be addressed within the larger community and society, but they do need to consider the place of religion in the curriculum. Society as a whole will benefit if students learn at school that religion has played and continues to play a role in history and culture. School districts may then discover less animosity from religious parents, and public education may be viewed more positively by parents and the public.

WHAT CAN YOU DO TO TEACH ABOUT RELIGIONS?

1. *Become better informed.* When teachers have ignored religious references in textbooks or avoided discussing religion for fear of violating what they mistakenly think the Supreme Court has ruled, there is a clear need for more and better information. We owe it to our students and ourselves to become better informed. (Some of the suggestions in this chapter come from the *Religion in the Public Schools: A Joint Statement of Current Law* [1995] that is reprinted in its entirety for your reference at the end of this chapter.)

2. *Accept the fact that religion is a sensitive issue, but it is not too hot to handle in an informed, descriptive, and impartial way* (Association for Supervision and Curriculum Development [ASCD], 1987). According to Carter, religion in public schools is a "minefield," but keeping religious and nonreligious views out of the classroom is not the answer (1993, p. 210). ASCD panelists pointed out, "Almost any classroom topic has the potential of outraging someone's sensitivity, trespassing on someone's wish to remain ignorant, or challenging someone's beliefs. This risk is routinely ignored in most school offerings—except those topics related to religion. . . . Educators must reexamine the assumption that any particular area of knowledge is too risky for the classroom. This assumption is subversive to the purpose of schooling and threatening to the growth of the intellect" (1987).

3. *Seek out professional development that is needed to help teachers know how to handle First Amendment issues.* Teachers in school districts that decide to make new efforts to acknowledge religious and nonreligious beliefs need help to develop the knowledge, skills, attitudes, and confidence to effectively include religion in the curriculum.

4. *Respect appropriate classroom boundaries.* ASCD panelists recommended that teachers "exert extreme care to avoid assuming the role of the family and the religious institution in students' religious, spiritual, and moral education and development" and reminded teachers that "your chief task in teaching about religion is to help students better understand faiths other than their own and the roles of religions in the life of their nation and that of other cultures" (1987).

5. *Take into consideration your own religious or nonreligious views.* In some ways, teachers who are strongly religious may seem to have an advantage, but some of them have gone out of their way *not* to talk about their religious faith out of fear they will say or do too much. It is especially difficult for Christian fundamentalist teachers whose evangelistic impulses may tell them that the best thing they can do for other human beings is to share the gospel (good news of salvation) with them. On the other hand, teachers who strongly oppose religion need to be just as careful about influencing students' attitudes and beliefs. Their antireligious impulses may be to nudge students away from what they perceive to be naive beliefs.

6. *Become as well informed as you can about what is and what is not appropriate at school for teachers in exercising religious freedom.* Some teachers overstep the bounds. When a fifth-grade teacher read his Bible during 15-minute silent reading, his principal told him to stop (Strope & Broadwell, 1990, p. 40). The school board said the behavior would violate the establishment clause. Eventually, the case ended up in court, where the court balanced the teacher's rights to read the Bible against his students' rights to be free of religious influence or indoctrination in the classroom. The court—noting the great influence teachers have as role models, especially for children— upheld the principal's mandate (p. 40). The same teacher had put two books into the classroom library, which were later removed because they were "considered strictly religious books with no secular qualities" (p. 42). Interestingly, the Bible had been removed from the school library, but it was put back based on the court's ruling that the school library is a "mirror of the human race, a repository of the works of scientists, leaders, and philosophers," and the Bible is considered by many "a major work of literature, history, ethics, theology, and philosophy. It has a legitimate, if not a necessary, place in the American public school library" (p. 42).

7. *Be prepared to respond when students ask tough questions.* When students ask, "But is it true?" or "What happens when we die?" or "Who made God?" the only safe answers may at first be frustrating for children who seek certainty: "Well, many people believe that . . . and on the other hand, many others think . . . " (Carter, 1993, p. 209). Noddings has recommended saying, "I believe . . . " or "So-and-so says. . . . " In terms of historical reporting, one might say, "What we know from what's been reported is . . . " or "What I'm aware of is . . . " (1993, p. xv). When working with college students, who are legally viewed as adults, some university leaders have argued that instructors and professors "should be open and direct in expressing their own religious convictions, when they have relevance either to the subject under study or to a student's concern" (Hoekema, 1996, p. 36). Instructors, Hoekema has insisted, "should be obliged to acknowledge their religious commitments when they bear on the subject under study." This acknowledgment seems especially important, given that within a class group there may be a student—or professor—who shares the views of militant atheists, Christians, Jews, Wiccans, or New Age mystics (p. 36).

8. *Be sure the study of religion is pluralistic.* "Pluralism involves the coexistence of comparable and competing positions that cannot be reconciled. Pluralism acknowledges that different persons and different groups may quite literally inhabit irreducibly different worlds" (Kliever, 1988, p. 9).

9. *Teach comparative religion.* The study of religion must not be structured by arranging various religions in an "evolutionary schema leading up to one normative tradition" or that reduces multiple religions to "one metaphysical essence of religion" (Kliever, 1988, p. 10).

10. *As much as possible, integrate teaching about religion and religions across the curriculum.* Include materials in reading and social studies curricula that demonstrate respect for religious pluralism and that ask students to learn about basic beliefs and the history of major religions. Teach the Bible, the Koran, the Torah, and other sacred texts, as literature, and teach about religion as both a positive and a negative force in history.

11. *Teach about creationism in social studies, comparative religion, or literature classes.* Science teachers may not teach creationism as science or refuse to teach evolution, and no teachers may ridicule students' religious explanations for life on earth.

12. *Teach about religious holidays and celebrate the secular aspects of the holidays.* You may use holiday dramatic productions that emphasize the cultural aspects of the holidays, but do not use the classroom to observe the holidays as religious events.

13. *Be open and honest with parents and community leaders about what, where, and when the school teaches about religion* (ASCD, 1987).

14. *Establish neutrality toward religion and nonreligion within the curriculum as a whole.* You can use individual sources and resources that are not neutral when multiple resources reflect multiple religious perspectives and worldviews.

15. *Display a religious passage such as the Ten Commandments on the wall of the classroom only if it is a temporary display for an educational purpose.* Similarly, display religious symbols only on a temporary basis as part of an academic program.

16. *Use religious music as part of an academic program, but do not use religious music to promote religious belief.* Lynn, Stern, and Thomas (1995) explained, "Sacred music may be sung or played as part of the academic study of music. School concerts that present a variety of selections may include religious selections. Concerts should avoid programs dominated by religious music, especially when they coincide with a particular religious holiday" (pp. 17–18).

17. *Include realistic fiction, historical fiction, biography, and nonfiction (also autobiography, diaries, other primary sources) that contain religious and spiritual themes and information.*

18. *Push for the creation of well-researched print and audiovisual materials about religion that are accurate, objective, honest, fair, and interesting* (ASCD, 1987).

HOW CAN YOU AND YOUR SCHOOL DISTRICT ACKNOWLEDGE RELIGION AND NONRELIGION?

1. *Accept the fact that religion and religious beliefs are part of many people's lives.* Respect the religious beliefs and practices—or the lack of faith—of students, parents, and colleagues.

2. *Excuse individual students from lessons that are objectionable to the student or parent on the basis of religion, following school district guidelines.* Also release students for off-premises religious instruction, according to school district policy.

3. *Protect the rights of students, both those who wish to speak on religious matters as well as those who do not wish to be compelled to listen to a sermon* (Lynn, Stern, & Thomas, 1995, p. 22).

4. *Rule out-of-order religious remarks irrelevant to the subject at hand but do not reject or correct students' work because it includes religious symbols or addresses religious themes.* Intercede to stop students' speech about religion if it turns into religious harassment aimed at a student or a small group of students (repeated invitations "in the face of a request to stop" constitutes harassment), but do not silence (or endorse or ridicule or rule out of bounds) students' remarks about views about religion or about abortion, and so forth (*Religion in the Public Schools,* 1995).

5. *Refuse to stereotype and to make assumptions about individual students and/or parents on the basis of their religious beliefs or practices.*

6. *When appropriate to the content area, accept—without discouraging or encouraging—students' written assignments about religion or religious experiences.* Do not limit students' expressive writing experiences (e.g., personal reflections and narratives, journal and log entries) and inquiry projects to nonreligious topics. Be sure students feel free to research religious topics and issues if such a project fits within the curricular guidelines.

7. *Promote tolerance and equality of multi-religious and nonreligious beliefs, being careful not to suggest either that religious belief matters or that it does not matter.* Be committed to the concept of a pluralistic and democratic society that accepts diverse religious beliefs and practices. Teachers must not engage in religious activities with students or participate in religious club activities (see the Appendix). Do not encourage or discourage participation such as in "see you at the pole" activities, and do not give outsiders access to the classroom to distribute religious or antireligious literature.

HOW CAN STUDENTS EXPRESS AND EXERCISE RELIGIOUS OR NONRELIGIOUS BELIEF?

1. *Students can pray at school.* Lynn, Stern, and Thomas have pointed out, "Nondisruptive individual prayer is permissible in the public school," but "asking schools to endorse such activities or imposing them on students who do not wish to participate simply cannot be accommodated within our constitutional system" (1995, p. 13).

2. *Students can discuss religious, nonreligious, or antireligious views, and they can present information about religion in the classroom.* They can express religious or antireligious beliefs in reports, homework, and artwork. They can even try to persuade their peers about religious topics and invite them to church. But they cannot conduct a religious service, and all students should be free of unwelcome religious persuasion in the classroom (*Religion in the Public Schools,* 1995).

3. *Students can distribute religious literature to schoolmates at a reasonable time and place as for all nonschool literature.* Students may also form religious clubs that can both meet and have access to the media to announce club meetings if the school receives federal funds and permits any other student noncurricular club to meet during noninstructional time (*Religion in the Public Schools,* 1995).

4. *Students can wear T-shirts, and so forth, with religious messages (that is, clothing carrying religious messages should not be singled out for suppression), and they may wear religious attire (such as yarmulkes and head scarves).* They also can refuse to wear gym clothes if they object on the religious grounds that the gym clothes are immodest (*Religion in the Public Schools,* 1995).

Religion in the Public Schools: A Joint Statement of Current Law

The Constitution permits much private religious activity in and about the public schools. Unfortunately, this aspect of constitutional law is not as well known as it should be. Some say that the Supreme Court has declared the public schools "religion-free zones" or that the law is so murky that school officials cannot know what is legally permissible. The former claim is simply wrong. And as to the latter, while there are some difficult issues, much has been settled. It is also unfortunately true that public school officials, due to their busy schedules, may not be as fully aware of this body of law as they could be. As a result, in some school districts some of these rights are not being observed.

The organizations whose names appear below span the ideological, religious and political spectrum. They nevertheless share a commitment both to the freedom of religious practice and to the separation of church and state such freedom requires. In that spirit, we offer this statement of consensus on current law as an aid to parents, educators and students.

Many of the organizations listed below are actively involved in litigation about religion in the schools. On some of the issues discussed in this summary, some of the organizations have urged the courts to reach positions different than they did. Though there are signatories on both sides which have and will press for different constitutional treatments of some of the topics discussed below, they all agree that the following is an accurate statement of what the law currently is.

Student Prayers

1. Students have the right to pray individually or in groups or to discuss their religious views with their peers so long as they are not disruptive. Because the Establishment Clause does not apply to purely private speech, students enjoy the right to read their Bibles or other scriptures, say grace before meals, pray before tests, and discuss religion with other willing student listeners. In the classroom students have the right to pray quietly except when required to be actively engaged in school activities (e.g., students may not decide to pray just as the teacher calls on them). In informal settings, such as the cafeteria or in the halls, students may pray either audibly or silently, subject to the same rules of order as apply to other speech in these locations. However, the right to engage in voluntary prayer does not include, for example, the right to have a captive audience listen to or to compel other students to participate.

Graduation Prayer and Baccalaureates

2. School officials may not mandate or organize prayer at graduation, nor may they organize a religious baccalaureate ceremony. If the school generally rents out its facilities to private groups, it must rent them out on the same terms, and on a first-come first-served basis, to organizers of privately sponsored religious baccalaureate services, provided that the school does not extend preferential treatment to the baccalaureate ceremony and the school disclaims official endorsement of the program.

3. The courts have reached conflicting conclusions under the federal Constitution on student-initiated prayer at graduation. Until the issue is authoritatively resolved, schools should ask their lawyers what rules apply in their area.

Official Participation or Encouragement of Religious Activity

4. Teachers and school administrators, when acting in those capacities, are representatives of the state, and, in those capacities, are themselves prohibited from encouraging or soliciting student religious or anti-religious activity. Similarly, when acting in their official capacities, teachers may not engage in religious activities with their students. However, teachers may engage in private religious activity in faculty lounges.

Teaching about Religion

5. Students may be taught about religion, but public schools may not teach religion. As the U.S. Supreme Court has repeatedly said, "[I]t might well be said that one's education is not complete without a study of comparative religion, or the history of religion and its relationship to the advancement of civilization." It would be difficult to teach art, music, literature and most social studies without considering religious influences.

The history of religion, comparative religion, the Bible (or other scripture)-as literature (either as a separate course or within some other existing course), are all permissible public school subjects. It is both permissible and desirable to teach objectively about the role of religion in the history of the United States and other countries. One can teach that the Pilgrims came to this country with a particular religious vision, that Catholics and others have been subject to persecution, or that many of those participating in the abolitionist, women's suffrage and civil rights movements had religious motivations.

6. These same rules apply to the recurring controversy surrounding theories of evolution. Schools may teach about explanations of life on earth, including religious ones (such as "creationism"), in comparative religion or social studies classes. In science class, however, they may present only genuinely scientific critiques of, or evidence for, any explanation of life on earth, but not religious critiques (beliefs unverifiable by scientific methodology). Schools may not refuse to teach evolutionary theory in order to avoid giving offense to religion nor may they circumvent these rules by labeling as science an article of religious faith. Public schools must not teach as scientific fact or theory any religious doctrine, including "creationism," although any genuinely scientific evidence for or against any explanation of life may be taught. Just as they may neither advance nor inhibit any religious doctrine, teachers should not ridicule, for example, a student's religious explanation for life on earth.

Student Assignments and Religion

7. Students may express their religious beliefs in the form of reports, homework and artwork, and such expressions are constitutionally protected. Teachers may not reject or correct such submissions simply because they include a religious symbol or address religious themes. Likewise, teachers may not require students to modify, include or excise religious views in their assignments, if germane. These assignments should be judged by ordinary academic standards of substance, relevance, appearance and grammar.

8. Somewhat more problematic from a legal point of view are other public expressions of religious views in the classroom. Unfortunately for school officials, there are traps on either side of this issue, and it is possible that litigation will result no matter what course is taken. It is easier to describe the settled cases than to state clear rules of law. Schools must carefully steer between the claims of student speakers who assert a right to express themselves on religious subjects and the asserted rights of student listeners to be free of unwelcome religious persuasion in a public school classroom.

   a. Religious or anti-religious remarks made in the ordinary course of classroom discussion or student presentations are permissible and constitute a protected right. If in a sex education class a student remarks that abortion should be illegal because God has prohibited it, a teacher should not silence the remark, ridicule it, rule it out of bounds or endorse it, any more than a teacher may silence a student's religiously-based comment in favor of choice.

   b. If a class assignment calls for an oral presentation on a subject of the student's choosing, and, for example, the student responds by conducting a religious service, the school has the right—as well as the duty—to prevent itself from being used as a church. Other students are not voluntarily in attendance and cannot be forced to become an unwilling congregation.

   c. Teachers may rule out-of-order religious remarks that are irrelevant to the subject at hand. In a discussion of Hamlet's sanity, for example, a student may not interject views on creationism.

Distribution of Religious Literature

9. Students have the right to distribute religious literature to their schoolmates, subject to those reasonable time, place, and manner or other constitutionally-acceptable restrictions imposed on the distribution of all non-school literature. Thus, a school may confine distribution of all literature to a particular table at particular times. It may not single out religious literature for burdensome regulation.

10. Outsiders may not be given access to the classroom to distribute religious or anti-religious nature. No court has yet considered whether, if all other community groups are permitted to distribute literature in common areas of public schools, religious groups must be allowed to do so on equal terms subject to reasonable time, place and manner restrictions.

"See You at the Pole"

11. Student participation in before- or after-school events, such as "see you at the pole," is permissible. School officials, acting in an official capacity, may neither discourage nor encourage participation in such an event.

Religious Persuasion versus Religious Harassment

12. Students have the right to speak to, and attempt to persuade, their peers about religious topics just as they do with regard to political topics. But school officials should intercede to stop student religious speech if it turns into religious harassment aimed at a student or a small group of students. While it is constitutionally permissible for a student to approach another and issue an invitation to attend church, repeated invitations in the face of a request to stop constitute harassment. Where this line is to be drawn in particular cases will depend on the age of the students and other circumstances.

Equal Access Act

13. Student religious clubs in secondary schools must be permitted to meet and to have equal access to campus media to announce their meetings, if a school receives federal funds and permits any student non-curricular club to meet during non-instructional time. This is the command of the Equal Access Act. A non-curricular club is any club not related directly to a subject taught or soon-to-be taught in the school. Although schools have the right to ban all non-curriculum clubs, they may not dodge the law's requirement by the expedient of declaring all clubs curriculum-related. On the other hand, teachers may not actively participate in club activities and "non-school persons" may not control or regularly attend club meeting.

The Act's constitutionality has been upheld by the Supreme Court, rejecting claims that the Act violates the Establishment Clause. The Act's requirements are described in more detail in *The Equal Access Act and the Public Schools: Questions and Answers on the Equal Access Act,* a pamphlet published by a broad spectrum of religious and civil liberties groups. (See * on page 190.)

Religious Holidays

14. Generally, public schools may teach about religious holidays, and may celebrate the secular aspects of the holiday and objectively teach about their religious aspects. They may not observe the holidays as religious events. Schools should generally excuse students who do not wish to participate in holiday events. Those interested in further details should see *Religious Holidays in the Public Schools: Questions and Answer*, a pamphlet published by a broad spectrum of religious and civil liberties groups.*

Excusal from Religiously Objectionable Lessons

15. Schools enjoy substantial discretion to excuse individual students from lessons which are objectionable to that student or to his or her parent on the basis of religion. Schools can exercise that authority in ways which would defuse many conflicts over curriculum content. If it is proved that particular lessons substantially burden a student's free exercise of religion and if the school cannot prove a compelling interest in requiring attendance, the school would be legally required to excuse the student.

Teaching Values

16. Schools may teach civic virtues, including honesty, good citizenship, sportsmanship, courage, respect for the rights and freedoms of others, respect for persons and their property, civility, the dual virtues of moral conviction and tolerance and hard work. Subject to whatever rights of excusal exist (see item 15) under the federal Constitution and state law, schools may teach sexual abstinence and contraception; whether and how schools teach these sensitive subjects is a matter of educational pol-

---

*Drafting Organizations:
American Jewish Congress, Chair
American Civil Liberties Union
American Jewish Committee
American Muslim Council
Anti-Defamation League
Baptist Joint Committee
Christian Legal Society
General Conference of Seventh-day Adventists
National Association of Evangelicals
National Council of Churches
People for the American Way
Union of American Hebrew Congregations

Endorsing Organizations:
American Ethical Union
American Humanist Association
Americans for Religious Liberty
Americans United for Separation of Church and State
B'nai B'rith International
Christian Science Church
Church of the Brethren, Washington Office

Church of Scientology International
Evangelical Lutheran Church of America, Lutheran Office of Governmental Affairs
Federation of Reconstructionist Congregations and Havurot
Friends Committee on National Legislation
Guru Gobind Singh Foundation
Interfaith Alliance
Interfaith Impact for Justice and Peace
National Council of Jewish Women
National Jewish Community Relations Advisory Council (NJCRAC)
National Ministries, American Baptist Churches, USA
National Sikh Center
North American Council for Muslim Women
Presbyterian Church (USA)
Reorganized Church of Jesus Christ of Latter Day Saints
Unitarian Universalist Association of Congregations
United Church of Christ, Office for Church in Society

icy. However, these may not be taught as religious tenets. The mere fact that most, if not all, religions also teach these values does not make it unlawful to teach them.

Student Garb

17. Religious messages on T-shirts and the like may not be singled out for suppression. Students may wear religious attire, such as yarmulkes and head scarves, and they may not be forced to wear gym clothes that they regard, on religious grounds, as immodest.

Released Time

18. Schools have the discretion to dismiss students to off-premises religious instruction, provided that schools do not encourage or discourage participation or penalize those who do not attend. Schools may not allow religious instruction by outsiders on premises during the school day.

HELPFUL RESOURCES

1. Americans for Religious Liberty is a nonprofit group "dedicated to preserving the American tradition of religious, intellectual, and personal freedom in a pluralistic secular democratic state." They publish a newsletter and books, such as *Religion and Public Education: Common Sense and the Law,* and have been involved in legal church-and-state cases. Contact: P.O. Box 6656, Silver Spring, MD 20916, (301) 598-2447.

2. Americans United for the Separation of Church and State frequently opposes the positions taken on issues by religious right organizations, such as the Christian Coalition. Articles in *Church and State,* published monthly, frequently focus on public education issues. Contact: 1816 Jefferson Place, N.W., Washington, DC 20036.

3. The Freedom Forum First Amendment Center at Vanderbilt University fosters a better public understanding of and appreciation for First Amendment rights and values, including freedom of religion, free speech and press, and the right to petition government and to assemble peaceably. Contact: 1207 18th Avenue, S., Nashville, TN 37212, (615) 321-9588, http://www.fac.org

4. Haynes, C. C., & O. Thomas (Eds.). (1994). *Finding Common Ground: A First Amendment Guide to Religion and Public Education* (rev. ed.). Nashville: The Freedom Forum First Amendment Center. This easy-to-use text is the most comprehensive but practical resource I am aware of for teachers who want accurate information and concrete ideas.

5. Lynn, B., M. D. Stern, & O. S. Thomas. (1995). *The Right to Religious Liberty*: *The Basic ACLU Guide to Religious Rights* (2nd ed.). Carbondale: Southern Illinois

University Press. A practical handbook filled with specific details about what is and is not appropriate for the classroom. This user-friendly, pocket-sized text is written for quick reading in a question-and-answer format.

6. The Rutherford Institute, Charlottesville, VA, is a network of activist attorneys who litigate church-state cases on behalf of conservative Christians. Linked to the Chalcedon group (see Chapter 3), they actively support local challenges to children's books, health education programs, school reform measures, reading series, and self-esteem curricula.

REFERENCES

Alley, R. S. (1996). *Public education and the public good.* Silver Spring, MD: Americans for Religious Liberty.

Association of Supervision and Curriculum Development. (1987). *Religion in the curriculum.* Alexandria, VA.

Barton, D. (1992, Oct. 2). America's Godly heritage. Report in *Congressional Record, 138,* E3069, E3071 (daily ed.) [transcript of videotape].

Bosmajian, H. A. (Ed.). (1987). The freedom to read. *The First Amendment in the Classroom Series, No. 1.* New York: Neal-Schuman Publishers.

Brinkley, E. H. (1994). Intellectual freedom and the theological dimensions of whole language. In J. Brown (Ed.), *Preserving intellectual freedom: Fighting censorship in our schools* (pp. 111–122). Urbana, IL: National Council of Teachers of English.

Brinkley, E. H. (1995). Faith in the Word: Examining religious right attitudes about texts. *English Journal, 84* (5), 91–98.

Carnes, J. (1994). About faith. *Teaching Tolerance, 3* (1), 28–33.

Carroll, J. D., W. D. Broadnax, G. Contreras, T. E. Mann, N. J. Ornstein, & J. Stiehm. (1987). *We the people: A review of U.S. government and civics textbooks.* Washington, DC: People for the American Way.

Carter, S. L. (1993). *The culture of disbelief: How American law and politics trivialize religious devotion.* New York: Basic Books.

Carter, S. L. (1994, Dec. 5). Let us pray. *The New Yorker,* pp. 60–74.

Coles, R. (1990). *The spiritual life of children.* Boston: Houghton Mifflin Co.

Gaddy, B. B., T. W. Hall, & R. J. Marzano. (1996). *School wars: Resolving our conflicts over religion and values.* San Francisco: Jossey-Bass.

Gerzon, M. (1996). *A house divided: Six belief systems struggling for America's soul.* New York: G. P. Putnam's Sons.

Green, W. S. (1996). Religion within the limits. *Academe, 82* (6), 24–32.

Haynes, C. C., & O. Thomas (Eds.). (1994). *Finding common ground: A First Amendment guide to religion and public education* (rev. ed.). Nashville: The Freedom Forum First Amendment Center.

Hill, M. (1997, Jan. 26). Bitter feud follows teacher's suspension for shamanism. *Kalamazoo [MI] Gazette,* p. A9.

Hoekema, D. A. (1996). Politics, religion, and other crimes against civility. *Academe, 82* (6), 33–37.

Holland, G. (1994, Dec. 23). Town of many churches angry over school prayer. *Kalamazoo [MI] Gazette,* p. A4.

Kliever, L. D. (1988). Religion and academic freedom: Issues of faith and reason. *Academe, 74* (1), 8–11.

Lynn, C. C., M. D. Stern, & O. S. Thomas. (1995). *The right to religious liberty: The basic ACLU guide to religious rights* (2nd ed.). Carbondale: Southern Illinois University Press.

Mah, L. S. (1994, Nov. 24). Ruling on Jesus image affirmed. *Kalamazoo [MI] Gazette,* p. A1.

Moshman, D. (1989). *Children, education, and the First Amendment.* Lincoln: University of Nebraska Press.

Noddings, N. (1993). *Educating for intelligent belief or disbelief.* New York: Teachers College Press.

Nord, W. A. (1995). *Religion & American education: Rethinking a national dilemma.* Chapel Hill: The University of North Carolina Press.

Peterson, M. D. (1994). Jefferson and religious freedom. *Atlantic Monthly, 274* (6), 113–124.

Reen, M. (1993, Oct. 26). Woman upset about school program. *The Daily Reporter [Coldwater, MI].*

Religion in the Public Schools: A Joint Statement of Current Law. (1995). Statement drafted by a committee of representatives from 12 organizations, chaired by American Jewish Congress.

Ruenzel, D. (1996, Mar. 27). Old-time religion. *Education Week,* pp. 30–35.

Shor, I., & P. Freire. (1987). *A pedagogy for liberation: Dialogues on transforming education.* New York: Bergin & Garvey.

Strope, J. L., Jr., & C. Broadwell. (1990). Academic freedom: What the courts have said. In A. S. Ochoa (Ed.), *Academic freedom to teach and to learn: Every teacher's issue* (pp. 31–47). Washington, DC: National Education Association.

Thomas, G. (1996). Does religious freedom have a prayer? *Christian American, 7* (2), 12–13.

Traditional Values Coalition. (n.d.). Why is a constitutional amendment necessary? *TVC Talking Points.* Anaheim, CA.

Whitehead, J. W. (1994). *The rights of religious persons in public education* (rev. ed.). Wheaton, IL: Crossway Books.

9 Character, Values, and Intellectual Freedom

The vigilant protection of constitution freedoms is nowhere more vital than in the community of American schools. The classroom is peculiarly the "marketplace of ideas." The Nation's future depends upon leaders trained through wide exposure to that robust exchange of ideas which discovers truth "out of a multitude of tongues," (rather) than through any kind of authoritarian selection.

—Supreme Court Justice Brennan,
Keyishian v. Board of Regents, 385 U.S. 589, 603 (1967)

Moral character and social values are almost as controversial as religion (Chapter 8) in the classroom. Disagreements focus on whether personal and social morality belong in the classroom, and if so, on which morals and values should be taught. There is less disagreement about intellectual freedom, on the surface at least, since virtually everyone pays lip service to this lofty ideal. Moral character, social values, and intellectual freedom do all play a role in public schools classrooms, though their presence is often implicit or invisible. Many teachers are not sure how to appropriately incorporate these values into the classroom or how to respond to parents and citizen groups with their own values agendas.

To be sure, there are fewer legal constraints on character, values, and intellectual freedom than on religion, and therefore, they require somewhat different thinking and planning. This chapter discusses the significance and place of moral character, values, and intellectual freedom and presents suggestions for integrating these values into the curriculum and classroom experience.

Views about Moral Character and Social Values

In a world filled with public discussion of personal morality, conservative and progressive groups alike agree that the people of the world are living in a moral crisis (Simonds, 1996; Wallis, 1994). But according to the public media, there is disagreement as to why the nation, and especially its young people, face a moral crisis. Some say it is because of an insatiable appetite for entertainment and an easy lifestyle, while others insist it is because of poverty, neglect, and crime. Poll-takers say there is great interest in the teaching of moral values, and statistics tracing students' personal moral decisions and behavior suggest there is great need: At least once a month, 44 percent of high school seniors say they have five or more drinks at one sitting; 22 percent of high school freshmen admit to being binge drinkers (Nord, 1995, p. 320). Some 65 percent of high school students say they would cheat on an important exam, and more than one-third of entering college freshmen are so focused on wealth and materialism that they believe it is important to be a millionaire by the age of 35 (p. 320).

A study of children and morality, headed by child psychiatrist Robert Coles, looked closely at children and teens' moral decision making. Coles and colleagues discovered that children and teenagers are missing "a strong, inarguable notion of right and wrong, good and bad" (Meade, 1990, p. 40). This major study involved more than 5,000 children in grades 4 through 12 who were asked 90 questions, such as "How do you decide what is right and wrong? What system of values informs your moral decisions?" The report showed that children do have "fairly complicated belief systems," though those belief systems do not reflect traditional values (p. 40). For example, the report found an "unmistakable erosion of children's faith in, and support for, traditional sources of authority" (p. 40).

Coles's study also found that young people increasingly turn to their peers for guidance on matters of right and wrong. Responses to questions about how children come to think about "what is right and what is wrong, what ought to be done and what ought not to be done" produced the following statistics:

- 16% call upon God, the Bible, church, or synagogue for major guidance;
- 19% look to what has traditionally been upheld as desirable or undesirable;
- 25% look to the world around them, to their neighborhood or community, to the nation and its standards;
- 10% look to what is useful for them, what seems to work;
- 11% have no clear-cut form of moral logic or reasoning to help them decide; and
- 18% essentially fall back upon themselves, their own wishes, feelings, interests, or moods. (Coles & Genevie, 1990, p. 43)

Coles and Genevie reported that almost 60 percent of children and teens rely on moral standards that have self-gratification as their main purpose. Moral decisions are based less on what they think is right than on what they think grown-ups expect, and parents sometimes model for their children such "slippery beliefs" as "winning is everything" and "me first." Surprisingly, the higher a family's income level, "the less clear a youngster is about right and wrong" (1990).

Coles believes the schools have a major role to play in educating the whole person and that it is the responsibility of the schools to "inculcate character" (Coles & Genevie, 1990, p. 41). Many others agree. In a 1993 Gallup survey, more than 90 percent of U.S. adults said they believe that public schools should teach "honesty, racial tolerance, belief in democracy, and the Golden Rule" (Carter, 1994, p. 73). Thomas

Lickona, author of *Educating for Character* (1991), sees an urgent need for teaching moral values and developing character, explaining that moral questions are among the great questions that a democratic society faces (pp. 20–22).

Controversy and Consensus

There is no universal agreement about whether to teach moral values or about how they might be taught. House Majority Leader Dick Armey has opposed school-sponsored values education: "I, for one, would not tolerate anybody having the presumption to dare to think they should define who my children are, what their values are, what their ethics are" (Cohen, 1995). Others, like Coles and Genevie, insist that children's values are unavoidably influenced by the curriculum and by school experiences (see Gaddy, Hall, & Marzano, 1996; Haynes & Thomas, 1994). Teachers do, to varying degrees, include character and values in their classrooms. Some teachers distribute and send home a code of conduct or a set of classroom rules at the beginning of the year. Some create classroom plans that feature conflict resolution strategies. Many engage students in discussion of morality as it appears in literature, psychology, and social studies. And many realize that we teach moral values by modeling them—that in a sense we do teach who we are.

The terms themselves—*morality, character,* and *values*—are slippery and highly charged. A publication from the Association for Supervision and Curriculum Development (ASCD) defines *morality* as having to do with *conduct* that relates to the "rights, duties, and well-being of others" without judging whether the conduct is right or wrong, as when one says that something is "a moral question." In its evaluative sense, *morality* involves "endorsing an act," as in the statement "being honest is a moral way to behave" (1988, p. 15). *Character* is described not as conduct but as a person's *attributes.* In its evaluative sense, character assesses the moral status of a person, as when one says a person "has character" (p. 16). When one talks about *moral character,* then, one ties personal conduct to personal attributes that determine personal decisions and actions. *Values,* on the other hand, are *principles* or *ideals* that one feels strongly about and that guide one's actions (p. 16). Thus, when speaking of *moral values,* one ties personal and/or social conduct to principles.

For some people, these concepts are closely tied to religious beliefs and values. And like religion, they generate considerable controversy in terms of how they can be incorporated into the classroom. The primary disagreement is about what should be included and/or emphasized—personal moral character and/or social values. The following commentary (from a manual for parent activists prepared by Citizens for Excellence in Education) explains the conflict about moral values from a religious conservative perspective:

> The liberal teacher's groups call a military build-up immoral. Many regard the U.S. economic policy as immoral. Planned Parenthood views abortion as moral and pro-life ideas immoral. Are not all these groups promoting their own moral views on others? Our posi-

tion is that traditional moral and family values should be taught in school for the well-being of our children and future generations. This is our American culture. (Simonds, n.d.)

The author does not define what he means by "traditional moral and family values" but implies by the negative comparison that school emphasis should be placed on personal (and family) moral values, not on social or civic values.

William Bennett, author of *The Book of Virtues* (1993), agrees. Bennett described a need for *moral literacy*, which children can achieve by seeing adults take morality seriously. He explained that his book is intended to provide children with specific reference points for their own actions through stories that help "anchor children in their culture, its history, and traditions" (p. 13). Bennett identified virtues that he believes should be taught: self-discipline, compassion, responsibility, friendship, work, courage, perseverance, honesty, loyalty, and faith. Interestingly, Bennett's introductory essay includes a political disclaimer. Anticipating criticism that his book does not include discussion of broader social issues—topics such as nuclear war, abortion, creationism, or euthanasia—he has insisted that "the formation of character in young people is educationally a different task from, and prior task to, the discussion of the great, difficult ethical controversies of the day. First things first" (p. 12). Bennett explained that the "tough issues" can be addressed later if parents want to (p. 13).

A Call to Character (Greer & Kohl, 1995) provides an alternative view of moral attributes worth promoting among children. Although Greer and Kohl explained a similar purpose—to "encourage young people to read, talk and think about moral issues"—they group a wider range of values into categories—those that (1) relate to one's self, (2) relate to people one knows, (3) relate to people one does not know and nature, and (4) relate to love.

The basic disagreement about whether to emphasize personal or social values has been magnified at the state level in Michigan. During the early 1990s, parent protest groups successfully lobbied state legislators to *eliminate* "values, attitudes, and beliefs" from the state's core curriculum. Apparently fearing that their own values, attitudes, and beliefs might be ignored or distorted by educators, they argued that such issues are family matters. But once religious conservatives gained control of the State Board of Education, virtually the same people quickly proposed and *promoted* an explicit moral code for students—with a heavy emphasis on personal, compliant behaviors:

1. I will accept responsibility for all my actions.
2. I will respect the dignity and property of my fellow students and teachers and will never seek to do them harm.
3. I will keep all the promises I make, fulfilling the trust that other people place in me.
4. I will complete projects and courses of study which I have begun.
5. I will strive for excellence in all my work and will respect achievement in my fellow students.

6. I will discipline myself to listen, learn and study, recognizing that long-run achievement is more important to my happiness than short-run pleasure.

7. I will not use any substance which will destroy my health and undermine my dignity.

8. I will respect the authority of my parents and teachers, because that authority is necessary for the welfare of my family, school and community.

9. I will train myself to be useful to others.

10. I will work together with others to improve my school, community and world.

Some of those who resist moral guidelines imposed by other groups feel comfortable themselves imposing their own moral values not only on their own children but on everyone else's children. This assumed superior moral stance on the part of some parents and community groups presents a major challenge for teachers across the country. Fortunately, broad discussions about moral and character education are taking place among educators and stakeholder groups, with a great deal of agreement about core or "universal" values that can be promoted by almost all. James Dunn, Joint Baptist Committee, identified justice, compassion, liberty, peace making, stewardship, and honesty as core values that are "compatible with" diverse religious perspectives (1987, pp. 82–84). His list includes both personal and social values. Likewise, character educator Thomas Lickona recommended that educators focus on both personal and social values—values he describes as "rationally grounded, nonrelative, [and] objectively worthwhile," that include *respect*—for oneself, for other people, and for all forms of life and the environment—and *responsibility*—paying attention to others and actively responding to their needs (1991, pp. 43–44). Lickona also recommended additional *personal* values—honesty, fairness, tolerance, prudence, self-discipline, helpfulness, compassion, cooperation, courage (p. 45)—and *democratic* values—respect for the rights of individuals, regard for law, voluntary participation in public life, and concern for the common good (p. 6).

Figure 9.1 compares the values espoused by Bennett, Greer and Kohl, Dunn, and Lickona. Only compassion and honesty show up as an exact match on all four lists, but I suspect that with slight shifts in language, all four would accept many of the items listed. There are differences, however, that suggest where possible disagreements about classroom emphasis might occur. For example, creativity, peace making, tolerance, and prudence seem not equally valued by all four.

Certainly, disagreements will continue to emerge as discussions continue about teaching moral values. What is more important than the disagreements, however, is the renewed interest in teaching moral values and the commitment of school districts who recognize the potential benefits of doing so. Stephen Carter, a Yale professor who sends his children to private schools for religious education, claims that parents care more about schools teaching *values* than they do about religion. He insists that including explicit instruction in values "will go a long way toward addressing parents' concerns without introducing religious indoctrination in the public schools" (1993, p. 203). If we want to address the deepest concerns of sincere parents, I believe we will not only acknowledge and teach about religions (Chapter 8) but we will also work to achieve enough consensus to teach moral values.

FIGURE 9.1   **Comparing Values**

Bennett	Greer and Kohl	Dunn	Lickona
Compassion	Compassion	Compassion	Compassion
Honesty	Honesty	Honesty	Honesty
Self-discipline	Self-discipline	Justice	Self-discipline
Responsibility	Responsibility	Liberty	Responsibility
Courage	Courage	Peace making	Courage
Loyalty	Loyalty	Stewardship	Fairness
Friendship	Fairness		Liberty
Work	Integrity		Respect
Perserverance	Creativity		Tolerance
Faith	Playfulness		Helpfulness
	Generosity		Prudence
	Empathy		
	Adaptability		
	Idealism		
	Balance		
	Love		

Teaching Character and Values

Redefining Values Clarification

In reading religious-conservative publications, I find that almost invariably discussions of teaching about morality or character focus on a firm rejection of *values clarification* theories and strategies that were popular in the mid-1970s. Critics have been particularly disturbed by the moral relativism they find in values clarification and by the casual treatment of serious issues: "At its worst," Lickona points out, "values clarification mixed up trivial questions ('Do you like to read the comics?') with important ethical issues ('Should capital punishment be abolished?')" (1991, p. 11).

In 1992, Sidney Kirschenbaum, one of the original developers and strong advocates of values clarification, reacted to many of the past objections to values clarification. Seldom does one hear professional educators come this close to saying, "Sorry, I was wrong." Kirschenbaum says there was "a major conceptual and political flaw" in the values clarification theory: "We insisted that values clarification *by itself* was a sufficient method for developing satisfying values and moral behavior in young people ... we implied that it was better to clarify than to inculcate values and that those who primarily inculcated values were perhaps even harming young people by denying them the decision-making skills for guiding their own lives in a complex world" (Kirschenbaum, 1992, p. 774).

Kirschenbaum (1992) now recommends a synthesis of both approaches and calls for "comprehensive values education" that:

- Is comprehensive in content—from choice of personal values to ethical questions to moral issues;
- Is comprehensive in methodology—inculcating and modeling as well as stressing responsible decision making and other life skills;
- Is comprehensive by taking place throughout the school—not limited to the classroom but also a part of extracurricular programs, counseling, awards, etc.; and
- Takes place throughout the community—involving parents, religious institutions, civic leaders, community agencies, etc. (p. 775)

Kirschenbaum (1992) offered examples that illustrate the range of occasions when educators might incorporate components of a comprehensive values education: "The elementary principal who, during morning announcements, thanks the student who turned in a lost wallet...the second-grade teachers who spend a whole month centering their students' reading, writing, and other activities on the value of 'kindness'" or the social studies teacher who discusses moral dilemmas in conjunction with a unit on the Civil War...or the principal who has the courage to cancel the rest of the football season because his school started a serious fight at the last football game" (p. 776).

Many schools no longer use the values clarification programs that were developed during the 1970s, but many teachers who were influenced by values clarification training still use its strategies to handle controversial subjects. Kirschenbaum's (1992) newer insights may make a lot of sense to classroom teachers and parents who are concerned about the limited moral judgment exhibited by students, as revealed in Coles's research. The call for comprehensive values education charts out a reasonable framework that cuts across the curriculum and that goes *beyond* the curriculum. It is a plan that provides a place to begin for teachers who want to address values more explicitly in their classrooms and in their schools.

In the Classroom and Beyond

Many teachers, however, do not feel comfortable teaching isolated lessons focused on morality, partly because we notice that morality is linked in many people's minds to religious conviction. Legally, there are fewer restrictions on how we treat moral values in the classroom than on how we treat religion, where the law is clear about preserving an overall neutral treatment. Charles C. Haynes, an authority on religious liberties in public education, and Oliver Thomas, a Baptist minister and member of the Supreme Court Bar, have provided a helpful clarification: "In public schools, where teachers may neither promote nor denigrate religion, these [moral] values must be taught without religious indoctrination. At the same time, teaching core [moral] values may not be done in such a way as to suggest that religious authority is unnecessary or unimportant" (1994, p. 14.2).

A reasonable course for teachers who want to address moral issues includes (1) acknowledging that many people make moral decisions based on their religious beliefs, (2) teaching moral character and social or civic values about which there is broad consensus, and (3) encouraging students to consult further with their parents and religious leaders about features of character and values about which there is considerable disagreement. Many teachers have found that the way to begin focusing on moral character and social values is through using conflict resolution and class meetings to help create a sense of classroom community and through content-related discussions that focus on the implications of personal values and social responsibilities.

Kindergarten teacher Janice Balsam Danielson (1993) has helped even very young children to tackle the tough issues of social responsibility. She would certainly not agree with William Bennett's assertion that young children should not be troubled with difficult issues. Kindergarten children, said Danielson, are already affected by troubling news events, and they bring related questions and queries with them to the classroom. Because television news coverage exposes young children to "frightening events and disturbing visual images," she often begins the morning meeting by asking the children if they heard anything on the news that they would like to talk about (p. 13). Over the years, her students have raised issues ranging from the famine in Ethiopia and the space shuttle *Challenger* accident to the meltdown of the nuclear reactor near Chernobyl. Danielson has been impressed by "the intensity with which they strove to interpret the confusing things they had seen and heard in ways which would be meaningful to them and consistent with their established views of the world" (p. 13).

Danielson (1993) has been careful, nonetheless, that the young children are not left "feeling overwhelmed and fearful" after discussing a catastrophe. She has been careful to end the day's discussion with a sense that they could do something to convey their feelings, such as sending a note to the victims' families (p. 21). She has also been careful to note individual students' responses and to speak with individual children later if she thinks it would help alleviate unnecessary fears (p. 21). Sometimes she has also sent parents a brief note describing the discussion and encouraging parents to see if their child wants to talk about it further (p. 21). Danielson's students are fortunate to learn from their wise teacher ways of thinking about and responding to disturbing information. The lessons her children learn during the class meeting discussions may well establish lifelong skills that they can build on as they grow up.

Responsible social action that goes beyond the classroom is a next step. For example, a group of students and their teacher, Michael H. Brownstein, called attention to a neighborhood "dope house." The teacher explained, "Despite all my calls and complaints to the police and the city, nobody seemed very interested in shutting the dope house down until some of my students and I went to the newspapers. We brought a box filled with 500 needles that we had collected during an angry visit to the house. The newspapers ran a story. A local television station sent cameras. Finally, the city had the building barricaded; it was eventually torn down" (1990, p. 6).

Surely one of the best things we can do to ease the concerns of sincere parent protesters is to demonstrate that public school is a place where both personal and social values are recognized and developed. In Figure 9.2, ASCD offers 10 recommendations for educators who are eager to make a place for moral character and sociopolitical values.

FIGURE 9.2 Planning a Moral Education Program

1. We urge all those involved in American education...to renew their commitment to promoting moral education in the schools....
2. We recommend that educators form partnerships with parents, the mass media, the business community, the courts, and civic, racial, ethnic, and religious groups to create a social and cultural context that supports the school's efforts to develop morally mature citizens.
3. We recommend that schools define and teach a morality of justice, altruism, diligence, and respect for human dignity....
4. We urge schools and school systems to make sure their moral education efforts extend beyond the cognitive domain to include the affective and the behavioral....
5. We recommend that moral education include, especially for younger children, socialization into appropriate patterns of conduct and, especially for older students, education for the critical thinking and decision making that are part of adult moral maturity....
6. We recommend that educators continually examine the institutional features of school life to ensure that climate and instructional practices contribute to the same moral growth.
7. We urge further research on what works in moral education, drawing on research findings from other fields and presenting those findings to the profession forcefully and clearly.
8. We recommend that educators regularly assess the moral climate of schools and the conduct of students and communicate the results of these assessments to their communities....
9. We recommend that schools establish and convey clear expectations for teachers and administrators regarding their roles as moral educators....
10. We recommend that teacher educators, both preservice and inservice, give major attention to moral education to ensure that teachers have the necessary knowledge, attitudes, and skills to fulfill their moral education responsibilities.

Source: From *Moral Education in the Life of the School: A Report from the ASCD Panel on Moral Education* by the Association for Supervision and Curriculum Development. Alexandria, VA: Association for Supervision and Curriculum Development. Copyright © 1988 ASCD. Reprinted by permission. All rights reserved.

WHAT CAN YOU DO TO TEACH MORAL CHARACTER AND SOCIAL VALUES?

1. *Focus explicitly on universally accepted values.* Elementary teachers in Dayton, Ohio, feature a moral theme in the form of a "word of the week," which is linked to discussion, assemblies, and readings. They report amazing effects: "In the first two years of the program, suspensions dropped drastically, teacher absenteeism declined, and PTA fund-raising increased. The principal reports that now children are sent to his office for compliments when they behave well" (Cohen, 1995, p. 7).

2. *Focus on moral character across the curriculum.* A similar, but more extensive values education program in Portland, Maine, integrates six noncontroversial values— respect, courage, honesty, justice, willingness to work, and self-discipline—throughout the curriculum and school day (Lickona, 1991, p. 166). Each year one of the six values is spotlighted as the "value of the year." Attention to self-discipline, for example, has been given in the following ways:

- Science and math teachers focused on lives of prominent people in these fields.... They called attention to the highly structured, disciplined methodology found in both courses of study;
- English teachers drew models of self-discipline from the study of literature, and students wrote compositions dealing with this trait;
- History teachers directed attention to specific moments in history when great men and women exhibited self-discipline;
- Art and music teachers examined the lives of great artists and composers as models of self-discipline;
- Home economics and industrial arts teachers stressed the role of self-discipline in designing and creating in wood, metal, clothing, etc.; and
- Physical education and health teachers showed students that one must maintain a certain degree of self-control to maintain a healthy body. (Lickona, 1991, pp. 166–167)

3. *Make morality a part of the ethos of the classroom and school community.* Kirschenbaum's (1992) comprehensive plan calls for moral values not only to be an explicit part of the curriculum but an unexpressed, modeled feature of the classroom and school environment, as well. That is, moral values should be a part of the ethos of the school, where teachers nurture moral values through the "examples set, the rules and regulations, the stories told, the history taught, and the personal relationships formed" (Nord, 1995, p. 339).

4. *Teach and use conflict resolution to solve problems.* Many teachers focus first on teaching moral values by using conflict resolution to address classroom behavior problems involving individuals. Judith Arbus, Conflict Resolution Advisor for the Toronto Board of Education, said that such programs "help students work at solving problems related to awareness, self-confidence, and social interaction" (1994, p. 8). To put a conflict resolution plan into action, teachers provide direct instruction on "active listening, listening for feelings, I-messages, and identification of problem-solving strategies" (p. 8). Children learn to become conflict mediators (sometimes called "conflict managers, peacemakers, peacekeepers, problem solvers, peer mediators, or facilitators") for their peers (p. 9). An elementary teacher uses a "Conflict Manager Report" (see Figure 9.3) form as part of her school's conflict resolution program. It suggests the formal process involved in many classroom and school-based conflict resolution programs.

Views about Intellectual Freedom

For many, "intellectual freedom" isn't an expression that pops into daily conversation. Instead, it is a lofty ideal that teachers believe in as a concept but that seems remote from what we do day-by-day in the classroom. If we do not take time to think through the significance and the boundaries of intellectual and academic freedom, we may take them for granted. The result is we either operate with a false sense of security or with an uncomfortable fear that we are somehow breaking the rules. The solution is to pull our heads out of the sand and claim the promises that intellectual freedom holds for teaching and learning.

FIGURE 9.3 Conflict Manager Report

- Do not interrupt.
- No name calling or put-downs.
- Be as honest as you can.
- Agree to solve the problem.

Date _____

Conflict Managers _____

What kind of conflict?   _____ Argument

                               _____ Fight

                               _____ Rumor

                               _____ Other _____

How did you find out about the conflict?

_____ Student   _____ Administrator

_____ Teacher   _____ Aide

_____ Counselor   _____ Yourself

What was the conflict about? _____

_____

_____

Was the conflict resolved?   _____ Yes   _____ No

Resolution:

Student #1 agrees to: Student #2 agrees to:

_____   _____

_____   _____

_____   _____

_____   _____

Source: Reprinted with permission of Linda Price, Kettering Elementary School, Newark, OH.

Intellectual freedom can be defined broadly as "freedom of the mind" (American Library Association, 1992, p. ix). It is a "personal liberty," but also a "prerequisite for all freedoms leading to action" (p. ix). Given the restrictions protesters sometimes want to place on student materials and experiences, we can only conclude that some parents today do not seem to want "freedom of the mind" or "personal liberty" for their children. Instead, they prefer classrooms where the curriculum focuses on single "right" answers to questions raised by the textbook or the teacher and where the teacher acts as absolute, unquestionable authority—so long, of course, as the teachers' views correspond closely to their own.

Some think of intellectual and academic freedom as being virtually the same, but it is helpful to distinguish *academic freedom* as "the freedom to teach and to learn" (Reichman, 1988, p. 6). Thus, it is a school-based form of intellectual freedom. It is most frequently applied to teachers' rights, although some use "academic freedom" to refer to the freedom of both teachers and students "to study, learn, teach, and express ideas" (Nelson, 1990, p. 21). Invariably, however, definitions of academic freedom come with a qualifier. Academic freedom "has its limits" and "means different things in different situations" (Reichman, 1988, p. 6). It is not license to do whatever we want. Instead, it is our right to teach and select classroom materials without interference but to do so "according to established policies and procedures" (Reichman, 1988, p. 6).

One of the lessons we are learning from the barrage of attacks on schools today is that both academic freedom for teachers and intellectual freedom for students are being challenged. This is serious business, indeed. Ultimately, intellectual freedom is the most important thing we teach, since a democratic form of government depends on who has the "freedom of the mind" to take action and to form policy. Our students need to learn how that process works by experiencing intellectual freedom in the classroom and by debating controversial matters. Teachers need to teach about the role that intellectual freedom plays in a democracy and to help students learn firsthand about their First Amendment rights.

Moshman explained that intellectual rights include "the right to use and develop one's intellect, including access to information and ideas, freedom to believe what one chooses, freedom to express one's beliefs, and perhaps freedom to act on those beliefs" (1986, p. 2). Given this broad understanding, intellectually free classroom settings can be described as places for wide and deep reading and discussion of a variety of texts and opinions; frequent opportunities for oral and written expression of student opinions and voices; investigation beyond textbooks and classrooms, stressing students' own inquiry projects; inclusion of multicultural knowledge and ways of knowing; examination of multiple perspectives when controversial issues are considered; and philosophical grounding in a constructivist model of education that assumes critical, creative, active learners.

The stakes for accomplishing these goals are high. The truth is, we need to teach so that even potential Oklahoma City bombers can learn within the safety of the classroom how to weigh ideas and make wise choices. If that were not challenge enough, we must face the daunting task of helping protesting parents and community members realize that permitting—and requiring—intellectual freedom in the classroom is in their own best interests. Parents' own perspectives will receive greater consideration and/or respect in classrooms where intellectual freedom exists. Providing a free exchange of ideas and few limits on access to materials and information means that individual parents' views will receive greater consideration and/or respect in classrooms. It means that text materials can address controversial topics and that teachers can insist that facts and arguments are supported and balanced by context, evidence, and commentary.

Our challenge, then, is to help students, parents, and community members understand their own stake in preserving intellectual freedom. First Amendment scholar Nat Hentoff has contended that most U.S. students do not really know their history as a free people and that they know little about the Bill of Rights or the Fourteenth Amendment or about what it took to gain our freedom and rights. More ominously, Hentoff has warned that "if they leave school with such ignorance, they are hardly likely, as adults, to fight to preserve their own liberties—let alone anyone else's" (1992, pp. 356–357). Therefore, it is time to bring to life the generalities that appear in lifeless history books, and to make intellectual freedom an explicit part of the curriculum and the ethos at work in every class.

Exercising Academic Freedom

Some religious conservatives who are concerned about adding religion and moral values to the curriculum, unfortunately, seem eager to *limit* the information and ideas that students are exposed to. Such parents spend little time, if any, fighting for intellectual freedom. By contrast, progressive and critical educators sometimes fight so aggressively against the oppression of disempowered groups and against the repression of ideas that they appear eager to replace existing dominant truths with potentially dominant truths of their own. Our challenge as teachers, therefore, is to create an intellectually free classroom in spite of the competing political, moral, and religious perspectives.

Toward that end, we can use James Beane's (1990, p. 143) identification of three kinds of affective content to consider how to handle particular topics and issues:

Affective Content	*Example(s)*
Ideas that may be *described* but not promoted	Both sides or multiple sides of controversial issues, such as abortion or gun control
Ideas that may be *promoted* but not insisted upon	Celebrating diversity or strict environmental protection
Ideas that may be *promoted and insisted upon*	Tolerance of differences

Individual teachers or groups that are planning curriculum can use Beane's categories to weigh which approach is more appropriate for which topics.

It is also helpful to know at least a little about what courts have decided in cases that involved teachers' academic freedom to teach and students' intellectual freedom to learn. Understanding the teacher-student relationship is an important place to begin. The Supreme Court decided in 1969 (*Tinker v. Des Moines Independent Community School District*, 393 U.S. 503 [1969]) that "students may not be regarded as closed-circuit recipients of only that which the State chooses to communicate," that school officials "do not possess absolute authority over their students," and that students "are possessed of fundamental rights which the State must respect, just as they themselves must respect their obligations to the State." The Court confirmed First Amendment rights for teachers as well as for students: "It can hardly be argued that either students or teachers shed their rights to freedom of speech or expression at the schoolhouse gate" (*Tinker v. Des Moines Independent Community School District,* 393 U.S. 503 [1969]).

The courts are also concerned about why and how materials and experiences are used in classrooms. Many teachers know that the selection of curricular materials and classroom experiences must be based on educational purpose. Determining educational purpose, however, is not as easy as it sounds. If we, as teachers, do not have a solid knowledge base of the content area(s) we teach, we will never be able to adequately defend our curricular decisions. That is why my undergraduate preservice teachers hear me say so often, "Yes, you must have a strong content base and know what you'll ask kids to do in the classroom. But for every 'what' that happens in your classroom, you must be able at any moment to articulate the reasons 'why' it's there. You must be able to defend the educational purposes for every book, every resource, and every activity."

Teachers need to know how particular curricular choices fit into the overall educational purposes of the school and/or district plans and policies for making curricular decisions. If, for example, a policy stipulates that teachers may not use any materials without receiving prior administrative approval, then teachers must abide by the policy. Even if there is no official policy but the principal tells teachers to have materials approved, the courts hold teachers responsible for following administrators' orders (see Strope & Broadwell, 1990).

Some say that the courts are more likely to uphold teachers' rights when teaching methods or strategies are involved than when course content or required materials are involved (Strope & Broadwell, 1990, p. 35). There are limits, however, and individual teachers' decisions about assignments will not always be defended. For example, the court ruled against a teacher who asked his students to write letters to his fiancee, who in turn wrote each a response describing herself as a communist (see Bosmajian, 1989, pp. 97–105). Most teachers who read about such extreme cases recognize the need to apply common sense to decisions about teaching strategies as well as to curriculum.

The courts usually support the inclusion of and access to information and ideas, even over strong opposition. They have ruled, for example, that textbooks and classroom experiences cannot be censored by individual parents or even by the majority within a community just because the materials or activities do not match individual parents' religious and moral beliefs. When parents in Tennessee protested against their children's reading textbooks on these grounds (*Mozert v. Hawkins County Board of Education,* 827 F.2d 1058 [6th Cir. 1987]), the court found that it would be "virtually impossible to provide any books that would satisfy their objections because only their view of the world was the correct view. In effect, the school board would have to develop a curriculum that would foster only the religious views of the plaintiffs" (Strope & Broadwell, 1990, p. 41). The threat to intellectual freedom was clear in this case. If the court had decided for the parents, it would have paved the way for parents to insist on a tailor-made curriculum reflecting only the views of a particular child's parents. Instead, the court clarified one of the purposes of schooling—to include, discuss, and examine a variety of contradictory views.

We teachers, like students, do not leave our rights at the schoolhouse door but carry our free speech rights with us into the classroom—up to a point. We know that we must take a neutral stand in the classroom toward religion. When expressing our own opinions about other controversial topics, we are advised not to rush to explain our own position. Instead, we can say something like, "I do have views on this issue, and I'd be happy to share them with you later. But I want to stay impartial for now, because the purpose of this unit is not for you to learn what I think. It's for you to evaluate carefully all the arguments and evidence and come to what you think is the most supportable position" (Lickona, 1991, p. 271).

Children's Intellectual Rights

Children had few physical rights and no intellectual rights at the beginning of the twentieth century. Those who were abandoned or impoverished lived on the streets and worked in factories. The system provided no safety net or protection. There was "no recourse against family abuse and neglect, including sexual abuse.... A juvenile delinquent might spend years in a juvenile hall or asylum for stealing a dollar or a loaf of bread" (Hempelman, 1994, p. xv). Legal reforms have gradually expanded the rights of children, so that today children are "major figures on the American legal scene" (p. xv). They have due process rights in juvenile court, First Amendment and other constitutional rights in public schools, and privacy rights in the area of birth control and abortion (p. xv).

Having the laws in place does not always mean, however, that they are enforced. Too often, the police and the courts act illegally against young people, and students are sometimes searched illegally and punished for exercising their First Amendment rights (Hempelman, 1994, p. xvi). Public school officials who overstep students' rights sometimes forget or ignore the Supreme Court's 1969 assertion that school officials do not have absolute authority over students and that students have fundamental constitutional rights. Given pressures from strong-willed groups with different agendas, we teachers need to know what is constitutionally protected and how intellectual freedom has been preserved so that we can decide how to respond to challenges and what action to take.

The concept of intellectual freedom was itself on trial in the case of *Smith v. Board of School Commissioners, Mobile, Alabama,* 827 F.2d 684 (11th Cir. 1987). Fundamentalist Christian parents protested against 44 U.S. history and home economics texts, claiming that they "inhibited Christian religions" and advanced "secular humanism" (Strope & Broadwell, 1990, p. 40). The charges leveled against the texts focused on what they taught students—"to make their own decisions, to use the scientific method, and to think for themselves." Ironically, the Court of Appeals agreed with the parents' characterization of the books. But the judge explained that rather than censor students' rights to make their own decisions, the court *affirmed* students' rights to think for themselves, which is "at the heart of the mission of public schools in this nation" (p. 40).

Another important issue to classroom teachers is whether the constitution protects children against political indoctrination and what rights children have to their own political beliefs. Many people admit that their political worldview has been influenced not only by their parents' views but also by the views of their K–12 teachers and university professors. Van Geel (1986, pp. 7–9) presents four models of the child-parent-state relationship:

1. *Traditional Model:* "The child enjoys no right not to be indoctrinated by either parents or government operating through a public school system—a system that parents are legally free to reject in favor of private schooling. Two important traditions lie at the heart of this model: respect for parental authority to control the upbringing of the child and respect for the authority of public schools to seek to inculcate students politically."

2. *Platonic Model:* "One way or another, it is the state that takes over the task of determining how the child should be indoctrinated. There is state inculcation in public schools and state regulation of private education to ensure that students are properly inculcated. Alternatively, parents could be required to send children to public institutions to be inculcated under state direction or even to enroll their children in residential schools to ensure that parents would have little or no opportunity to undertake their own private programs of inculcation."

3. *Open Future Model:* The child enjoys a right to be "free from the efforts of both parents and government to instill unshakable political beliefs." Educational programs provided by parents and the government allow the child the freedom, as an adult, to take a political direction of his or her own choosing.

4. *Asymmetrical Model:* The authority of parents to inculcate and the authority of public schools to inculcate are treated differently; parents are permitted to seek to inculcate their own beliefs and values, but public schools are prohibited from deliberate indoctrination.

Those of us who have a generation of teaching experience can probably identify schools whose practices fit each category. Some we recognize from our own school settings; others we know from the news and from professional publications. We might describe our own student experience as fitting the traditional or the asymmetrical models. We might associate the platonic model with our understanding of education in the former Soviet Union. And we have at least heard about Summerhill or other schools known to be based on an open future model.

Van Geel (1990) recommends the asymmetrical model, which allows parents and schools to *inculcate* (i.e., to impress something on the mind of another by frequent instruction or repetition). The difference lies with what gets inculcated. Parents can teach "their own beliefs and values"; they can, if they choose to, also *indoctrinate* (i.e., to instruct in a body of doctrine or principles or imbue with a partisan or ideological point of view). But public school teachers should refrain from indoctrination.

Regardless of the political child-parent-state model involved, children's intellectual freedom is not without limits. Wringe explained that children's freedom, especially their right to access to knowledge, may sometimes be restricted "in the interests of the child's own (welfare) right to guidance and protection" (1986, p. 55). The key issue is, of course, where to apply reasonable limits. Wringe articulated a position that is fairly conservative but that many teachers and parents feel is sound, especially for young children:

> It is not unreasonable to fear that a precocious knowledge of sexual license and perversity, of the prevalence of drug taking, and of such dishonest practices as petty theft might increase the risk of a young person's becoming involved in these activities, especially if they are widely seen as the mark of adulthood. Also, detailed and explicit knowledge of what takes place on battlefields, in slaughterhouses, operating theaters, and some kinds of brothels might at some stages be acutely distressing, not to say traumatizing. (p. 56)

Wringe urged caution in permitting too much information for young children:

> If we even suspect that significant harm may result from an experience or situation, it is incumbent upon us to keep the child away from that situation until we are reassured that our fears are groundless.... When the avoidance of harm is concerned ... the point at which the line is to be drawn is not the average, but rather that at which most individuals can cope without risk of harm. To let people of a certain age do something that can safely be done by the average person of that age is to expose half the age group to danger. (pp. 57–58)

Court decisions during the 1980s focused on students' age and maturity levels as a rationale for limiting students' intellectual freedom, referring explicitly to the age and immaturity of the students in question (Moshman, 1989, p. 31). Moshman insisted that "it is the burden of the government to show that a specific situation is so exceptional as to justify restrictions on children or adolescents greater than those that would apply to adults" (p. 91). However, classroom teachers need to remember that the courts usually provide K–12 students less academic freedom than that permitted for college students, who are considered adults.

Students' Speech and Expression

In the case of *Tinker v. Des Moines* (1969), for the first time the Supreme Court declared a government action unconstitutional on the ground that it violated minors' rights to freedom of expression" (Moshman, 1989, p. 11). This case involved students wearing black armbands to school in protest over Vietnam. It clarified that children have First Amendment rights because they are persons under the Constitution and showed that students have a right to communicate ideas of their own (p. 14).

However, in the area of freedom of speech, as any parent and teacher knows, students sometimes test our good intentions and the limits of what is generally acceptable and what is not. The *Bethel v. Fraser* case of Matthew Fraser, a high school student, is one of two cases (the other is *Hazelwood v. Kuhlmeier;* see Chapter 4) that reveal the courts' willingness to restrict students' freedom of speech. When Fraser gave a nominating speech for one of his friends, these were his remarks in a school assembly:

> I know a man who is firm—he's firm in his pants, he's firm in his shirt, his character is firm—but most of all, his belief in you, the students of Bethel, is firm.
>
> Jeff Kuhlman is a man who makes his point and pounds it in. If necessary, he'll take an issue and nail it to the wall. He doesn't attack things in spurts—he drives hard, pushing and pushing until finally—he succeeds.
>
> Jeff is a man who will go to the very end—even the climax, for each and every one of you. So vote for Jeff for A.S.B. vice president—he'll never come between you and the best our high school can be. (Strope & Broadwell, 1990, p. 43)

The Supreme Court found the speech to be "indecent, obscene and lewd," and not protected by the First Amendment. They explained that such speeches would not be permitted in "adult public circumstances" and that school administrators had a responsibility to prohibit such public speaking in the school setting (Strope & Broadwell, 1990, p. 43). The speaker was given a two-day suspension (Hempelman, 1994, p. 21). Apparently more than just the words of the speech and the double entendres were considered as the Court made its decision upholding the school's right to discipline the student. The assembly audience consisted mainly of 14-year-olds, who apparently responded to the speech by "hooting, shouting, and embarrassment." The speech was said to have disrupted classes and caused confusion among many of the students (p. 21). The Court ruled that the school didn't violate Fraser's First Amendment rights by disciplining him, but they did acknowledge that the speech might have been "protected" if the student had delivered it in a different setting and to older students (p. 22).

Clearly, the effect of both the *Fraser* decision and the *Hazelwood* decision (see Chapter 4) was to place new limits on the free speech rights of students that had seemed so strong in the *Tinker* decision. Eveslage (1988) asserted that both the *Fraser* decision and the *Hazelwood* decision are less about students' rights than they are about *administrators'* rights. The *Bethel* case involved whether a *principal* should have suspended a student whose school assembly speech was considered inappropriately vulgar. The *Hazelwood* case involved whether a *principal* unconstitutionally censored articles in a student newspaper. In both cases, the Supreme Court ruled in favor of the administrator.

When all is said and done, some argue that the general public does not really believe in free speech: "We all believe in it for ourselves, for those who agree with us, and some of us, even for those who don't disagree too much. But we are generally not eager to defend the rights of those whose views trouble us, or frighten us, or threaten us" (D. Kagan, cited in Hentoff, 1992, p. 113). Hentoff quoted Oliver Wendell Holmes, Jr. (*U.S. v. Schwimmer,* 1928): "If there is any principle of the Constitution that more imperatively calls for attachment than any other it is the principle of free thought—not free thought for those who agree with us but freedom for the thought that we hate.... The history of intellectual growth and discovery clearly demonstrates the need for unfettered freedom, the right to think the unthinkable, discuss the unmentionable, and challenge the unchallengeable" (p. 115).

The answer to the expression of speech by "those whose views trouble us, or frighten us" is, according to Hentoff, "to answer it with more and better language of your own" (1992, p. 161). Hentoff has encouraged teachers to remind students of their free speech rights, especially when politically controversial subjects are raised. Teachers might say, for example, "I want everyone here to be able to think and speak without fear of intimidation. Remember, it takes courage to take a minority position, and history often applauds those who did. Remember, too, that there is no shame in changing your mind or in withholding judgment if you're not sure what you think" (Hentoff, 1992, p. 276).

Teaching Intellectual Freedom

Educators and First Amendment scholars alike defend teachers' academic freedom and students' intellectual rights, not only to help teachers do a better job of teaching but also to help students do a better job of learning. There is broad agreement that the continuation and growth of democracy depends on the freedom to teach and learn, and teachers, along with parents, hold the key to developing responsible citizenship. Fege has said that public schools are public not only because they are free but also because they are charged with "creating" citizens: "Shaping character, transmitting common civic values, and nourishing critical thinking to future generations are as vital tasks as teaching reading" (1990, p. 49).

Many teachers begin by building classroom dialogue and decision making into the classroom structure and schedule. One teacher, for example, teaches intellectual freedom as she and her students negotiate rules during the first few weeks of school. The fifth-grade students write out their own rules, and then together they study and analyze them and eventually establish the rules derived from their discussion (Charney, 1992). As students try to abide by the rules, they sometimes discover that not all of the rules work, but even that experience presents a new opportunity for teaching about democratic processes. In this case, the teacher could tell her students were making the right connections later in the year when they studied the Constitution and a student commented, "Hey, they did it like us!"

Even younger students have been taught about intellectual freedom and democracy (Fisher, 1994) by making them responsible for class government. Fisher has one committee for each curriculum area, each of which checks its clipboard daily and performs any committee work that needs to be done to get ready for the day. Early in the year, class meetings are used to brainstorm jobs that each committee can do. Some are standard jobs, others change with the curriculum. Fisher uses class meetings to strengthen the classroom community. In a circle, students discuss positive ways of working and playing together. They concentrate on specific school-related problems that need to be solved. On those occasions, Fisher acts as scribe to write the decisions and rules on chart paper.

When there is a problem (e.g., whether to allow cutting in line or how to include everyone who wants to play tag on the playground), Fisher and her students "talk the problem" and consider answers to such questions as "what is the problem? what do we want to have happen? what are some ways to solve it? what way shall we try?" After they try the solution for two days, they reflect on such questions as "was the solution a good one? and do we need to talk about the problem some more?" (Fisher, 1994).

Teachers like Bobbi Fisher use conflict inside the classroom in a positive way to teach individual moral character and the civic values of the group as well. Many of the most significant issues in the world grow out of conflict and controversy, but often in school we avoid them like the plague. In our attempt to avoid the unpleasant, too often we accept censorship and control— which many of us believe is too great a price for students and society to pay for short-term conformity (Nelson, 1990, p. 24).

Too often, we kill students' interest. A study conducted by People for the American Way (Carroll et al., 1987) concluded that much of the blame should be placed on publishers of social studies textbooks for killing students' interest in the controversies that are essential to spark an interest in democracy:

> What is missing, in a word, is controversy. Eighty percent of the civics books and half of the government books minimize conflict and compromise. The dynamic sense of government and politics—the fierce debates, colorful characters, triumphs and tragedies—is lost. Controversies like school prayer and civil rights that have ignited passions at all points along the political spectrum are ignored or barely mentioned. The vitality of political involvement and the essential give and take between people and their elected officials is neglected. One text drily asserts, "Conflicts . . . between citizens and government may be settled according to law."

* * *

> The result of this dry recitation of facts is texts that encourage young people to be bystanders in democracy rather than active citizens. These texts fail to instill a sense of civic responsibility, challenge students to think critically, or urge them to get involved in public life. Textbooks should be inspiriting as well as informative, compelling as well as comprehensive, fascinating as well as factual. (Podesta, 1987)

Although social studies teachers who confront lifeless texts can always lobby for new textbooks, they and their colleagues in all content areas need to develop a range of strategies and resources that will allow them to use conflict and controversy to protect and teach intellectual freedom. Bob Peterson, fifth-grade teacher at La Escuela Fratney in Milwaukee, tries to foster in his students what has been called "civic courage," which encourages concern and interest in social change. Peterson believes that struggle and conflict should be part of the curriculum, that history should focus more on social movements instead of primarily focusing on rulers. He recommends teaching critical thinking and social responsibility through community activities, such as adopting a section of beach on a lake or river and keeping it clean, interviewing people involved in a local strike or community struggle, raising money for earthquake or famine relief, and so forth (1991, p. 177).

In another case, Hentoff reports that when a North Carolina ninth-grader wore a Confederate flag sewn on the back of his denim jacket, the principal asked him not to wear the jacket to school and then forbade him to enter if he persisted. The student's parents talked to attorneys, the school principal, and superintendent and, amazingly, they "agreed that rather than get into a court battle, they would hold an assembly and let the kids hear the conflicting points of view." Hentoff points out that there had been Black-White tensions at the school before and many had bristled at the sight of the jacket. Hentoff was an observer when several students and others spoke at the assembly, which turned out to be an opportunity to focus on conflict about the First Amendment rights of those who hold unpopular opinions (Hentoff, 1992, pp. 361–363).

One of the attorneys participating in the assembly that Hentoff described made the most lasting impression when he told students:

> Today the Confederate flag is not very popular with school officials. Twenty years ago, the symbols of the civil rights movement were not very popular with many school officials. In the 1960s, black people marched in all parts of the South to bring down legalized racism. . . . Everywhere they marched they offended many white people who believed things were fine just the way they were. Those marchers faced angry white crowds who were disturbed by the marchers' message. If the hostile reaction of those crowds had justified bans on demonstrations and marches, there would be no Civil Rights Act or Voting Rights Act or integrated restaurants and motels. (Hentoff, 1992, p. 361)

After the assembly, students had debates in each classroom and in a schoolwide meeting of classroom representatives on whether hateful speech, in this case in the form of the Confederate flag, should be protected. Hentoff reported, "Out of all this robust exchange of views throughout the school, there came an understanding on the part of most of the kids—from hearing viewpoints other than their own—that maybe this free-speech thing should apply to everybody" (1992, p. 362).

Parents do have the right, if they choose, to send their children to a private school that will discourage them from forming or expressing their own ideas and that will instead "systematically indoctrinate" students' particular views and deny them access to contrary opinions (Moshman, 1989, p. 171). Although it sometimes makes us uncomfortable, the Constitution requires us to "tolerate the intolerant" (Moshman, 1989, p. 182). But one of our biggest challenges as teachers and as citizens is to figure out new ways to handle our deepest differences about issues that involve morality, values, and intellectual freedom.

WHAT CAN YOU DO TO PRESERVE INTELLECTUAL FREEDOM?

1. *Build a strong knowledge base.* When we welcome controversy into the classroom, we need to know our content area(s) broadly and deeply, and we need an open-minded attitude toward ideas and issues and a deep understanding of multiple perspectives on significant content-related topics.

2. *Read multiple viewpoints.* Especially if highly charged issues like abortion are considered, students deserve to hear a variety of positions articulated by those who hold them. We need to be able to teach our students strategies for comparing and contrasting multiple perspectives.

3. *Let students lead and facilitate discussion.* When teachers lead all of the discussion of controversial issues, we run the risk that some students will stop listening and will not think critically for themselves.

4. *Use debate and panel discussion.* Use classroom debates and panel discussions to address highly controversial ideas. Anticipating and preparing to respond to opposing views drives students to do more research and thought about both sides of issues. Assign switched positions. Aristotle said that we should know our opponent's position as well as we know our own. Asking students with strongly held positions to switch positions results in new respect for opposing views.

5. *Use an inquiry approach to teaching and learning involving primary sources and texts written from a variety of perspectives.* Inquiry-based teaching and learning depends on teaching students to "inquire" about topics, to dig deep to find information. Often the digging involves finding and reading primary sources. Students learn from such projects to weigh one perspective, or one argument, against another. They learn to think critically as they begin to question some of the assumptions made by authors. Eventually, they learn to shape their own arguments in order to express their own informed ideas and be heard.

6. *Use multimedia materials.* Many teachers have discovered curricular materials, such as the award-winning books and videotapes produced by the Southern Poverty Law Center, that tell the stories about the injustice and anguish that society's greatest conflicts have caused and about how they have been resolved. Such materials breathe life into deadly social studies textbooks, like those surveyed by People for the American Way. Hentoff, who has worked in schools across the country, explained, "I have yet to be in a classroom where—once the Constitution becomes inhabited by actual people—students are not eager to search further into that suddenly compelling document" (1992, p. 357).

7. *Support a free and responsible student press* (see Chapter 4) *taught by qualified advisers.* An open forum student press provides student journalists and their readers real life models and experience with First Amendment free press principles.

HELPFUL RESOURCES

1. American Civic Liberties Union is a liberal watchdog group organized to defend the Constitution and intellectual freedom. They are sometimes criticized when they defend behaviors that most people find reprehensible, but all citizens benefit from their hard work to defend First Amendment rights. Contact: 132 West 43rd Street, New York, NY 10036-6599.

2. Bosmajian, H. A. (Ed.). (1989). *Academic Freedom.* The First Amendment in the Classroom Series, No. 4. New York: Neal-Schuman Publishers. Bosmajian provides accurate information and details that are useful when a particular issue arises or when you simply want a better understanding of what your own intellectual rights are as a teacher. He tells the stories of significant court cases, offering factual information in a relatively easy-to-read format.

3. *Democracy in Education* (IDE) is a "partnership of all participants in the educational process—teachers, administrators, parents and students—who believe that democratic school change must come from those at the heart of education. IDE promotes educational practices that provide students with experiences through which they can develop democratic attitudes and values. IDE works to provide teachers committed to democratic education with a forum for sharing ideas, with a support network of people holding similar values, and with opportunities for professional development." Contact: Institute for Democracy in Education, College of Education, 119 McCracken Hall, Ohio University, Athens, OH 45701-4531.

4. Lewis, B. A. (1991). *The Kid's Guide to Social Action.* Minneapolis: Free Spirit Publishing. This practical paperback is subtitled *How to Solve the Social Problems **You Choose**—And Turn Creative Thinking into Positive Action.* It is full of examples from real "kids in action" classrooms and it details nuts-and-bolts information that most citizens, not just kids, have little experience with—including, for example, power interviewing, power fundraising, and initiating or changing laws.

5. Lickona, T. (1991). *Educating for Character: How Our Schools Can Teach Respect and Responsibility.* New York: Bantam Books. This comprehensive book is packed with concrete suggestions and strategies for the classroom. It is highly recommended by many classroom teachers.

6. Moshman, D. (1989). *Children, Education, and the First Amendment.* Lincoln: University of Nebraska Press. This insightful book is not a quick read but it provides extensive interpretation that will deepen your understanding of classroom implications of the First Amendment.

REFERENCES

American Library Association (ALA). (1992). *Intellectual freedom manual* (4th ed.). Chicago: Author.

Arbus, J. (1994). Building a successful school conflict resolution program. *Primary Voices K–6, 2* (4), 6–11.

Association for Supervision and Curriculum Development (ASCD) Panel on Moral Development. (1988). *Moral education in the life of the school.* Alexandria, VA: Author.

Beane, J. A. (1990). *Affect in the curriculum.* New York: Teachers College Press.

Bennett, W. J. (Ed.). (1993). *The book of virtues: A treasury of great moral stories.* New York: Simon & Schuster.

Bosmajian, H. A. (Ed.). (1989). *Academic freedom. The First Amendment in the Classroom Series, No. 4.* New York: Neal-Shuman Publishers.

Brownstein, M. H. (1990, Mar.). Needles on the sidewalk. *Teacher Magazine,* p. 6.

Carroll, J. D., W. D. Broadnax, G. Contreras, T. E. Mann, N. J. Ornstein, & J. Stiehm (1987). *We the people: A review of U.S. government and civics textbooks.* Washington, DC: People for the American Way.

Carter, S. L. (1993). *The culture of disbelief: How American law and politics trivialize religious devotion.* New York: Basic Books.

Carter, S. L. (1994, Dec. 5). Let us pray. *The New Yorker,* pp. 60–74.

Charney, R. S. (1992). Be nice! . . . and other classroom rules. *A Newsletter for Teachers.* Greenfield, MA: Northeast Foundation for Children.

Cohen, P. (1995, Spring). The content of their character. *Curriculum Update* [Association for Supervision and Curriculum Development].

Coles, R., & L. Genevie (1990, March). The moral life of America's school children. *Teacher Magazine,* pp. 42–49.

Danielson, J. B. (1993). Controversial issues and young children: Kindergartners try to understand Chernobyl. In S. Berman and P. La Farge (Eds.), *Promising practices in teaching social responsibility* (pp. 13–26). New York: State University of New York Press.

Dunn, J. M. (1987). Personal belief and public policy. In F. S. Bolin & J. M. Falk (Eds.), *Teacher renewal* (pp. 76–86). New York: Teachers College Press.

Eveslage, T. (1988). *A reversal on regulation of student expression.* ERIC Digest, No. 8. Bloomington: ERIC Clearinghouse on Reading and Communication Skills.

Fege, A. F. (1990). Academic freedom and community involvement: Maintaining the balance. In A. S. Ochoa (Ed.), *Academic freedom to teach and to learn: Every teacher's issue* (pp. 48–59). Washington, DC: National Education Association.

Fisher, B. (1994). Getting democracy into first grade—Or any grade. *Teaching Pre K–8, 25* (1), 87–89.

Gaddy, B. B., T. W. Hall, & R. J. Marzano (1996). *School wars: Resolving our conflicts over religion and values.* San Francisco: Jossey-Bass.

Greer, C., & H. Kohl (Eds.). (1995). *A call to character: A family treasury.* New York: HarperCollins.

Haynes, C. C., & O. Thomas (Eds.). 1994. *Finding common ground: A First Amendment guide to religion and public education* (rev. ed.). Nashville: The Freedom Forum First Amendment Center.

Hempelman, K. A. (1994). *Teen legal rights: A guide for the '90s.* Westport, CT: Greenwood Press.

Hentoff, N. (1992). *Free speech for me—But not for thee: How the American left and right relentlessly censor each other.* New York: Harper Perennial.

Kirschenbaum, H. (1992, June). A comprehensive model for values education and moral education. *Phi Delta Kappan,* pp. 771–776.

Lickona, T. (1991). *Educating for character: How our schools can teach respect and responsibility.* New York: Bantam Books.

Meade, J. (1990, March). Introduction: The moral life of America's schoolchildren. *Teacher Magazine,* pp. 39–41.

Moshman, D. (1986). Children's intellectual rights: A First Amendment analysis. In D. Moshman (Ed.), *Children's intellectual rights* (pp. 25–38). San Francisco: Jossey-Bass.

Moshman, D. (1989). *Children, education, and the First Amendment.* Lincoln: University of Nebraska Press.

Nelson, J. L. (1990). The significance of and rationale for academic freedom. In A. S. Ochoa (Ed.), *Academic freedom to teach and to learn: Every teacher's issue* (pp. 21–30). Washington, DC: National Education Association.

Nord, W. A. (1995). *Religion and American education: Rethinking a national dilemma.* Chapel Hill: The University of North Carolina Press.

Peterson, R. E. (1991). Teaching how to read the world and change it: Critical pedagogy in the intermediate grades. In C. E. Walsh (Ed.), *Literacy as praxis: Culture, language, and pedagogy* (pp. 156–182). Norwood, NJ: Ablex.

Podesta, A. T. (1987). Foreword. In J. S. Carroll et al., *We the people: A review of U.S. government and civics textbooks.* Washington, DC: People for the American Way.

Reichman, H. (1988). *Censorship and selection: Issues and answers for schools.* Chicago: American Library Association and Arlington, VA: American Association of School Administrators.

Simonds, R. (n.d.). *How to help your school be a winner! Who speaks for the children?* Costa Mesa, CA: National Association of Christian Educators/Citizens for Excellence in Education.

Simonds, R. (1996, July). *President's report* [National Association of Christian Educators/Citizens for Excellence in Education].

Strope, J. L., Jr., & C. Broadwell (1990). Academic freedom: What the courts have said. In A. S. Ochoa (Ed.), *Academic freedom to teach and to learn: Every teacher's issue* (pp. 31–47). Washington, DC: National Education Association.

Van Geel, T. (1986). The Constitution and the child's right to freedom from political indoctrination. In D. Moshman (Ed.), *Children's intellectual rights* (pp. 7–23). San Francisco: Jossey-Bass.

Wallis, J. (1994). *The soul of politics*. New York: The New Press.

Wringe, C. (1986). Three children's rights claims and some reservations. In D. Moshman (Ed.), *Children's intellectual rights* (pp. 51–62). San Francisco: Jossey-Bass.

CHAPTER

10 Taking Action

Policies and Strategies

*Legal precedent has left no doubt that at the very least, school boards should
have some articulated policy for selecting and retaining instructional
materials. When a board appears to have acted capriciously, the courts show
concern, and nothing gives the appearance of caprice so strongly as the lack of
a policy.*

—Mary Sheehy Moe (1995)

As teachers, we focus primarily on our classroom world because it consumes our time
and passion. We do not teach in a vacuum, however. The issues addressed in this chapter focus on what we can do as we face each day knowing our classroom curricular
resources and methodology are subject to scrutiny, criticism, or attack from concerned
individual parent protesters and from political groups organized to undermine public
education.

Classroom teachers can play a unique role—explaining and defending curricular choices, working with parents and community in positive ways, and becoming an
activist and advocate for public education. When we apply First Amendment principles to classroom decisions, we can avoid self-censorship, anticipate confrontation
with protest groups, and consider ways to address challenges. When we help plan and
establish school- or districtwide policies and procedures for selecting and retaining
materials and methodologies, we help teach all of those we work with—parents,
school board members, teachers, and the community—about academic and intellectual freedom.

The costs are high for school-based censorship and controversy. Huge chunks of
time can be diverted from teaching and learning. Expenses incurred to defend teachers
and curricula can drain personal and school district bank accounts. Educational consultant Janet Jones has warned about other potential ill effects:

- Loss of momentum within the curriculum
- Undermined staff effectiveness and trust
- Deterioration of school-community relations
- Frustration and hostility turned inward on the self
- Staff leaving the district
- Self-censorship
- Board becoming the mouthpiece of a parent protest group. (1990, p. 99)

Many teachers have learned from the wisdom and long experience of Ken Donelson, censorship scholar and classroom teacher. Donelson explained, "No matter how the book protesters . . . came to me, and some were jovial and confiding and others were antagonistic and untrusting, they all challenged my right as a teacher to select books for students" (1987, p. xiv). Included among the lessons Donelson learned from experience are the following:

- That parents aren't necessarily going to trust my judgment simply because I was a teacher
- That some people can't be placated
- To respect the sincerity and honesty of the protestor without giving in, though I have always believed that any parent has the right to control the reading of his or her child and no one else
- That I caused many of the problems that I labeled censorship by not communicating with parents about both what I taught and, more important, why I taught as I did
- That there are rarely only two sides to an issue
- That other teachers . . . were sometimes under attack for their ideas or books. . . . We all ought to band together to face attacks. (Donelson, 1987)

Donelson candidly has blamed educators for poorly handling censorship attempts and especially for not being willing to take a stand. Some teachers, he has insisted, favor indoctrination rather than education, and some are "gutless wonders" who are "incapable of fighting or unwilling to fight for education and against censorship" (p. xv). As a teacher, Donelson explained, he learned that he could expect no support from his superintendent or administrators and to *expect* censorship attempts and not be frightened if they came. Writing the Introduction to a set of books about court cases, Donelson reported that he was much slower at learning about court decisions but that from them he realized that court cases offered reassurance that teachers have a place to turn (pp. xiv–xvi). From Donelson and a host of others cited in this book, we can learn to work together with colleagues, parents, and organizations to reduce the likelihood of challenges without self-censoring and to be ready when they come. And even if we feel more or less alone, there are steps we can take and resources we can use.

Making a Plan

Filling out the checklist in Figure 10.1 will serve as a review of some of the issues addressed in earlier chapters and also as a blueprint to help you sense needs and issues that still need to be addressed.

FIGURE 10.1   Circumventing Censorship

Directions: Check a YES, NO, or DON'T KNOW (DK) for each question and, to the best of your ability, complete the narrative sections.

__ Yes __ No __ DK   **1.** Does your district have an up-to-date policy manual?

__ Yes __ No __ DK   **2.** Does your district have policies for both the selection and reconsideration of instructional materials?

__ Yes __ No __ DK   A. If so, have they been formally adopted?

__ Yes __ No __ DK   B. Have they been reviewed/revised in the last 3 years?

__ Yes __ No __ DK   **3.** Does each policy contain explicit details regarding timelines, responsibilities and definitions of terms?

__ Yes __ No __ DK   **4.** Does the policy require a procedural inquiry of the material before any action can be taken to change or remove it?

__ Yes __ No __ DK   **5.** Is there a procedure for parent complaints which requires their written documentation?

__ Yes __ No __ DK   **6.** Does the school system regularly communicate with civic, religious, educational and political organizations in your community? (This means using methods other than a newsletter once a month.)

__ Yes __ No __ DK   **7.** Has your district actively defined and promoted the concept of intellectual freedom for both the staff and the community?

__ Yes __ No __ DK   **8.** Is there an academic freedom policy or negotiated academic freedom clause in the teachers' contract?

__ Yes __ No __ DK   **9.** Would you say, currently, that the vast majority of the teaching staff, administrators and board of directors agree on a definition of intellectual freedom?

__ Yes __ No __ DK   **10.** Does your district stay aware of local, state, and national organizations that are most likely to challenge curricula and school district practices?

_____

_____

__ Yes __ No __ DK   **11.** Has your district kept track of organizations who are most likely to be knowledgeable and supportive of public education and intellectual freedom?

_____

_____

__ Yes __ No __ DK   **12.** Do most district employees understand the "language of censorship" in relation to their particular subject area, grade level or job responsibility?

Source: Adapted from "Circumventing Censorship" by Janet L. Jones in *No Right Turn: Assuring the Forward Progress of Public Education,* 1993, Washington Education Association. Reprinted by permission of Janet L. Jones.

Effectively facing censorship and controversy requires a specific plan, a plan that might grow out of responses to the "Circumventing Censorship" checklist. Any "don't know" responses call for further investigation—asking questions and seeking out the right people to check with. The "no" responses can become a working plan and a "talking points" sheet to be used to encourage colleagues and administrators to work together.

Then comes the tougher task of volunteering to help establish or revise school- or districtwide materials selection policies, procedures, and philosophy statements, if action is needed. It is reasonable to ask administrators or the school board for professional development time for an ad hoc committee to work together to research and plan. Also, it will take time to gather and read source materials recommended in this book.

The ideal is to work with colleagues who can all read and discuss the same materials or divide the materials and report on important information and ideas gleaned from several sources. Eventually, parents, community members, and students can be invited to participate in discussions and planning, especially when new ideas and plans are being considered.

Learning about Censorship

Teachers and Administrators

First Amendment scholar Nat Hentoff has reminded us that censorship is not an appropriate way to squelch views with which we disagree. This is especially true for professional educators. Indeed, believing in intellectual freedom means that we will fight against the suppression of ideas and information—even ideas that we hate (Hentoff, 1992). Consider the following public dialogue between two librarians:

> Do I have the right to make available to children a book that might do them harm? Suppose, a woman novelist—a fine, compelling writer—were to write a vivid, powerful novel against a woman's fundamental right of privacy to choose to have an abortion. A beautifully written novel in which the pro-life characters were so attractive they could make you cry, and the pro-choice people were cold and selfish. And in which the writer repeatedly calls abortion "murder." Should I allow such a novel to poison the minds of young people, to give them so misleading and distorted a sense of what's at stake in a woman's right to decide so deeply personal a question? . . . If being true to the First Amendment means that I am free to warp young people's minds in the name of intellectual freedom, is that what I should be doing? Maybe I could do with a little less freedom.
>
> *Response:*
> I want to make sure that I understand what you're saying. Are you saying that we should put limits on what children learn and think and explore—so that they will be able to think for themselves when they grow up? So that they'll be more free when they grow up? (Hentoff, 1992, pp. 372–373)

The first speaker's position may sound reasonable. But the second speaker shows us why the first speaker is wrong. I think of librarians as generally having a deeper understanding of the dangers of censorship and a deeper appreciation of intellectual freedom than most of us as classroom teachers possess. If even librarians—who have been more rigorously trained to handle censorship attempts—still need to be reminded of intellectual freedom issues, then surely we as classroom teachers need it even more so.

Many teachers, in fact, know little about the significance of censorship and intellectual freedom issues, as Kathie Krieger Cerra's research has revealed. She asked 348 Minnesota elementary teachers about how they selected books for their classrooms: "When you are warned that a favorably reviewed book which you have read is risky because of its subject matter, what action do you take when considering purchase of the book for your classroom?" From the responses, she learned that only 15.8 percent "purchase the book anyway, and do not limit student access," that 24.7 percent "purchase the book, but limit student access," and that 59.5 percent "do not purchase the book" (Cerra, 1994, p. 47).

One reason many teachers do not understand how to handle such curricular decisions well is that their professional preparation may not have adequately addressed these issues. When Cerra asked 373 elementary teachers about their preservice experience, only 135 respondents (37.1 percent) said yes, they had attended a class session devoted to intellectual freedom, while 229 respondents (62.9 percent) said no, they had not attended such a session (1994, p. 50). Clearly, citizens and educators need to insist that preservice teachers learn more about censorship and intellectual freedom.

When I asked a group of preservice teachers to think of a time when they had experienced censorship, most of them could not do it—not because it had not happened, we later realized, but because school censorship is so often invisible to its victims. Now I work harder to focus preservice teachers' attention on censorship and intellectual freedom issues. For example, in a reading course I taught recently for preservice elementary teachers, we experimented with literature circles. Rather than give students a free choice of literature to read, I asked them to select among recently published adolescent novels that focused in some way on controversial issues—homosexuality, religion, racism, censorship, or incest. Students were grouped by the text they selected. As we read and responded to the texts, we reflected not only on what we read but also on the literature circle experience and on the classroom implications of using or not using such texts in their future classrooms. This experience sparked vigorous discussion and debate. In the end, several students still had reservations about whether and how they would use these particular texts in their own classrooms, but as a result of this experience, they all will face their "selection" tasks with more thought and insight.

Students

Janie Hydrick (1994), an elementary teacher in Mesa, Arizona, has stayed alert to current challenges and looks for ways to turn the news into a learning experience for her students. When she read in her local paper that *Slugs* by David Greenburg was being reviewed by another school district's book complaint review committee, she immediately thought of her own children's love of the book and the fact that the author had visited in her daughter's classroom the day before and her daughter had brought home an autographed copy of the book.

Hydrick was not deterred when she discovered that her third-grade teaching colleagues were not willing to risk criticism by reading the controversial book to their students. We can all learn from the skillful lesson that she created for her own third-graders: She read the book aloud to her third-graders and showed them the illustrations. She noted to herself that her students' reactions ranged from "Yea! Rad! Neat!" to "Yuck! Sick! Gross!" Then without interjecting her own opinion, she asked, "Well, what did you think?" When the first student's reaction was "It was awful," Hydrick said, "I can understand why you feel that way.... And do you know what? There's a group of moms who agree with you." She showed students the newspaper article and explained that some parents wanted the book taken off the shelves. At that point, other students began to express more positive responses to the book: "But I liked it. I thought it was funny."

Hydrick then skillfully took the side of the parents and explained where their actions might lead, all the while hinting by her tone that the opinions she expressed were not her own: "Sorry, guys, you're out of luck on this one. Alison doesn't like *Slugs* and neither do these moms." Then, returning to Alison, she said, "Are there any other books that you feel strongly about? There wouldn't be any problem removing them from our class library. And we could probably get Mrs. Edgell to remove them from our school library. And—if enough kids and moms agree, we could probably have them removed from the city library."

When some students began naming books they did not like, Janie volunteered to write the titles on the board. For each title suggested, however, another student protested. Hydrick followed the students' leads, offering each protester the opportunity to decide what to censor: "Maybe it's Tyson's list we should go by and not Alison's?" When a student asked, "Why should we go with Tyson's list?" Hydrick continued in her devil's advocate role: "You obviously don't understand. If a book bothers someone, we need to see that the book is removed from the library so that it won't bother anyone else." Eventually after other titles were condemned and defended, students began to suggest, "Well, they don't have to read it.... Let them get something else to read." Later that day, two students wrote an article for the class newspaper, which concluded: "Some of us liked it, some of us didn't. *Slugs* is on any library shelf. If you want to read it you can and then you can decide if you like it or not." In retrospect, Hydrick realized that although her students did not use the word *censorship* that day, what this experience taught stuck with them during the course of the year. From time to time she heard them remind each other that people have different likes and dislikes and she knew that they had learned from the insight expressed in their own words: "some of us liked it, some of us didn't" (Hydrick, 1994, p. 202).

This kind of explicit teaching about censorship and controversial issues can easily take place across the curriculum. A library media specialist recommends a cross-curricular focus on the First Amendment (Scales, 1995). When studying the Constitution in social studies courses, students can read and react to contemporary novels that deal with censorship issues in their English language arts class. Students can research various First Amendment issues and provide a forum to express their views regarding the subject of intellectual freedom. These activities will help them understand their personal options regarding the use of books and materials that might offend them. Other practical classroom ideas include (Scales, 1995):

- Displaying banned books and asking students to consider what they would say to someone who told them that one of the books was inappropriate for them to read
- Conducting polls, such as asking 25 adults why they feel scary stories are harmful to children and teenagers, then polling 25 peers, asking the same question, and charting the results
- Discussing ways families can deal with controversial books, movies, and music without forbidding their use
- Discussing access to offensive Internet materials and whether online services should be controlled or monitored.

Parents

In some communities, teachers or librarians have organized sessions for parents to read and discuss controversial books used in the curriculum. The results have been very positive: "Complaints were replaced with strong community support for the books and praise for the dedication of the teachers" (Franks, 1986). Such plans carry some risk, of course, given that individual parents or groups might use the occasion to promote a particular extremist agenda.

Following a school media specialist's plan might increase the likelihood of success. Gretchen V. Swibold set up an evening of discussion with teachers and parents called "Changes in Children's Literature: The Children's Books of Judy Blume" (Boardman, 1993). She planned the session very wisely. Children were not included in the discussion but were invited in advance to respond in writing to their reading of Blume's books. The students' comments expressed how Blume reflected real life and how the books made them think. Even more important, Swibold asked each adult attending to have read at least one book by Judy Blume. She then designed the session around discussion of the students' written comments about the books and the following questions:

- What is the value, for an adult, of reading Judy Blume's children's books?
- Someone has described Blume's books as didactic. If you agree with that description, do you object to that quality?
- Many children obviously enjoy Blume's books. Do you think there are other good reasons for reading them?
- Do you like the children in Blume's books? Do they seem real to you as an adult?
- Do you think Blume's adults are honestly conceived?
- Is sexuality conceived as an evil or a good in these books?
- Changes in children's literature have brought us books about all kinds of 'new' subjects; are these changes good ones in your view? (Boardman, 1993, pp. 1.10–1.11)

Such questions effectively kept the focus on Swibold's primary goal of helping parents recognize for themselves the value of books about controversial issues.

Establishing Policies and Procedures

Anyone who researches school censorship issues quickly discovers the admonition to be sure there are established, school-board approved curricular selection policies as well as reconsideration policies and procedures. But in practice, classroom teachers have not always valued such policies and procedures. I once heard a young teacher describe her classroom experience using a book titled *Monster,* written by a former Los Angeles gang member, with alternative high school students. She reported that, although her students responded very positively to the book, she cannot teach it any-more. She explained that the school district did not have a selection policy before but "unfortunately, they do now." She said that it was the book's language that parents objected to, and so, "I offered to use white-out so I could still use it, but. . . ." I hoped she was being facetious, but I could not tell for sure.

This teacher had operated on the premise that she would take the risk and do what she wanted until someone told her not to. Such a policy—or lack of one—works well for some who teach in districts with little conflict and who have enough experience to operate by instinct. Many teachers, however, have little or no such protection and may not have even the support of their colleagues when they face challenges.

Teachers who have experienced long-term school conflict usually realize that carefully prepared policies and procedures carry several benefits for all concerned: They provide a "front-end process" that provides a context for teachers' choices and that demonstrates a high standard of professionalism (Myers, n.d.). They often reduce distress, panic, anger, frustration, and confrontation, and they provide for a response to challenges. Moreover, they assure various groups—parents, administrators, and others—that teachers "have chosen materials responsibly and reflectively, with intensive knowledge of both their discipline and their students" (Myers, n.d.). Moe pointed out that policies also provide legal protection for school boards, explaining that "nothing gives the appearance of caprice so strongly as the lack of a policy" (1995).

Those who prefer to operate without formal policies are right to want the freedom to make their own curricular choices, but that does not mean they do not need selection and reconsideration policies. It means that teachers who help design such policies will want to work hard to create policies that *reduce,* rather than increase, constraints on classroom choices. The remainder of this chapter can serve as a blueprint for classroom teachers to consider while thinking through the policies and procedures needed to focus on issues that have impact at the classroom, school, district, community, state, and national levels.

Philosophy Statements

Work with others to create or review a board-approved philosophy statement that guides education in your community or area. Concurrently or alternatively, articulate your own philosophy statement as a teacher. Write it out, post it in your classroom, and discuss it with students and parents.

Many school communities have developed philosophy or mission statements that express their overarching goals. Often, they consist of carefully worded, paragraph-length vision statements describing what they hope each student will gain and/or what the students' education will provide. It takes time to participate in the development process, but if your district does not have a philosophy statement, you will want to encourage administrators and colleagues to begin the process of developing one. Once in place, the philosophy statement is the "guiding light" (Moe, 1995, p. 2) for selection policies and procedures. That is, it will steer materials selection processes as well as "direct the attention of the courts toward a [school] board's own intent, should a challenge occur" (p. 2).

The *Rethinking Schools* group in Milwaukee has developed a set of principles that is more progressive and critical than many school districts and communities might create. I include it, in summary form, not as a model philosophy statement as much as a place to start in thinking about the possibilities that philosophy statements hold (see Figure 10.2).

FIGURE 10.2   Philosophy Statement

What if a school district used the set of principles articulated in *Rethinking Our Classrooms* as the basis for developing a philosophy statement that would guide the district's curricula and selection policies? In that case, the statement might say something like the following:

Selection decisions demonstrate the attempt to provide all students with a wide range of materials and experiences that are:

- *Grounded in the lives of our students:* rooted in students' needs and experiences; exploring the ways their lives connect to, and are limited by, the broader society
- *Critical:* equipping students to "talk back" to the world; posing essential critical questions
- *Multicultural, antiracist, projustice:* striving to include the lives of all those in our society, especially the marginalized and dominated
- *Participatory, experiential:* allowing concepts to be experienced firsthand; encouraging students to make real decisions and collectively solve problems
- *Hopeful, joyful, kind, visionary:* organizing classroom life to make students feel significant and cared about; creating a "community of conscience"
- *Activist:* encouraging students to think of themselves as truth-tellers and change makers; offering opportunities to act on ideas
- *Academically rigorous:* equipping students to maneuver in the world that exists; inspiring levels of academic performance exceeding those motivated or measured by grades and test scores
- *Culturally sensitive:* learning from our students; calling on parents and culturally diverse community resources for insights into the community we serve

Source: Excerpted and adapted from B. Bigelow, L. Christensen, S. Karp, B. Miner, & B. Peterson, (Eds.). (1994). Creating classrooms for equity and social justice. In *Rethinking Our Classrooms* (pp. 4–5). Reprinted with permission from *Rethinking Our Classrooms*, Rethinking Schools, 1001 E. Keefe Ave., Milwaukee, WI 53212; 414-964-9646.

Selection Policies and Procedures

Work with others to create or review board-approved policies for selecting materials, resources, and teaching methodologies. The policy document should include statements that address the definition of materials and resources covered, the guidelines for selection decisions, and the responsibility for selections.

Definition of Materials and Resources Covered

1. Selection policies should define and identify curricula and course-related materials and/or methodologies that can be assigned for or used with whole class groups, small groups, and individual students.*

2. Selection policies should address not only materials that have been purchased but also those that are loaned or donated. Education consultant Janet Jones has recommended that such materials not be included in the curriculum unless and until they are approved by a selection committee in accordance with selection criteria (1993, p. 94).

3. The policy should state that a selection group will discuss every work under consideration for ongoing, regular, routine inclusion, giving extended attention to works that are likely to be assigned for whole-class reading or viewing. But selection policies should "recommend that the scope of the policy not unwittingly stifle spontaneity and creativity in teachers by requiring a formal selection process for all materials used for instructional purposes" (NCTE *Guidelines*). Teachers and students should be permitted to use materials that do not lend themselves to the formal selection process—for example, current newscasts, television programs, articles, student writing samples, and materials for short-term projects. Such supplemental materials may be selected or approved by the teacher, with the understanding that they meet the general selection criteria of educational relevance and ability to meet student needs (NCTE *Guidelines*).

4. The policy should address distinctions between library resources and classroom resources. In the past, courts have granted more leeway in selecting library items for students' voluntary use and much tighter constraints on classroom resources, based on the practice of all students being assigned the same texts and experiences. Individual and small-group inquiry projects blur such distinctions and call for careful attention as policies are developed.

5. Policies should reflect the understanding that the school's curricula and each class's curriculum are comprised of a collection of instructional materials that as a whole need to create a balance and emphasis in the curriculum (NCTE *Guidelines*). A statement to this effect will serve as a safeguard against potential community proposals that every individual resource should reflect values that are endorsed by the school or district.

---

*This suggestion and several of those that follow apply to all content areas but have been drawn from or adapted from the National Council of Teachers of English (n.d.) *Guidelines for Selection of Materials in English Language Arts Programs.* Copyright by the National Council of Teachers of English. Reprinted with permission.

Guidelines for Selection Decisions

1. All school personnel should strictly adhere to the policies and procedures.

2. Selection is part of sound program planning within the district. The selection process should be part of each school's annual schedule, and adequate time must be set aside for the selection process. Goldstein recommended that selections not be based on similar selections that have been made by other school districts, regardless of their reputations, unless that district's curricula and academic emphases are carefully reviewed (1989, p. 23).

3. Selection committees must have a charge that is clearly specified and understood by all. For example, all selections should be made on the basis of the materials' strength according to the criteria set forth in the selection policy document.

4. Curricular materials should align with the general philosophy and philosophy statement of the school or district, with the goals and objectives of the curriculum as a whole, and with the specific objectives of the particular course or grade level (NCTE *Guidelines*).

5. Selection policies and procedures should reflect mandated and recommended state and national standards and assessments that are aligned with best practice.

6. Age appropriateness alone is not sufficient reason to include particular materials in the curriculum, but materials should be suited to the maturity level of the students for whom they are intended. Age appropriateness is an important factor for sensitive topics, including (1) obscenity, profanity, and vulgarity; (2) the subject of sex; (3) religious and moral objections; and (4) violence and brutality (Moe, 1995). "The answer to creating guidelines regarding offensiveness," according to Moe, "may lie in connecting topic-sensitivity with age-appropriateness."

7. Materials must be selected with an eye toward coordinating instruction within and between grade levels, courses, and discipline. This is not an argument for a fixed, lock-step curriculum but for a collegial sharing of goals and ideas for instructional materials as teachers engage in the process of selecting materials (NCTE *Guidelines*).

8. Materials must be selected with the understanding that some of the curricula and classroom experiences will be negotiated between teachers and learners within classroom communities. That is, teachers should be empowered to use their wisdom to make curricular decisions consistent with the district's guidelines and with recommended best practice. Also, students should be able to make at least some decisions about some assignments and classroom experiences.

9. The policy should include a statement affirming both students' intellectual freedom and teachers' academic freedom. It should also express the value of including and addressing controversial issues. For many years, the courts have been clear about recognizing the inevitability that the curriculum will include controversial ideas and issues. Although access to cable television, newspapers, books, radios, and computers with Internet connections make it impossible to exclude controversial ideas from children's lives, protest groups still try to keep controversy out of the classrooms. Thus, selection policies should include a statement affirming the value of "examining a wide range of viewpoints" (Moe, 1995) and using resources that "give students a sense of both the range and limits of ongoing public debate," so that students will understand that a middle ground exists between "blind adherence to a monolithic orthodoxy" and the "nihilistic belief that no idea is better than any other" (Stewart, cited by Moe, 1995).

10. Consideration of major texts should involve review of several texts or text series. An evaluation sheet for materials being considered should be developed that will reflect the school or district's philosophy and selection criteria. Reviewing texts in use should occur on a regularly scheduled basis.

11. The selection criteria should be made public in written form. NCTE recommends that the list of materials be made available for comments by students, parents, and the public at any time, with the understanding that further informal selection and changes are sometimes made as teachers perceive opportunities during the course of the year to better meet students' needs through other materials (NCTE *Guidelines*).

Responsibility for Selections

1. Typically, selection policies dictate who has the authority to make decisions about classroom and library materials. Court cases in the 1980s indicate that the building principal ultimately has the authority to make those decisions for the school, and the superintendent to make decisions for the district, but because the superintendent is appointed by the school board, the school board itself has the final say. NCTE (whose members are primarily classroom teachers) has recommended that administrators and schools boards (who are legally responsible for selection decisions) should delegate this responsibility to teaching professionals (NCTE *Guidelines*).

2. The reason classroom teachers are usually the best selection decision makers is that those responsible for selecting curriculum and resources must have enough experience and knowledge to make sound choices and to be able to defend those choices. This means experience and knowledge not just related to students' backgrounds and learning experiences (as parents would have), but also of "students' abilities, interests, and learning styles"; not just of educational objectives, but of the "best practices and range and quality of materials for meeting them" (the knowledge that teachers bring); not just of the particular work being considered, but of its "place within the medium, genre, epoch, etc., it represents" (NCTE *Guidelines*).

3. Policies should provide for school-based textbook selection committees composed mainly of teachers in appropriate content areas. The Minnesota Civil Liberties Union has cautioned against district self-censorship: "Only administrative reasons (for example, costs) and educational judgments should be used as the basis for rejecting teachers' choices of educational resources and teaching methods, never the personal, political, religious, social or aesthetic beliefs and biases of principals, superintendents or school board members or the worry that some members of the community will complain or think that the content of the educational resources is controversial" (n.d.).

Rationales

Once selections are made—or even as selections are made—the selection committee(s) should create and then maintain a file of written rationales.

I admit that developing rationales is time-consuming work, but it is work that is important and worthwhile. Writing rationales forces us to articulate why we teach what we teach and gives us the chance to help parents and administrators better understand how and why teaching and learning happen as they do in our classrooms. However, every item brought into the classroom does not require an extensive written rationale. Given that some nationally organized groups have called for school board approval of every item used in the classroom, even for an hour, it is essential that selection policies state explicitly that not everything needs to go through the formal selection and rationale process. Brown and Stephens (1994) have suggested a range of rationale options:*

1. *Informal Selection Committee Notes:* A brief written statement of purpose for using a particular book—the *why* for using it and *where it will fit in the curriculum*—is sometimes all that is needed. Brown and Stephens have cautioned that such notes must be *written:* "Just thinking about the reason is not enough to demonstrate thoughtful planning, if a protest should arise, nor does it provide teachers with opportunities to be reflective about their decisions."

2. *Formal Rationales Prepared by Teachers:* Formal rationales are often produced using a given format established by a school district. The rationale form in Figure 10.3 has been used by countless teachers and districts since it was first published in 1979.

3. *Published Rationales:* In the past, teachers have used collections of rationales published by professional organizations (Brown & Stephens, 1994). Professional organizations are beginning to develop CD-ROM programs that provide database rationales.

4. *Supplementary Materials:* Teachers can also use published reviews to build a defense for particular texts and resources. Student comments about the materials and resource are also valuable to demonstrate the positive impact of the materials.

Rationale Guidelines

I recommend that rationales be prepared for major materials, resources, and methodologies used as an ongoing part of the curriculum and for major resources used less often but that are potentially controversial. State and national standards documents can provide easily identified data to begin the process of gathering support for the inclusion of particular resources. The following recommended elements build on and adapt Brown and Stephens' rationale guidelines (1994):

1. The *bibliographic citation*.
2. The *intended audience*—that is, the type of class, range of grade levels, how the material or resource will be used, and reasons why it is being used.

*Copyright 1994 by the National Council of Teachers of English. Reprinted with permission.

FIGURE 10.3   Teacher's Rationale

School:

Teacher:

Title:

Grade or Course:

Approximate date(s) a book will be used:

This book will be (check one or more):
__ Studied by the whole class
__ Studied by small groups
__ Placed on a reading list
__ Placed in a classroom library
__ Recommended to individual students
__ Part of a larger study of (explain):
__ Other (explain):

Ways in which the book is especially appropriate for students in this class:

Ways in which the book is especially pertinent to the objectives of this course or unit:

Special problems that might arise in relation to the book and some planned activities which handle this problem:

Some other appropriate books an individual student might read in place of this book:

Source: Shugert, D. (1979). How to write a rationale in defense of a book. In J. Davis (Ed.), *Dealing with censorship*. Urbana, IL: National Council of Teachers of English. Copyright by the National Council of Teachers of English. Reprinted with permission.

3. A *brief summary and/or description* of the work that provides an overview, sometimes reflecting aspects of a work that the teacher considers most important and aspects that relate to its educational significance.
4. The *purpose* for using the material or resource and its relationship to the program. As a part of the total program, the book or other resource should be consistent with the ongoing objectives of the class and with any applicable state or national standards. The rationale should address *how* a book or resource will be used, including the teaching methodology and methods of assessment.
5. The *impact* of the book or resource—that is, ways in which it may "open new perspectives" for students or affect their behavior or attitudes.

6. *Potential problems* with the work and how such problems might be handled.
7. Available collection of *information about the book or resource,* such as published reviews, especially those that address any controversial issues in the materials or resource.
8. Available collection of *supplementary information,* such as biographical information about the author, especially if it includes any critical assessment of the author's work.
9. Available collection of *books of rationales* that cite the particular book or resource.
10. *Alternate works* an individual student might read or view instead of a particular resource. It is especially important that rationale documents ask that alternative resources be listed for whole-class assignments involving the study of a particular book or nonprint resource that seems likely to be challenged. Parents who are concerned about particular materials will welcome provision for "excusal policies," especially if the substitutions can be made without embarrassment or calling attention to the students involved. The rationale document in Figure 10.4 incorporates all of these criteria.

Rationales are more problematic than selection policies since they sometimes ask the teacher to identify and thus call attention to "special problems" that might arise in using a particular resource. Brown and Stephens (1994) recommend including such items. The rationale in Figure 10.4 includes this item as an option. Some school districts and teachers will want to use it, probably following item 7. But it is not always wise to call undue attention to and to name potential problems. Some teachers believe that the "potential problems" question results in self-censorship, since teachers are reluctant to write down anything critical about any of the materials they want to select. In any case, it is important for teachers to at least *think through* the ways a particular item might be construed as controversial or problematic. And it is just as important to think through ways any difficulties or controversy might be responded to and addressed. I am convinced that we need to understand and anticipate parents' expressions of concern about particular resources—not so we will self-censor but so we can decide how best to address the concerns. But perhaps a better question to ask is: What merits of the material or resource override or compensate for any potentially controversial characteristics? Or framed even more positively: What makes the material or experience a sound curricular choice? Ultimately, the point is to weigh the merits of the resource by the extent to which it fulfills district guidelines and carries forward the curricular goals.

Most guidelines for rationales focus on books and nonprint resources. But teachers whose classroom practices have been challenged know that sometimes protesters raise objections to teaching methods, educational philosophies, learning strategies, and discussion topics as well. For example, frequently protested are the classroom use of calculators, whole language philosophy, guided visualizations, and discussions about evolution and/or creationism. Figure 10.5 illustrates how such a rationale form can be used to address a learning strategy—in this case, using "learning logs" in an Earth Science class.

FIGURE 10.4   Rationale for Curricular Resources

1. Class: Level:

2. Description of resource and how it will be used:

3. Major curricular goal(s) this resource helps achieve:

4. Resource categories:
   ___ Books and materials formally approved and purchased by school district for classroom use
   ___ Books and materials in the school library/media center
   ___ Internet and World Wide Web resources
   ___ Invited guest speakers
   ___ Books and materials provided by classroom teacher
   ___ Books and materials provided by students
   ___ Books and materials provided by parents
   ___ Other: _____

5. This resource will be used:
   ___ By entire class
   ___ As limited choice by small groups within the class
   ___ As individual choice as part of a focused or thematic unit
   ___ As individual free choice

6. Ways in which this item is especially appropriate for the *age* and the *intellectual, emotional, and/or social development* of students in this class:

7. In what ways and/or to what extent is this resource consistent with school district philosophy statement and selection policies? What makes it a sound curricular choice?

   [**7A.** optional] Ways this work might be controversial/difficult/problematic:
   [**7B.** optional] Ways difficulties might be overcome/problems resolved:

8. Appropriate materials that an individual student might use in place of this item:

9. Comment/other considerations:

Note: The use of a particular material or resource in the classroom does not necessarily mean the school or teacher endorses the ideas and information included. Teachers in this district strive to offer materials that speak from multiple perspectives on many issues, thereby providing an overall neutral view on highly controversial topics about which the general public holds a variety of opinions.

FIGURE 10.5   Rationale for Curricular Resources and Experiences

1. Class: *Earth Science*   Level: *8th grade*
2. Description of resource and/or experience and how it will be used:

   Learning logs—students will do quick-writes in class and at home in response to readings and class experiences. Sometimes students will be asked to record observations and respond to specific prompts about assigned topics. Students will be invited but not required to share some log entries with classmates.

3. Major curricular goal(s) this resource or experience helps achieve:

   Promotes reflective and critical thinking and expressions; uses writing, speaking, and listening to extend learning of Earth Science facts and concepts.

4a. Resource categories:
   ___ books and materials formally approved and purchased by school district for classroom use
   ___ books and materials in the school library/media center
   ___ invited guest speakers
   ___ books and materials provided by classroom teacher
   ___ books and materials provided by students
   ___ books and materials provided by parents
   ✓ other: _____ *class-related experiences* _____

4b. Experience categories (circle any that apply):

   reading; (writing;) (speaking/discussing;) (listening;) viewing; constructing/designing; role-playing; telephoning/emailing; interviewing; teaching/leading/demonstrating; attending; recording;
   other: _____

5. This resource/experience will be used/experienced:
   ✓ by entire class
   ___ as limited choice by small groups within the class
   ___ as individual choice as part of a focused or thematic unit
   ___ as individual free choice

6. Ways in which this item is especially appropriate for the *age* and the *intellectual, emotional, and social development* of students in this class:

   Encourages all to participate by thinking and writing, even shy students who might feel self-conscious expressing opinions in class as a whole. Extends opportunities for private dialogue about Earth Science concepts between teacher and student. When pieces are shared, encourages students to learn from each other.

7. In what ways and/or to what extent does this resource/experience fit school district criteria for selecting curricular materials and classroom experiences? What makes it a sound curricular choice?

   ■ Grounded in the lives of our students
   Personalizes students' engagement with Earth Science concepts, allows them to build on their personal knowledge and strengths.

   (continued)

FIGURE 10.5 Continued

- Critical
  Allows students to pose critical questions and consider possible responses.
- Multicultural, antiracist, projustice
  Promotes respect for all students' voices.
- Participatory, experiential
  Encourages participation by all and allows for hearing a variety of shared responses.
- Hopeful, joyful, kind, visionary
  Values students' individual ideas and opinions.
- Activist
- Academically rigorous
  Enhances learning of Earth Science, clarifies students' understanding, extends writing fluency and expression.
- Culturally sensitive
  Students aren't required to write about personal beliefs or family experiences. Students aren't required to read log entries aloud to classmates.

8. Comment/other considerations:

Not every teacher and district will want to develop formal rationales for classroom practices; however, we all should routinely think about our philosophies, methods, strategies, and discussions in a rationale-like way. If we do, we will be better able to handle questions about our practices when we are called on to defend them.

Reconsideration Policies and Procedures

Establish, in writing, a clearly defined method for handling complaints.

According to People for the American Way (PFAW) reconsideration policy should apply uniformly to *all* complaints, regardless of whether they originate with parents, students, school personnel, school board members, or community members (Hulsizer, 1989). An important part of this policy should address formal reconsideration procedures, deadlines for each step of the process, and the pledge to retain use of the materials until the reconsideration process has been completed.

A form should be used to identify the parent or citizen's specific concerns. Figure 10.6 provides a basic format recommended by NCTE several years ago that can be adapted as needed by particular school districts. The American Library Association's

FIGURE 10.6   Citizen's Request for Reconsideration of a Work

Author _____   Paperback _____

Hardcover _____

Title _____

Publisher (if known) _____

Request initiated by _____

Telephone _____ Address _____

City _____ Zip Code _____

Complainant represents

_____ Himself/Herself

_____ (Name organization) _____

_____ (Identify other group) _____

1. Have you been able to discuss this work with the teacher or librarian who ordered it or who used it?

_____ Yes   _____ No

2. What do you understand to be the general purpose for using this work?
   a. Provide support for a unit in the curriculum?

   _____ Yes   _____ No

   b. Provide a learning experience for the reader in one kind of literature?

   _____ Yes   _____ No

   c. Other _____

3. Did the general purpose for the use of the work, as described by the teacher or librarian, seem a suitable one to you?

   _____ Yes   _____ No

   If not, please explain. _____

4. What do you think is the general purpose of the author in this book? _____

5. In what ways do you think a work of this nature is not suitable for the use the teacher or librarian wishes to carry out? _____

6. Have you been able to learn what is the student's response to this work?

   _____ Yes   _____ No

7. What response did the students make? _____

(continued)

FIGURE 10.6   Continued

---

8. Have you been able to learn from your school library what book reviewers or other students of literature have written about this work?

    _____ Yes   _____ No

9. Would you like the teacher or librarian to give you a written summary of what book reviewers and other students have written about this book or film?

    _____ Yes   _____ No

10. Do you have negative reviews of the book?

    _____ Yes   _____ No

11. Where were they published? _____

12. Would you be willing to provide summaries of the reviews you have collected?

    _____ Yes   _____ No

13. What would you like your library/school to do about this work?

    _____ Do not assign/lend it to my child.

    _____ Return it to the staff selection committee/department for reevaluation.

    _____ Other; please explain. _____

14. In its place, what work would you recommend that would convey as valuable a picture and perspective of the subject treated?_____

Signature _____ Date _____

Source: The Student's Right to Read, NCTE, 1982, pp. 12–13. Copyright 1982 by the National Council of Teachers of English. Reprinted with permission.

Intellectual Freedom Committee has offered a shortened "Statement of Concern about Learning Center Resources" document (Figure 10.7) that conveys a somewhat more positive tone and is appropriate for classroom as well as library use.

A broad-based committee that includes parents and other citizens as well as school personnel should be established to review challenged materials. In fact, the Minnesota Civil Liberties Union recommends that there be a reconsideration committee appointed at the beginning of each school year rather than waiting for a specific complaint to be made. It should have at least teachers, librarians, and academic area specialists as members of the committee. It should have clearly defined procedures for functioning and indicating to whom the decision is to be referred. PFAW recommends that reconsideration committees should be broad based, including not only teachers, librarians, and administrators, but also parents and, if appropriate, students.

FIGURE 10.7   Statement of Concern about Learning Center Resources

(A Simplified Request for Reconsideration Form)

Name _____ Date _____

Address _____ Phone # Home _____

City _____ State _____ Zip _____ Work _____

1. Resources on which you are commenting:

____ Book   ____ Audiovisual Resource

____ Magazine   ____ Content of Library Program

____ Newspaper   ____ Other

Title _____

Author/Producer _____

2. What brought this title to your attention?

3. Please comment on the resource as a whole, as well as specifically on those matters that concern you. (Use other side if needed.)
Comment:

Optional
4. What resource(s) do you suggest to provide additional information on this topic?

Source: Reprinted by permission of the American Library Association.

Ideally, such committees schedule a widely publicized annual meeting, perhaps in the fall, with a program that provides information about curricular selections and possibly a speaker who addresses school-based intellectual freedom issues. Even if attendance at such meetings is small, there is considerable value in the message that is conveyed to the public about the existence of such a committee and its work.

Nonprint Media and the Internet

Nonprint media—television, music video, videotape, film, radio—and Internet resources present challenges for classroom teachers that were unheard of when many of us started teaching. Deciding how best to use these resources requires significant thought and time, but the pace of technology developments is so fast that we have to realize that we are probably going to make some mistakes along the way. Most teachers, however, understand the enormous value that technological media and resources provide and take the time to seek ways to use them effectively.

The most useful guideline to keep in mind, regardless of the type of media involved, is that resources and experiences of all kinds must be used in a way that is consistent with a school district's philosophy or mission statement and must serve an educational purpose. For films, television, music videos, and so on, the National Council of Teachers of English has published a helpful booklet that addresses the use of nonprint media in classrooms. If your district does not already have established guidelines for nonprint media, you can (perhaps with the help of the NCTE booklet) work with colleagues to establish them, being careful to specify that curricular materials will identify the nonprint media to be included and what educational purpose each will serve. In the guidelines you create, you will want to include important reminders about previewing materials ahead of time and preparing rationales for their use. And as you teach, you will want to put the film or other work into a context that will make it clear to students and to parents how the material fits with current study and class experiences. The NCTE booklet also reminds teachers to follow copyright law and current fair-use laws of broadcast programming for educational purposes (NCTE, n.d.).

Fortunately, many resources are now available to help teachers determine how to make the most of Internet resources. It seems even more important that you make a point to identify curricular purposes for online resources, in part so that you will not be lulled into thinking that time online, regardless of how students use it, is time well spent.

Parents are understandably concerned about how online time is spent, and teachers have an obligation to address those concerns. Eileen Giuffré Cotton, author of *The Online Classroom* (1998), suggests that teachers need to begin by admitting the potential dangers that come with Internet access—"cyberporn, advocacy of violence, invitations to buy things that are prohibited to underage people, inappropriate e-mail invitations from people with perverted intentions for the naive and innocent" (p. 58). Cotton recommends that one of the best ways to establish ground rules for Internet use is for school districts, or individual teachers, to develop an Acceptable Use Policy (AUP). The AUP document will demonstrate for everyone involved—students, parents, and community members—that the Internet is being used as a tool for educational and curricular purposes (p. 60). Commonly included in AUPs are the following points:

- Standards for security and safety;
- Guidelines about the amount of time allowed on the Internet, who is responsible for enforcing the AUP, and Netiquette (network etiquette);
- Consequences for misbehavior; and
- Consent forms to be signed by parents/guardians and the student. (Cotton, p. 61)

Once the AUP is drafted, it should be approved by the school board and by school district attorneys. Then, students and parents should be informed and sign it. Some school districts, such as the Los Angeles Unified School District, require that students pass an Internet Test before they are permitted to log on to the Internet. Los Angeles even issues those who pass the test an Internet Driver's License (IDL). Cotton points out, "This might sound like a gimmick, but it does inform your students you are serious about enforcing the rules and regulations for accessing the Internet in your classroom" (p. 62). She encourages teachers to ask students to display their IDL before they log on as their promise that they will follow the guidelines set forth in the AUP.

Cotton also outlines practical procedures that will help you monitor students' online experience. She suggests, for example, that you face the computer monitors so that you can see the screens and enlarge the font size so that you can see at a glance what is being viewed. To keep students on task, she encourages the use of "Website Logs" in which students tell about the websites they have visited and what they have learned from them (p. 65).

Some school districts apparently are adding a "nonconsent line" to the AUP form to give parents the option of not permitting their children to use the Internet. I would be tempted, if I were faced with parents who wanted to make this choice for their children, to invite them to weigh the potential value against the possible harm. I would also ask them to consider the comment of a high school teacher who understands both the promise and the problems of classroom Internet use: "To prohibit the Internet because it contains offensive material is like banning a dictionary so a child cannot look up a dirty word" (Lyman, 1998).

WHAT CAN YOU DO WHEN CHALLENGED?

1. *Do not panic or act in haste.* Do not defend materials on the spur of the moment. Take the time to present your views thoughtfully and carefully. That may mean rereading or reviewing the material in question, even though you may already be familiar with it. Identify its strengths. Write down *why* you believe it is proper and useful in your teaching program (NCTE, 1978, p. 10).

2. *Attempt to resolve the challenge informally.* An informal discussion may solve a problem. According to Jenkinson, many teachers and librarians have "warded off full-blown protests by having the opportunity to talk—informally and amicably—to the person considering the possibility of making a challenge" (1990, p. 74). Many parents simply want to know how a book is treated or why it is selected. If the parent or citizen still wants to challenge the material, the school official should provide the formal request-for-reconsideration form. Many educators have learned that the very existence of a reconsideration form will discourage parents from registering a formal complaint. However, that is not the purpose of the form. The point is to get parents to state clearly what they find offensive, why they find it to be so, and what they would recommend as suitable alternative plans for their children.

3. *Take no action to review challenged materials until a written request for reconsideration is filed.* The reconsideration procedures should then be started immediately and the school board informed of the details. Follow established procedures to the letter. Educators, school board members, and the public should be reminded that materials will not be removed or restricted during the reconsideration process, which should be conducted openly with the community kept informed of progress and decisions.

4. *Do not isolate the public or students from the challenge or controversy.* Educators and school board members need to be ready to listen to those who articulate the issues from the perspective of the challengers and to provide a public forum for doing so. Students can also exercise their rights and speak about the issues, and they should be informed about the controversy and how it is being resolved. Such experiences can be powerful opportunities for learning appropriate ways that controversy can be addressed.

5. *When faced with a broad community challenge, Jones (1993) has recommended that teachers identify and call attention to any misrepresentations, generalizations, and half-truths used by the protesters.* Jones has suggested that teachers and citizens be aware of how some organized groups use confrontations to their advantage—answering questions with questions, bringing new policy statements to the school board as alternatives to existing ones, citing "authoritative sources," and redefining educational terms, then demanding administrators defend or deny *their* definitions (p. 91).

Many of the preceding suggestions have been incorporated into the "Selection and Reconsideration Policy of Riverside (California) Unified School District" on pages 245 to 250. The policy statements covering "learning resources" appear in the left-hand column, and my commentary appears in the right-hand column (statements covering library resources have been omitted). Such documents provide legal support for curricular decision making.

Selection and Reconsideration Policy of Riverside (California) Unified School District—Plus Commentary

I. Definition of Learning Resources

1. For the purpose of this statement of rules and regulations, the term "learning resource" will refer to any material (whether acquired or locally produced) with instructional content or function that is used for formal or informal teaching learning purposes. Learning resources include print and non-print materials and community resource people.

Comment

1. "Computer-accessed information" should be listed among the items identified as "learning resources." It is tempting to recommend that "teaching methodologies" or "class-related experiences" be included, as well. Itemizing teaching methodologies and class-related experiences, however, produces an endless list (e.g., direct instruction, cooperative learning groups, lab experiments, interviews, individual reading, writing, speaking, workbook exercises, listening, videotaping, recording, viewing, debating, singing, and so much more). Perhaps a statement such as the following would provide helpful clarification: "Teaching methodologies and class-related experiences used will be consistent with the spirit of this policy."

2. The primary objective of learning resources is to implement, support and enrich the educational program of the district. It is the duty of professional staff to provide students with a wide range of materials in a variety of media at varying levels of difficulty that present different points of view.

2. The role of school is clearly seen as a marketplace of ideas.

II. Selection of Learning Resources

1. The RUSD Board of Education delegates the selection of learning resources to the professional staff employed by the school district.

1. *Professional staff* is a broad enough label to include classroom teachers as selection decision makers.

2. At the school level, selection of learning resources involves many people (administrators, teachers, librarian/media specialists, students, community persons). Responsibility for coordinating and/or delegating the selection of learning resources rests with the principal. Periodically, the principal should review the selection and reconsideration procedure with the teaching staff.

2. This position is consistent with the *Hazelwood* decision (see Chapter 4), but it spells out the principal's right to delegate selection decisions to teachers.

3. Selection of learning resources for the district Instructional Media Services collection is made on the recommendation of subject area teacher evaluation committees and IMS certified personnel.

3. This position identifies subject or content-area teachers as appropriate curricular decision makers but through committees, not as individuals.

4. Books, subscriptions, or any other materials donated to school libraries will be gratefully accepted with the understanding that the items will be evaluated by a building level or district level library/media specialist against the same selection criteria as listed in the section below and should be accepted or rejected on the basis of those criteria. If a community or individual wishes to pre-purchase materials for our school collections, they should order those materials from our approved book list or have the materials reviewed and evaluated by our librarian staff prior to purchase. Cash or other funds donated to school libraries should be given with the understanding that the funds will be used for items which meet the selection criteria and are approved by a building level or district librarian/media specialist. Donations of money for the purchase of library resources should be placed in the school's Library Book Account and/or the Instructional Materials Account.

4. This statement would be strengthened by expanding it to include donated or purchased materials that are offered as *classroom* resources, in which case the items could be evaluated by the classroom teacher against the district's selection criteria.

5. It is the responsibility of the professional staff to select learning resources according to the following guiding principles:

- To provide materials that will support and enrich the curriculum, taking into consideration the varied languages, interests, abilities, learning styles and maturity levels of the students served;

- To provide materials that will stimulate growth in factual knowledge, literary appreciation, aesthetic values, and societal standards;

- To provide materials on various sides of controversial issues so that students may have an opportunity to develop under guidance the practice of critical analysis and therefore learn to make informed judgments in their daily lives;

- To provide materials representative of the many religious, ethnic, and cultural groups and their contributions to our local and national heritage and the world community;

- To place principle above personal opinion and reason above prejudice in the selection of materials of the highest quality in order to provide a comprehensive collection of learning resources appropriate to the school community.

- This statement recognizes that a variety of materials is needed for students with diverse needs and interests.

- This statement recognizes the need for materials that serve diverse purposes.

- This important provision makes it clear that the district values critical thinking and the learning that occurs from considering controversial issues.

- This statement expresses the district's intention to recognize a pluralistic and multicultural society.

- This statement expresses the district's decision not to select or remove materials on the basis of personal opinion or prejudice.

III. Challenges to Learning Resources
1. Despite the care taken to select materials for student use, occasional objections to learning resources may be made by members of the community. If materials are challenged, the principles and procedures for the reconsideration process described below will be followed.

1. This statement acknowledges curricular challenges as an expected, natural part of the curricular decision-making process. In the second sentence, I suggest changing the word *if* to *when*.

2. The following principles of intellectual freedom shall guide the RUSD staff involved in the reconsideration process:

- No parent has the right to determine reading, viewing or listening matter for students other than his/her own child.
- The major consideration in the reconsideration process is the appropriateness of the material for its intended educational use.
- Access to challenged material shall not be restricted during the reconsideration process.
- A decision to sustain a challenge shall not be interpreted as an indication of irresponsibility on the part of the professionals involved in the original selection and/or use of the material.
- RUSD supports the American Library Association "Library Bill of Rights."

- The principle of the freedom to read/listen/view shall be defended.

3. The following procedures for reconsideration of challenged materials shall guide the RUSD staff:

- The school or district person receiving a complaint regarding a learning resource shall try to resolve the issue informally.

The principal or other appropriate staff member shall explain to the complainant the school's selection procedure, criteria, and the qualifications of those persons selecting the resource.

2. These principles are wisely chosen to reflect judicial decisions about challenged books and materials.

This item is especially helpful as a reminder for educators and the public not to unjustly accuse or ostracize teachers whose curricular decisions are challenged.

This widely distributed document is reprinted in the American Library Association's *Intellectual Freedom Handbook.*

3. The procedures described are all consistent with the recommendations of censorship scholars.

I suggest changing *complainant* wherever it appears to the more neutral *parent or citizen.*

The principal or other appropriate staff member shall explain the particular place the questioned resource occupies in the educational program and its intended educational use or shall refer the complainant to someone who can identify and explain the use of the resource.

- Should the complainant not be satisfied, the complainant will be invited to file objections in writing. Complaints must be submitted on Request for Reconsideration of Learning Resources form.

The Request for Reconsideration of Learning Resources form shall be signed by the complainant and filed with the principal or the principal's designee.

The Request for Reconsideration shall be referred to the District Reconsideration Committee for reevaluation of the resource.

- The District Reconsideration Committee is a standing committee appointed by the Administrator of Instructional Media Services which shall consist of a school administrator, a librarian/media specialist, two teachers, two parents and may include one high school student. The purpose of this committee will be to reevaluate learning resources which have been formally challenged.

- The reconsideration committee shall proceed as follows:

Examine the challenged resource. All members will read/listen to/or view the resource in its entirety.

This item puts a heavy responsibility on committee members but is crucial to the process so that all committee members can speak knowledgeably about the materials.

Determine professional acceptance by reading critical reviews of the resource.

Weigh values and faults and form opinions based on the material as a whole rather than on passages or sections taken out of context.

Discuss the challenged resource in the context of the educational program.

This item clarifies that balance is important across the curriculum, not that every individual resource needs to reflect a balanced perspective.

Consult with school district staff members and/or community persons with professional knowledge of the material or its subject matter.

Invite the complainant to discuss the challenged item with the committee.

This promises the parent or citizen an opportunity to speak in person to the committee.

Make a decision as to the disposition of the challenged material.

Prepare a written report and submit it to the Superintendent and subsequently to the complainant.

Source: Reprinted with permission from Riverside Unified School District, Riverside, CA 92501.

HELPFUL RESOURCES

1. Doyle, R. P. (1996). *Banned Books 1996 Resource Guide*. Chicago: American Library Association. This annual publication of the ALA provides a wealth of information that helps you know about books and materials that have been challenged during the past year and what challenges might occur in your own district. It also provides suggested activities and promotional ideas for classroom teachers and librarians to use in demonstrating "that censorship is far more dangerous to freedom than the ideas expressed in books."

2. Hentoff, N. (1982). *The Day They Came to Arrest the Book*. New York: Dell Publishing. In what has become a classic novel about high school censorship of *The Adventures of Huckleberry Finn,* Hentoff brings the First Amendment to life for student readers, especially since the students in the story actively participate in the rethinking that takes place throughout the school and wider community once the book is challenged.

3. Hentoff, N. (1992). Bringing the First Amendment (live!) into the schools. In *Free Speech for Me—But Not for Thee: How the American Left and Right Relentlessly Censor Each Other* (pp. 356–386). New York: HarperCollins. This chapter features discussion of effective programs that teach students what free speech means and why it must be preserved.

4. Jones, J. (1993). *No Right Turn: Assuring the Forward Progress of Public Education.* Federal Way, WA: Washington Education Association. This reference book is written by a teacher and consultant who speaks candidly about threats to public schools from religious conservatives. She provides a wealth of practical information about targets for attack and strategies for fighting back.

5. Miles, B. (1980). *Maudie and Me and the Dirty Book.* New York: Knopf. A novel about a sixth-grade student who sparks a local censorship battle when she reads to a group of first-graders. Similar plot to Hentoff's novel but for a younger audience, it focuses on the sequence of events and the varying perspectives involved in a censorship challenge. A variety of other children's and adolescents' books address censorship and First Amendment issues, such as Avi's *Nothing But the Truth,* Kathryn Lasky's *Memoirs of a Bookbat,* Richard Peck's *The Last Great Planet on Earth,* and Stephanie S. Tolan's *Save Halloween!*

6. Moe, M. S. (1995, Aug.). Selection and retention of instructional materials—What the courts have said. *SLATE Starter Sheet.* This six-page document is filled with invaluable information and insight for teachers of all levels and all content areas. Contact: National Council of Teachers of English, 1111 W. Kenyon Road, Urbana, IL 61801-1096.

REFERENCES

Bigelow, B., L. Christensen, S. Karp, B. Miner, & B. Peterson (Eds.). (1994). Creating classrooms for equity and social justice. In *Rethinking our classrooms* (pp. 4–5). Milwaukee: Rethinking Schools.

Boardman, E. M. (1993). *Censorship: The problem that won't go away.* Worthington, OH: Linworth Publishing.

Brown, J. E., & E. C. Stephens. (1994, April). Rationales for teaching challenged books. *SLATE [Support for the Learning and Teaching of English] Starter Sheet.* Urbana, IL: National Council of Teachers of English.

Cerra, K. K. (1994). Self-censorship and the elementary school teacher. In J. E. Brown (Ed.), *Preserving intellectual freedom: Fighting censorship in our schools* (pp. 36–50). Urbana, IL: National Council of Teachers of English.

Cotton, E. G. (1998). *The online classroom* (3rd ed.). Bloomington, IN: ERIC Clearinghouse on Reading, English, and communication and EDINFO Press.

Davis, J. (Ed.). (1979). *Dealing with censorship.* Urbana, IL: National Council of Teachers of English.

Donelson, K. (1987). Foreword. In H. A. Bosmajian (Ed.), *The freedom to read* (pp. xiii–xvi). New York: Neal-Schuman Publishers.

Franks, B. A. (1986). Children's intellectual rights: Implications for educational policy. In D. Moshman (Ed.), *Children's intellectual rights* (pp. 75–87). San Francisco: Jossey-Bass.

Goldstein, W. (1989). *Controversial issues in schools: Dealing with the inevitable*. Bloomington, IN: Phi Delta Kappa Educational Foundation.

Hentoff, N. (1992). *Free speech for me—But not for thee: How the American left and right relentlessly censor each other*. New York: Harper Perennial.

Hulsizer, D. (1989). *Protecting the freedom to learn: A citizen's guide*. Washington, DC: People for the American Way.

Hydrick, C. J. (1994). *Slugging it out*: Censorship issues in the third grade. In J. E. Brown (Ed.), *Preserving intellectual freedom: Fighting censorship in our schools* (pp. 198–202). Urbana, IL: National Council of Teachers of English.

Jenkinson, E. B. (1990). Lessons learned from three schoolbook protests. In A. S. Ochoa (Ed.), *Academic freedom to teach and to learn: Every teacher's issue* (pp. 60–76). Washington, DC: National Education Association.

Jones, J. L. (1990). Appendix. In A. S. Ochoa (Ed.), *Academic freedom to teach and to learn: Every teacher's issue* (pp. 77–104). Washington, DC: National Education Association.

Jones, J. L. (1993). *No right turn: Assuring forward progress of public education*. Washington, DC: National Education Association.

Lyman, H. (1998, Jan.). The promise and problems of English on-line: A primer for high school teachers. *English Journal, 87* (1), 56–62.

Minnesota Civil Liberties Union. *Written policies* [handout sheet].

Moe, M. S. (1995, Aug.). Selection and retention of instructional materials—What the courts have said. *SLATE [Support for the Learning and Teaching of English] Starter Sheet*. Urbana, IL: National Council of Teachers of English.

Myers, M. (n.d.). *Guidelines for selection of materials in English language arts programs*. Brochure. Urbana, IL: National Council of Teachers of English.

National Council of Teachers of English. (n.d.). *Guidelines for dealing with censorship of nonprint materials*. Booklet. Urbana, IL: National Council of Teachers of English.

National Council of Teachers of English. (n.d.). *Guidelines for selection of materials in English language arts programs*. Brochure. Urbana, IL: National Council of Teachers of English.

National Council of Teachers of English. (1978). *Censorship: Don't let it become an issue in your schools*. Urbana, IL: National Council of Teachers of English.

Scales, P. (1995). Studying the First Amendment. *Book Links, 1,* 20–24.

Shugert, D. (1979). How to write a rationale in defense of a book. In J. Davis (Ed.), *Dealing with censorship*. Urbana, IL: National Council of Teachers of English.

11 Taking Action as Teacher, Citizen, and Advocate

Above all things, I hope the education of the common people will be attended to; convinced that on this good sense we may rely with the most security for the preservation of a due degree of liberty.

—Thomas Jefferson

I am not inclined to believe that either parents or the state should have the sole right to determine the nature of education. Parents should have rights over the education of their children; *states should have rights over the education of their* citizens *[emphasis added].*

—Warren A. Nord (1995)

There is a crisis in education, we are told repeatedly by news columnists, politicians, and business and community leaders, but there is little agreement about the source(s) of problems or the potential solutions. Whether we believe the crisis is real or manufactured (Berliner & Biddle, 1995), teachers know that the problems and the needs of public education are real.

This book was written to help you think about school-based censorship and controversies within schools and communities. Often, the censorship challenge or controversy is sparked by a local incident but reflects broader concerns and negative views of public education, as well. Thus, we, as teachers and as citizens, must be concerned about both local incidents and about the broader national issues and negative perceptions that raise concern. This chapter describes serious threats to public education and practical, reasonable action that teachers can take to support and strengthen public schooling. It also invites teachers to rethink life beyond the classroom and to consider an advocacy role as a citizen in community, state, and national arenas.

Perceived Problems and Real Needs

No wonder teachers sometimes lose heart. A national report generated newspaper headlines in my community that read, "State Teachers Get Failing Grades"

(McMichael, 1996). The article beyond the headline revealed, in fact, that one of the primary complaints was that so many classroom teachers are not fully certified to teach the subject areas to which they are currently assigned. Local teachers rose to the occasion and wrote angry letters to the editor, challenging the misleading headline. They rightly pointed out that teaching assignments are made by *administrators,* not teachers. The paper's next edition carried a follow-up article, titled "Teachers Angered by Poor 'Grade' Reported in Gazette"—a statement that again was technically accurate but misleading (McMichael, 1996). In fact, both headlines reflected an editorial position that discredits teachers. More accurate headlines might have read, "Teachers Make the Most of Difficult Circumstances" for the first article and "Teachers Set the Record Straight" for the second. Instead, those who read only the headlines probably assumed that teachers are at fault and also defensive about it.

Teachers also must reckon with the public's perceptions about curricular issues. Newspapers regularly play up professional disagreements among educators about content and methodology. Education reporters and columnists do not always report just the facts about curricular controversies but often at least implicitly favor one method—usually the one that is more traditional and familiar—while mildly ridiculing newer strategies and reforms. Too often, the messages that resonate most with the public are overly simplistic ones, such as William Raspberry's praise for "one easy solution" for public education offered by E. D. Hirsch: "Decide precisely what information should be taught in each grade, then make sure every child learns it" (Raspberry, 1997).

A survey of 1,200 citizens conducted by Public Agenda (see Chapter 3) found that the public is "distrustful of new approaches to education" and wants to "recapture the advantages of traditional schooling" (Willis, 1995). The public, according to Public Agenda, blames educators for three things: "for using counterintuitive teaching methods that don't work; for claiming that social problems prevent them from producing better results; and for evading accountability" (Willis, 1995). Such charges are hard for us as educators to hear, especially when we are convinced the public does not know the whole truth, but such charges deserve a public response from teachers. When we read about "counterintuitive teaching methods that don't work," we often sigh in frustration. We are surprised to learn that "86 percent of Americans say students should memorize the multiplication tables and learn to do arithmetic 'by hand' before using calculators" (Willis, 1995). We know that some new methods and reform ideas are unfounded and faddish, but we need to do a much better job of gathering the data and documentation from our classrooms to demonstrate the advantages and effectiveness of our curricula and teaching strategies.

As teachers, we know that many of the real needs in public schools do reflect the problems in society as a whole—underemployment, lack of skills, and loss of spirit; cut-throat competition and high-paced demands on time and energy; violence as a way of settling differences; crime glamorized as entertainment; lack of community, compassion, and civility; and lack of family nurture and support, loss of personal connection, and loss of meaning. Teachers know that to varying degrees students bring these burdens and more with them to school.

The charge about evading accountability is somewhat more legitimate. Often, we do resist standardized tests imposed by school districts and by state legislators because large-scale, multiple-choice tests typically reduce knowledge to isolated bits of factual information. We especially resist the influence such tests have on curriculum—crowding out the richness and depth of carefully designed classroom experiences that provide the context and integration of ideas and information. And we are appalled when state funding for public schools is determined solely by students' performance on standardized tests and cringe when opponents of public education use test scores to serve political purposes.

But there is more we can do than just fight the use of state tests that ask students to identify someone else's "right" answers in a multiple-choice format. The public does have a right to hold public schools accountable, and we can work as educators to find better ways of measuring student achievement and school effectiveness. One way is to replace outdated, standardized tests with more valid, large-scale performance assessments and to agree that traditional standardized tests in fact function as a form of censorship since they prevent students from demonstrating the range and richness of their own knowledge and skills on tests that carry high stakes.

Teachers can also offer firsthand testimonial evidence of real problems and practical needs that grow out of everyday experiences at school. Elementary teachers who teach 30 or more students at a time know the frustration of stretching to meet the individual needs of 30 multitalented and multichallenged young learners. Secondary teachers who work with 150 or more adolescent students every day know the virtual impossibility of meeting that many teenagers' individual needs.

Those who teach in less affluent communities can testify to the range of additional practical problems many teachers face. Not only do they lack adequate library and computer facilities but they also sometimes face leaking ceilings and crumbling walls. All teachers face the real problem of too little time to carry out basic plans for teaching and learning and for professional development. Public school teachers operate without the time and resources that corporations and industry provide for their trainers, but many classroom teachers nevertheless shoulder enormous responsibilities and manage to take responsibility for their own professional growth, as well—usually by squeezing time away from family and other personal interests.

Not all teachers are willing to make such sacrifices, however. Thus, another real problem is the fact that some teachers do not seem to care as much as we think they should. They do not read professional publications and they resist change. They say, "If I'm not getting paid extra to stay late to talk to my colleagues about curriculum, I won't be there." Unfortunately, some teachers seem to respect neither their profession nor their students, and they sometimes do more damage than we like to admit. We laugh at the "bad" teachers in the movies, but occasionally they show up in real life, too.

Crisis Rhetoric

A crisis gets manufactured because somebody has an agenda that is best served by its creation. Though we do not agree on what the real problems are or how to solve them, clearly we need to understand the part that crisis rhetoric plays in discussions and attitudes about public education. To be fair, we need to acknowledge at the outset that the idea of a public education "crisis" does serve educators' purposes to some degree. Focusing on schools in crisis means we can justify asking for more funds, more materials, better pay for teachers, and smaller classes.

It is interesting to compare fund-raising letters mailed by conservative and by liberal and progressive organizations. Both highlight worst-case scenarios to build a case for urgent action. Americans United for Separation of Church and State, for example, opened its 1996 back-to-school letter with the following:

> Imagine this scene . . . In a high school English class the teacher begins the lesson: reading and discussing Shakespeare's *Romeo and Juliet*. A week later, the teacher gets a call. The parent of one of her students demands that this classic be removed from the lesson plan. Why? Because, insists the parent, *Romeo and Juliet* deals with an issue that has no place in public schools—teen suicide. After discussion with the principal, who fears a lawsuit, the teacher gives in to the parent's request and switches the class to *Macbeth*. The next day, another parent calls to demand that *Macbeth* be removed because of 'occult' elements, like the three witches. (Lynn, 1996)

These parents' concerns may sound extreme until we consider the following excerpt from an undated mailing from Beverly LaHaye, president of Concerned Women for America:

> In Chelmsford, Massachusetts, a group of parents sued school officials when their children were forced to sit through a 90-minute presentation by "Hot, Sexy, and Safer Productions, Inc." In this so-called "group sexual experience," children were made to engage in activities some parents considered outrageous and pornographic. One little boy was told to "lick a condom." The court decided against the parents, stating that mothers and fathers did not have a right to know and consent to this sexually explicit program before their children were required to attend. (LaHaye, n.d.)

Such stories and rhetoric are effective for fund-raising and for heightening the public's anxiety. Most of us know we face a losing battle if we try to defend or refute what is depicted in either of these worst-case scenarios. Unless there is full documentation provided, no one knows for sure where the truth lies. But it is helpful to consider the stance revealed by the rhetoric and the issues various groups use to call attention to their agendas.

It is especially helpful to pay attention to the rhetoric of public education's most outspoken critics. Robert Simonds, president of Citizens for Excellence in Education, claims to be protecting children "from the chilling effect of anti-Christian teachers or administrators who are discriminating against our children of faith, many times openly persecuting them and their parents" (1997). Similarly, Pat Robertson, past president of the Christian Coalition, has called public education an "anti-Christian movement" that should be changed. "Put Christian principles in and Christian pedagogy in," he recommended. "In three years, you would totally revolutionize education in America"

Source: © 1992 Huck/Konopacki: Teacher Cartoons. Reprinted by permission.

(quoted in People for the American Way, n.d.). Robertson's rhetoric reveals an assumption that he speaks for all Christians and that he knows how to "revolutionize" education. He neglects the fact that as public citizens, we *are* the "state" from which he would remove education. For Robertson, and so many others who take similar stands, the recommended remedy for real and perceived problems within public education is to destroy public education itself.

Control of Education

Not long ago, I testified at a town meeting sponsored by the Michigan State Board of Education. As I listened to others' testimony, I was surprised that only one religious-conservative organization seemed represented among those testifying. I had expected to see clusters of angry parents demanding vouchers to release their children from what they believed to be the tyranny of ineffective public schools. Then it dawned on me that the religious-conservative groups did not *need* to be there because their candidates had gained the majority of seats on the State Board of Education.

Legislative Agendas

Major legislative proposals serve as a focal point for those who want to control children's education. State and nationally organized protest groups have learned from experience that local efforts to protest against curricular materials can be successful in ridding districts of specific sources to which they most object. But they have also learned from experience that such efforts take enormous time and commitment and often do *not* lead to the censorship they ask for and thus do *not* achieve their goals. They are learning that much broader goals can be accomplished through legislation. Such measures still require enormous time and energy but can be achieved much more efficiently by networking with like-minded groups, by consolidating their talents and efforts and by pressing for legislation. (Such plans are dependent, of course, on being reasonably confident that enough legislators share similar goals—or are eager enough for the groups' support—to work within the legislative process to accomplish the organizations' goals.)

Religious Freedom

Passage of the Religious Freedom Amendment to the U.S. Constitution, introduced in 1995 by Rep. J. Ernest Istook, Jr., and supported by Rep. Henry Hyde, is at the top of religious conservatives' education agenda: "To secure the people's right to acknowledge God according to the dictates of conscience: The people's right to pray and to recognize their religious beliefs, heritage or traditions on public property, including schools, shall not be infringed. The government shall not require any person to join in prayer or other religious activities, initiate or designate school prayers, discriminate against religion or deny equal access to a benefit on account of religion." The Christian Coalition has promised to spend up to $2 million lobbying for the amendment (Burrell, 1997), which Ralph Reed described as "the most important legislation dealing with religion that Congress has voted on in over 10 years" (Reed, 1997).

In 1996, Rep. Martin Hoke proposed a Freedom of Religious Expression Act to allow public school students to express their beliefs in school, specifically targeting four areas: group prayer and religious discussion, religious beliefs expressed in school assignments and homework, distribution of religious literature, and the communication of religious messages, including messages on clothing (People for the American Way [PFAW], 1997c).

People for the American Way has warned that such legislation as these proposed bills "would allow expensive lawsuits and huge damage awards against school districts and even individual teachers if they simply made an inadvertent mistake on complex legal questions concerning religion in the schools" (PFAW, 1997c). When I first learned about the proposals, I wondered why religious-conservative groups felt the need for additional legislation. I knew that all four of the targeted areas mentioned in the Freedom of Religious Expression Act had already been protected under the Constitution and the Religious Freedom Restoration Act (RFRA). (The RFRA was backed by a large interfaith coalition of both liberal and conservative groups and had passed the Senate by a vote of 97–3. It overturned a 1990 Supreme Court ruling that had made it easier for government to curb religious practices.) In 1997, however, the Supreme Court ruled against the RFRA, apparently because of a disagreement with Congress about whether it could overturn a Supreme Court ruling.

But both the Religious Freedom Amendment and the Freedom of Religious Expression proposals were drafted *before* the Supreme Court's 1997 decision. Thus, it seems likely that religious-conservative groups—including the Christian Coalition—who supported the RFRA ignored it after it was passed because it did not go far enough to accomplish their goals. That is, it addressed their need for less interference with religion, but it did not fulfill their political agenda. Thus, their newsletters and promotional materials continued to focus on the horror stories that supposedly demonstrated the need for additional legislation.

Parental Rights

Another key piece of legislation is the Parental Rights and Responsibilities Act that has been proposed for all 50 states and for the U.S. Constitution. In Massachusetts, parents' right legislation was proposed but defeated (Boston, 1996). It would have required Massachusetts public school officials to "give parents written notice at least 10 days before presenting 'any information involving a morally or religiously sensitive topic.' Students would not be permitted to hear such discussions without written parental consent." Listed as *morally or religiously sensitive* were such topics as human sexuality, sexual orientation, contraception, abortion, sexual or physical abuse, alcohol or drug use, marriage, divorce or family life, moral decision making, suicide, coping with personal loss, or religious practices and beliefs (Boston, 1996). PFAW believes the bill is so broad it would threaten public schools with "chaos" (1997a).

Clearly, religious-conservative parents and legislators feel the need to have a stronger say about what materials and experiences their children encounter at school. Included among the 26 items included in a parents' and students' "Bill of Rights" (Citizens for Excellence in Education, n.d.) are the following statements:

- Parents have the right and responsibility to inspect all instructional materials used by a public school, before and during their use. Copies of all curriculum, special courses, outside speakers, texts and textbooks must be publicly available for parental perusal before and during use in the public schools.
- Parents have the right to know that all curriculum materials, speakers and instructional materials that are used, even for a single class period, have been approved by the duly elected and accountable school board.

Such stipulations convince me that parental rights legislation would virtually cripple classroom teachers' ability to make curricular decisions, because any parent could veto any materials—and conceivably every parent could veto all materials.

Colorado voters defeated a parents rights bill in 1996 that was phrased as a simple statement: "The right of parents to direct the upbringing and education of their children shall not be infringed." Rob Boston, editor of *Church and State,* pointed out that in spite of its simplicity and its reasonable sound, this legislation, like the Religious Freedom Amendment, is not needed and might be dangerous (1996). In fact, if such legislation is passed in other states or at the national level, Boston insisted that the use of a particular book or a health curriculum in a public school could be declared an "infringement" of parents' rights, and religious education could be declared a "parental right," with vouchers mandated by the courts. Many also feared that the bill might protect child abuse (Boston, 1996).

A group called Of The People is leading the effort for passage of the parental rights bill. Boston pointed out that Of the People is "strangely reluctant to explain exactly what the amendment is intended to do" (1996, p. 8). The group's leaders insist that parents' rights are trampled on by the government, but they could provide little evidence to support the charge. When asked for a specific example, the group's leader Betsy DeVos (Amway family, Grand Rapids, MI), pointed to an unnamed public school that allegedly subjected a child to counseling without his parents' knowledge, saying, "They were changing the personality of this child through the counseling" (Boston, 1996, p. 8).

Such vague, undocumented charges suggest that there is another agenda at work. Indeed, Boston discovered that the real agenda focuses on voucher programs that permit public money for private schooling. A speaker from the Heritage Foundation was asked, during a panel discussion about the voucher movement, if the Parents' Rights Amendment would provide "additional firepower" in the courts. The speaker responded, "It surely does . . . if you put it in terms of who should be sovereign over children—parents or some state government bureaucracy—you win that battle pretty niftily, and then you just ease on in to choosing where a kid goes to school, so I do see it as very helpful" (Boston, 1996, p. 9).

Public, Private, and For-Profit Schools

A religious-conservative author, Paul deParrie, uses a metaphorical description to explain his preference for children's education: "Hothouse plants are *stronger and more productive.* Just as the weed-free, well-watered environment of the greenhouse produces a stronger plant, so home school, Christian school, church, and selected friendships will improve a child's chances of resisting the world's tug" (deParrie, 1991, p. 79). Individual parents, according to deParrie and others who share his view, should have the entire say about what happens to their children, even if it means isolating them from outside influences entirely. Clearly, what these parents seek is a private school experience—that is, owned and controlled by individuals and operated with little public scrutiny.

Parents have the right, of course, to send their children to any private school that they can afford and that will accept their children as students. They have the right to create new private schools and to home-school their children. What is troubling, however, is that parents and legislators today want the government to pay to send their children to the school of their choice. In Michigan, for example, a foundation has been established to fight for new state legislation that would institute a school voucher plan. Paul DeWeese, head of the TEACH Michigan Education Fund, explained, "We believe the infrastructure has been created which will ultimately allow private and religious schools to be chartered while remaining independent of government control" (Guyette, 1996). This statement exposes the political agenda that could dismantle the current public school system and disperse public money to private and religious groups.

In Michigan, the path toward complete privatization has produced "public school academies" or "charter" schools, which allow private individuals and profit-making corporations (though not overtly religious groups), to receive state funds for their programs. The State Board of Education approves agencies, typically universities, that can charter schools and collect a 3 percent management fee from the approximately $5,500 per child that the charter school receives. The chartering agency is also ultimately responsible for overseeing the work of the schools that receive a charter. Each charter school creates a school board made up of people who are not *elected* by citizens in the area but who are *selected* by the charter school itself and ultimately *approved* by the chartering agency. Thus, there is no publicly elected oversight to monitor how the school is run or how it spends the money received from the state. Meanwhile the state has also eliminated certification requirements for school administrators and allows noncredentialed persons to teach if they have a bachelor's degree plus five years of employment in their field.

Operating now in a defensive stance, school districts must devote more and more of their time, energy, and funds to promotional materials and advertising: "Some districts are putting the hard-sell on schools and programs by promoting itself through advertising and marketing because competition has increased between the districts" (Bonnette, 1996). Districts are setting up "marketing committees" of parents, community leaders and school officials to help promote their schools. They are "advertising in newspapers and hiring marketing experts to promote schools and hopefully attract new students.... Marketing is a whole new animal for school districts, some superin-

Source: Reprinted by permission from Gary Packingham, *Muskegon Chronicle,* November 1, 1995.

tendents say" (Bonnette, 1996). I wonder, what percentage of public schools' budgets for marketing would constitute good use of taxpayers' money?

In a bizarre twist of the law, a "cash-strapped" public school district outside Detroit planned a for-profit school in midtown Detroit "with the explicit purpose of making money" (Bradsher, 1996). The "pirate" public school district would collect $5,500 a year in state money for each student taught at the new for-profit school in Detroit and planned to hire a small, private company to run the school for $4,240 a student. The difference would become "profit" for the invading public school district (Bradsher, 1996). Fortunately, this pirating plan was eventually rejected, but such schemes generate new, disturbing questions. Is this the way to create the "competition and innovation" that public schools supposedly need? Under what circumstances might such practices produce better education for all students?

For-profit corporations have also contracted to operate some public school districts, but there is no evidence that they produce better results. In fact, the National Education Association (NEA) reported, "Corporate takeovers have failed to improve student achievement wherever they've been tried" (1995). In Baltimore, for example, Education Alternatives, Inc., promised to raise student achievement and reduce costs, but student achievement did not increase and the districts spent a lot more money. And what if they *could* save money? In Michigan, one charter school gave each teacher a supplies budget but allowed the teachers to keep any funds left over at the end of the year. NEA pointed out, "The reality is that any savings in the operation of privatized schools are pocketed as profit by the corporations that run them, not returned to taxpayers or reinvested in communities" (1995). For public schools, the bottom line is *student learning;* for private companies, the bottom line is *profit.*

A Dangerous Trend

Parents Training Children to Resist Classroom Ideas

Teachers need to know that some of their students' parents may feel so strongly about protecting their children from the "dangers" at school that they follow advice offered in books with titles such as *Children at Risk: The Battle for the Hearts and Minds of Our Kids* (Dobson & Bauer, 1990) and *Ravaged by the New Age: Satan's Plan to Destroy Our Kids* (Marrs, 1989). From a teacher's perspective, I know that such thinking can create a barrier to learning. What a handicap for students to come to school suspicious of all that is offered there. On the other hand, I learned though similar warnings by my parents and Sunday School teachers to be a critical thinker. That is, I was taught to question and challenge the ideas, information, and experiences that I encountered at school. I was taught to filter these things through my understanding of Christian faith and to reject anything that was contradictory—much the same way, in fact, that teachers who embrace critical pedagogy encourage students to question and challenge the "secret education" of films and fairy tales (Christensen, 1994) and to reject what contradicts their understanding of equity and justice. Franks has insisted optimistically,

"No matter what children see, hear, and are exposed to, they invariably think for themselves, to some degree. It is impossible to control every thought another person has, no matter how strictly an educational or moral treatment is applied. Sooner or later, most children will begin to think for themselves and to question the values and beliefs of their parents; this is part of becoming an adult" (Franks, 1986, p. 83).

Some of you will find this form of spiritual coaching more troubling than I do. Parents do have the right to advise their children at home about how to respond at school. And most parents, even ultra-conservative religious parents, want their children to become critical thinkers by the time they are adults. Still, one of our primary challenges is to help all parents learn through their interactions with us and their children to place new value on critical, independent thinking.

Taking Control of Local and State School Boards

Those who want to control their children's education, and possibly their children's thinking, use multiple strategies to accomplish their goals. While they seek national legislation that will redefine *public* education to include for-profit *private* schools, they encourage like-minded individuals in local communities to take control of their local school boards: "Most elections are won on 1 percent to 3 percent of the vote. . . . If only 10,000 vote in your district, that means 100–300 voters could elect the entire new school board" (Simonds, quoted in Hill, 1992). Church resources are another tool for gaining control: "There's a minimum of 10 evangelical churches for every school district! And so, politically, they don't even have a prayer. We can vote who we want in and out" (Hill, 1992).

Parents of any theological or political persuasion have the right, of course, within a democracy to run for school board. They also have the right to try to win office for a slate of candidates of their choice so that they can promote their agenda after being duly elected. What is more troubling is the idea of stealth candidates—those Ralph Reed of the Christian Coalition spoke of as working "under cover of night" (Goldin, 1993). I worry when those who claim to possess the truth, who claim religious superiority, feel no compunction for concealing their reasons for running—of being elected under false pretenses. I especially worry when people who would conceal their real agenda seek control not only of the education of their own children but of all children in the district.

"Family-Friendly" Libraries

Since the early 1970s, would-be censors have shifted their primary attention from library books to books used in the classroom, then to teaching methodologies, and then to school board control and finally to legislation as a way to change and/or control both the substance and spirit of public education. Censors have discovered how difficult it is to get library books, even school library books, removed from circulation. Perhaps society has come full circle, however, considering the new efforts to censor or restrict public library materials.

Source: Reprinted by permission from Gary Packingham, *Muskegon Chronicle,* June 25, 1995.

A group euphemistically called Family Friendly Libraries has targeted the Internet, sexuality education books, and books about homosexuality. An Oklahoma City group has pressured the local library to allow parents to draw up a list of 50 books they do not want their children to check out. The group, with close ties to the Christian Coalition and the American Family Association, also has succeeded in getting books written from the conservative Christian perspective, such as *You Don't Have to Be Gay*, purchased for public libraries (Garza, 1997). A spokesperson for Family Friendly Libraries has made clear that the group's purpose is to regulate the content of public libraries: "Right to read? It's a bunch of hogwash. . . . You don't have the right to read anything you want. We have to protect each other from dangerous material" (PFAW, 1997b).

Those who listen to the messages of the Family Friendly Library group do not hesitate to criticize the American Library Association for "ignoring" parental rights. They downplay the number of "banned" books, insisting that some books were "merely transferred to a different shelf within the library" (Maier, 1995). They encourage "opt-in" or "opt-out" policies that allow parents to identify books that their children are not permitted to read without parental permission: "Parents should request, at the beginning of the school year, a list of books that will be used. Parents have the right to opt a child out of a book requirement that is offensive to their family" (Maier, 1995). But for the sake of all children, especially those who have grown up in families that have heavily censored their reading and experience, we all need to fight to protect the right to read.

Technology as a Form of Parental Control

It is interesting to notice that parents who want to bring censorship to local libraries and who want the power to create unmonitored chartered schools favor using technology to teach their children. What they seek is not, however, unlimited access to website information resources. The proposed Noah Webster School in Michigan shows just how much control and privatization—financially and educationally—some parents want. The Noah Webster plan called for the purchase of computer equipment that the school would place in the houses of home-schooled students, whose parents would monitor their children's distance learning. The "school" would provide the lessons via distance learning for its widely dispersed students, and for that service they would collect $5,500 per home-schooled student per year from the state. The Noah Webster charter school model was supported by the president of the State Board of Education and his colleagues but was eventually rejected by the State Superintendent of Instruction, who soon thereafter lost his job.

Such plans are disturbing not only because they represent a misuse of public education funds and not only because the students' education would suffer. Such plans could potentially isolate students entirely and completely eliminate the role public schools can play in educating citizens. Columnist Cal Thomas has praised the Live Interactive Network Classroom, developed at Bob Jones University. While lessons are transmitted by satellite, all that is needed at home is an adult "facilitator." Thomas dismisses concerns about "the loss of 'socialization' and other supposed benefits of the current system" in favor of a system that would "allow all parents the freedom to choose what they believe is best for their children, at a reasonable price, and without the indoctrination that passes for education in the currently intellectually and spiritually closed system all must subsidize" (1996). A privately published newspaper distributed in my community praised similar distance learning plans because "parents can bring information directly into their own homes, personally and carefully selecting and screening the material presented to their children" (Dumont, n.d.).

Fortunately, I do not think my parents would have enrolled my brother, sister, and me in such a "school" even if such a plan had been available when I was growing up. But given the experience of growing up in a conservative Christian home and church community, I sometimes wonder how different my school experience might have been if I had attended a private, church-sponsored elementary or secondary school. I wonder about the different person I might have become under those circumstances. I have tried, for example, to imagine being taught science and mathematics and geography and American literature by the teachers who taught my Sunday School classes. Each was very sincere and many were passionate about their faith. However, most knew a lot less about how to teach than my public school teachers did. And what they taught was strict adherence to a narrow view of the Christian's place in the world. Fortunately, what I heard on Sunday was offset by what I learned from my public school classmates from a variety of cultural and theological perspectives represented in my school community—including Jewish, Syrian, and Lebanese families in my immediate neighborhood, African American families just a few blocks away, and the semirural families who lived in the outlying areas. Fortunately, the "world" was not described simply as "sinful" in my public school classrooms.

Taking Action as a Teacher and a Citizen

Most classroom teachers are not by nature a combative group. What we care most about is what happens to kids and to learning. The last thing most of us want is conflict, but on bad days many of us are feeling besieged. Our awareness of pressure groups (Chapter 3) gives us some sense of what we are facing. Although we are justified in criticizing groups that generate conflict and denounce public education, we recognize that some of their concerns and agendas are partially valid. One primary goal, therefore, must be to speak to deep concerns in order to work toward lasting solutions at every level from the classroom to the U.S. Congress.

In many cases, legitimate concerns about religion, moral character, social values, and intellectual freedom drive individual parents and protest groups to seek alternatives to public schools. Warren A. Nord and Stephen Carter, authors I have quoted extensively in Chapter 8, both advocate school vouchers, but *only* as a last resort if public schools continue to omit the study of current major religions and of religion's role in history and the arts, and the acknowledgment of religion as a force in today's society and culture. Vouchers, they insist, offer a remedy only if public education does not resolve the problem with "hostility" to religion in public schools. It seems reasonable to suggest that adding religion in appropriate ways that preserve the separation of church and state might save genuine public education.

Public Charter Schools

In a number of districts across the country, teachers admit that the curriculum *has* sometimes become overly rigid and the bureaucracies *have* sometimes become unresponsive to students' needs. Teachers who find themselves in these circumstances sometimes find the plans for new charter schools appealing. They would welcome being given the freedom to design their own curriculum. And some prominent educators are doing just that.

If genuine choice of programs to meet individual needs and interests of students is a high priority, then *public* charter schools operated within existing public school districts may be an answer for some students. Charter schools, however, are defined in many ways across the country. Although they have the potential to provide new and creative ways of teaching and learning, if they are unmonitored, they also may allow unqualified people to open schools—sometimes with the best of intentions—and to undermine education.

In 1993, the National Education Association passed a resolution and created a framework to ensure that charter schools would be consistent with this country's commitment to free and universal public education with equality of educational opportunity for all. The following criteria can be used by citizens trying to sort through the complex issues raised by the advent of charter schools and voucher plans. The criteria could also be used by educators who are drawn to the possibilities for innovation that charter schools offer:

- No negative impact on the regular public school program
- No diversion of current funds from public schools
- Voluntary staff and student assignment to charter schools
- Direct involvement of all affected school employees in the charter school's design, implementation, and governance
- Adequate safeguards covering contract and employment provisions for all employees
- Appropriate procedures for assessment and evaluation at preestablished periods within the term of the charter
- Licensed professional staff
- Health and safety standards for all students and employees
- Nondiscrimination and equal educational opportunities
- Adequate and equitable funding, including start-up monies
- Equitable procedures on student admission and retention
- Appropriate safeguards to ensure against racial and ethnic segregation (NEA, 1995)

Regaining Public Confidence

It is difficult to know how much of the crisis of public education is manufactured and how much is real. But one common cry from educators is that the public does not have enough accurate information. Citizens tend to "know" only what they see on televised news reports or what they hear about on radio talk shows. As teachers, we often feel helpless, especially when the critics blame us for the "failures" of education and dismiss our suggestions as self-serving. But as educators and as citizens, we need to move beyond a state of helplessness. Jean Johnson, vice president of Public Agenda, insists that "the public is really in a 'show-me' mood" and needs to see new approaches in their local schools (cited in Willis, 1995). Thus, the challenge for teachers and for local school district communities is to get parents and community members "in the schoolhouse door to see for themselves" (Willis, 1995).

I am grateful to a Michigan colleague, Jan Loveless, who has described a program that shows the public the reality of classrooms and schools in action and that provides the occasion for the public to ask and get straight answers to their questions without the "hype" that sometimes accompanies showcase programs.

Inviting the Public Back into Public Education*
Jan Loveless, Midland Public Schools, Midland, MI

The Midland (MI) Public Schools learned rather gently, in retrospect, that school districts in the 90s must be proactive about telling their stories. The district wanted to float a bond issue to support what administrators and teachers felt was a cinch: a technology plan that would bring our students the hardware and software they needed to get real

*This section printed with permission of Jan Loveless.

preparation for the twenty-first century, and a building renovation/addition plan to support the growth we were expecting. Three 1994–95 Board of Education public hearings showed us the error of our assumptions.

The community feedback to the Board was loud and clear: "Go ahead with this bond issue, and we'll vote it down."

The Board and the administration were stunned by the reaction of a citizenry that had passed every school tax bill for more than 30 years. Some of the loudest nay-sayers were people who used technology in their jobs every day. Others were retirees from a major chemical company with a global market.

What had happened to their support for our schools? One-on-one conversations with protestors gave us the answers. The community was reeling from the "rightsizings" of two of its four largest corporate employers. Rumor had it that more layoffs were on the horizon. The A&P store had recently closed and left town. Yes, the community was growing, despite these events. But people were afraid for their jobs. Employee morale was at an all-time low even among the "survivors" of the downsizings. These people were not monsters, but they remembered when Midland High had gotten along fine with a larger student population, before the second high school was built. And besides, they had succeeded in their own careers by learning technology after high school graduation. They had read the dismal national news about education, and this bond issue talk looked like more evidence that educators were spending carelessly when other industries were forced to do belt-tightening. Most of the protestors' own children were out of college now, and they had done just fine with the educations they had gained in the Midland Public Schools.

Our analysis showed that we were dealing with the strong opinions of a well-educated group of citizens, the backbone of our community. We had been so focused on communicating with our Parent Teacher Organizations that we had failed to notice that the community had changed. Sixty to seventy percent of local voters no longer had children in school. The members of our Rotary and Kiwanis Club, our city council members, our Chamber of Commerce officers, our community foundation leaders— the major opinion leaders in our town had aged while we had our backs turned.

Our 1990s education system had changed dramatically from what they had experienced in the 1940s and 50s. We knew that—but what could we do to change *their* opinions, to help them understand that we had a burgeoning special education population, and lots more kids on free and reduced price lunches? We needed to use our existing classroom space for more hands-on learning than we did in the past. And we needed more space. In our own minds, everything had changed except our buildings, which had looked the same for 30 years, since our newest had been finished in 1969.

We came up with a multi-pronged solution. First, we would have to revise our plans for funding renovations, including technology. Districts that lost funding elections dug public relations holes we could not afford. Second, we needed to get our stakeholders in to see what we were doing. Our most important process for accomplishing that goal became the VIP (Very Informed Person) Tours of the Midland Public Schools. We began these Tours in May of 1995. April 30, 1997, marked our fourteenth tour.

VIP Tour ingredients come down to a simple recipe that any district can follow:

- Prepare a videotape that gives the history of the district, showing how education has changed from the presentational model to constructivism (Warning: Make sure the video avoids "educationese" like I just used at all costs!) and detailing the challenges the district faces now. Have a local corporate leader talk on tape about the qualities the corporation looks for in its current new hires; segue from that information to what education must look like to help students achieve those qualities. On the tape, show all district employee groups as they do their parts toward the district's mission. (Everybody in the district must work together on these tours; if we don't, we'll all "hang" together.)
- Identify the groups who are the opinion leaders in your community.
- Send a targeted batch of those individuals invitation letters personally signed by the superintendent, accompanied by a "formal" invitation to a VIP Tour.
- Offer a choice of two dates close together, and ask for RSVPs. When people call, ask which level building they would like to tour; have buildings at all three levels on each tour.
- Invite guests to arrive at 8:30, and greet them with delicious treats prepared by school food service. Have the superintendent welcome guests warmly, then show the videotape as part of an orientation to the morning. (Our tape is 20 minutes and gets rave reviews.)
- Have buses waiting when the tape is finished. Make sure bus drivers greet guests enthusiastically and offer to answer questions. Deliver guests to a building at the level they have selected. The principal of each building on tour on a given day rides the bus with guests and starts comments as the bus approaches the building.
- Conduct building tours that include at least the following: visits to numerous classrooms, offices, laboratories, food preparation areas, and, last but not least, boiler rooms. Involve parents, students, secretaries, and custodians as well as teachers and administrators in hosting the tour. Alert everyone involved that we are not selling anything. We are just showing our guests a *good regular day* of school. (The cardinal rule: Absolutely No Whining to This Captive Audience.)
- Deliver guests back to the administration center for more treats and a 20- to 30-minute question/answer session with a panel that includes at least the superintendent and his or her direct reports, the head of the teachers' union, and several teachers. Have a Q&A moderator invite any sort of question guests want to ask. (Have someone record these questions to be disseminated with tour feedback to all staff members involved.) Coach panel members in advance to answer questions cheerfully, honestly, and nondefensively. About 10 minutes before the scheduled time ends, draw names for "door prizes." We give away attractive sweatshirts donated by our teachers' association. The sweatshirts read, "I've Been Back to School."
- Then ask guests to complete written evaluations of the morning, specifically asking for more information on anything they would like to know more about. Invite them to come again, and thank them for spending the morning with you. End the session precisely when the agenda said you would. Our tours end at 11:45.

Instruct staff members to linger in a friendly manner as guests gather their things and leave.

Over the course of two years, this tour recipe has made a *huge* difference in our community's attitude about the Midland Public Schools. Tour evaluations have been overwhelmingly positive, with most guests leaving wanting more time to visit. (Caution: Do not lengthen your tour; half a day is the longest time you will get the people you need.) Some tour alumni have returned for second and third tours. Others have made testimonials at their Kiwanis Club meetings. Still others have recommended our tours to their colleagues, spouses, and neighbors. We have had wonderful press coverage, including a glowing editorial from our local editor himself. Some groups have begun to call and ask for special tours. Of course, we have obliged. Last summer, our biggest employer asked us to do three summer tours to help them entice 110 employees from Granville, Ohio, to transfer to Midland.

In February, 1997, we passed a 10-year local school tax initiative by an overwhelming margin.

The moral of this story is that times have changed. No longer can we depend on our communities to value what we do if we don't tell our own stories, show them what is happening in our classrooms, and project an eagerness to answer their questions. We must reinforce that we are their employees, working together for what we all want—the best possible future for our children.

To be successful educators in the communications age, the age of school choice and political infomercials, we must become master communicators. Powerful communicators get to know their audiences. The trick is to reach out to them before barricades to listening go up on either side. If we genuinely listen to our constituents, show them that we value their ideas and are grateful for their interest, they will reward us with their support.

Positive School Reform

Ironically, those on the far right as well as those on the far left believe that public education in the United States is beyond repair. Those on the far right focus on their own children's needs and believe that public schools, like almost every government function, will never work as well as a privatized system. Those on the far left are committed to providing education for all children but believe that the current system of public education is so constrained by outdated, oppressive ideologies and bureaucracies that the only hope is to start over. In *Do We Still Need Public Schools*, writers for the Center on National Education Policy, Washington, DC, pointed out that "There are ways to improve the schools without undermining the essential concept of a system of public schooling" (1996, p. 22). These writers remind us that public school in the United States was developed "to unify our nation and to provide for the common good." Thus, we should raise the following fundamental questions about proposed solutions for the problems of public schools:

- Will this reform prepare all Americans to become responsible citizens, or will the reform benefit only some citizens?

- Will it improve social conditions or exacerbate social ills?
- Will it promote cultural unity or sharpen divisions within our society?
- Will it help all people become economically self-sufficient, or will it leave some citizens out of the economic mainstream?
- Will it enhance the happiness and enrich the lives of many individuals or only a few?
- Will it dispel inequities in education or aggravate them?
- Will it ensure a basic level of quality among all schools, or will it aid only some schools? (Center on National Education Policy, 1996, p. 23)

Taking Action as a Citizen and an Advocate

Working outside the system is another way that teachers, working alongside citizens from many walks of life, can make a positive difference.

Grass-Roots Organizations

A few years ago, a group of parents and other concerned citizens in Mississippi gathered for a living room meeting to discuss their concerns about parents opting out of the public school system. That meeting eventually led to the development of Parents for Public Schools (PPS), a national organization of grass-roots chapters dedicated to recruiting students, involving parents, and improving public schools. Members of PPS believe that "offering every child the highest quality of public education is vital to American democracy" and that "by mobilizing parents who reflect our diverse culture, we build excellent schools and better communities."

Unlike school-based organizations, Parents for Public Schools establishes independent, community-based groups whose members serve as "critical friends" that create a bridge between schools and communities. They tackle local issues that the parents decide need attention and action. The Jackson, Mississippi, group, for example, drew up a proposal for a special program for disruptive students and presented it to the school board. The PPS local president explained, "This momentous action represented a real turning point for this school district. Through organization and patience, we realized the strength of the parent voice in systemic changes."

In 1994, I met with a handful of Michigan friends in conversations that eventually led us to create a grass-roots organization, Michigan for Public Education. We were concerned about local efforts to defeat what we knew to be good classroom practice, and we knew about controversy in other parts of the state that left school boards at the mercy of candidates who conducted misleading "stealth" campaigns to get elected so that they could control the district's decision-making process. We also knew that newly elected State Board of Education members were boldly ambitious about promoting an agenda that involved reinstituting prayer in schools, teaching Creationism, and establishing publicly financed but privately owned "charter" schools. When we read in the newspapers a comment made by a state legislator calling an emphasis on multicultural diversity a "bunch of garbage" (Hornbeck, 1994), we knew it was time for somebody—for us—to do something. At first, we were not sure what, but we decided that doing something was more likely to help than doing nothing.

We invited a variety of people to meet with us to talk about what we, as concerned citizens, might do. Over the course of a few months, we eventually decided to form a nonprofit organization focused on state-level issues affecting public education. Thus, a new grass-roots organization, Michigan for Public Education (http://www.ashay.com/mpe) was born. Since then, we have learned so much from so many experiences, some more successful than others and some that may have had no effect whatsoever. But there are signs that our work has made a positive difference, particularly as we have networked with a host of other local, state, and national organizations.

We are not a huge group—just a few hundred members from across the state. But we are passionate about what we believe in and not afraid to speak out boldly at state board of education meetings, legislative hearings, and citizen panels. We have discovered that we are more confident when we are part of an organization, that we are more likely to take the time to investigate the issues and to take a stand. We have also learned the value of carefully articulating issues in a straightforward way. One of our strengths as a group is to create materials—newsletters, fact sheets, statements for public testimony—that explain complex issues *with the insight of professional educators* but with a keen awareness of the agendas of pressure groups and of the general public's perceptions. Most of all, we have discovered that defending against attacks on teaching and learning takes a commitment to do what all of us can, individually and together, to speak out to support and strengthen public education (see Brinkley, 1997).

Moral Will

Throughout this book, I have discussed dozens of controversial issues and problems within public schools and have presented dozens of suggestions as to what teachers can do to support and strengthen public education. The needs are great. Public schools need to be more responsive to the communities they serve; their bureaucracies need to be reduced. School-to-home and home-to-school communication needs to be improved. Citizen organizations need to take a public stand to support and strengthen public education. Parents and community leaders need to be convinced that positive change is possible—and is actually happening—within publicly run public schools. Private businesses need to demonstrate their concern for public education by paying their fair tax share to support local schools. We all could add to the list of needs.

Perhaps we in education can learn to work together from the experience of groups who meet to talk about abortion—those who oppose it meeting with those who favor it. They look for areas where they can agree without compromising their individual beliefs and hope eventually to understand and respect each other's positions, and perhaps unite on other issues. But I also join those who warn against too great a press for civility, who explain that we cannot improve civility "until we recognize the concept's dual essence, which encompasses not merely gracious manners, but also social responsiveness" (Hilliard, 1996). Hilliard has stated that sometimes the only way for an "outsider" to be heard is to make enough noise until finally "what began as a whisper" escalates to a shout. We need to be ready to hear the shouts, even the whispers, when they come and to learn from them, as well. And we need to be ready to become shouters ourselves when the need arises.

Some teachers take the time to seek common ground with those who hold very different views, and some teachers find the courage to "shout" when there is a need. In some ways, it does not take a lot to look for common ground, or to speak out for what we believe in, or even to decide to support and strengthen public education. But it *does* take moral will. That is the hardest part—deciding to take action as a citizen and having the moral will to do it. If we want to make a positive difference, we need as much energy and passion for preserving intellectual freedom and for supporting and strengthening public education as our opponents have for fighting it.

WHAT CAN YOU DO AS A TEACHER AND A CITIZEN?

1. *Resolve to do all that you can to address the deepest concerns of sincere protesters.* For example, use great care to protect students' and families' privacy. Although students often volunteer personal and family information, they should not be *required or expected* to reveal such information in the classroom. Parents, especially those who have felt that their faith and values were outside the mainstream, have rightfully been concerned that their children's and families' privacy be protected and that private family matters not be the basis for any required assignments.

2. *Learn to separate the pedagogical issues from those that are theological/philosophical or political.* As a teacher, you will probably be most effective when you talk about teaching and learning. Remember to respect parents' rights to hold a variety of perspectives and to make ultimate decisions about their children's education. It is also important to maintain your professionalism even when parents and citizens are rude.

3. *As a teacher and a citizen, you can become an articulate advocate, striving to support and strengthen public education and the broader societal issues that confront education.*

4. *Teach students and the wider community about censorship and about living positively in a controversial world.* Encourage the development of what Giroux has called "civic courage" that students "will be moved to challenge the social, political and economic forces that weigh so heavily upon their lives" (1985, p. 201).

5. *Document what students are learning in your classroom and teach students to be reflective and articulate about their own learning, so they can demonstrate their learning for others.*

6. *Do not be defeated.* Organize a grass-roots support group, a counterinsurgency group that gives you a chance to do something about the issues for which you care most passionately. Our Michigan for Public Education group has learned from experience that it is true that together we have a voice, together we make a difference.

7. *Seek out existing groups where you can find others who share your interest and passion about education issues.* In some cases, you can build on the work of existing public engagement initiatives. For example, Phi Delta Kappa International provides guidelines for conducting a forum on the purposes, effectiveness, and changes needed in public schools (P.O. Box 789, Bloomington, IN 47402-0789).

H E L P F U L   R E S O U R C E S

1. Center on National Education Policy (now the Center on Education Policy). (1996). *Do We Still Need Public Schools?* Bloomington, IN: Phi Delta Kappa, and Washington, DC: Center on National Education Policy. This 24-page booklet can be a useful tool to help teachers, parents, and community leaders refocus on public education. It provides brief historical context explaining the rise of public education and addresses why public schools and public funding for education are needed.

2. Lewis, Barbara A. (1991). *The Kid's Guide to Social Action*. Minneapolis: Free Spirit Publishing. This text provides step-by-step guides to social action, ready-to-use materials, and resources that work not only for kids but for adults, as well. Teachers who want to become public education activists and work individually or with others in a grass-roots group can learn from the information about petitions, news releases, and so on.

3. Lowe, R., & B. Miner (Eds.). (1996). *Vouchers, Selling Out Our Schools: Markets, and the Future of Public Education*. Milwaukee: Rethinking Schools. This inexpensive collection of 36 articles—by such leaders as Linda Darling-Hammond, Jonathan Kozol, and the editors of *Rethinking Schools*—addresses the issues of vouchers and market ideology, public choice and charters, and the conservative agenda.

4. National Education Association. *The People's Cause: Mobilizing for Public Education*. Washington, DC: Author. A fat notebook's worth of practical information and strategy ideas has been prepared as a resource for teachers who want to take action.

5. Parents for Public Schools. PPS is a national organization of grass-roots chapters dedicated to recruiting students, involving parents, and improving public schools. Contact: P.O. Box 12807, Jackson, MS 39236-2807, 800-880-1222.

6. People for the American Way's Right-Wing Watch Online mailing list. This website provides current information on a variety of issues and legislation that threaten public education. Contact: http://www.pfaw.org/press/list.htm

7. Simonds, R. (1993). *A Guide to the Public Schools: For Christian Parents and Teachers, and Especially for Pastors*. Costa Mesa, CA: NACE/CEE. Written by an outspoken critic of current public education curricula and teaching practices, this book provides an overview of issues that have galvanized parent protest groups and advises parents how to practice "impact evangelism" to influence school policies. Teachers who hear issues discussed from this perspective are less likely to be caught off guard by parent and community protesters.

8. Courage to Teach. A teacher renewal program that provides quarterly retreats over a two-year period. The focus is not on teaching techniques or reforming the system but rather on "renewing that which is closest to us—the inner life of the teacher." Some of the activist teachers whom I know find strength and energy in this program to face the school-based challenges about which they care the most. Contact: The Fetzger Institute, 9292 West KL Avenue, Kalamazoo, MI 49009-9398, 616-375-2000.

REFERENCES

Berliner, D. C., & B. J. Biddle. (1995). *The manufactured crisis: Myths, fraud, and the attack on America's public schools.* Reading, MA: Addison-Wesley.

Bonnette, J. (1996, Sept. 22). Schools of choice having little impact on area districts. *The Herald-Palladium [Benton Harbor, MI],* pp. 1A–3A.

Boston, R. (1996, June). The parent trap. *Church and State,* pp. 8–11.

Bradsher, K. (1996, Sept. 27). Educational piracy? For-profit school opens. *Kalamazoo [MI] Gazette,* p. B4.

Brinkley, E. (1997, Nov.). Believing in what's possible, taking action to make a difference. *Language Arts, 74,* 537–544.

Burrell, C. (1997, April 1). School prayer campaign announced. *Kalamazoo [MI] Gazette,* p. A2.

The Center on National Educational Policy. (1996). *Do we still need public schools?* Bloomington, IN: Phi Delta Kappa, and Washington, DC: Center on National Education Policy.

Christensen, L. (1994). Unlearning the myths that bind us: Critiquing fairy tales and films. In B. Bigelow et al. (Eds.), *Rethinking our classrooms: Teaching for equity and justice.* Milwaukee: Rethinking Schools.

Citizens for Excellence in Education. (n.d.). *Parents and students' Bill of Rights.* P.O. Box 3200, Costa Mesa, CA 92628.

deParrie, P. (1991). *Satan's seven schemes: An overcomer's guide to spiritual warfare.* Brentwood, TN: Wolgemuth & Hyatt.

Dobson, J., & G. L. Bauer. (1990). *Children at risk: The battle for the hearts and minds of our kids.* Dallas: Word Publishers.

Dumont, C. R. (n.d.). Education and techonology: There's good news ahead. *Biblically Speaking* [Webberville, MI], pp. 1 & 10–11.

Franks, B. A. (1986). Children's intellectual rights: Implications for educational policy. In D. Moshman (Ed.), *Children's intellectual rights* (pp. 75–87). San Francisco: Jossey-Bass.

Garza, M. M. (1997, May 25). Effort to make libraries "family-friendly" is one for the books. *Chicago Tribune,* p. 1.7.

Giroux, H. (1985). *Theory and resistance in education.* South Hadley, MA: Bergin & Garvey.

Goldin, G. (1993, April 6). The 15 per cent solution. *Voice,* pp. 19–22.

Guyette, C. (1996, June 26–July 2). Onward Christian scholars. *MetroTimes [Detroit],* pp. 10–15.

Hill, D. (1992, Nov./Dec.). Christian soldier. *Teacher Magazine.*

Hilliard, C. (1996, Dec. 29). In search of manners: Rethinking the debate on a civil society. *Chicago Tribune,* p. 1.19.

Hornbeck, M. (1994, Nov. 20). Multicultural curriculum in hands of GOP. *Detroit News,* pp. 1A–3A.

LaHaye, B. (n.d.). Bold new bill would give authority over children back to parents. Letter.

Lynn, B. (1996, Sept.). Americans united for separation of church and state. Letter.

Maier, H. (1995, Dec. 6). Libraries battling "censorship" ignore parental rights. *The Herald-Palladium [Benton Harbor, MI],* p. 10A.

Marrs, T. (1989). *Ravaged by the New Age: Satan's plan to destroy our kids.* Austin, TX: Living Truth Publishers.

McMichael, E. (1996, Sept. 19). Teachers angered by poor "grade" report in Gazette. *Kalamazoo [MI] Gazette,* p. A1.

National Education Association (NEA). (1995). Corporate takeovers: Myths and realities. *The people's cause: Mobilizing for public education.* Washington, DC: Author.

Nord, W. A. (1995). *Religion and American education: Rethinking a national dilemma.* Chapel Hill: The University of North Carolina Press.

Parents for Public Schools. (1997, April). PPS chapters are tackling status quo. *Parent Press.* Newsletter.

People for the American Way. (n.d.). The two faces of the Christian Coalition. Fact sheet.

People for the American Way Action Fund. (1997a). Campaign to destroy public education. Website.

People for the American Way Action Fund. (1997b). "Family friendly" libraries: Extending the culture war to your local library. Website.

People for the American Way Action Fund. (1997c). Rep. Hoke's dangerous and unnecessary legislation. Website.

Raspberry, W. (1997, Sept. 2). There's one easy solution. *Kalamazoo [MI] Gazette,* p. A8.

Reed, R. (1997, May). Letter from Christian Coalition.

Robertson, P. (1990). *The new millennium: Ten trends that will impact you and your family by the year 2000.* Dallas: Word Publishing.

Simonds, R. (1997, May). *President's Report.* National Association of Christian Educators/Citizens for Excellence in Education.

Thomas, C. (1996, Jan. 28). Classroom of the future is in space. *Lansing [MI] State Journal,* p. 8A.

Willis, S. (1995, June). Responding to public opinion: Reforming schools in a climate of skepticism. *Education Update.* Alexandria, VA: Association for Supervision and Curriculum Development.

INDEX

Abington School District v. Schempp, 172
Academic freedom:
  defined, 206
  teachers' rights, 207–208
  while handling controversial topics, 209
Accountability:
  performance assessments, 255
  public's interest in, 254–255
  standardized test scores, 56–57
Adams, Marilyn, 84
Administrators:
  censorship by, 43–45, 94–96, 126
  First Amendment role of, 172
  rights of, 212
  view of student publications, 90
Adolescent literature, 39, 132–133
  rationales for, 141
Adventures of Huckleberry Finn, The, 123,
    129, 250
Advocates:
  for public education, what can you do?,
    273–274
  teachers taking action as, 253
Age appropriateness for curricular materials,
    231
"America first" policy, 12
American Center for Law and Justice, 61
American Civil Liberties Union, 31
American Family Association, 63, 152, 264
American Library Association, 26, 264
Americans for Religious Liberty, 191
Americans United for the Separation of
    Church and State, 191, 256
Anticipating censorship and controversy, 24–26
Aquarian Conspiracy, The, 68
Assembly on Literature for Adolescents,
    National Council of Teachers of English
    (ALAN), 141
Attack, as type of challenge, 37
Attacks on Freedom to Learn, 26

Banned books, 32, 264
Banned Books Resource Guide, 49
Basal reader series, 123

Baseline Essays, 113–114
Basics, the, 55
Bauer, Gary, 63
Bethel v. Fraser, 212
Blum, Judy, 123, 127–128
Books, challenges of, 8
Broad-based complaints, 10
  as type of challenge, 37
Brookins-Fisher, Jodi, 147
Bruno, Giordano, 106

"Capitalist state," pressures from, 63
  corporate takeovers of public schools, 262
Carter, Stephen, 167
Censorship:
  contrast with selection, 41
  defined, 11, 32–37
  determining acts of attempted censorship,
    36–37
  of learning, 46–47
  levels of incidents leading to, 36
  political categories of, 33
  students learning about, 225–227
  teachers learning about, 225
  of teaching practices, 38
Center on Education Policy, 274
Chalcedon, 69
Chall, Jeanne, 84
Challenges:
  categories of challenges to curriculum, 8
  most frequently challenged books and
    materials, 1982–1996, 9
  number of censorship and related challenges
    to public education, 10
  to school and school library materials, 9
  what can teachers do when challenged?,
    243–244
Character:
  conflict resolution, 204–205
  defined, 197
  moral character across the curriculum,
    203–204
  teaching and teaching about, 195–203
Charter schools, 266–267

Children, Education, and the First Amendment, 217

"Choosing" curricula, contrast with "excluding," 41

Christian Coalition, 61, 256, 258, 263–264

Churches, impact on school board elections, 62

Cinderella, 3, 26

Citizens, teachers taking action as, 253

Citizens for Excellence in Education, 54, 61, 152, 256

Classroom censorship, what can you do?, 47–49

Classroom controversy, 50–55
  teaching students about censorship, 225–227

Common ground, 70

Competition, 64, 66

Complaints:
  oral, 36
  written, 36

Computers, 2–3, 90, 241–243

Concerned Women for America, 63, 152, 256

Conservative censorship, 33

Controversy, first impulses, 21
  ignoring or minimizing signals, 21
  launching an aggressive counterattack, 23
  making concessions, 22
  searching for appropriate action, 24

Corporate partnerships with public schools, 65–66

Corporate pressures on public schools, 63–66

Covert censorship, 46

Creation Research Society, 110

Creation science, 110–111

Creationism, 107, 110, 187–188
  prohibition in science classes, 111

Crisis in education, xv, 51
  Manufactured Crisis, The, 57
  Nation at Risk, A, 57

Critical literacy, 134–135

Critical teacher, 67–68
  defined, 67

Critical thinking, 55, 115–117
  parents' control of, 262
  teaching, through classroom dialogue, 213

Culture of Disbelief, The, 167

Darwin, Charles, 107–108

Death, fascination with, 45

Democracy, teaching, 214–215

civic courage, 214

"Devil" tales, 130

E-mail, 3, 90, 241–243

Eagle Forum, 63, 152

Educating for Character, 217

Education Research Analysts, 63

Educational purpose of curricular materials, 40, 44

Endorsing ideas in curricular materials, 45

Engel v. Vitale, 172

Epistemologies (ways of knowing), science, 102

Evangelicals, defined, 60

Evolution, 107–108, 110–111, 187
  Statement on Teaching Evolution, National Association of Biology Teachers, 119

Experienced teachers, vulnerability of, 16

Expression of concern, 36

Extremists, pressures from, 69

Family privacy, 88–89, 93
  in sexuality education, 149

Family Research Council, 63

Ferguson, Marilyn, 68

First Amendment, 170
  inappropriate religious expression, 170
  religious rights, guarantee of, 30
  tolerance of religion, 168

Focus on the Family (FOF), 62, 152

Finding Common Ground: A First Amendment Guide to Religion and Public Education, 191

Freedom Forum First Amendment Center, 191

Freedom of press, students', 94–96

Freedom of speech, students', 90

Fundamentalists, defined, 60

Gabler, Mel and Norma, 63, 129–130, 133

Galileo, 106

Good, Ronald G., 101

Goodman, Kenneth, 84

"Governing state," pressures from and within, 59

Grammar, 87

Grass-roots organizations, 271
  Michigan for Public Education, 271
  Parents for Public Schools, 271

Guided imagery, 101, 131–132

Guidelines for Teaching about Religion,
National Council for the Social Studies,
171

Halloween, 130
Haynes, Charles, 191
Hazelwood decision, 90
Hispanic students, 56
Holt, Dan, 94
Home schooling, 4
potential effects of technology, 265
Homosexuality, 91
homophobia, 152

Imagination, 123
imaginative truth vs. literal truth, 126
Impressions textbook series, 12, 62, 97, 130
Inculcation, 210
Indoctrination, 211
Inquiry, as type of challenge, 36–37
Intellectual freedom, 204
child-parent-state relationships, 210
class meetings, 213–214
classroom dialogue, 213
controversy, what can you do?, 215–217
critical thinking, 55, 115–117
defined, 205
Newsletter on Intellectual Freedom, 26
political indoctrination, 210
students' rights, 206, 209–213
teaching, 213–215
International Reading Association (IRA), 97
censorship statement, 136–137
Internet, 241–243
Acceptable Use Policy (AUP), 242–243
Internet Driver's License (IDL), 243
online ground rules, 242–243
website logs, 243

Jones, Janet, 223
Journal writing, 88
biology, in, 119–120
personal and family privacy, 88–89, 93
Journalism, student, 94
open forum, 94
Judgment calls, about student behavior, 39–40

Kanawha County (West Virginia) textbook
war, 29–31

Kids' Guide to Social Action, The, 72
Kozol, Jonathan, 66

Legislators, 20
Lemon v. Kurtzman, 177
Lewis, Barbara A., 217
Liberal censorship, 33
Libraries and librarians:
"family-friendly" libraries, 263
response to censorship, 35
Lickona, Thomas, 217
Literary magazines, 25
Literary merit, for curricular materials, 138
Literature, 123
adolescent, 39, 132–133
Adventures of Huckleberry Finn, The, 123,
129, 250
children's, 143
classics, 125
classroom libraries, 136
controversial language in, 139
controversy, what can you do?, 135–141
defending books, 142
gender stereotypes, 129–130
happy endings, 132
imaginative truth, 126
multicultural, 133–134, 135
offensive language in, 127
parents, informing, 139–141
racial stereotypes in, 129
sexuality in, 127–128
value of, 124–125
violence in, 128–129
witchcraft and Satanism, 130–131
Loveless, Jan, 267–270
Luksik, Peg, 19–21

Militia groups, 33, 69
Money, impact of, 66
Moral will, 272
Morality and moral character:
defined, 197
moral education program, 203
moral relativism, 200
personal code of conduct, 198–199
students deciding about right and wrong,
196
teaching and teaching about, 195
Moshman, David, 217

Multicultural texts, 30
controversy about, 133
cultural intolerance, 133–134
literature, 133–134
pluralist perspective, 134

National Council against Censorship, 49
National Council of Teachers of English
(NCTE), 97, 230–243
National Education Association (NEA), 31,
266, 274
National Writing Project, 89
Nature as censor, 115
Neutral treatment of religious and nonreligious
beliefs, 175
New Age, impact on literature, 131
New Age Spiritualists, pressures from, 68–69
New teachers, vulnerability of, 15
Newsletter on Intellectual Freedom, 26
Newspapers, student, 94
advisor's stance, 95
censorship by administrators, 95
*No Right Turn: Assuring the Forward
Progress of Public Education,* 223
Nonprint media, need for previewing, 242

Of the People (organization), 63, 260
Offensive language, 39, 92, 127
On the Origin of Species, 107
Online resources, 2–3, 90, 241–243

Parent protesters, 4, 18–21
aggressive counterattacks, 23
early signs of, 21
ignoring, 21
making concessions to, 22
Parents:
control exerted through "opt-in" and "opt-
out" provisions, 264
learning about controversial books, 227
Parents for Public Schools, 274
Parks, Rosa, 133, 135
Pentecostals, defined, 60
People for the American Way, 26, 32
Personal experience, curricula linked to, 12
Philosophy statements, 228–229
Phonemic awareness, defined, 76
Phonics:
conservative Christian perspectives, 77

controversy, what can you do?, 83–86
controversy about, 75–79
explaining role of, 78
impact of overemphasis on, 76–77
political perspectives, 78
theology, links with, 77, 85
Play-it-safe teachers, vulnerability of, 15
Policies and strategies, 221
circumventing censorship, 223
need for, 221–224
nonprint media and the Internet, 241–243
philosophy statements, 228–229
rationales, 233–238
reconsideration policies and procedures,
238–241
selection policies and procedures, 230–233
*Selection and Reconsideration Policy of
Riverside (CA) Unified School District,*
245–250
Political education:
contrast with politicized education, 68
defined, 68
Political stance, teachers taking, 13
Politicized education:
contrast with political education, 68
defined, 68
Prayer-in-schools amendments, 173
Pressure of belief systems on classrooms, what
can you do?, 71
Pressure groups, effects on teachers and
classrooms, 51, 57–69
Previewing curricular materials, 48
Primary sources, research using, 47
Professional knowledge of teachers, 40
Progressive teacher, defined, 67
Public attack, 36
Public education, control of, 257
private and for-profit schools, 260–262
public charter schools, 266
Public education, legislative agendas, 258–267
parental rights, 259
real needs, 253–255
religious freedom, 258
Public education, public perceptions of:
crisis rhetoric, 255–257
the "good old days," 52
need for public relations campaigns, 261
perceived problems, 253–255
surveys and polls, 53–54

VIP (Very Informed Person) Tours, 267–270

Public forum, student publication designation, 90

Public pressure, teachers feeling, 59

Publications, student, 90
  administrators' role, 90
  Hazelwood decision, 90
  open forum, 94
  school newspaper, 90
  self-censorship, 91
  topics addressed, 91

Racial bias, 30, 32, 47–48, 67
  controversial language in literature, 139
  stereotypes in literature, 129

Radical censorship, 33

Radio talk shows, 13, 91

Rationales, 233–238
  for books, 39, 233
  for curricular resources, 236
  for curricular resources and experiences, 237–238
  guidelines, 233–238
  potential problems, whether to identify, 235

Reactions to parent protests, 21–26

Reading:
  aesthetic stance toward, 82
  conservative Christian perspectives, 77
  constructivist view, 83
  controversy, what can you do?, 83–86
  controversy about, 75–86
  critical stance toward, 82, 97
  cueing systems, 78
  efferent stance toward, 79
  money spent on teaching, 77
  political perspectives and involvement, 78, 84
  power of, 38
  purposes for, 79–83
  risky activity, 38
  theology, links with, 77, 86

Reconsideration policies and procedures, 238–241, 249
  citizen's request form, 239–240
  reconsideration committee, 240
  statement of concern, 241

Reed, Ralph, 60–61, 258, 263

Religion in the classroom, 163

acknowledging religion and nonreligion, 168

acknowledging religion and nonreligion, what can you do?, 183
  elective courses, 169
  endorsement, avoiding, 167
  excusal policies, 183
  omission of, 166
  People for the American Way study, 167
  religious pluralism, 169
  students' religious rights, 184–185, 188, 189, 191
  teachers' religious rights, 182
  teaching about religions, 168, 171, 187
  teaching about religions, what can you do?, 181
  textbooks, religion in 176
  3Rs Project, 170
  unbelief, 169

Religion in the Public Schools: A Joint Statement of Current Law, 186–191

Religion in schools:
  antireligion vs. nonreligion, 176
  distributing religious literature, 188
  "endorsement test," 178
  inappropriate religious expression, 170
  Lemon v. Kurtzman, 177
  neutral treatment of religious and nonreligious beliefs, 175–179
  prayer and Bible reading, 172–174, 186–187, 189
  religious holidays, 189
  separation of church and state, 168, 170

Religious right, defined, 60

Religious rights amendments, 173

"Religious state," pressures from, 59

Research, students conducting, 89–90
  Internet and e-mail links, 90, 242–243

Research studies:
  National Science Foundation Report, 56
  Sandia National Laboratories Report, 56

Rethinking Schools, 72, 229

Risk-taking teachers, vulnerability of, 14

Riverside (CA) Unified School District, selection and reconsideration policy, 245

Role of schooling, 164–166
  inculcation, 164
  indoctrination, 164
  marketplace of ideas, 166

noninculcative teaching, 164
Rushdoony, R. J., 69
Rutherford Institute, The, 192

Schlafly, Phyllis, 63
School boards, 4–5, 261, 263–264
  churches, impact on school board elections,
    62
  control of, and controversy, 48, 62
School reform, criteria for evaluating proposed
    solutions, 271
School-sponsored censorship, 43–46
Schools, vulnerability of, 17–18
Science:
  censorship, links to history of science, 106
  censorship, what can you do?, 117–120
  censorship in, 101
  critical thinking in, 103
  defined, 102
  epistemologies (ways of knowing), 102
  multicultural arguments, 112–113
  nature as censor, 115
  nonscience, 108
  private, 109
  pseudoscience, 108, 110–111
  public, 109
  science literacy, 105, 111
  scientific inquiry, 103–104, 110
  theory, in natural sciences, 104, 109
Scopes, John, 107
Secular humanism, 60, 176, 209
Selection of curricular materials, 40
  selection vs. censorship, 40–43
Selection policies and procedures, 230–233
  books and resources, 230, 246
  responsibility for selections, 232
  selection decisions, 231
  textbook selection committees, 232
Self-censorship, 43–46
Separation of church and state, 168, 170
  Barton, David, 174
  historical facts, 174
  inappropriate religious expression, 170
  Madison, James, 174
Sexuality education:
  abstinence-based curriculum, 154–156
  abstinence-only curriculum, 154–156
  censorship in, 147
  churches supporting, 150

comprehensive sexuality education,
    curriculum, 159–160
comprehensive sexuality education, defined,
    148
controversy, what can you do?, 156–161
family life education, 148
HIV education, 150
homophobia, 152
moral and religious values links, 150–151
organizations opposing or seeking control
    of, 152–153
pregnancy, 151
questions students ask, 157–158
sexually transmitted diseases (STDs),
    149–151
teacher training in health education,
    156–157
values activities related to, 160
Sherrill, Anne, 34
Shor, Ira, and Freire, Paulo, 67, 74, 175
Shymansky, James A., 101
Simonds, Robert, 62
Social justice and action, 67, 72
  Kid's Guide to Social Action, The, 217
  writing for, 89
Social values:
  civic courage, 214
  teaching about, 195
  teaching social responsibility, 202
Speech and expression, students', 92
  administrators' rights, 212
  Bethel v. Fraser, 212
  controversy, what can you do?, 93–96
  First Amendment rights, 211
  freedom of speech, 212
  self-censorship, 92
Spelling, 87
Standards, 55, 233
Student Press Law Center, 98
Supreme Court decisions:
  Abington School District v. Schempp, 172
  Bethel v. Fraser, 212
  Engel v. Vitale, 172
  Lemon v. Kurtzman, 177

Taxes, corporate, impact on schools, 65
Teachers:
  ideological stances of, 67
  vulnerability of, 14

Teaching and learning:
    traditional teaching, 55
    transmission model, 46
Teaching Tolerance, 72
Technology, 4, 114
    Internet, 241–243
Test scores, 56–57
Textbooks, use of, 1
Theory, in natural sciences, 104
Topic sensitivity of curricular materials, 231
Totalitarian censorship, 33
Traditional teacher, defined, 67
Training, corporate, comparison to education,
    64
"Transformation state," pressures from, 66–78
Transmission model of teaching and learning,
    46, 175
Two New Sciences, 107

Values:
    comprehensive values education, 201
    controversy, whether to teach, 197
    defined, 197
    democratic, 199
    identifying and comparing, 200
    personal, 198
    respect, 199
    responsibility, 199

    social values, 199
    teaching and teaching about, 195
    universal, 199, 203
    values clarification, 200–201
Videotaping, 92
Vista, California, 48

Ways of knowing (epistemologies), science,
    102
Whole language, 62,
    controversy, what can you do?, 83–86,
        97–98
    controversy about, 75–79
    defined, 75, 80–81
    theology, links with, 85
Witchcraft and Satanism in literature, 130–131
Writing, student:
    controversy, what can you do?, 92–96
    controversy about, 86–96
    form and structure, emphasis on, 86
    freedom of press, 94
    grammar, emphasis on, 87
    journal writing, 88, 119–120
    research, 86
    self-censorship, 91
    spelling, links with, 87

Yore, Larry D., 101